The Harriman Alas
Expedition of 1899

The Harriman Alaska Expedition of 1899

*Scientists, Naturalists, Artists
and Others Document
America's Last Frontier*

JOHN J. MICHALIK

McFarland & Company, Inc., Publishers
Jefferson, North Carolina

ISBN (print) 978-1-4766-8423-9
ISBN (ebook) 978-1-4766-4325-0

LIBRARY OF CONGRESS AND BRITISH LIBRARY
CATALOGUING DATA ARE AVAILABLE

Library of Congress Control Number 2021033625

Front cover image: members of the Expedition bartering with the Eskimos,
Plover Bay, Siberia—"A doubtful bargain." *Left to right*: Dr. George F. Nelson,
Captain Peter Doran, Dr. Lewis Rutherford Morris, Daniel G. Elliot;
photograph by Edward S. Curtis
(University of Washington Libraries, Special Collections, NA 2116)

Printed in the United States of America

*McFarland & Company, Inc., Publishers
Box 611, Jefferson, North Carolina 28640
www.mcfarlandpub.com*

For CLARKE CHAMBERS—a promise kept

Contents

Contents

Part V. In the Wake of the Expedition

Acknowledgments

It is incumbent upon me to first acknowledge the participants in the Harriman Alaska Expedition for their role in this book. The story told in the following pages relies heavily on the now more than century-old primary materials they generated: diaries, memoranda, letters home, field journals, photographs, and their varied and legion post–Expedition writings, reminiscences, and interviews. I also owe much to those scholars who have collectively built an impressive library of biographical information about the lives of E.H. Harriman and those who traveled to Alaska with him and his family in the summer of 1899.

In the course of researching and writing this book, I have drawn on the collections and resources of more than two dozen institutions—the repositories of much of the participant-generated material referred to in the previous paragraph. While the Internet and the digitalization of materials has revolutionized research through making so much available from the comforts of home and office, there remains, still, something indispensable about long, solitary hours in quiet library reading rooms poring through boxes of original, hard-copy materials retrieved from storage. The feel and look of the originals, the stories the physical documents themselves tell, the finding of faded notes and jottings, the effort sometimes required to accurately decipher scribbled sentences and paragraphs, the squinting at the screens of microfilm readers, and the actual time spent in the reading rooms and stacks of great libraries, all have their own rewards.

Those rewards include the unfailing knowledge, assistance, patience, and hospitality of the staffs of those institutions. My particular thanks to Jeffery Flannery, head of the Reference and Reader Services Section in the Manuscript Division of the Library of Congress, and Carol Armbruster, Grant Harris, Elizabeth Faison, and many other LOC staffers in the Madison Building Reading Room whose names I sadly neglected to note; Ted Bennicoff, archivist at the Smithsonian Institution Archives, who provided patient assistance in the long days I spent there; Gina Bardi, reference librarian at the San Francisco National Maritime Historical Park, who dug up the blueprints for the steamer *George W. Elder*, and supplemented my notes and drawings with her own photos of those blueprints; Suzanne Peurach, collections manager at the USGS Patuxent Wildlife Research Center, and Craig Ludwig, assistant chair for collections at the Smithsonian Institution National Museum of Natural History—they both went the extra mile, at a very busy time for them, in making A.K. Fisher's field notes and journal available; John Bolcer, University of Washington archivist, together with Rebecca Baker and Gary Lundell of Special Collections at the UW's Allen Library; Nathan Sowry, reference archivist at the Smithsonian's National Museum of the American Indian Cultural Resources Center; and Professor Donna

McCrea, head of Archives and Special Collections, and Kellyn Younggren, archives specialist, at the University of Montana's Mansfield Library in Missoula.

I am especially indebted to the *numerous*, wonderfully helpful folks at the Sterling and Beinecke libraries at Yale—especially those at Beinecke, where my visits coincided with their temporary quarters and reading room at Sterling while their own building was closed to the public for extensive remodeling. Day after day, despite the difficulties and inconveniences involved in accessing materials at Beinecke, and all the challenges and tumult of construction, they were invariably cheerful and never missed a beat in finding and fulfilling my wants and needs for materials.

For their help, consistent courtesies, and willing attention, I also wish to thank the staffs of the Eberly Family Special Collections Library at Pennsylvania State University; the Robert Frost Library at Amherst College; the Massachusetts Historical Society in Boston; the Bancroft Library at the University of California, Berkeley; the Green Library at Stanford University; the Division of Rare and Manuscript Collections at the Cornell University Library; the Seattle Public Library; the Holt-Atherton Center for Pacific Studies at the University of the Pacific; the Archives and Special Collections Library at Vassar College; the Alaska State Library in Juneau; and the resources and staff of the Klondike Gold Rush National Historical Park at its units in Skagway and Seattle.

When I was an undergraduate history major at the University of Minnesota, my faculty advisor was Professor Clarke Chambers. I took a number of courses from Clarke, including a graduate-level seminar or two that he somehow got me into—though I lacked some of the prerequisites. Papers I wrote in those seminars received high marks; caused a mixture of pride and embarrassment when he passed copies of one of them out to everyone in that class as an example of "thorough scholarship"; and, I assume, played a role in his encouraging me to think about a career in history and teaching, rather than law. I, however, stayed the course, graduating with that degree in history and moving just a little ways across the Minnesota campus to the School of Law. During the next three years, I stopped in to see Professor Chambers from time to time. The last such occasion was in the spring of my senior year, shortly before graduation, and with my first position as a newly-minted lawyer about to carry me away to upper New York State. As we shook hands when I left his office that day, he again encouraged me to find time, as life went on, to return to research and writing in his discipline. I remember nodding my head, and casually shrugging my shoulders. He fixed me with his distinctive, somehow always twinkling eyes. After a moment, I said, "I will. I promise." That promise wasn't the impetus for this book, but promises are meant to be kept, and it was certainly there, kind of lingering in the background all these years, until finding its fulfillment here. Clarke Chambers died at age 94 in July 2015. To his memory, his interest in his students, and his indisputable character as a teacher and a person, this book is dedicated.

Finally, most importantly, a word of inadequate thanks to Diane Michalik for the understanding, forbearance, support, and wry good humor she brought to the demands of this project; as she has to so many other of my ventures, diversions, and pursuits on the long path of life we travel together. She is unexcelled in providing motivation and inspiration—to say nothing of the skill and patience she brings to the daunting task of being my wife.

—John J. Michalik

Preface

under recognized event of importance

In the declining years of the twentieth century, one of America's most prominent historians, the late Henry Steele Commager, characterized the Harriman Alaska Expedition as "an almost forgotten episode in the history of American exploration." It has remained largely so into the twenty-first century—forgotten or, at best, dimly remembered; unrecognized in terms of its importance, then and now; and with little comprehensive, scholarly treatment.

Lost in the forgotten nature of the broader story is the extraordinary make-up and ground-breaking interdisciplinary character of the members of the scientific and artistic party that made up Mr. Harriman's "guest list." There was, at the close of the nineteenth century, a singular wealth of capacity and strength in the American scientific community, which was populated by men whose work and ideas would impact the development and shape of their emerging disciplines for years to come; in fact, to this day. The cream of that crop journeyed together to Alaska—accompanied by an equally impressive group of writers, artists, and photographers to record and preserve what was observed, discovered, measured, and collected.

This book tells the story of what was, in fact, a remarkable journey of exploration and discovery, enriched by the interactions of the participants and by unexpected adventures. The heart of the narrative follows two intertwined threads.

One of those involves the substance of the journey: where they went and what they learned—including the discovery of unknown features of the land and early, hard evidence of glacial retreat; consideration and evaluation of the nature, current exploitation, and future of coastal Alaska's natural resources; mapping activities that filled in the gaps and voids of much of the Alaskan coastline; important scientific discoveries stemming from the observations of the members of the party and the accumulation of an astonishing collection of specimens; and contributions to general public knowledge of Alaska through a comprehensive written record and the thousands of photographs taken during the journey.

An equally important thread is built around the personal stories of the party that traveled together for two months. The backgrounds of all the members of that party, and their achievements and lives in the years before and after the Harriman Alaska Expedition, are covered in some depth; creating a story that weaves multiple biographical strands into the narrative of the journey, its results, and the experiences that the party—including the ship's crew and the Harriman family—shared in their odyssey in Alaskan waters. These experiences include their interactions with each other; their activities not just as scientists, but as tourists; and their extended and varied contacts with defeated prospectors, successful entrepreneurs, government

glacial retreat, evidence for

1

officials, early settlers, cannery workers, whaling ship captains, and the native Aleut, Tlingit, and Inuit populations. Finally, and as another important result of this forgotten episode of exploration, the story tracks the development of ongoing, long-term relations between members of the party, leading to future, post–Expedition cooperative efforts, including the campaign for expansion of Yosemite National Park and federal regulation of pelagic sealing operations in the Bering Sea.

The research path for this book, like the route of the Expedition, has had many ports of call, but the overriding sources are the primary materials—particularly in diaries, letters home, and post–Expedition writings—generated by the members of the party during the journey and shortly thereafter. Those materials are archived and held by institutions stretching from Massachusetts to Southern California, from Alaska to Washington, D.C. A number of those personal diaries, letters, unpublished autobiographies, and other writings have not been referenced in other published materials on the Harriman Alaska Expedition: they play an important part, and provide new perspectives, in the pages that follow.

departure fr Seattle

Introduction

It was the last day of May 1899. In the failing light of evening, amid the misty remnants of a day-long, drizzling rain, the steamer gathered in its heavy mooring lines and slowly pulled away from the wharf at the foot of Seattle's Seneca Street, moving into the open waters of Elliott Bay, bound for Alaska. On deck, many of the ship's passengers braved the weather to gather at the rails and watch the departure; waving to the spectators who crowded together under umbrellas on the wharf. Those headed north on the steamer that evening were embarking on what was not only the last major scientific expedition of the nineteenth century, but an expedition that was unique, at the time, in its destination and purpose, and extraordinary, at any time, in its origin, its participants, and its results.

The expedition was the brainchild of E.H. Harriman, head of the Union Pacific Railroad and one of America's wealthiest men. Harriman had initially envisioned a sabbatical for himself and a vacation for his family, and decided on a two-month cruise to Alaska—still, more than thirty years after its acquisition by the United States, a largely unexplored frontier territory best known to the general public through the excitement of the Klondike Gold Rush of 1897–1898. As the planning progressed, the size of the ship Harriman had chartered, coupled with the myth and mystery of the destination and the opportunities for exploration that would be presented in travels extending along much of Alaska's coastline, caused him to consider including some guests who would add to the "interest" of the journey. To that end, he decided to invite and take along, entirely at his own expense, a party of "scientific men" who could "gather useful information and distribute it for the benefit of others."[1]

Among those accepting the invitation were well-known university professors, the leaders of several U.S. Government research agencies, and men who were the nation's acknowledged experts on Alaska. The final contingent included leading naturalists and early, pace-setting environmentalists and conservationists, as well as ornithologists, geologists, biologists, botanists, paleontologists, and mineralogists, together with the country's chief geographer and its first professional forester. In fact, the Harriman Alaska Expedition foretold the practices of twentieth and twenty-first-century science by involving a truly interdisciplinary team. The ranks of that team included established professionals with already impressive credentials, as well as others who were up-and-coming in their fields. In addition, as a group they were educationally-oriented, attuned to wilderness and wildlife preservation, and forward-looking: the roster included founders of organizations such as the National Geographic Society, the Audubon Society, the Sierra Club, the American

innovative interdisciplinary quality

Ornithologists' Union, the Boone and Crockett Club, and the American Museum of Natural History.

In addition to the "scientific men," the guest list included some of the country's best known and widely published nature writers; two landscape artists, and a bird artist who would soon rival John James Audubon; and an exceptional photographer whose experiences and contacts on the journey would help propel him into a thirty-year photographic project and ethnological study of unequaled proportions. The combined expertise and efforts of these men would contribute to a comprehensive and detailed record, in pictures and in words, of the Harriman Alaska Expedition.

In terms of a summary description of the essential, distinguishing features of Mr. Harriman's Alaskan cruise, it would be difficult to improve upon that provided by the historian Maury Klein. Writing of the origins of the Expedition in his biography, *The Life and Legend of E.H. Harriman,* Klein observes: "Nothing like it had ever been conceived. No individual or even government had gathered experts from so many fields on a private ark and taken them to explore wilderness from their own perspectives in a setting where they were free to interact, exchange ideas, and determine their own agenda. Even more remarkable, the benefactor who made the venture possible was himself going along to share the adventure."[2]

If the participants were an extraordinary and unprecedented group, so too the circumstances of the times and the destination and plan of the journey were particularly propitious. Exploration at the close of the nineteenth century was less about discovering unknown lands and blazing new trails than about advancing scientific and popular knowledge through such things as accurate mapping, in-depth study of the nature and uses of natural resources, and identifying and describing flora and fauna in detail. It was also an age of scientific acquisition, with new species being discovered and categorized, and the collections of the country's great museums of natural history being built and expanded. No area presented a more fertile and expansive ground for all that activity than Alaska: then, as it arguably still is more than a century later, America's last frontier.

After leaving Seattle, the party would travel almost 9,000 miles on its Alaskan journey, making, generally as the result of collective choices and decisions, over fifty stops: sometimes brief visits of a few hours but often involving much longer excursions, where small shore parties would be left for as long as ten days before the ship would circle back to retrieve them. "The general plan pursued," one member of the party would write afterwards, "was to follow the coast, making brief stops at numerous points for the purpose of making observations and collections."[3] Thus, the Harriman Alaska Expedition was primarily a sophisticated reconnaissance—providing a contemporary snapshot and baseline, scientific and otherwise, of conditions, the land itself, and life of all types in coastal Alaska at the close of the century.

The nature of the Expedition and the status, individually and collectively, of Harriman's guests, confined (though for the most part comfortably and amiably) together in close contact for two months, and all focused on subjects and activities of diverse yet mutual interest, created an atmosphere and a shared life on ship and shore that stretched beyond the scientific purposes of the journey and added much to it. The prospect of the interactions and the society they would create and share was recognized in advance by many, such as the young mineralogist Charles Palache who, writing home from Seattle before the steamer's departure on that last day of May, would enthuse that the journey "is a wonderful opportunity ... to meet on equal terms a most interesting body of men of science and affairs such as are not often thrown thus together."[4] Later that summer, a few weeks after the return to Seattle and the scattering of the party, no less a personage than John Muir would provide a retrospective, noting that on the ship "I found not only the fields I liked best to study, but a hotel, a club, and a home, together with a floating University in which I enjoyed the instruction and companionship of a lot of the best fellows imaginable...."[5] The experience, companionship, and benefits of the club, home, and university were consistently shared and often enriched by the involvement of the Harriman family party, as well as the ship's physicians and chaplain, the hunters and packers who supported the scientists, and by many of the ship's sixty-five officers and crew members. In truth, no one who participated in any capacity in Mr. Harriman's Expedition could fail to have been affected by the experience.

The story of the Harriman Alaska Expedition in the following pages is told in large measure in the words of its participants. As a group, they generated for publication a thirteen-volume series of books featuring essays and scientific reports covering their observations and findings on a broad range of topics, including details of the vast collections that they amassed and the results of the study and analysis of those collections in the years following the Expedition. Individually, many returned home to write articles for publications including the *National Geographic Magazine*, and a number of them were the subject of newspaper and magazine interviews. Most importantly, during the course of their travels and explorations many members of the party kept extensive personal diaries and field journals, and a significant number were prolific writers of letters home to spouses, other family members, and friends. The personal observations, revelations, and detail in these unpublished writings are at times extraordinary, enhanced by the fact that many of the authors were superb writers. While one might expect that sort of thing from scientists attuned to recording their daily activities in the field, and certainly from the professional writers in the party, there are also significant contributions, often involving events, perspectives, and nuances not mentioned by others, from the likes of the party's chaplain, the group's chief hunter and scout, and the taxidermists who worked with the hunters and collectors.

I have, albeit vicariously, been privileged to tread the decks of that nineteenth-century steamer, and to travel the waters and shores of Alaska with Harriman and his guests during the seven-year gestation period of this book. I hope that through this story you will also come to know them and to share the experience of what was truly, from many angles and perspectives, the event of a lifetime.

Prologue:
The Rise of E.H. Harriman

The story of the Harriman Alaska Expedition has its prologue in the improbable rise of its patron and namesake, and that in turn has roots extending back to a time more than a hundred years before the Expedition party set out from Seattle.

= ◆ =

Unlike the tired, the poor, and the huddled masses depicted in Emma Lazarus's sonnet,[1] and who would in later years be welcomed at Liberty Island in the vast harbor of New York City, the eighteenth-century immigrant who established the Harriman family line in the newly independent and fledgling America was relatively well-to-do for the times. His son and, with one notable exception, his grandsons would also be successful businessmen. The exception would struggle; but in turn his son would be the stuff of a fourth-generation Horatio Alger story, rising from the streets to the heights of financial and business success, power, and no little controversy.

The immigrant family patriarch was William Harriman, a successful London stationer who sailed for America in 1795 and settled in New Haven, Connecticut. He was not without resources: his neighbors in New Haven referred to him as "the rich Englishman,"[2] and he soon set himself up in the West Indies trade through a number of vessels he either bought or chartered. Shortly after the turn of the century, he moved his family to New York City, and began to move from shipping to a more general commission business. That business prospered, and the Harrimans soon lived comfortably in a neighborhood populated by many of New York's established families. William's business success was offset by tragedy in the family's personal life: of seven sons, three were lost at sea and three others died in childbirth. Following William's death in 1820, the family name and business fell to the sole surviving son, Orlando.[3]

Orlando carried on and grew the family business. He and his wife, Anna, settled in a stately home in the same neighborhood his father had lived in; he became a notable figure in the business world of New York; and they moved in a social circle that included many prominent families. With others, he suffered significant losses from the great fire that devastated much of the city's business district in 1837, but he was able to recover from those losses as the years passed. His many sons would join their father in his business as they came of age—except for the eldest, also named Orlando.[4]

This Orlando graduated from Columbia University, entered the ministry, and in

1841 was ordained a deacon in the Episcopal Church. While this was a career and a calling that interested him, he was apparently not fully suited for it: "he possessed a cold, austere personality,"[5] and was not a person whom parishioners would necessarily be attracted to follow. After serving for a year as an assistant rector, he obtained a parish of his own at St. George's in Hempstead, Long Island. In 1842, prior to answering the call to St. George's, Orlando married Cornelia Neilson, the daughter of a distinguished physician and with a family tree that included Stuyvesants, Livingstons, Fishes, and other well-connected families. They would have six children, the fourth of whom, Edward Henry Harriman, was born in St. George's rectory on February 25, 1848.

As his family grew, Orlando faced increasing financial difficulties and pressure. St. George's was a small congregation that had trouble keeping current with what little was owed him. Prospects were grim until 1850, when he received and accepted an offer from a parish in the mountains of California.

Leaving his young family behind, he traveled west alone; electing to avoid the long journey across the continent and to take the less time-consuming but riskier route by sea to Panama, followed by an overland traverse by foot and on mules through the jungles of the Isthmus, and concluding with a sea voyage to San Francisco. During the trip across the Isthmus he fell ill with fever, and was forced to spend more than a month recuperating in Panama before he could resume his journey to San Francisco. On arrival, he found that the vestrymen of the church he had been called to had assumed, in the absence of any communication from him since he left New York, that he was not coming, and they had engaged someone else to fill the position. He would spend most of the next year wandering through small towns and preaching in mining camps, hoping to establish himself in some place to which he could bring his wife and children. In March 1851 he gave up and made his way back to New York.[6]

He soon moved his family to Jersey City, where he latched on as a curate in one of the city's churches. He also tried his hand at business in partnership with two of his brothers, who were engaged in the family firm of William Harriman & Company. This effort lasted, with little personal success, until 1857. He searched again for a parish of his own, eventually finding two small churches and taking positions at both: on Sundays he preached at one church in Jersey City in the morning and then would walk to the other, in West Hoboken, to conduct afternoon services. This arrangement lasted until the fall of 1866 when, with the West Hoboken church owing him two years back salary, he left that post.[7] He would spend the latter part of his life as a bookkeeper in New York's Bank of Commerce.[8] In many ways, he and Cornelia were poor relations who often scraped by only because of the charity of the Harriman and Neilson families.

＝ ◆ ＝

Orlando and Cornelia Harriman's son Edward Henry was, from the outset, small of stature and not at all an imposing figure, though as the years passed he achieved not only physical fitness but also proved in his business dealings to have an aggressive and combative personality, as well as remarkable strength of will. Beginning early in life—and though he never particularly cared for either of his given names—he was referred to within the family as "Henry."

His formal education was brief. He started in the Jersey City public schools, but when he was twelve his parents found the money to send him to Trinity School in New York—largely because at Trinity the children of ministers were accepted at a fraction of the normal tuition. Every weekday he would make his way in the early morning darkness to the Jersey City ferry, ride that across the river, and then walk another mile to school. After two years, he had had enough of Trinity. In 1862, at the age of fourteen, he informed his father that he was quitting school and going to work; nothing Orlando could say was able to sway or deter his son.[9]

Young Harriman immediately gravitated to Wall Street, where he started in the firm of Dewitt C. Hays. In the absence of electricity and stock tickers, the brokerage business of the day was paper intensive, and his first position was as a messenger carrying securities between the Hays firm and the offices of other brokers and bankers. He quickly graduated to being a "pad shover"—one of a cadre of boys who hurried about the Street, from office to office, with current stock prices and offers to buy or sell scribbled on pads of paper. Harriman demonstrated great attention to detail, possessed an accurate and retentive memory, and proved trustworthy and reliable in a place where those qualities were paramount.[10]

As a pad shover, and later when Hays promoted him to managing clerk, Harriman began to delve beyond the transactions he wrote up and helped to facilitate, and to explore the reasons for fluctuations in the prices of stocks and bonds; he learned to connect market activity with causes and larger events, giving him a wider view of business and the world of financing. He also developed an intense desire to strike out on his own. In the summer of 1870, at the age of twenty-two, and using funds borrowed from his uncle Oliver Harriman, he bought a seat on the New York Stock Exchange and opened the firm of E.H. Harriman & Co. on the corner of Broad Street and Exchange Place.[11]

The 1870s were a volatile time on Wall Street: spurred by a major depression early in the decade, by 1879 over four hundred firms on the New York Stock Exchange had closed their doors. Though new to the game, Harriman prospered while others failed. One reason for his success was that—by natural inclination and interests, the contacts he made and reputation he established while working for DeWitt Hayes, and his innate business sense—he attracted solid clients and quickly developed close relations with many of the contemporary speculators and wielders of capital. He handled orders for John Jacob Astor, Jay Gould, Commodore Vanderbilt, and August Belmont. And the family connections on his mother's side helped build a wealthy client base among Livingstons, Fishes, Neilsons, and Van Burens. Though he engaged in active trading in his own account, his early wealth accumulated to a far greater degree through commissions earned off the successful investments, often based on his recommendations, of others.[12]

As he grew his business and his business sense, Henry branched-out socially. He joined the fashionable Travelers' Club, soon became one of its directors, and was a regular attendee at the Club's Saturday night dinners, which were frequented by some of the best known and up-and-coming young men in New York. He also wheedled memberships in the Union and Racquet Clubs, and became a private in the Tenth Company of the Seventh Regiment, a unit of the New York militia that was popularly referred to as the "society company" because its ranks were filled with men from the best families.

The social set of young men that Henry became a part of was athletic and competitive, and a perfect fit for someone who loved sports and the outdoors, though he didn't look the part. He was short, perhaps five feet five; slight in build and somewhat bow-legged; and had a face featuring a prominent forehead, large ears, dark eyes magnified by thick wire spectacles, and what would become a formidable walrus mustache. He became a crack shot with a rifle, developed a love of trotting horses and in time became a skilled racer, and was an "unusually quick and clever" boxer— he took boxing lessons and occasionally sparred with the light heavyweight champion, Billy Edwards.[13] And he grew to be an avid outdoorsman: a favorite haunt then and throughout his life was the wilderness camp and hotel maintained by Paul Smith in the remote northernmost reaches of the Adirondacks, where Harriman hunted, fished, camped, and enjoyed roaming the woods.[14]

Through his membership in the Union Club, Henry became friends with George C. Clark, a member of Clark, Dodge & Co., one of Wall Street's most respected firms. Clark's mother was involved in the Wilson Mission School, which provided industrial training for girls from the tenements in New York's Tompkins Square neighborhood. Henry was visiting that school with her one day in 1875 when he heard the school's matron complain about how gangs of boys teased and harassed the girls and threw stones at the windows of the school. He began to develop the idea of a club for boys that would get them off the streets, provide interesting activities, and help them mold their lives along constructive lines. He enlisted the aid of a policeman in the precinct to recruit boys for a meeting to discuss the idea.

While only three boys ventured to show up, they formed a core that slowly grew, and early in 1876 Harriman rented the basement of the building occupied by the Wilson School and opened the Tompkins Square Boys Club, probably the first of its kind in the world. Harriman financed the club's activities and devoted his evenings to running it. As the club grew, he recruited his friends to serve as volunteer group leaders, and personally oversaw an expansion of its activities that grew to include a library, lectures, musical events put on by the boys, athletic teams, and a program of summer trips that eventually evolved into a permanent summer camp. Full-time staff were added, and when the club outgrew its facilities in the Wilson School, Harriman dug into his own pocket to purchase several nearby lots and erect a five-story building to serve as the club's home and headquarters. The Boys Club would become a lifelong commitment for Henry and succeeding generations of the Harriman family.[15]

It was at George Clark's home in 1878 that Henry met Mary Williamson Averell, who was a cousin of Clark's wife and the daughter of William J. Averell, a banker in the northern New York town of Ogdensburg. Mary had a matronly air, was energetic and well-educated, and was a "people person" whose life revolved around family, friends, church, civic causes, and welfare activities.[16] She was interested in many of the same things that appealed to Henry, including his development of the Boys Club. They were married in Ogdensburg in September 1879.

=== ◆ ===

By the early 1880s, Harriman had cemented his position as a broker on Wall Street. In his mid-thirties, "having worked long and hard with persistence and success, he was well-to-do, master of a considerable fortune."[17] Contemporary writers looking at his career estimated that "young Harriman had acquired several hundred thousand dollars before he was thirty-five."[18] Though successful as a broker, he also developed other, deeper interests: particularly regarding investments not just in terms of the trading of securities, but in the underlying businesses and their opportunities. His focus and attention turned to railroads.

As a broker, Henry couldn't ignore railroads: they were America's first big business. In 1885, of roughly 150 stocks listed on the New York Stock Exchange, 125 were railroad issues. On the bond side, that market was, apart from federal and state government issues, also dominated by the railroads. Henry's first exposure to the railroad business, as opposed to railroad securities, came when his father-in-law, who was president of the Ogdensburg & Lake Champlain Railroad, gave him a seat on that company's board of directors.

One of his fellow directors was Stuyvesant Fish, whose prominent family was connected to the Harrimans via Henry's mother and the Neilson family. Henry may have met Fish through that connection, or when Fish was working on Wall Street with Morton, Bliss & Company, where he would have had business with Dewitt Hays's office.[19] Fish had left Morton Bliss in 1877 to join the board of the Illinois Central Railroad, where his duties included securities placements, loans, and other financing. He was soon sending some of that business to E.H. Harriman & Company. It is likely that that relationship had a great deal to do with Fish, who had no other connection to the Ogdensburg road, joining Henry on its board of directors.[20]

Fish and Harriman had embarked on what would be a thirty-year business relationship. Initially that involved financing and other matters for the Ogdensburg & Lake Champlain, as well as other small roads in New York State. However, the major Fish-Harriman collaboration, a defining enterprise in both of their careers, involved the Illinois Central.

The Illinois Central was the first land-grant railroad. Conservatively managed and embracing over 1,300 miles of track, it had a diversified traffic and, unlike many other lines, it was profitable and paid regular dividends throughout the depression years of the 1870s. As the depression ended, the competitive environment grew, and railroads in the West faced pressures to expand to meet the needs of a growing population. The Central's board was soon split between conservatives loathed to change the existing formula for success, and a more aggressive group, led by Stuyvesant Fish, who felt expansion was the key to continued prosperity.[21] Fish realized that expansion required finding creative ways of handling increased financial burdens and of allaying the fears of the conservatives on the board.

In 1881, the Illinois Central sought to sell bonds issued by one of its subsidiary lines. E.H. Harriman & Co. made a successful bid on the entire $2.5 million lot and an option for another $1.5 million. Despite a depressed market following the assassination of President Garfield, Harriman held on to the bonds and eventually sold them at a substantial profit, including buying such quantities for his own account that his partners were frightened. "It won't cost us a cent to carry," he reassured them, "the shorts will carry it for us," and he proved correct: he bought steadily, but just as steadily the "shorts" appeared to borrow and carry it.[22] The success with this bond issue opened the door for Harriman to become involved with the Illinois Central's financial affairs on a continuing basis.

Fish continued to work to gain control of the Illinois Central board through seating his own candidates, including Harriman, as directors until he finally obtained a majority in the spring of 1884. The last vestiges of the old guard were replaced in 1886, and Fish assumed the presidency of the railroad in the spring of 1887. Harriman was elected vice-president in September of that year.

Over the next half dozen years, Fish and Harriman worked to further elevate and strengthen the Illinois Central. The effort involved a systematic approach to three major initiatives: restructuring the railroad's financial obligations, enlarging the system, and instituting and underwriting improvements of all types to elevate the road's efficiency. Harriman played a major role in all three areas.[23]

As to the Central's financial obligations, he tied restructuring to underwriting expansion, including issuing new bonds at the lowest saleable rates and using the proceeds to retire older, higher obligation issues. Harriman and his firm handled most of the new bond issues and ongoing stock sales. His skills as a railroad financier and a reader of market conditions were, then and throughout his career, uncanny. Some forty years after his death, Robert A. Lovett, son of Harriman's longtime legal counsel, noted that as to the Illinois Central of the 1880s and 1890s, "somehow or other, it never had any bonds for sale except in times when bonds were in great demand; it never borrowed money except when money was cheap and plentiful."[24]

Harriman also played a leading role in the enlargement of the Illinois Central system. One acquisition, the purchase of the Dubuque & Sioux City Railroad, brought Harriman into the first of a number of clashes with the country's most powerful financier, J. Pierpont Morgan.

For twenty years the Illinois Central had operated the Dubuque under a lease that was set to expire in October 1887, but which would be renewed in perpetuity unless the Central terminated it in advance. While not profitable, the line was important to Fish and Harriman because it secured the Central's Iowa connection. They couldn't afford to lose use of the trackage, but they were not satisfied with the road as it was, and concluded that the best course was to terminate the lease and buy the Dubuque outright. The Dubuque board of directors, which included Morgan and controlled a majority of the Dubuque's stock through a committee, had other ideas based on holding the stock and forcing sale to some willing buyer for at least par or, alternatively, obtaining a new, more lucrative lease.

Harriman's efforts to, at a price below par, buy stock that would give him a controlling stake in the Dubuque failed. However, he ultimately secured victory based on his discovery that company elections had for years ignored Iowa law that prohibited voting stock by proxy. Two weeks before the Dubuque's annual meeting in February 1887, Harriman had a friendly stockholder file suit against the Dubuque and the committee to void the casting of proxy votes based on and represented by their shares. At the annual meeting, the only stock whose voting rights were recognized produced a board friendly to the Illinois Central, though at a separate meeting the Morgan forces used the disputed proxies to elect their own board. The controversy was soon in the hands of the lawyers and the courts.

In the meantime, the Illinois Central gave notice of terminating the lease. As the termination date approached, and with no other buyers stepping forward, the Morgan forces had to accept Harriman's offer to buy their stock; since if the lease simply expired, the line would have little independent value at any price approaching the Harriman offer. Harriman biographer Maury Klein notes that "this first clash with Morgan cast a pall over their relationship that was lifted only on Harriman's deathbed." Klein also reasons that what was involved for Morgan was not just a small railroad but his personal code of honor, and offense to his sense of propriety through Harriman's use of what Morgan felt were "devices and technicalities," as well as a clash of personalities where "Harriman's combative nature and abrasive style guaranteed friction with a man like Morgan."[25]

≡ ◆ ≡

Harriman's growing involvement in the Illinois Central found a parallel in the growth of his family. After their marriage, he and Mary had taken up residence in New York City and by 1884 they had welcomed two daughters and a son—Mary, Cornelia, and Henry Neilson. And as his young household grew, biographer Klein would find it clear that "in the years after 1880 nothing shaped Henry's world more than his family. He doted on his wife and children, did everything with them, and insisted they do everything together."[26] That view was also voiced by business associates and personal friends who were close to Harriman throughout his career, such as family friend and physician Lewis R. Morris, who wrote that no day was "too short or too full of affairs that [Harriman] did not find time for the children."[27]

That dedication to his family, combined with his love of nature and the outdoors, made Harriman receptive to an opportunity to acquire a substantial, heavily-forested property in the Ramapo Highlands in New York State's Orange County, about forty-five miles north of Jersey City, west of the Hudson River, and south of the West Point Military Reservation. The property, involving 7,863 acres, had gone into receivership and in September 1886 was the subject of a foreclosure sale. Alerted to the sale, Harriman attended, bid $52,500—approximately $6.67 an acre—and left the county courthouse the owner of a significant estate. Harriman gave the estate the name Arden,[28] and over the next several years bought some forty different farms and wooded tracts which adjoined his property. Eventually the estate grew to an area of nearly thirty square miles of mostly forested lands, and was "perhaps the most extensive country estate in the vicinity of New York."[29] And, as time passed, he commenced construction of what would become a massive yet practical home on Arden's heights.

A year after the Arden purchase, in September 1887, Harriman became vice president of the Illinois Central, a position that meant moving to Chicago. The still growing Windy City was a different living environment from New York, and Harriman also found that he no longer had an up-to-the-minute finger on the pulse of Wall Street. And personal tragedy soon struck when four-year-old Henry, "Harry" as he was called, contracted diphtheria and died in February of 1888. Years later, speaking of Harry's death, his younger brother Averell would say, "My father always said that was the thing that made him feel he should make railroading his career. He felt his son had died because he was working on the railroad, and he wanted to justify the sacrifice of his son by dedicating himself to railroading."[30]

It seems likely that Harriman had actually made the beginnings of a commitment to "railroading" prior to his son's death, and at least concurrent with assuming the responsibilities of being vice president of the Illinois Central, as evidenced by his studied decision to step back from the routine business of Wall Street. Beginning in 1888, the brokerage firm of E.H. Harriman & Co. had been run by his brother, Willie Harriman, and Nicholas Fish, the older brother of Stuyvesant Fish. Henry had become a special partner in the firm. Nonetheless, in February 1888, early in the month when his son passed away, Henry wound-up the business of E.H. Harriman & Co., and transferred its contracts to the other family house, Harriman & Co., whose partners included the sons of the Uncle Oliver who had helped Henry buy his seat on the New York Stock Exchange.

Young Harry's death may also have been one of the influences that contributed to what his leading biographer has referred to as the "partitioning of Harriman's life." Like many of the self-made, self-confident businessmen or "tycoons" in the industrial era, Harriman developed something of a split personality: "Doctor Jekyll was the dutiful, considerate husband and father, the genial master of the household, who could be the soul of kindness and hospitality to his friends. At work, however, he became Mr. Hyde, the cold, lynx-eyed businessman who prided himself on his single-minded dedication and ability to shut feelings or sentiment out of decisions."[31]

Those traits would become increasingly conspicuous as Harriman's railroading career advanced, particularly in the early twentieth century when he emerged from virtual obscurity and life out of the public eye to a more prominent, controversial spot on the national stage and in the press.

= ◆ =

The late 1880s and substantial parts of the 1890s, were a time of turbulence and adjustment in the railroad industry. In the world of the Illinois Central, tensions arose between President Fish, in New York, and Harriman, in Chicago, where the latter's duties as vice president were vaguely-defined and at times at apparent odds with authority which had for years been vested in the line's chief operating officer. These issues were eventually worked out, in many ways to Harriman's advantage, including a decision by the Illinois Central board to move the office of the president back to Chicago. That set in motion a chain of events that led to Harriman's return to New York—where he submitted his resignation as vice president in June 1890 and reverted to being chairman of the Illinois Central's finance committee.

The big turbulence in the railroad industry was the all-pervasive financial storm of 1893—the most serious depression the country had yet experienced. The panic had its beginnings when railroads, with heavy borrowing from banks, expanded their operations beyond existing demand. More than seventy railroads—including the Reading, the Erie, the Northern Pacific, and the Union Pacific—quickly fell into bankruptcy, compromising banks unable to recoup their loans and forcing them to call in the loans of all their borrowers. Small businesses and heavily mortgaged farmers who could not cover their notes also went bankrupt. Predictably, frightened depositors rushed to withdraw deposits and hundreds of banks became insolvent. Within twelve months, more than four million jobs were lost.[32]

Conspicuously missing from the list of failed railroads was the Illinois Central. Between 1890 and 1892, pursuing the Fish-Harriman policy, the Central spent millions on improvements and it continued spending through the years of the depression. It posted solid earnings in the 1893–1897 depression years and kept paying dividends. Using its cash reserves, it was able to expand by investment in existing railroads such as the Louisville, New Orleans & Texas and the Chesapeake, Ohio & Southwestern. By 1896 its trackage was nearly four times what it was in 1877.[33]

Not Every attempt by the Illinois Central at investment and acquisition ~~did not meet~~ met with success, nor did all of Harriman's efforts in other related ventures, but even in the losses he added to his knowledge and mastery of railroad affairs. A prime example involved the bankruptcy of the Erie Railroad, and its reorganization under the aegis of none other than J.P. Morgan.

The Erie's situation was complicated by a peculiar, layered debt structure, with many of its securities held abroad. Morgan's plan of reorganization involved major simplification of the railroad's capital structure, including large sacrifices from the foreign securities holders. The plan raised a storm of protest, not only in Europe but among several U.S. financial houses. Many of the protesters formed a protective committee to oppose Morgan's plan and, though his holdings in the Erie were small, Harriman soon found himself chairing that committee.

When the Morgan plan gained enough support to go into effect, Harriman brought suit to enjoin its implementation; and as with the Dubuque & Sioux City in 1887, he and Morgan again locked horns. In the course of this process, Harriman went to the Morgan offices to lay out the objections to the plan, and when asked who he represented, retorted, "Myself!"[34] While the court declined to grant the request for an injunction and Morgan's plan went into effect, it soon proved unworkable and Morgan had to scrap it in favor of one essentially based on that proposed by Harriman's protective committee.

If the Erie's situation in bankruptcy was complicated, it paled in comparison to that of the Union Pacific—and Harriman's involvement in its restructuring and future marked not only the point of no return in his commitment to railroading, but in his ascension to the ranks of railroad power with the likes of James J. Hill and Morgan, as well as to the rarified regions of wealth.

The Union Pacific was a storied railroad. Chartered and created during the Lincoln administration under the Pacific Railroad Act of 1862, it was part of the first transcontinental rail line, ceremonially completed on May 10, 1869, when the Central Pacific and the Union Pacific were joined at Promontory Summit in Utah. When it went into receivership in 1893 it was beset by many issues: its earnings were in decline, its trackage amounted to a staggering 7,700 miles, and the system was believed by many to be in need of major repairs. And its future was partially in the hands of Congress because of a massive government loan dating back to its charter. In essence, the government held a second mortgage on the Union Pacific, and as an unusually powerful creditor it could either cancel the debt, extend it, refund the debt at a lower interest rate, or demand cash payment to clear the debt. The last alternative was probably the most desirable and potentially the most advantageous, though raising some $52 million in a depressed market was a daunting prospect. In the final analysis, and though several such efforts had already failed, getting a refunding bill through Congress, however problematic, seemed to be the only viable approach.

A further complication was that the task of reorganizing the Union Pacific was beyond the resources of most banking houses. J.P. Morgan dismissed it as a lost cause, characterizing the Union Pacific as "two streaks of iron rust across the plains."[35] An early reorganization committee disbanded in 1895 after failing in its attempt to get a refunding bill from Congress. Finally, later that year, Jacob Schiff, the powerful head of the Kuhn, Loeb & Company investment house, decided to take the chance.

Schiff put together a new committee, which developed a reorganization plan based on a revised capital structure. To avoid a foreclosure sale, a new refunding bill was introduced in Congress in March 1896, with seemingly bright prospects of passage. Those prospects quickly dimmed: minority bond- and stock-holders suddenly and unexpectedly balked at settlement terms, criticism in the press grew, and enthusiasm for the refunding bill in Congress seemed to mysteriously wane and the process slowed. Considering these obstacles, and that it all seemed too coincidental, Schiff suspected that the hand of the rival house of Morgan was involved, but Morgan denied any involvement and instead told Schiff, "It's that little fellow Harriman, and you want to watch him carefully."[36]

Following up on the tip from Morgan, Schiff met with Harriman and asked him point blank whether he was the force opposing the reorganization committee. Harriman replied, "I am the man," and that he in fact planned to issue $100,000,000 in Illinois Central bonds and use the proceeds to reorganize the Union Pacific himself. When Schiff inquired whether there was a way they could work together, Harriman replied that he would join forces if Schiff would make him the chairman of the executive committee of the reorganized company. Schiff rejected that offer as "out of the question," and the meeting ended.[37]

Schiff moved ahead, but his refunding bill was rejected by the U.S. House of Representatives in January 1897. Further troubles arose when Schiff reluctantly came up with a foreclosure plan, which the government determined was underfunded. In May, Schiff again met with Harriman—this time reiterating that he couldn't make him chair but proposing that, if Harriman would join with him, he would put him on the executive committee and "if you prove to be the best man on the committee, you will get the chairmanship."[38] Harriman quickly agreed.

From that point on, the reorganization of the Union Pacific moved on largely unabated. Apparently, Harriman's only actual role in that process, other than staying out of the way, was to take a share—a bit north of $3 million—in the underwriting syndicate that would pay off the government loan. However, with a sense of what the reconstituted Union Pacific could be in the future, and counting on his own ability to significantly increase the value of the railroad, Harriman invested heavily on his own account in the company itself, buying large blocks of its common stock throughout the remainder of 1897 and into 1898 at prices ranging from $20 to $30 a share. In the market in those months the stock "was considered to have very little intrinsic value, and no dividends were in sight even for the preferred, much less for the common stock.... But within less than ten years from the time Mr. Harriman had made what then appeared a preposterous prediction, Union Pacific had been placed upon an annual dividend basis of 10%, and was selling in the market at close to 200."[39]

The foreclosure sale took place in November and the reorganized Union Pacific opened its New York offices in January 1898. Schiff kept his promise and put Harriman on the executive committee, where he was one of many: respected for his work with the Illinois Central but otherwise not well known and not yet possessing the wealth or record of achievement of his fellow directors. With an eye toward the positions and interests of those other directors, one of them, Otto Kahn, described Harriman as a "freelance, neither a railroad man nor a banker nor a merchant."[40]

Harriman would prove himself to be all of those things and, while continuing his responsibilities with the Illinois Central, he quickly took on many of the difficult, complicated, and time-consuming tasks incident to the start of the restructured company and for which his fellow committee members had little time. They quickly grew

E.H. Harriman. Science History Images/Alamy Stock Photo.

to rely upon and trust him, and in May 1898—almost exactly a year to the day from when Jacob Schiff had told him he might get the chairmanship if he proved to be "the best man on the committee"—Harriman was elected chairman. Within a year "he placed himself at the head of the board, and became the ruling spirit, the dominating force of the enterprise."[41]

≡ ◆ ≡

In June 1898, less than a month after becoming chairman of the executive committee, Harriman set out to personally travel over and inspect the entire Union Pacific system. Although he had already made a careful study of the road from all the information and reports available, he needed to verify that information, perfect his knowledge, and fill in the gaps between what he was told and what he needed to know. As usual, he was, in the final analysis, willing to fully rely on no one other than himself.

He borrowed Fish's private car from the Illinois Central and put it at the head of a special Union Pacific train, with the locomotive at the rear. That arrangement put Harriman at the front of the train, in an "observation" car where he could sit, inspect, and take notes on the grades, curves, rails, ballast, buildings, and equipment of the line, as well as the countryside and towns along the route. He took along the Union Pacific's president, chief engineer, general manager, freight traffic manager, and general passenger agent—those he felt would have the most to tell him (and perhaps explain and justify to him) as they traveled the road. And the traveling party was expanded to allow Harriman to mix business with family time. By 1897, the Harriman brood had grown to five with the addition of a third daughter, Carol, in 1889, and two boys, Averell in 1891 and Edward Roland in 1895. While those three were very young, his two oldest daughters, Mary and Cornelia, were in their teens, and Harriman couldn't pass the opportunity to take them along and give them a unique summer adventure.

The train pulled out of Kansas City, "backing up" with the engine pushing from the rear. They traveled only during the daytime, and at a rate that allowed Harriman to look at and question everything in sight. They stopped at important stations, where Harriman quizzed officials, investigated conditions, and regularly grilled the Union Pacific officers traveling with him. In the three weeks that they traveled the West, Harriman "became thoroughly acquainted with the physical condition of the road, estimated the value of its equipment, interviewed the shippers who made use of it, gauged the mood and prospects of farmers along its route, judged the characters of the officials locally in charge of it, and not only devised plans for its immediate improvement, but, in many cases, put such plans into operation without waiting for approval of the executive committee."[42] Little escaped his attention: as one division superintendent reported, "He saw every poor tie, blistered rail, and loose bolt on my division."[43]

The train ran northwest to the end of the line in Portland, rode the rails of the Southern Pacific south to San Francisco, and completed its twenty-three-day, 6,200-mile journey by traveling the original transcontinental railway route east through Promontory Point and on to Omaha. Along the way, Harriman and the girls took time to explore the Garden of the Gods and Pikes Peak in Colorado. In Salt Lake City, they visited Temple Square and found time for a swim in the Great Salt Lake. They took pictures of Indians in Montana, rode horses in the countryside, and Harriman did some solitary trout fishing. In California, they visited Mount Shasta and Monterey, and spent two days roaming about San Francisco.[44]

The trip not only provided Harriman with a greater overall view and understanding of the Union Pacific than anyone else associated with it, but also fostered a strong belief in the agricultural potential of the West and the possibilities it held for the railroad if it was put in the shape needed to capitalize on that potential. As the trip ended, he took two dramatic steps.

First, at dinner on the train on the last evening of the trip he announced, "I have today wired New York for 5000 shares of Union Pacific preferred at 66, and any one of you are welcome to take as few or as many shares as you like"—a statement that in the minds of the Union Pacific officers at his dinner table was a stunning personal commitment in a business that was coming out of bankruptcy; and those who took him up on the offer reaped the results.[45]

Harriman also telegraphed the executive committee in New York for authority to immediately spend $25 million—a staggering sum for the times and under the circumstances—on new equipment and improvements.[46] Harriman had seen signs of coming prosperity all along the route, and the developing availability of more business than the road could handle. In his mind, while the time was short, the opportunity was there to get the Union Pacific in shape to meet and capitalize on that demand.

There was, one imagines to put it mildly, "much doubt in the board as to whether Mr. Harriman's recommendation should be followed," and apparently at least one director felt that if the $25 million expenditure was authorized "the Union Pacific would find itself in receiver's hands again before two years had passed."[47] The matter was put over until Harriman returned to New York in July; when, after a long and heated board meeting, the request was approved.

Almost immediately Harriman put the wheels in motion for a spectacular effort, extending over the next three years, to carry out the projects he had in mind. While an initial $2.7 million was marked for new equipment, the true focus of the expenditures was on reducing grades, straightening curves, rerouting the line where needed, and taking other dramatic steps to create a straighter, wider roadbed with the heavier rails and added ballast that were needed to handle what Harriman saw would soon be larger payloads and the need for more frequent, faster trains. Among the challenges perhaps the largest was dealing with the Sherman Hill and Dale Creek area near Cheyenne, Wyoming. Sherman Hill was the highest point on the Union Pacific: at over 8,200 feet it required helper engines to assist trains up the slope. Nearby stood the Dale Creek Bridge: 130 feet high and 650 feet long. Together they formed a costly, huge bottleneck in a division of the line that already carried heavy traffic and suffered from the worst weather on the system. Harriman's engineers decided the solution was to eliminate both problems by going through Sherman Hill and filling up Dale Creek: a project involving relocating thirty miles of track and boring an 1,800-foot tunnel through solid granite. Rock from the tunnel and other areas at Sherman Hill, to the tune of 475,000 cubic yards of gravel, would be dumped off the Dale Creek trestles to fill the creek bed. Eventually the Sherman Hill/Dale Creek project would involve a work force of 131,000 men.[48]

Throughout the remainder of 1898 and into 1899, Harriman devoted much of his time to rebuilding the Union Pacific, keeping an eye and a hand on all of the massive equipment upgrading and line reconstruction projects going on across the West; that process would continue for the next decade.[49] At the same time, he set about recapturing important pieces of the Union Pacific that had been abandoned or sold off during the five years the railroad had been in receivership: by the end of 1899, he had pulled over 1,100 miles of branch lines back into the system.

Although Harriman was center stage in one of the great industries and businesses of the country, all of this activity received little notice outside of financial circles and Wall Street, and he "reached the age of nearly fifty years without attracting any great attention."[50] Even when he became chairman of the Union Pacific, his name seldom appeared in the newspapers, and when it did it was mostly in passing and with little elaboration about the man behind the name. In terms of the Union Pacific the stories were of the railroad, not the man who was rapidly making things happen and becoming its master. While the situation would change dramatically in the years ahead, as 1898 faded into 1899 E.H. Harriman enjoyed the quiet and privacy of being basically unknown to the general public.

Harriman powerful but obscure to the public as he became a railroad tycoon

PART I

A Ship's Company

ONE

A Vacation Becomes an Expedition

"To be a member of it would be the event of a lifetime."—C. Hart Merriam

The Harriman Alaska Expedition was born in the wintry, early months of 1899. "The expedition," Harriman would later write, "was originally planned as a summer cruise for the pleasure and recreation of my family and a few friends. It was intended to extend along the Alaska coast only as far as Kadiak Island,* my attention having been directed to that place by a chance conversation with Mr. D.G. Elliot, who especially interested me in the opportunities there offered for hunting the Kadiak bear, said to be the largest in the world."[1]

With that sort of vacation in mind, Harriman set about making plans and arrangements. A critical component was a serviceable vessel, large enough to provide ample room and assure safety for his family. Harriman turned to the Oregon Railway and Navigation Company, a rail and steamship line in which he had an interest. He obtained one of its steamers, the *George W. Elder*, and took steps to have it overhauled and comfortably refitted. The *Elder* was no small ship, and its size caused Harriman to rethink the trip, and to hit upon the idea of a scientific expedition: "Our comfort and safety required a large vessel and crew, and preparations for the voyage were consequently on a scale disproportionate to the size of the party. We decided, therefore, if opportunity offered, to include some guests who, while adding to the interest and pleasure of the expedition, would gather useful information and distribute it for the benefit of others."[2]

Harriman's comments on the origins of the trip, and its evolution from a wealthy family's private cruise to something of a far greater scope, have—in the minds of some—not adequately answered the question of *why*, with his vast projects on the Union Pacific underway and a myriad of acquisitions and critical activities swirling about him, he would take a two-month sabbatical, especially to a remote area as far across the North American continent as possible from New York, his base of operations and the center of the financial and business worlds.

One proffered rationale for the journey is that "the family doctor, his close friend

---

*Within the text of this book, and to preserve the accuracy of quotations such as this, many usages current at the time of the Expedition have been retained, particularly with regard to Alaskan place-names. Thus, "Kadiak" is used here and elsewhere when it reflects the spelling used in the writings of the members of the Expedition party; though "Kodiak" also appears, again reflecting the same type of contemporary usage which members of the party discovered on reaching that place. So too, where words have accepted spelling variations, such as "fiord" and "fjord," the spelling actually used in quoted diary entries, letters, and other writings is retained. Where necessary, names and usages are explained in the notes.

Lewis Rutherford Morris, ordered him to rest from business for several weeks on an extended vacation."[3] That assertion, in terms of mandated "doctor's orders"—implying a serious health issue—as the driving reason for the trip, finds scant support.[4] That said, it is not hard to imagine that with his growing portfolio of interests and positions of responsibility, as well as the schedule he had maintained, Harriman felt the simple need for some time off. Indeed, he had recognized that need as recently as September 1898, after his cross-country Union Pacific inspection tour and its immediate aftermath; noting that he was "a little used up more than I realized while working under pressure," he had left the railroad world behind and spent a week with his family at Paul Smith's remote outpost in the Adirondacks.[5] He may well have been feeling that way again in early 1899, and conceivably could have been under some friendly prodding from his family and others to take another break. As noted in the Prologue to this book, spending time with his family was always a priority with Harriman. And at this stage of the major and literal rebuilding of the Union Pacific, he may well have also been looking for a more relaxed atmosphere—away from the usual daily hum and interruptions of business—to reflect, think, and plan. There is, however, no evidence that he was experiencing any significant or serious health issues, and mandated "doctor's orders" as the rationale for the journey seems to be a grasping at the straw of an overly- and loosely-used expression in some search for a justification or deeper reason for a wealthy family's vacation.

As to the specific destination, some have asserted that he may have chosen to explore Alaskan waters because he was "beginning to visualize the most grandiose railroad scheme of all; a line that would circle the world" including, as a first step, "a railroad connecting Alaska to Siberia."[6] However, it seems clear that while an around-the-world project (though with a route which did *not* include an Alaska-Siberia railroad) eventually intrigued Harriman, it was not conceived until some years later, and then under the direct impetus of the opportunity he saw to obtain control of the South Manchuria railway, which Japan had acquired from Russia in 1905 via the Treaty of Portsmouth.[7] One of the more exhaustive studies of the Bering Crossing, and its role as the frontier between East and West, states that "there is no foundation" to the story that Harriman wanted to build a railroad causeway across the Strait or that he intended to construct a rail line across Alaska to facilitate such a Crossing project—both ideas are characterized as "myths" and "all rumor."[8] And Harriman biographer Maury Klein concludes that "there is not a shred of evidence" that Harriman had already begun to think along the lines of an around-the-world project in 1899, and that, at most, the Alaskan journey may have "helped nurture the germ of such an idea."[9] As a practical matter, it is also the case that if exploration of an Alaskan railway route were in any way or in any context the purpose of the trip, Harriman would not likely have let others plan the Expedition's route of travel, but that's essentially what he did. Shortly after the party left New York by train for Seattle, "he called together the members of the Expedition and announced that it was not his desire to dictate the route to be followed," and the group organized itself into committees, one of which was a Committee on Route and Plans to which the ship's route was entrusted, "so that from day to day and hour to hour her movements were made to subserve the interests of the scientific work."[10]

In the final analysis, Harriman's own comments about the initial plan for relaxation and a family summer cruise "only as far as Kadiak Island," and the reasons for the later decision to expand that family vacation into something far greater, are the most likely, pervasive, and persuasive answers to "why," with a number of considerations playing into the general plan and the ultimate specific focus on Alaska. For one thing, it was less than a year since he had taken his lengthy inspection trip of the Union Pacific and discovered much of what, to him, was the unknown West; and the Expedition would in fact begin with another cross-country rail trip that would create new chances to see the vast country, this time with his entire family. There was also the clear opportunity for, in the context of Harriman's life, unprecedented rest and relaxation, and the prospect of time to collect himself and reflect on next steps in his complicated business empire. In addition, there was the appeal of wilderness and the outdoors—always a part of Harriman's make-up and something he may have felt with special intensity as to Alaska, a land still a mystery to many, recently prominent in the stories of the gold rush in the Klondike in the years following 1896, and the home of that trophy Kodiak bear. So too Klein notes that once the scientists and scholars had been added to the mix, their presence "would turn the ship into a floating classroom, and the children would benefit greatly from the experience."[11] And as the idea of adding those "guests" matured, it might have crossed Harriman's mind that he had the chance to do something no one—not even the likes of Andrew Carnegie and John D. Rockefeller, pioneers in the great age of philanthropy—had done, and to have a personal role in doing it.[12]

Motives or reasons aside, the world of the appropriate scientists and scholars to invite as his guests was not one that Harriman frequented. He needed an organizing hand, with all the necessary contacts, to identify and approach those who would form a respected ship's company in many disciplines; a distinguished group that could "gather useful information and distribute it for the benefit of others." While there is no direct evidence, and there are certainly other possibilities, it seems that for advice in recruiting that organizing hand and leader he might have turned to Daniel G. Elliot, who had interested him in hunting the Kodiak bear. Elliot was then serving as Curator of Zoology at the Field Columbian Museum in Chicago, and among other things was one of the founders of the American Ornithologists' Union. The AOU's founders also included Dr. C. Hart Merriam, chief of the U.S. Biological Survey, one of the founders of the National Geographic Society, and someone who was known to Elliot to be respected and extremely well-connected throughout the scientific and academic communities.

Whether on Elliot's recommendation or otherwise, in March 1899, and accompanied by his friend Dr. Morris, Harriman traveled to Washington, D.C., to confer with Merriam.

= ◆ =

Across most of the country, and particularly on the East Coast, the late winter of 1899 had been exceptionally severe. Heavy snows had buried the city of Washington as late as Valentine's Day, and an area of extreme high pressure, combined with clear skies and a deep snow cover, had, on February 11, created the coldest morning in the Capital's history, with the thermometer registering an official -15° F.[13] However, by the morning of Saturday, March 25, temperatures had moderated and the remaining significant traces of snow in Washington were generally found scattered under the trees in Rock Creek Park and in the shadows on the sheltered north sides of the most imposing government buildings. While the weather was cool, it was a fine morning to be outdoors.

Saturday was a normal working day for many, including Hart Merriam, who could easily walk to his office at the U.S. Biological Survey on what was then B Street (and is now Independence Avenue) from his home on 16th Street, a short distance north of the White House. Merriam was then forty-four years old and a national figure in the scientific community. As a boy growing up in Lewis County, New York, on the western edge of the Adirondack Mountains, and like his contemporary the young Theodore Roosevelt, Merriam learned taxidermy and put together his own wildlife museum.[14] His collection was impressive enough that in 1871, when Merriam was sixteen years old, Professor Samuel Baird, then the Assistant Secretary of the Smithsonian Institution, was astounded when he saw it, noting that every specimen of bird or mammal was perfectly embalmed.[15] At about the same time, pursuing another interest, Merriam struck up a correspondence with John Muir regarding glaciation in California's Yosemite Valley. A year later, and through the combined influence of his father, a one-time U.S. Congressman, and Professor Baird, he joined a cadre of soon-to-be-prominent young naturalists, geologists, and botanists attached to the government's Hayden Survey; he spent the summer in the Yellowstone region, collecting birds, their nests and eggs, and in classifying the animal populations. His resulting report was highly acclaimed in the zoological community.

He soon developed a desire to make medicine and surgery his career, and after receiving his early education at Yale he studied at the College of Physicians and Surgeons of Columbia University, receiving his M.D. in 1879. For the next six years, Merriam practiced medicine in Locust Grove, New York, but he was also active and engrossed in studying the local fauna, in building up his collections, in correspondence and personal contact with others of like mind, and in developing a growing interest in mammals as well as birds. In 1883 he became one of the founders, and the first secretary, of the American Ornithologists' Union. That position notwithstanding, by that time his primary focus had turned from ornithology to mammalogy, and his private collection of mammals had reached a total of some seven thousand specimens. His expertise and reputation in both areas would also draw him into the group of thirty-three scientists and explorers who founded the National Geographic Society in January 1888; he would go on to serve on its Board of Directors for fifty-four years.

In 1885 Congress authorized the establishment of a section of ornithology in the Department of Agriculture. The American Ornithologists' Union was consulted in the choice of someone to head the new enterprise and Merriam was soon offered the position, with the title of Ornithologist. The section's mandate was later expanded to include mammalogy, and in 1896 it became the Division of Biological Survey—often and commonly referred to as the U.S. Biological Survey—with Merriam as its head.[16]

And Merriam was no stranger to Alaska. In 1891 he was appointed by President Benjamin Harrison as one of two American members of an international commission charged with looking into pelagic fur sealing operations and jurisdictional rights in the Bering Sea. In his work as a commissioner, he headed north and spent that summer in the Pribilof Islands, becoming versed in fur seals and the sealing industry.

However, Alaska might well have been one of the furthest things from Merriam's mind that last Saturday in March 1899. The routine of the office and his work were interrupted by the arrival of an unexpected visitor. Recalling that morning, Merriam would write:

> He came unannounced and told me in an unassuming, matter-of-fact way that he was planning a trip along the Alaskan coast in a privately chartered steamer and desired to take along a party of scientific men. He asked my cooperation in arranging plans for the expedition and in selecting the scientific men and outfits necessary for the work.[17]

Merriam listened, cautiously and with more than a dose of skepticism: he had never heard of Harriman, knew nothing of the man's resources, and the trip his visitor envisioned and outlined as he sat across from Merriam was on a scale and of a nature that had no precedent, particularly as a private undertaking. During the conversation, Harriman

Clinton Hart Merriam in 1901. Library of Congress.

remarked that he was "a railroad man," and after his departure Merriam made inquiries of a railroad official he knew and was assured that Harriman "was a man of means and a rising power in the railroad world."[18] With that information, Merriam was more engaged when Harriman, accompanied by Dr. Morris, called at the Merriam residence later in the day and expanded on his plans.

Harriman noted that the *George W. Elder* had been chartered and was being refitted. He also mentioned that he had already secured a number of books and maps relating to Alaska, and wanted Merriam's advice as to others that would be needed to build a substantial ship's library. Also, and while his plans were still in the early, formative stages, Harriman thought that the make-up of the cadre of scholars and scientists should include two men in each important field of science. When Merriam observed that few members of the scientific community could stand the cost of such a trip, Harriman replied that all would be his guests and at his sole expense. Merriam suggested that further planning meetings include paleontologist William Healey Dall, whose many trips to Alaska had made him the recognized authority on the region, and Grove Karl Gilbert, a geologist with an impressive resume of exploration and fieldwork in the American West. Harriman agreed, suggested another meeting at his hotel, and invited Merriam to bring Dall and Gilbert with him.[19]

The next day, at Harriman's hotel, the three scientists were quickly and completely impressed by his planning and commitment. "He was," Merriam would recall, "very much in earnest, and we realized that the expedition was bound to go, that it would afford the opportunity for scientific research, and that to be a member of it would be the event of a lifetime."[20] Dall and Gilbert quickly accepted the invitation to join the scientific party and over the next few days, and prior to Harriman leaving Washington, a series of meetings developed and fleshed-out further ideas and plans. In the waning days of March, Merriam and Dall traveled to New York City for dinner with Harriman on the evening of March 31 at the Metropolitan Club; they discussed a number of potential invitees, with Harriman authorizing Merriam to extend invitations to those men and entrusting him with the task of selecting and inviting the other members of the Expedition's scientific party.[21]

Looking back on the organizing meetings in Washington and New York, Harriman would write that with associates such as these "there was much pleasure and recreation in working out the details of the expedition, and almost imperceptibly its scope expanded and its membership grew."[22]

═ ◆ ═

On the train back to Washington following the dinner at the Metropolitan Club, Merriam and Dall undoubtedly exchanged ideas about who else to invite to join them on the Expedition. Harriman had again suggested that "there should be two men of recognized ability in each department of natural science—two zoologists, two botanists, two geologists, and so on—and that each should have an assistant."[23] While the idea of "assistants" was eventually dropped, the number was still formidable and the time was short: Harriman was intent on leaving Seattle for Alaska at the end of May, and it was now the first of April.

Recruiting such a party, even on an all-expenses-paid basis, would be complicated by the short notice; by the existing commitments and schedules of the potential invitees, who would be men with significant ongoing responsibilities; and by the fact that the journey would require a commitment of over two months, into the middle of summer. Balancing the scales was the "opportunity of a lifetime" involved in the trip by virtue of its still uncommonly known destination, coupled with the chance to be part of an unprecedented and interdisciplinary collection of accomplished men, and the intellectual exchanges that company would foster and provide. There was also the driving force of Harriman's clear and appealing purpose to "gather useful information and distribute it for the benefit of others." And Merriam had built-in recruiting tools in the largesse of Harriman, and in the stature of the core of the party that was already built around himself, Dall, and Gilbert.

William Healey Dall was an anthropologist, paleontologist, zoologist, and the country's acknowledged expert on Alaska. As a young twenty year old, Dall had first traveled to what was then Russian America in 1865, shortly after the end of the Civil War, as the naturalist with the Western Union Telegraph Extension Company's project to establish an overland and trans-Pacific telegraph line through Russia's Alaska territory and Siberia to Europe. This project was born out of the need to connect the world's ever-expanding telegraph networks, and the failure of attempts in 1857 and again in 1858 to connect North America and Europe by trans-Atlantic submarine cable. He was engaged in work on the proposed telegraph line for the next two years, working both in the interior and in sounding and bottom-sampling across the shallow water of the Bering Sea to Plover Bay in Siberia. Dall wintered two seasons in Alaska: the first near St. Michael, where the temperature dropped to -68° F. The work was abruptly halted in July 1867 with the news that an Atlantic telegraph cable had at last been completed, leading to abandonment of the Alaskan-Siberian enterprise. Dall stayed on at his own expense to complete exploration of the lower Yukon River and its delta,

William Healey Dall. Smithsonian Institution Archives.

and was at Nulato on the Yukon in February 1868 when he learned that Alaska had been purchased by the United States from the Russian government almost a year earlier.

With that news, Dall wound-up his work and six months later left for San Francisco. In 1870 he published *Alaska and Its Resources*, a benchmark work based on his observations and experiences during 1865–1868. From 1871 to 1884 he worked for the U.S Coast & Geodetic Survey, including charting stretches of the Alaska coastline, and continued his work in Alaska after he became paleontologist in the U.S. Geological Survey in 1884. On one of his trips he had explored and named the Malaspina Glacier, and his pre-eminent expertise in all phases of Alaskan exploration and discovery was reflected in a wealth of plants, animals, and places bearing his name—including Dall Sheep, which the Smithsonian naturalist and explorer Edward W. Nelson had named for him in 1877. The Harriman Expedition would be his unprecedented fourteenth trip to Alaska.

Unlike Dall, Grove Karl Gilbert had never been to Alaska, but he possessed an impressive resume of exploration in the American West and was generally recognized as the top field geologist of his day. He had joined the U.S. Geological Survey when it was formed in 1879, and had been transferred to the USGS Washington, D.C., office in 1881 when the legendary John Wesley Powell became the agency's director. Like Dall and Merriam, he was one of the founders of the National Geographic Society. Gilbert had an abiding interest in astronomy and made frequent use of the telescope at the U.S. Naval Observatory to study the craters on the Moon. He was one of the first to theorize that those craters were not the result of volcanic activity but were impact craters; though his 1893 paper on that subject drew scant notice from professional astronomers until the 1960s, when it was rediscovered and recognized as not only ahead of its time but one of the most important papers ever written on the subject. Among the large and tight circle of scientists in Washington in the late nineteenth century, Gilbert was held in high esteem for both his accomplishments and his character. The Harriman Alaska Expedition came along at a propitious time for the fifty-eight-year-old Gilbert: his invalid wife had died on March 17, and when approached by Merriam—who was a long-time, close friend—he had just given up the couple's residence, moved into a temporary apartment, and was at loose and somewhat lonely ends.

With Dall and Gilbert on board, Merriam would later note that "thus early was the nucleus of the scientific party established and the high character of the expedition assured."[24] After returning to Washington, he set to work on filling out the roster.

Grove Karl Gilbert. U.S. Geological Survey, Denver Library.

Initially, Merriam relied heavily on the eminent circle of scholars, scientists, and men of letters he knew through the Washington Academy of Sciences and through the Cosmos Club. The Cosmos Club had been founded in 1878 by a group headed by John Wesley Powell, and its home was on the eastern side of Lafayette Square, near the Merriam residence. Since its founding, the Club's quarters had been a comfortable haven and gathering place for Washington's rapidly growing community of scientists and intellectuals, men who "came to serve in various government agencies ... some to explore, survey and understand the geography and resources of the United States ... others to expand its intellectual and cultural foundations ... or build its economic, social, medical, and industrial prowess ... or set forth on expeditions to learn the world's secrets...."[25]

An early recruit, and one of those discussed at the meeting with Harriman in New York on March 31, was fellow Cosmos Club member Frederick V. Coville, a well-known botanist ... and a distinct prodigy. Tall and handsome, he graduated from Cornell University—where he enjoyed academic and athletic success—in 1887. After a brief stint at teaching, he became a career employee of the U.S. Department of Agriculture. Coville was an important participant in an 1891 Death Valley Expedition (which Merriam had organized and launched prior to his departure for service on the Bering Sea Commission), and his resulting writing on desert plants became an ongoing classic. In 1893, at age twenty-six, he became the USDA's Chief Botanist and the Curator of the National Herbarium, and throughout his career was an enthusiastic and leading member of many biological surveys in the West.

Also quickly on board was ornithologist Albert K. Fisher, a college classmate of Merriam's, with him one of the founders of the American Ornithologists' Union, and a colleague at the Biological Survey. Like Merriam, he had trained for the medical profession, but in 1885 when Merriam was named to head the newly-established section of ornithology in the Department of Agriculture, he persuaded Fisher to give up further thoughts of practicing medicine and join him in developing this new section. In 1891 Dr. Fisher served as ornithologist for the Death Valley Expedition and prepared an extensive report on the birds observed in Death Valley and adjacent poorly-known areas in California, southern Nevada, and parts of Utah and Arizona. Fisher had a growing reputation as one of the country's leading ornithologists based on his fieldwork and upon his publication, in 1893, of a monumental work on the hawks and owls of the United States.[26]

Two key members of the growing Harriman Expedition party were, like Merriam, relative youngsters when they traveled west with the government's 1871 Hayden Survey in the soon-to-be Yellowstone National Park: at that time Henry Gannett and Robert Ridgway were, respectively, twenty-five and twenty-two years old.

Gannett would go on to serve as topographer of the western division of the Hayden Survey until 1879, when he played a leading role in consolidating the government's various surveys into the United States Geological Survey. He became Chief Geographer of the USGS in 1882. Gannett's contributions to surveying, mapping, and the "face" of America were legion. His 1893 publication, *A Manual of Topographic Methods*, became the authority for methods to be used in performing topographic surveys; in the 1890s he organized and chaired the Board of Geographic Names, which identified common names for thousands of locations in the U.S., eliminated multiple or similar town names existing in the same state, and researched the name origins for the majority of the country's cities, towns, rivers, and prominent geographic locations; and in 1896 he began the nationwide system under which topographical survey crews placed the now-familiar permanent U.S. Geological Survey markers, which Gannett correctly believed would be of lasting importance to future surveys and in establishing exact locations. During his career as Chief Geographer more territory was mapped under his supervision than was ever mapped by any other man, and by 1899, at age fifty-three, he had already been dubbed "the Father of Government Mapmaking."[27]

Unlike Gannett, but like Fisher, Robert Ridgway was an ornithologist. In 1874, after his participation in the Hayden Survey, he had accepted an initial position with the Smithsonian Institution—a career relationship that continued until his death in 1929. In the early days of that relationship, the Secretary of the Smithsonian Institution lived in the Smithsonian building, and a number of the workers, Ridgway among them, also had living quarters assigned to them in various tower rooms. Here he was associated with other young naturalists, including Dall and Merriam, who had connections with the Smithsonian. In 1886 he became the Smithsonian's first Curator of Birds, a title he held throughout the remainder of his life. In his lifetime, he was unmatched in the number of North American bird species that he described, and in the course of some sixty years, beginning when he was eighteen years old, he published more than 500 titles and 13,000 printed pages, almost all relating to North American birds. As he grew settled in his position, he became increasingly averse to travel, and when approached by Merriam had some initial reluctance about joining the Expedition. Once having overcome that reluctance, he would note, in writing to a friend at Harvard, "It seems that at last I am to have an opportunity of seeing the North West Coast, having been favored by an invitation to join the Harriman Expedition. For many reasons I have hesitated about accepting the invitation, but have concluded that I ought to take advantage of the opportunity, which is one that may never occur again."[28]

In addition to the personal invitations he could extend by visiting with the leading government scientists in their Washington offices or in the comfort of the lounges of the Cosmos Club, Merriam reached across the country by letter and telegram to extend invitations to a broad range of the best and the brightest in a variety of disciplines ... including three men whose credentials were less confined to specific areas of study but who would in a later time be denominated as leading "environmentalists" and "conservationists," as those terms developed and took on meaning. They were also men who were already well-known to large segments of the American public.

One was George Bird Grinnell, owner and editor of *Forest and Stream*, one of the most popular outdoor magazines of the time. Grinnell, who proudly traced his ancestry back to the *Mayflower*, was raised in and around New York City. When he was seven years of age, his family moved to Manhattan Island and a home in Audubon Park, the estate of the naturalist and renowned bird artist John James Audubon. Grinnell's early education included tutelage by Audubon's widow. In his early twenties, after completing his undergraduate education at Yale (where, later, he would receive a Ph.D. in osteology and vertebrate paleontology), he served as a naturalist on General George Armstrong Custer's 1874 expedition to the Black Hills, almost accidentally planting the roots of a lifelong interest in the culture and welfare of Native Americans, especially the Blackfeet, Cheyenne, and Pawnee tribes. Year after year he returned to the West to expand his knowledge: in the process learning several tribal dialects and acquiring some proficiency in the sign language of the plains Indians. Those annual western trips included extended, pioneering exploration of the mountains and glaciers of western Montana, where his name soon became attached to features such as the Grinnell Glacier and Mount Grinnell, and started him thinking about acquiring land in that area from the Blackfeet and turning it into a national reservation or park.[29]

Grinnell's experiences, particularly as naturalist on an 1875 reconnaissance of the future Yellowstone National Park, also convinced him of the pending demise

of many wildlife species, particularly big game such as the buffalo; in submitting his zoological
report, which became a part of the
official government publication of
the papers of the reconnaissance,
he included a "Letter of Transmit-
tal" which decried the commer-
cialization of game, its systematic
destruction, and the threat to the
extinction of many species—that
Letter may have been the first official protest of its kind.[30] In *Forest
and Stream*, he launched sustained
campaigns against market hunting and for the adoption of realis-
tic game laws, and also gradually
expanded the magazine's focus
and editorial balance to encompass
broad-based conservationism. He
developed a close relationship with
Theodore Roosevelt, and they sub-

George Bird Grinnell. Library of Congress.

sequently organized the Boone and Crockett Club to promote the conservation and
management of wildlife.[31] The two co-edited the Club's various publications for many
years, and worked together on legislation to protect Yellowstone Park from commer-
cialization and to safeguard its wildlife. Similar fears about the extinction of game
birds and others, including birds killed solely to obtain feathers as adornment for
women's hats, moved Grinnell to found, in 1886, the first Audubon Society. The Society's spectacular membership growth—within six months it counted 10,000 members—led him to launch *Audubon Magazine* in January 1887.[32] Ten years later, as a
member of the Board of Managers of the New York Zoological Society, he played a
major role in planning the zoo that would cover over 260 acres in Bronx Park, and
which opened its doors in late 1899. Grinnell was a prolific author who was working
on a number of books when he received Merriam's invitation to join the Harriman
Expedition.

John Muir was already America's legendary naturalist. Fitting almost no single, easily definable characterization, Merriam would later admiringly eulogize
him as "a famous wanderer."[33] He would be simply identified in the official Harriman Expedition roster as "Author and Student of Glaciers." Muir's home was in the
San Francisco Bay Area. When he received Merriam's invitation he was skeptical,
uncomfortable, and perhaps suspicious: Harriman's name was unfamiliar to him,
the all-expenses-paid aspect of the trip made him concerned about being somehow
indebted to the man he learned was a railroad mogul, and he was by nature inherently
committed to maintaining his independence. Only when Merriam provided a reas-
suring follow-up, including the observation that the trip would likely include areas of
Alaska that even the well-traveled Muir had not visited, did he agree to sign on; noting rather enigmatically that "I at last decided to go, leaving proud compensation to

again, Harriman little known at the time

John Muir. Library of Congress.

any chance opportunity that might offer."[34] At age sixty-one, Muir was a veteran of a half-dozen, often quite extended previous trips to Alaska, beginning in 1879–1880 when he traveled the Inside Passage and dispatched numerous articles back to the *San Francisco Daily Evening Bulletin*. He became a recognized authority on glaciers and Glacier Bay, and one of the largest glaciers there had already been named for him. In Alaska over the years, Muir had many encounters with the Tlingit natives, who dubbed him "Great Ice Chief."[35] Apart from his Alaskan experiences, Muir's writings had become a personal guide to nature for many individuals, and he was established in the public's eye as an ecological thinker and as the nation's emerging environmental conscience. In 1892, he was one of the three co-founders of the Sierra Club, and began a twenty-two-year run as the Club's first president.

The third member of the conservationist/environmentalist triumvirate was John Burroughs, whose name was often linked with Muir's. They had much in common, including age, long and lanky frames, flowing beards, compatible philosophies of life, dedication to nature and the environment, and national reputations. Burroughs had combined careers as a federal bank examiner and an essayist until the 1880s, when he moved to the Catskill Mountains in New York. There, he embarked on a singularly focused and successful writing career that would encompass hundreds of articles on flora and fauna and natural wonders, as well as two dozen "nature" books that cumulatively sold over two million copies. For the next fifty years, until his death in 1921, he was the most famous and widely published nature writer in America. Reflecting the views of many, Theodore Roosevelt had hailed Burroughs as "foremost of all American writers on outdoor life," adding that "I can scarcely suppose that any man who cares for existence outside the cities would willingly be without anything that he has ever written."[36]

Like Muir, Burroughs was initially reluctant to join the Harriman Expedition, but for very different reasons: he was not a scientist and was very much a homebody, content and at peace for solitary weeks on end in the Adirondack-style retreat cabin that he called "Slabsides." As one of his biographers would note, in the spring of 1899 "happy in his woodland cabin poking about the woods, burning brush, rowing on the Shettega, and nibbling betimes at his pen, there came a disturbing proposition—an invitation to go on the Harriman Alaskan Expedition. With all his curiosity about new lands, he shrank from such a departure from his quiet life."[37] But after debating the question (with himself) he finally agreed to go and to serve as the Expedition's historian.

John Burroughs. Library of Congress.

An invitation that was much more quickly accepted was the one extended to zoologist Daniel G. Elliot, who had interested Harriman in Alaska and the prospect of hunting the Kodiak bear. In addition to his position with Chicago's Field Museum, Elliott had been a founder of the American Museum of Natural History in New York City.

Merriam also reached into academic circles with a number of his invitations, including one to William H. Brewer, an experienced and respected botanist and geologist who had held the Norton Chair of Agriculture at Yale University's Sheffield Scientific School since 1864. At seventy-one, Brewer would be the oldest of the Harriman party scientists. He was a veteran explorer, including a journey in 1869 into the seas of Greenland on the steamship *Miranda*, which was wrecked near the Arctic Circle, exposing the people on board to a long period of isolation and very real danger before they were rescued.

An early acceptance also came in from Benjamin K. Emerson, professor of geology at Amherst College and, simultaneously, a geologist with the USGS. Perhaps indicating that Emerson's participation had been hard-won with the college administration, Merriam, in a note acknowledging Emerson's acceptance, stressed the academic benefits that would inure from the Expedition, advising Emerson that "your college authorities must not look on this expedition as a 'junketing trip' or vacation. On the contrary, it is a phenomenal opportunity to obtain material and illustrations for future work and lectures."[38]

Merriam also asked Emerson to bring along an assistant, and Emerson promptly extended the invitation to thirty-year-old Harvard mineralogist Charles Palache, whose early field work already included uncovering the first evidence of rifts and fault lines in San Francisco Bay, presaging the seismic activity along those lines in 1906. Palache was set to be married in Cambridge on June 21; but after consulting with his fiancée, the wedding was postponed and Palache accepted the invitation.[39]

Another young scientist was the budding zoologist and entomologist Trevor Kincaid, who had drawn national acclaim for achievements while still an undergraduate student and laboratory assistant at the University of Washington. In 1897, culminating four years of work, he sent some 1,300 specimens of bees to Theodore D.A. Cockerell, then recognized as "the greatest expert on bees in America." Kincaid's collection included forty-one new species, several of which Cockerell named in Kincaid's honor. Cockerell kept one series of the Kincaid Collection and sent another duplicate series to the Smithsonian Institution.[40] Kincaid also had Alaskan experience, having traveled to the Pribilof Islands in 1897 as part of a study undertaken by the American Fur Seal Commission. These and other activities had drawn the attention of Dr. L.O. Howard of the National Museum, who recommended him to Merriam when the latter sought his advice regarding an Expedition entomologist.[41] Kincaid was ready to graduate in the spring of 1899, but missed, by a day, the University of Washington commencement exercises when he departed Seattle with the Harriman Expedition.

As the roster of scientists and scholars continued to grow, Merriam—and Harriman himself—turned to assembling those who, with Burroughs, would help to document, record, and preserve the scenes, evidence, and accomplishments of the upcoming Expedition. A photographer was a must, and Merriam quickly thought of a young Seattleite he had met

Charles Palache. National Academy of Sciences Biographical Memoirs.

not all that long ago, under some trying circumstances, on the side of Washington's Mt. Rainier.

It was a midsummer evening in 1898, and Merriam and George Grinnell[42] were in a party of six men who were on the mountain for scientific study and to support the campaign to protect Mt. Rainier—a campaign which achieved success the following March when it became the county's fifth national park. They were on the five-mile long ice field of the Nisqually Glacier when they were engulfed in rapidly moving clouds and fog that soon dramatically reduced visibility on the treacherous terrain. Just before they disappeared from view, they had been spotted from above by a climber who was taking

Edward S. Curtis—self portrait. University of Washington Libraries, Special Collections [UW2807].

pictures from a platform he had set up high above the glacier. He heard their echoing shouts, packed up his camera, and carefully picked his way down to the group; which he then guided to Camp Muir, a spot 10,000 feet up the mountain, above the worst of the encroaching fog. Around the campfire that evening, the rescued found that their rescuer was Edward S. Curtis. Talking with Curtis and seeing his work a few days later at his studio in Seattle, they soon learned that he was an accomplished landscape and portrait photographer, who also knew a good deal about Native Americans—his pictures of Indians around Puget Sound had recently been chosen for a touring exhibition sponsored by the National Photographic Society, and he already had achieved some notoriety for his iconic photograph of Princess Angeline, the ancient and last surviving child of Chief Seattle.[43] He was also an experienced and expert mountaineer, and he and his brother Asahel (destined to become a famous photographer in his own right) had journeyed to Alaska in the early stages of the Klondike Gold Rush, leading to a riveting photojournalism article, "The Rush to the Klondike," that had appeared in the March 1898 issue of the respected *Century Magazine*. In April of 1899, Merriam and Grinnell readily agreed that Curtis was ideally suited to be the Harriman Expedition's official photographer, and he quickly accepted the position.

Harriman himself apparently reached out to recruit landscape artists to capture the Alaskan scenes he anticipated, perhaps hoping to emulate the work of those artists who had accompanied earlier expeditions—such as the painter Thomas Moran and his work on the Hayden Geological Survey of the Yellowstone region. He invited Robert Swain Gifford, whose work included illustrating Theodore Roosevelt's book *Hunting Trips of a Ranchman,* and who was a long-time and respected teacher at the Cooper Union School in New York. The sixty-year-old Gifford's artist colleague on the Expedition would be Frederick Dellenbaugh, who had developed an interest in landscape painting at an early age. While still in his teens, Dellenbaugh had served as an artist and as an assistant topographer with Major John Wesley Powell's second expedition on the Colorado River in 1871–1873, where—and like many of the scientists and scholars he would accompany to Alaska—he had developed the habit of keeping a daily journal of his extensive travels. The two artists both seemed excited about the Harriman Expedition and opened an early correspondence—as April drew to a close, Gifford enthusiastically wrote to his younger colleague that "we can do a great deal together when the other specialists are entirely absorbed in their respective pursuits. On such a trip there should be, if possible, 'two of a kind.'"[44]

The two-of-a-kind landscape artists would be joined by a bird artist, Louis Agassiz Fuertes. At twenty-five, Fuertes's career was in its early stages, but he had already

achieved critical success with his illustrations in the birding magazine *The Osprey* and for the more than one hundred drawings he did for the noted ornithologist Elliot Coues's multi-volume book *Citizen Bird*—which was sub-titled *Scenes from Bird-Life in Plain English for Beginners.* Fuertes had also done a series of pen-and-ink drawings for a book, *A-Birding on a Bronco,* by Merriam's younger sister, Florence Merriam, and it was likely that Florence recommended him to her brother, who would have already been familiar with Fuertes's work and the esteem in which he was held by Coues.

In addition to photographers and artists, it was thought that it would be convenient to have stenographers available during the journey and two were recruited: Louis F. Timmerman from New York City, where he may already have been in Harriman's employ, and Julian T. Johns of

Frederick Dellenbaugh. History and Art Collection/ Alamy Stock Photo.

Washington, D.C., apparently a Merriam recruit. So too, the preservation of the specimens that were sure to be collected by the scientists would require taxidermists,
and Merriam tapped Edwin C. Starks, then in his employ at the Biological Survey, and Leon J. Cole, a student at the University of Michigan. Starks had just been
appointed—with Merriam's knowledge and support—to a position at the University
of Washington, which would commence with the fall term, shortly after the Expedition returned, and he was looking forward to making his home in Seattle.[45] Like many
of the other younger members of the Expedition party, Starks and Cole were destined
to develop important careers, in their particular cases stretching far beyond physical
preservation activities.

═ ◆ ═

From the outset, Harriman had sought to insulate the plans, the traveling party,
and, not surprisingly, himself from publicity and, in simplest terms, from being
bothered. If there was a fly in that ointment, it buzzed to the surface in the Sunday,
April 23, 1899, edition of the *New York Herald*. Under a modest page six headline
that read "Many Scientists to Invade Alaska," subtitled "Mr. Edward H. Harriman Has
Invited Distinguished Company to Visit Little Known Country," the paper reported
on the "quiet arrangements" that were being made for a trip "of national importance."
The story noted the projected hunt for the Kodiak bear, whose "skull, at least, if not
the entire skeleton of this animal, is much wanted by the American Museum of Natural History," and that "the expenses of the expedition will be enormous, but Mr. Harriman and his friends decline to talk figures." The report went on to correctly identify
Merriam, Dall, Grinnell, Brewer, and a handful of others as members of the party,
and also confidently asserted that others, including ornithologist Frank Chapman of
the American Museum, "will go," and listed "Professor Pritchard of the United States
Coast Survey" as among those who "will also be of the party."

The *Herald* story did not quote a source, and other than declining "to talk figures"
it seems unlikely that Harriman would have supplied much, if any, information. Merriam would cryptically note, "The Harriman exped. Matter has leaked out & a notice
of it appeared today in the New York Herald—glad the leak was not in the Washington
end of the line."[46] While the source of the leak is not known, the *Herald* story provides
some evidence that, despite all the inducements, not all of the invitations extended
were or could be accepted.[47] "Frank Chapman of NYC" and "H.S. Pritchett of the US
Coastal Survey" were among those discussed at the March 31 dinner meeting in New
York, and Merriam had recorded them as among those he was authorized to invite.[48]
And at least in Chapman's case the fact that the invitation was extended, but could not
be accepted, seems implicit in a post-expedition August 19, 1899, letter he wrote to
A.K. Fisher, where he noted that the fact that he missed meeting Fisher "is the crown-
ing disappointment I have had in connection with the Harriman Expedition."[49]

The most significant impacts of the *Herald* story may have been in accelerating
the recruiting process, and in tightening the secrecy of the information that circulated among all those preparing to travel.

═ ◆ ═

As April progressed and turned into early May, the final roster of the scientific party fell into place. Perhaps the most—to some—eccentric or "out of the

mainstream" (though perhaps more so at later points in his life) member of the Expedition was Charles Keeler, a biologist and ornithologist by training but increasingly a poet, architect, and spiritual-seeker, who was the director of the Museum of the California Academy of Sciences in San Francisco. Another California based recruit was William E. Ritter, a zoology professor at the University of California, Berkeley, who was an expert in sea and coastal marine life, and who was also the newly-elected president of the same California Academy of Sciences that employed Keeler.

Also wiring his acceptance was Bernhard E. Fernow, the Prussian-born former chief of the Division of Forestry in the U.S. Department of Agriculture, who had left that position in 1898 to become the founding dean of the New York State College of Forestry at Cornell University, the first four-year forestry school in the United States. If not so already, Fernow was on the cusp of becoming recognized as the father of North American forestry.

Another academic recruit was Wesley R. Coe, a zoologist and an assistant professor of Comparative Anatomy at Yale, whose central interest and expertise was in the taxonomy and natural history of marine invertebrates, especially nemerteans (ribbon worms) and bivalves. Three men who were primarily botanists were Thomas H. Kearney from the Department of Agriculture; De Alton B. Saunders, who had done substantial work on West Coast algae and seaweed, and was a professor of botany and entomology at the South Dakota Agricultural and Mechanical College in Brookings, South Dakota; and William Trelease, a botanist, entomologist, and plant taxonomist who was director of the Missouri Botanical Garden in St. Louis, and who had served, in 1894, as the first president of the Botanical Society of America. And the party acquired a noted mining engineer in Walter B. Devereux, who was based in Glenwood Springs, Colorado, but also had a business office in New York and traveled the world examining and evaluating mining sites for many companies.

In a late addition to the party, the combination of Grinnell and Merriam that had led to the recruitment of Edward Curtis came into play again with the addition of the well-known scout and frontiersman Luther "Yellowstone" Kelly as the Expedition's Chief Guide. Kelly's adventurous life began in early 1865 when, not yet sixteen, he joined the Union infantry shortly before Lee's surrender at Appomattox. Kelly's unit was then sent west to the Dakota Territory, where he completed his enlistment and then continued on, in a civilian capacity, as Chief Scout for the military District of the Yellowstone. Over the next dozen years he had a number of significant encounters with Indian war parties; served throughout the Sioux War of 1876–1877, including the pursuit of Sitting Bull in the months following the battle of the Little Bighorn; and was on hand in October 1877 when Chief Joseph and the Nez Perce surrendered in Northern Montana. Those exploits led to popular comparisons of Kelly with other frontiersmen such as Daniel Boone, Kit Carson, and Buffalo Bill Cody.[50] In the spring of 1875, Kelly met George Bird Grinnell; the first of many times that their paths would cross. In 1880 he moved to Colorado, married, and spent the next decade as a rancher, hunting and fishing guide, and justice of the peace. In 1891, the Kellys moved to Chicago, and he began a seven-year career as a government clerk. Successive transfers would eventually take the Kellys to Washington, D.C. There, in February 1898, his experiences in the West and his military contacts led to his being recruited for one of three planned War Department expeditions to Alaska, each of which was to survey key areas of that territory in light of the issues and needs that had arisen following the gold discoveries along the Klondike. Kelly was attached to the Glenn Expedition, which departed Seattle in April 1898, to explore northeastward from Prince William Sound in search of routes of travel to the Copper and Susitna Rivers and, thereafter, to move to Cook Inlet, where the objective was to find a direct, usable, year-round route to the Tanana River.

The Glenn Expedition completed its work in October, and Kelly returned to Washington, D.C. At loose ends in the spring of 1899, Kelly met with Grinnell, who mentioned the ongoing recruitment of the party for the Harriman Expedition and apparently referred Kelly to Merriam. On May 3, Kelly visited Merriam, who then raised the subject with Harriman, assumedly noting Kelly's background as a scout and his recent experience in Alaska with the Glenn Expedition.[51] Thereafter, Kelly joined Merriam and others at a dinner hosted by Harriman in New York City on May 9, and the next morning the two met at Harriman's office—resulting in Harriman including Kelly in the Expedition. "My business," Kelly would recall, "was to be to take charge of the packers to be engaged, and assist in the hunting and exploring work." Apparently to get Kelly on the ground and involved in recruiting packers and seeing to adequate equipment for the hunting parties, Harriman instructed him to "proceed without unnecessary delay to Portland, Oregon where the ocean steamer was being put in shape to carry the expedition."[52] Kelly returned to Washington and entrained for Portland on May 12, becoming one of the first of the party to head for the Pacific Northwest.

= ◆ =

In less than two months, Merriam had assembled a stellar roster of the type Harriman had in mind, qualified to gather "useful information" and, ultimately, "distribute it for the benefit of others." In early May, Merriam had also secured the cooperation of the Washington Academy of Sciences, whose endorsement put an additional and significant stamp of credibility and scientific importance on the Harriman Alaska Expedition. In the meantime, work on the *George W. Elder* continued on the West Coast, and the "guests" themselves were busy preparing for travel and for being absent from their normal pursuits for upwards of two months.

While some members of the party, including those from the West Coast, would join the Expedition in Seattle, most would travel cross country from New York City by train. To those, a letter dated May 12 and over Harriman's signature advised that "at a meeting of the Invitation Committee held on the 8th instant, it was arranged that the party for Alaska will start from the Grand Central Depot, Forty-second Street, New York, by special train, on Tuesday afternoon, May 23rd, 1899," adding (perhaps with an eye to the leak of information that precipitated the *New York Herald* article in late April) that the hour of departure would "be advised later by telegram."[53] The promised telegram set 2:00 p.m. as the departure time, and, just so the point wouldn't be missed, a follow-up letter from Harriman concerning baggage noted again that "it is particularly desirable that the time and place of departure be not made public."[54] Harriman seemed bound and determined that his Expedition would get underway quietly, and without undue attention and fanfare.

avoiding publicity

Two

Riding the Rails
to the Pacific Northwest

"A night's run west of Omaha a change comes over the spirit of nature's dream."—John Burroughs

The East Coast members of the Expedition spent the morning of Tuesday, May 23 in last minute preparations as they eyed the afternoon's two o'clock departure time. There were put-off purchases to be made, bags to be packed, final good-byes to be tended to, and loose ends to be tied-up in light of the fact that, once they left Seattle in a week's time, communications with home and office would be at best difficult, certainly irregular, and at times actually impossible for the next two months. And the precision and tone of Harriman's letters and telegrams, the anticipation about the Expedition, and the natural desire to get off on the right foot with their fellow travelers—including a benefactor most of them had yet to meet—were all undoubtedly on the minds of many in arranging their activities to ensure they would be on time for the scheduled departure.

As with a number of the out-of-towners, Charles Palache arrived in New York City on Monday. He had a meeting that evening regarding an article on jade that he was reviewing and editing for a colleague. Early on Tuesday morning, and with an eye to his delayed wedding, he reported on that meeting in the first of what would be many letters to his fiancée, Helen Markham, and also passed on to her the details of a visit he made to Tiffany & Company, where the renowned mineralogist and gem expert George Frederick Kunz "poured a handful of glorious sapphires out for me to dabble in a new sensation."[1] Frederick Dellenbaugh, like others of the party, had more mundane tasks to attend to, including stopping "at the umbrella man's in Astor Park where I was having my sketching umbrella repaired," and then meeting fellow artist Swain Gifford at the Century Club for lunch before they headed for Grand Central Station.[2]

Two other men making final travel preparations in the hours before noon reflected Harriman's concern for the health and spiritual needs of both his family group and the cadre of eminent scientists and scholars who would be his guests. One was old family friend Dr. Lewis Morris, who—not surprisingly—would serve as the Expedition's physician. Morris would be assisted by both Edward L. Trudeau, Jr., who was about to enter his final year of study at the College of Physicians and Surgeons at Columbia University, and a trained nurse, a Miss Adams.[3] The other man was the Rev. Dr. George F. Nelson. Nelson was then acting as Secretary to New York's

Episcopal Bishop Henry Potter, and would serve as chaplain on board the *George W. Elder.*

It was also a frantically busy morning in the Harriman household on East Fifty-First Street. In addition to the Harrimans and their five children, the traveling party that assembled that morning in advance of boarding carriages for the rail station included three maids[4] and Miss Dorothea Draper, the daughter of Mr. and Mrs. William Draper, family friends who lived nearby on East 47th Street. Dorothea, whose grandfather Charles Dana was editor and publisher of the *New York Sun*, was a friend of the two older Harriman daughters, Mary and Cornelia. As for E.H. Harriman himself, his thoughts that morning probably wandered from time to time to the train that would be carrying the party across the country.

That traveling party was no small group: thirty-five people would board the train in New York and ten more would join along the way. The route planned was not replicated by any regular rail service and schedule; and, in any event, being tied to such a schedule would not have suited Harriman's purposes. Perhaps thinking of the side trips he and his daughters had made on his Union Pacific inspection trip the previous autumn, Harriman wanted both to avoid publicity and to have the flexibility to adjust the schedule as the trip across the country and opportunities along the way developed. A "special" train (in the sense of one running apart from any regular schedule) was needed, and for those arrangements Harriman had enlisted the help of the Union Pacific office in Omaha.

Putting the train together was in itself not a simple task: Harriman's Union Pacific was a western railroad and its equipment was located almost exclusively in the territory west of the Mississippi and Missouri Rivers. However, the business of The Pullman Palace Car Company was nationwide and, in fact, leasing Palace Cars from Pullman for long- and short-term purposes was de rigueur.[5] Although they had to do some scrambling, the men in Omaha put together a five-car train consisting of two sleeping cars, a dining car, and a combination smoker/baggage car, all hired from Pullman, and—since Harriman did not yet have his own private car—Union Pacific business car number 100 for the personal use of Harriman and his family.[6]

Omaha also had to tackle some complex routing issues. Most of the trip would require use of trackage owned by railroads other than the Union Pacific, with the special's travels and schedule needing to be coordinated to allow for the passage of the regular trains that operated on those tracks every day. Though arrangements of this sort were complicated, railroad officers routinely extended the courtesy of use of their tracks to each other. In the case of the Harriman special the pieces ultimately fell into place, and on its way west the train would travel over seven lines: North Central & Hudson River (New York City to Buffalo); Lake Shore & Michigan Southern (Buffalo to Chicago); Chicago & Northwestern (Chicago to Council Bluffs): the Union Pacific (Council Bluffs to Granger, Wyoming); Oregon Short Line (Granger to Huntington, Oregon); Oregon Railway and Navigation Company (Huntington to Portland); and the Northern Pacific (Portland to Seattle).[7]

⇒ ◆ ⇐

At Grand Central Station, Expedition members worked their way through the midday crowds to an unmarked gate where, upon identifying themselves, a guard let them through to the train. Prior to boarding, in the midst of wisps of building steam, they mingled on the platform: renewing old acquaintances, introducing themselves to those they did not know, watching the porters as they expertly gathered-up trunks and luggage, and examining the train they were about to board.

The exteriors of Pullman cars of the age were impressive, with highly-finished wood that was painted and adorned with elaborate scrolls and bars, striping, and lettering. Pullman gave names to each of its sleeping, dining, and smoking cars, and the names of the car's comprising the special were prominently displayed on the outside of each of them: wandering down the platform next to the cars, the Reverend Nelson recorded that the two sleepers were "Borachio" and "Horatio," the dining car was "Gilsey," and the smoking car was named "Utopia."[8]

On boarding, Nelson and the others found interiors which reflected "the opulence and extraordinary artistry" that were standard on Pullman Palace Cars of the late nineteenth century, including "heavy rich fabrics, etched and beveled glass, brass ornamentation, wood carvings, and dark wood panels adorned with beautiful inlays of various designs."[9] The two sleeping cars had a number of private compartments with facing window seats, berths for two (in some cases three), a lounge chair or two, a clothes locker, and luggage storage. "Utopia" featured one of Pullman's standard set-ups for such a car: smoking and reading areas with comfortable wicker armchairs and settees, a buffet, a barber shop, and—taking up about a quarter of the car's length and space—a baggage room. Harriman had gathered a small library of books and maps in the smoking car, along with several brands of fine cigars.

With all present and accounted for, the special got underway promptly at two o'clock. As it pulled out of the station, Harriman worked his way through the cars and compartments to welcome his guests—some of whom jumped up so quickly at his approach that they banged their heads on the closed upper berths above their seats. The botanist Thomas Kearney would recall his embarrassment when he became the latest to do so, and that Harriman waved it off with a laugh and said, "You are the fifth man who has done that."[10]

After Harriman had made his rounds, and as the guests enjoyed a respite from the busy activities of the day, John Burroughs sat alone at a window as the train rolled up the Hudson Valley, within sight of his quiet farm. Still anxious and unsure about his place on the Expedition and in the party of "scientific men," he pulled out his journal and made his first entry.

> Join the Harriman expedition to Alaska today in New York. Pass my place on the Hudson at 4 p.m. Look long and fondly from car window upon the scenes I am to be absent from till August. The sun is shining warmly. I see the new green of the vineyards. Wife is waving her white apron from the summer-house. I sit alone in my room in the Pullman car and am sad. Have I made a mistake in joining this crowd for so long a trip? Can I see nature under such conditions? But I am in for it.[11]

Burroughs spirits may have been buoyed at dinner. Settled in, and randomly seated in groups of four, the guests enjoyed a casual setting for conversation. At each place in the dining car they found a card with a printed Bill of Fare that featured Little Neck Clams, Baked Bluefish, and Prime Roast Beef.[12] "Our table," Palache would record, "was in a constant roar.... Altogether there is a spirit of friendliness and good fellowship which promises well for the expedition. There is all the feeling of a house party—every guest at liberty to speak to every other as he wishes or to remain silent if he chooses."[13]

At midnight, with most of its passengers asleep, the special pulled into Rochester to pick up the Cornell University forester Bernhard Fernow, as well as Mrs. Harriman's brother William Averell, his wife, and their daughter Elizabeth. The two teen-aged Harriman girls and Dorothea Draper stayed up to welcome Elizabeth—as a group, they were destined to soon be christened the "Big Four" by John Muir.

The next morning, after a quick stop in Toledo to board the taxidermist Leon Cole, Harriman called the group together in the smoking car Utopia and announced, as Merriam would recall, that as to the upcoming cruise he desired "to leave the details of the route and itinerary to those most familiar with the region and the opportunities it was likely to afford."[14] To make that happen, he proposed to create a series of committees to deal with details ranging from a "Committee on Route and Plans," to committees in various scientific disciplines from "Botany" to "Zoology," and to other committees responsible for things like "Big Game," "Lectures," and "Music and Entertainment." By late afternoon, a dozen committees had been formed, involving most of the guests and also including Mrs. Harriman, Mrs. Averell, and the Big Four. The Committee on Route and Plans included Harriman and Merriam, together with the chairmen of each of the scientific discipline committees, plus Dr. Morris and Captain Peter Doran of the *George W. Elder*. Looking back on the committee structure and how it operated, Merriam wrote that it was "an organization which perfected its plans in advance and took advantage of every opportunity for work, thus accomplishing results out of all proportion to the time spent in the field."[15]

Later that day, as the train made its way through Indiana, Emerson and Palache watched the passing, sun-bathed countryside and Emerson "regaled" his young companion with a "cheerful account" of a train accident he had been involved in some years earlier, at a point on the line they had passed by that morning, and in which he had sustained broken ribs, a broken leg, and a broken arm. "For all that, he is alive and cheerful now," Palache would record, though also noting that Emerson mentioned he was only 55 years old, "instead of the 70 he looks and I thought him."[16] Like Emerson, Palache himself also had occasion to wax nostalgic, recalling how his mother had travelled to the Pacific Coast in a prairie schooner drawn by oxen on a six months journey, covering at best eight miles a day. "While he was telling this," Nelson would observe, "we were speeding along at the rate of 65 miles an hour."[17]

In Chicago, Daniel Elliott, William Trelease, and De Alton Saunders joined the traveling party. There was enough time in the Windy City for one group to visit the Field Museum, for another group to explore the campus of the University of Chicago, and for the whole party to meet for dinner before returning to the train. That evening, Palache described the day's events in a long letter to Helen Markham, including that he had sat at lunch with Mrs. Harriman, who proved to be quite aware that he had delayed his wedding to be a part of the Expedition. After reporting that, because of the postponement, Mrs. Harriman had said "We ladies consider it our duty to be specially kind to you," Palache hastily cautioned Helen not to be afraid, since "the ladies except the married ones are much too young to be dangerous!" A little later that evening he composed a second letter to send with the first, alerting Helen that he had learned "we shall probably receive no mail after leaving Seattle until our return there," and advising her to "address any letters you may write to Seattle General Delivery, care Harriman Alaska Expedition" and he would pick them up on the Expedition's return in early August. He added that "we can send mail more often than we receive it

Harriman Special Train on the Continental Divide in Wyoming. Photograph by Mary Harriman Rumsey. National Museum of the American Indian, Smithsonian Institution [NMAI AC 053_010_000_L00688].

and should be able to let you hear four or five times I hope."[18] He would prove to be far more prolific than that in writing to her.

Coming out of Chicago the morning of Thursday the 25th, the special switched to the tracks of the Chicago & Northwestern Railroad as it ran across Illinois and Iowa. "All west of the Mississippi was new land to me," Burroughs mused, "and there was a good deal of it. Throughout the prairie region I, as a farmer, rejoiced in the endless vistas of beautiful fertile farms, all busy with the spring planting, and reaching from horizon to horizon of our flying train."[19] While others camped at the windows and enjoyed the scenery, Harriman was busily composing telegrams to the Union Pacific offices in Omaha regarding last minute details, ideas, and arrangements. On their arrival in that city, they left the train in favor of trolley transportation, provided by Union Pacific President Horace Burt, to the Greater American Exposition—which was a follow-up to the Trans-Mississippi and International Exposition "world's fair" that Omaha hosted in 1898. Burt added his private car to the special and hitched a ride to the UP construction sites in Wyoming.

As the train moved west, Burroughs found a different countryside.

A night's run west of Omaha a change comes over the spirit of nature's dreams. We have entered upon that sea of vast rolling plains; agriculture is left behind; these gentle slopes and dimpled valleys are innocent of the plow; herds of grazing cattle and horses are seen here and there; now and then a coyote trots away indifferently from the train, looking like a gray homeless kill-sheep shepherd dog; at long intervals a low hut or cabin, looking very forlorn; sometimes a wagon track leads away and disappears over the treeless hills. How I wanted to stop the train and run out over those vast grassy billows and touch and taste this unfamiliar nature.[20]

There was more in store for Burroughs than running over "vast grassy billows." Passing Dellenbaugh in the dining car that afternoon, Dr. Morris announced, "I have just given John Burroughs the sensation of his life—riding on the front of the engine for the last 25 miles."[21] Burroughs, predictably, waxed a bit more eloquent about the experience.

I had my first ride upon the cowcatcher, or rather upon the bench of the engine immediately above it. In this position one gets a much more vivid sense of the perils that encompass the flying train than he does from the car window. The book of fate is rapidly laid bare before him and he can scan every line, while from his comfortable seat in the car he sees little more than the margin of the page.... How rapidly those two slender rails do spin beneath us, and how inadequate they do seem to sustain and guide this enormous throbbing and roaring monster which we feel laboring and panting at our backs. The rails seem ridiculously small and slender for such task; surely, you feel, they will bend or crumple up or be torn from the ties.... During this ride of twenty-five miles we struck two birds—shore larks—and barely missed several turtle doves.[22]

News of the Morris-Burroughs adventure spread quickly; later in the day other members of the party found spots on the "bench" for similar rides. "I do not think I care to repeat the ride," Palache noted after he had taken his turn, "but am bound to get into the cab for a trip before we come to the end of our journey. This is one of the privileges of being with railway magnates on a special train."[23] And Palache experienced another "privilege" early in the day, and again in the evening, when he twice visited Harriman's private car—visits he dutifully described to Helen.

The car is last on the train and the last third of it is an observation room with big plate windows from floor to roof on end and sides. Comfortable chairs—electric fans—maps conveniently hung—flowers, books—candy, and all the other "comforts of home" including the company of the four girls who are jolly and simple and not in the least spoiled by the luxury of their surroundings. We talked and read there nearly all the morning. [*And as to the evening visit*] There was a grand sunset with high piled masses of silver lined dark clouds and fleecy gold veils and after that was over the girls took some of us back to the observation car for some "singing" (God save the mark!). I also sang as you will be distressed to learn but they all stood it nobly and indeed there were some no better than myself. We all enjoyed it anyway and I was thinking of you all the time and so I know was Miss Mary Harriman for the girls are of an age to take a romantic interest in anything like our separation. Altogether both the young ladies and Mrs. H. are very nice and show their millions absolutely not at all, which is delightful.[24]

By the morning of the 27th the party had left Wyoming. The morning wake-up chimes at 5:00 a.m. found them stopped at Shoshone Station on the Snake River in Idaho. Harriman had telegraphed ahead for transportation to Shoshone Falls, some twenty-five miles away. The notice had been short, and the local resources had been sorely taxed to provide sufficient transportation for the group. As they gathered after breakfast they found "a big Concord coach holding about 12–15 people with six horses—a 2-seated, 2 horse wagon for 6 people, Mr. Harriman's 2-horse buggy, and ten saddle horses."[25] The party divided themselves up over the coaches, wagons, and horses for the three-hour trip, with Burroughs securing a lofty place beside the driver of the old stagecoach. As with the ride on the front of the engine, this new experience ate away at his brooding: "The day was clear and cool and the spirits of the party ran high. That ride over the vast sagebrush plain in the exhilarating air, under the novel conditions and in the early honeymoon of our journey—who of us can ever forget it?"[26] At Shoshone Falls, they clambered down to the river to board a ferry that took them across to the other bank for a spray-soaked, closer view of the waterfall. At 2 p.m. and after lunch at the little hotel above the rushing water, they began the return trip. Whether by a different route, or just at a slower and more leisurely pace, the ride back took nearly two hours longer than the morning's trip out to the Falls. "By 6:30 p.m. we are back to the train, have washed the dust out of our throats with a magnificent glass of cask beer from the saloon ... and the dust from our bodies with a towel bath, and at 7:30 sit down to a game and fish dinner with the appetites of wolves and satisfaction beaming from every face," Palache would write, concluding that "it was a rare experience—a perfect day."[27]

The special train arrived in Boise just at sunrise on Sunday morning, and was met by a welcoming delegation from the Board of Trade, whose leaders escorted the party onto electric trolley cars and drove them down to the Boise Natatorium, where everyone had a chance to enjoy the mineral hot springs.[28] It being the Sabbath, after everyone had bathed and dressed, Starks would observe that "Cleanliness was followed by Godliness," and in a brief service Dr. Nelson "delivered a platitudinous sermon that I think perhaps did none of us any particular harm."[29] By noon the special was back underway, riding the rails west to Oregon.

During the night, the train entered Washington and passed through Walla Walla. Breakfast was being served as the station in Pullman, Washington flashed by, and they were soon slowing to a stop a little further along the line in the town of Colfax. Here Harriman had arranged for another day-trip. The party soon transferred from its train to a small Northern Pacific special that took them down a winding side canyon to Lewiston, Idaho: a trip that came to an abrupt halt at a point where the tracks were blocked by the final cleanup of a train wreck. The last of the derailed but intact freight cars to be righted was in the grip of a wrecking engine, and had been swung out over a steep embankment as the crew labored to hoist it back on the track. The Northern Pacific officer accompanying the train carrying the Harriman party advised the foreman of the wrecking gang that the Harriman train couldn't wait, and that he should just drop the freight car down the bank into the ravine below. The foreman pleaded for ten more minutes; and soon succeeded in getting the car on the track, allowing the reassembled freight train to move ahead and out of the way. With the tracks cleared, the party completed its trip to Lewiston, where they crossed the Snake River on a rickety ferry to board a stern-wheel steamer for a 150-mile scenic river cruise. That evening the steamer tied-up below a bridge near the junction of the Snake with the Columbia River, and all aboard were sent scrambling up through the twilight to the tracks on the bridge, where they were soon picked up by their own train, which had come around from Colfax.[30]

On Tuesday, as the special ran down the Columbia River Gorge, Charles Palache made good on his vow to ride in the engine cab. And as they drew near Portland the train made a brief stop at Multnomah Falls, which Burroughs would later describe as "perhaps the most thrillingly beautiful bit of natural scenery we witnessed on the whole trip.... I hardly expected to see anything in Alaska or anywhere else that would blur or lessen the impression made by these falls, and I did not, and probably never shall."[31]

Expedition members aboard ferry crossing the Snake River. Photograph by Grove Karl Gilbert. University of Washington Libraries, Special Collections [Harriman 8].

≋ ◈ ≋

As the Harriman special needed west, Charles Keeler and John Muir boarded a regularly-scheduled train in San Francisco late in the day on Friday, May 26, bound for Portland, where they would meet up with the main party en route to Seattle. The two men, acquainted but not yet friends, shared a compartment on the train, and both had misgivings about their participation in the Expedition.

While when first invited Muir had been hesitant because of the all-expenses paid nature of the Harriman Expedition and his fear of somehow becoming indebted to a railroad tycoon, it now appeared that he was also simply tired and worn-out. Writing to his editor and friend Walter Hines Page on the day before leaving San Francisco, he lamented, "I start tomorrow on a two month trip with Harriman's Alaska expedition. John Burroughs and Professor Brewer and a whole lot of good naturalists are going. But I would not have gone, however tempting, were it not to visit the only part of the coast I have not seen.... This has been a barren year and I am less the willing to go.... I lost half the winter in a confounded fight with sheep and cattlemen and politicians on behalf of forests. During the other half I was benumbed and interrupted by sickness in the family."[32] Keeler, on the other hand, was simply dreading the absence from his wife Louise and their young daughter, Merodine. The family's financial situation and the apparent delicate health of all three of them were constantly on his mind, as reflected in his many letters home. On the first day out from San Francisco he concluded a letter to Louise, "I feel very well and we must both get stronger during the next two months."[33] By the 28th he was already writing his fourth letter home, noting,

"There is little to tell you, dearest, except that I am thinking of you and miss you all the time. It has been a sacrifice for both of us to have me go on this trip and I only hope there will be enough compensation in the end."[34] The last reference apparently related to hoping that the trip would provide material for articles he might write and sell to various magazines.

The misgivings the two men felt gave way, at least in part, as they traveled together and developed a friendship. Muir felt fortunate to have Keeler as a travel partner, finding him a "charming companion."[35] And Keeler quickly found that Muir "delights in talking"—the naturalist kept a weather eye out on the passing scenery, identifying species of trees they passed, talking about the geology of the mountains, and also sharing accounts of his travels and adventures.[36]

On the train, Muir encountered William Holabird, a long-time railroad man who was then working for the Southern Pacific. Holabird told Muir he was going to Portland to meet Harriman with regard to the purchase of a seventy-five-mile section of railroad in southern California. Perhaps via an introduction from Muir, Keeler also passed some time with Holabird and gained a greater appreciation of Harriman's position when Holabird described him as "the president of the board of managers of five or six railroads ... and one of the leading railroad men of the country."[37]

Muir and Keeler arrived in Portland on the 29th and checked into the Portland Hotel to await the arrival of the main party. In the hotel lobby, Muir encountered the president of the Mazamas, a local mountaineering club. That chance meeting may have played a part in a delegation of the Mazamas being on hand—along with Keeler and Muir—as a welcoming party when the special pulled into the train station at noon on May 30. It was Decoration Day, with parades and other celebrations around town. And news of the Harriman Expedition made the Portland papers: an editorial in *The Oregonian* called the trip "a striking example of the beneficent possibilities of great wealth," and lauded Harriman as a man who "has done his country and the cause of human learning a signal service."[38] There is no record of any reaction by Harriman to the newspaper editorial.

That evening, Muir and Keeler got their first taste of the sort of adventures the main party had been experiencing in their cross-country journey when they boarded a boat that would take them all to Kalama, Washington. In a letter to Louise dated the 31st, Keeler wrote, "When we left Portland yesterday we took a new boat (the fastest stern wheel steamer in the world) and she made her first trip with our party, humming along at a speed of 25 miles an hour. All the boats in port whistled salutes as we passed."[39] Arriving in Kalama, they found the special train waiting and soon settled in for a late dinner as, using the tracks of the Northern Pacific, they headed north through the night for Puget Sound and the city of Seattle.

⸺ ◆ ⸺

Yellowstone Kelly was already in Seattle. After leaving Washington, D.C., on May 12, he had traveled cross country through Salt Lake City on his way to Portland, where the *George W. Elder* was being refitted and refurbished. Part of Kelly's assignment as an "advance man" for the Harriman party was to hire hunters and packers for the Expedition, and it appears that in traveling west Kelly took an initial step in that direction by contacting Colorado ranchman and hunter C.H. Fredell; Fredell caught a train in Big Piney, Wyoming, on the 24th and traveled to Portland, where he boarded the *Elder*.[40] After Fredell's arrival, Kelly headed overland to Seattle to engage packers, probably intending to pick from among the many mountaineers, outdoorsmen, and failed miners that populated the waterfront in that city. On arriving, however, he found that Edward Curtis had already recruited a cadre of packers. "I learned later," Kelly would write, "that the so-called packers were mostly young college students who had little or no experience in packing," though "Robb, one of them, was an experienced packer, had been a seal hunter, and was an experienced boatman."[41] Kelly's concerns about the packers would prove to be prescient.

Also arriving in Seattle a day or two in advance of the main party were George Bird Grinnell, who had been at the Blackfeet reservation in Montana, and William Ritter. And on Monday, May 29 the *Elder*, carrying a crew of sixty-five under the command of Captain Peter Doran, and with Fredell also on board, arrived from Portland, maneuvered along the Seattle waterfront, and tied up at the foot of Seneca Street.[42]

An iron-hulled passenger/cargo steamship, 250 feet long and 38 feet wide, the *Elder* was launched in 1874. She had a triple expansion steam engine rated at 900–1000 horsepower, and like many steamships of the time was equipped for sail if needed, with tall masts forward and aft of the stack. Acquired by the Oregon Steamship Company in 1876, the *Elder* became a fixture and a familiar sight in West Coast shipping, particularly after being sold to the Oregon Railway and Navigation Company in 1880. Operating primarily out of Portland, and under a number of different captains, she served Victoria, British Columbia and Alaskan ports including Juneau, Douglas, Glacier Bay, and Sitka. Drawing only 16 feet of water, she was well-suited for visiting a variety of small ports and undeveloped coastal areas.

Nonetheless, like many ships of the time, the *Elder's* life in the North Pacific was not without incident. On one occasion she ran aground two miles west of Point Wilson, near Port Townsend in Washington. Several tugs were able to float her off without significant damage. In September of 1890, the *Elder* clipped an iceberg in Glacier Bay while on its way to Victoria: the steamer was beached to avoid sinking, and then refloated and dry-docked for repairs at Esquimalt, British Columbia. The *Elder* secured a place in history on July 30, 1897, when she was the first ship to leave Portland for Skagway at the start of the gold rush, and it remained in service to ports in southwest Alaska until chartered for the Harriman Expedition.[43]

⸺ ◆ ⸺

The special arrived in Seattle shortly before midnight and its passengers woke on the morning of May 31 to overcast skies, light winds, and an intermittent, spitting rain. At the waterfront, the task of loading supplies and equipment onto the *Elder* got underway early—and it quickly became clear it would be a long process, consuming more of the day than planned, and leaving the members of the traveling party to their own devices.

Keeler and Palache went for the mail right after breakfast: Palache finding two letters from Helen Markham, and Keeler overjoyed at receiving two from Louise. Keeler's mood was dampened less by the rain than by hearing, probably from Palache, that "no attempt is to be made to forward mail," so, he wrote to Louise, "unless a letter you sent to Sitka or some other point reached me by the merest chance I will have no further word." Still, he continued, "I hope you will try to reach me each time the steamer sails, with a short word, and if I do not get them they will return to you."[44]

Muir and Burroughs set out together and "sauntered about town most of the day," brunched at the Rainier Club with other members of the party, and were interviewed by a newspaper reporter who, Muir noted, "wrote a queer notice of 'Two famous men.'"[45] Others stopped at Curtis's studio on Second Avenue, where the photographer and his young assistant, Duncan Inverarity, were packing and loading glass plates and photographic equipment for transport to the *Elder*. The thirty-one-year-old Curtis was an imposing figure: husky, 6'2" tall, with a mustache and a Vandyke beard, he often sported a broad-brimmed hat, tipped rakishly to one side and festooned with a silk-ribbon hat band.

Last minute shopping was in order for some, and there were plenty of outfitters along the streets bordering the docks and wharfs. The shoppers may have had in hand a memo that William Healey Dall had sent out to Emerson and, apparently, others under the head "Notes on Outfit for Alaska Trip," advising:

> I have found wash-leather gauntlets comfortable wear, and, if one is to penetrate the shrubbery any distance from the shore, a mosquito net or veil will be found convenient at times. For camping where there is shrubbery, away from the sea, a piece of mosquito netting is sometimes indispensable for a good night's rest. On such occasions, as every traveler knows, old clothes and a negligee flannel shirt are the proper wear. It is well to have a good supply of handkerchiefs, as laundresses are rare; and (except at one or two places) starched linen cannot be done up.
>
> If anyone has any pet medicines, soap or similar trifles, which they are accustomed to, they should take them along; as they are not likely to meet with such specialties at the shops in the Alaskan towns.[46]

Palache was one of those wandering through the shops, and he would report to Helen, "I purchased a suit of what is called Mackinaw—a sickly yellow sort of woolen garment said to be dry and warm and much used by lumbermen and such. I hope it will do. Otherwise I had nothing to get but odds and ends—a supply of tobacco and a hair-cut all of which are now accomplished."[47]

While his guests busied themselves, Harriman stood in the drizzle, mostly on the wharf, at times on the *Elder's* hurricane deck with Captain Doran, watching as the ship was loaded. Doran had already seen that a newly-acquired steam launch and two naphtha-powered launches were secured on deck: those boats would transport the parties that would be put ashore at various points during the journey. Throughout the day a crowd of curious citizens braved the rain and watched as a seemingly endless stream of supplies and equipment arrived and disappeared into the ship: trunks and innumerable smaller pieces of personal luggage, Curtis's cameras and photographic supplies, foodstuffs, tents, sleeping bags, folding canvas canoes, surveyors' tripods and transits, painters' easels and canvas, guns and ammunition, hunters' traps, a piano and two violins, boxes of books and cases of cigars and champagne, lantern slide projectors, a graphophone that could both play and record voices, and all sorts of paraphernalia.[48]

The loaded cargo also included a menagerie of farm animals, which were in some ways a precaution. Burroughs would explain that "we have hunting parties among us that expect to supply us with venison and bear meat, but to be on the safe side we take aboard eleven fat steers, a flock of sheep, chickens, and turkeys, a milch cow, and a span of horses. The horses are to be used to transport the hunters and their traps and to pack out the big game. The hold of our ship looked like a farmer's barnyard."[49]

It was while the animals were being loaded that Mrs. Harriman arrived with the younger children: nine-year-old Carol, Averell, who was seven, and Roland, then three and a half, all attired in nautical gear. Searching his mind years later for his earliest memory in life, Roland would recall that "the first thing I distinctly remember … was a crateful of squawking chickens dropped into the water between a steamship and a dock."

> I was standing at the rail of the steamship in Seattle, watching the last-minute preparations before departure, and among other things some live poultry, pigs and even a cow were put on board. The reason for the cow was to produce milk for one young passenger, Roland. Well, one of the crates of chickens slipped out of the net and into the water and that is what I first remember in life. The desperation of those chickens! Fortunately, I am glad to say, they were rescued, and they and their eggs were eaten on the trip.[50]

While eyeing the loading operation, Harriman also greeted his guests as they came on board in small groups, spending a few extra minutes with the newcomers—Ritter, Grinnell, Kincaid, Curtis, and Inverarity. With all now accounted for, and perhaps still unsure of where he himself fit in, Burroughs would record—and muse—that "our completed party now numbered over forty persons besides the crew and the officers of the ship (126 persons in all), and embraced college professors from both the Atlantic and Pacific coasts—botanists, zoologists, geologists, and other specialists, besides artists, photographers, two physicians, one trained nurse, one doctor of divinity, and at least one dreamer."[51]

specialties

professions

The passenger accommodations on the *Elder* for the "dreamer" and his fellow travelers were spread over two decks, with refinished, repainted, and newly furnished individual staterooms. The forward half of the Upper Deck, beginning behind the Pilot House and the Captain's Cabin, had staterooms that opened onto a promenade extending around the entire ship and wide enough to accommodate deck chairs.[52] Keeler found himself in stateroom number 49, "only one removed" aft of the Captain's cabin, with William Brewer in the intervening room. He soon found that he would not have these quarters to himself. Writing home, he reported that "Mr. Muir's stateroom had to be given up for the pilot, so they have put him in with me. Of course we are a trifle crowded but how great a privilege to be cooped up for two months in a room with John Muir!" and enclosed a sketch showing that on the *Elder's* port side the rooms aft of the shared Muir & Keeler cabin were occupied by Ritter, Burroughs, and then the Harriman family party.[53] Aft of midships, the Upper Deck contained additional perimeter staterooms and an interior Social Hall, complete with a stage and ample seating. Completing the Upper Deck, and extending to the ship's stern, was a large, furnished Smoking Room.

The Upper Deck's Social Hall was at the head of stairs leading down to the "Dining Saloon," located on the Main Deck and extending all the way aft to the stern. Staterooms on the Main Deck ran the length of the Dining Saloon on both sides and opened into the dining area. "Most of us young fellows are on the lower deck," Louis Fuertes advised his parents, adding that "we will probably form a sort of little club to jolly the upper deckers who are either old or aristocrats or something."[54] With the help of some of those "aristocrats," the Harriman girls, Fuertes secured a studio on the Upper Deck just forward of the Social Hall and "right up in the skylights over the engine room—a place painted white, with a course of windows all around and skylights overhead."[55] And Fuertes was not alone in having found room to work: Trevor

Kincaid was delighted to discover that space on the deck below the Main Deck had been "partitioned off to form small laboratories in which we could spread out and organize our materials."[56]

As people unpacked and settled in, the long, rainy day of delay and anticipation finally gave way to departure. At six o'clock the lines were pulled in and the ship's whistle echoed on the Seattle waterfront. In his diary, Dellenbaugh wrote that "we cast off, the wharf being full of people who had waited to see us start—a few friends and the rest idlers. The graphophone horn was put out of the window and music by the band floated distinctly on the air and we moved away."[57]

THREE

The Land to Which They Were Going

"At present few people go to Alaska to live; they go to stay until they have made their stakes."—Henry Gannett

The Harriman Alaska Expedition could not and did not take place in a vacuum divorced from the history of its destination or from what Alaska was—both in reality and, somewhat differently, in America's collective mind's eye—at the close of the nineteenth century when the *George W. Elder* steamed out of Seattle.

While the *New York Herald* headline of April 23, 1899, that spoke of the Expedition party setting out for "Little Known Country" may have reflected some degree of eastern provincialism, for the majority of the *Herald's* readers, and the country's citizenry in general, it was an apt and accurate characterization that in a short phrase of only three words covered the territory's history, its geography, its Native peoples, its existing and potential resources, and almost everything else pertaining to Alaska. The fact of the matter was that comparatively little was commonly known, and a good deal of that purported "knowledge" was the stuff of myth and misinformation. The situation had changed very little since 1875 when, in a report to the U.S. Treasury Department, the naturalist Henry Wood Elliott wrote: "On the subject of Alaska, it is safe to assert that no other unexplored section of the world was ever brought into notice suddenly, about which so much has been emphatically and positively written, based entirely upon the whims and caprices of the writers, and, therefore ... the truth in regard to the Territory does frequently come into conflict with many erroneous popular opinions respecting it."[1]

As to what *was* generally and accurately known, much of that was narrowly focused on the purchase of Alaska from Russia thirty-two years earlier, and on the excitement generated by the Klondike Gold Rush beginning in the summer of 1897.

Even as to the parameters and size of the land, and despite three decades of American ownership, Henry Gannett, the country's Chief Geographer, would note shortly after the Expedition's return that "the exact area of Alaska cannot at present be known, owing to the fact that the boundaries are as yet located only approximately. The seacoast, which forms by far the greater part of the boundary, has not been accurately mapped, except in small part, while the land boundary on the southeast, which separates our territory from Canada, has not been defined, except in the general terms of the treaty of cession from Russia."[2]

The very vastness of the Alaskan subcontinent made the country, in its various parts and as a whole, comparatively unknown even to its scattered Native peoples. The Tlingit, Haida, and Tsimshian of Alaska's southeastern coast had but imperfect knowledge of the Aleuts and the island chain they inhabited; the coastal Indians and the Aleuts were, by distance and towering mountain ranges, separated from the Athapaskan groups and their homelands in the interior and the subarctic north; and all had little sustained contact with the culture and lives of the Inupiat and Yupik Eskimos in the far reaches bordering the Bering Sea and the Arctic Ocean. That is not a surprising situation, considering that the territory covered some 600,000 square miles with over 33,000 miles of coastline. And that vast expanse of Native-occupied lands was very sparsely populated: although at one time undoubtedly at least somewhat higher, in 1900 the total combined and recorded Native population was less than 30,000.[3]

At the dawn of the twentieth century, William Healey Dall, speaking from a European and American perspective of what counted as "history," wrote that "the history of Alaska is practically the history of exploration and trade along its coasts and within its borders."[4] The primary players in that history of exploration, over a period covering a little more than 150 years, were Russians and Americans. And that history— together with all the natural ingredients and make-up of the territory itself—shaped the Alaska of 1899 that awaited the members of the Harriman Alaska Expedition.

⇒ ◆ ⇐

The non–Native history of Alaska dates back to one of the last acts of Czar Peter the Great. In the fading light of his reign, in late December 1724—he'd live for just another month—Peter named the Danish-born and trained Russian Navy veteran Vitus Bering to traverse the vast emptiness of Siberia and explore the largely unknown Russian Pacific. Bering's travels and exploits under Czar Peter's mandate would occupy him for most of the next twenty years and involve two separate expeditions. His efforts throughout that time were often and much delayed: in part because of continuing political issues in Saint Petersburg following Peter's death, and to an even greater extent because of the difficulties not only in marshaling large numbers of men and huge volumes of supplies, but in moving them across the wild, sparsely-settled, weather-battered, and seemingly endless expanses of Siberia. It would be nearly four years after receiving the Czar's commission before Bering would first set out into the Pacific.

In 1728, in a sixty-foot long, two-masted vessel they built on-site, Bering and a crew of forty men sailed from the Kamchatka Peninsula on Siberia's Pacific coast. They explored north to the Chukchi Peninsula and into the Strait that would eventually carry Bering's name, but they did not cross to the North American continent.

That would happen on Bering's second expedition, which set sail from the Kamchatka port of Petropavlovsk in June of 1741. The party was divided into two ships: the *Saint Paul*, under the command of Lieutenant Aleksey Chirikov, and the *Saint Peter*, which served as Bering's flagship. Sixteen days out into the Pacific, the ships lost contact with each other in heavy fog and drizzle. They never saw each other again, though both would sight the Alaskan coast and Bering would make landings at various points. Under Chirikov, the *Saint Paul* reached parts of the Alexander Archipelago west of present-day Ketchikan, and came within sight of various islands in the Aleutians as it slowly worked its way back to the Russian coast, arriving there in mid–October. The *Saint Peter's* journey lasted much longer. Bering and his seventy-six-man crew would sight the volcanic peak of what would later be named Mount St. Elias; they would make landfall on Kayak Island off the southern coast of Prince William Sound; and as they sailed an erratic return course westward they would anchor at various points in the Shumagin Islands, including at Bird Island, where they met their first Natives—Aleuts who came out to the ship in kayaks. The voyages of both ships provided the first European descriptions, though limited ones, of the land and people of Alaska.

All this came at a high cost. The *Saint Peter* struggled to find its way home; its crew suffered heavy losses to scurvy; and in mid–November 1741, as the ship lay at anchor in a bay that those on board thought was on the Kamchatka Peninsula, a terrific storm severed the anchor cables and beached the ship—which sank, taking with it much of the party's gunpowder and supplies. And rather than being back in Mother Russia, the ship had actually anchored in a channel in the Commander Islands, about 109 miles east of the Kamchatka Peninsula. Stranded, and continuing to be swept by scurvy and other ailments, fourteen men would die in the next two months, including Bering, who was buried on an island that would eventually be named for him. The survivors scrambled to make it through the winter, slowly working to construct a new ship from the wreck of the *Saint Peter*. That make-shift vessel was ready by summer, and in August 1742 they weighed anchor and after a two-week voyage reached their home port of Petropavlovsk.[5]

The return of the *Saint Peter* survivors and their news of the lands across the ocean created far less excitement than what they brought with them. While stranded, and even as they built their new ship, the crew succeeded in killing more than 700 sea otters, and they brought those furs back to Petropavlovsk.[6] The returnees reported on the great numbers of marine mammals they had encountered, such as whales and sea lions, but especially fur seals and those sea otters.

Pursuit of the riches of the fur trade quickly got underway: an early voyage brought back 1,600 sea otter and 2,000 fur seal pelts, and in the second half of the eighteenth century small Russian merchant companies completed over one hundred fur-hunting expeditions. In the process, fur-bearing animals on the islands closest to Kamchatka were quickly exterminated, and the seafarers pushed through the Aleutian chain and toward the North American coast.

As the fur operations stretched farther and farther east, the higher operational costs of longer and longer voyages pushed the smaller operators out: by the mid–1780s a government-sanctioned enterprise, eventually to be known as the Russian-American Company, began to assume a dominant and exclusive position. While the Russian-American Company was primarily focused on its monopolistic position in the fur trade, it was also "required to organize settlements, promote agriculture, commerce, discovery, and the propagation of the Greek Catholic faith, and to extend Russian influence and territory on the Pacific so far as it might without trespassing on the territory of any foreign power."[7]

The Russian-American Company's greatest commercial successes were achieved in 1790–1818, when its chief manager in Russian America was Alexander Baranov. Baranov established a series of settlements and posts at locations including present-day Seward and Sitka, and impressed Native laborers to support the company's operations. Particularly in the Aleutian Islands, conscription of large numbers of young, able-bodied males to work in fur hunting and processing had a disastrous effect on the ability of the Native population to support itself: in the absence of those men who provided subsistence and protection to the settlements, starvation and hardship began to haunt and erode the Aleut way of life and their population. And through the decades of Russian rule the Aleuts also suffered from sweeping epidemics, including a smallpox outbreak on Kodiak Island in 1837–1838 which claimed over seven hundred lives. How destructive the Russian presence was is difficult to measure, since there are no hard figures as to what the original Aleut population was. But that population clearly diminished significantly, due at least in part to the disruptions caused by the use of forced labor: most estimates place the decline at 75–80 percent.[8] Baranov also crossed swords—literally—with the native Tlingit population, particularly in 1804 in New Archangel (now Sitka), where the Russian-American Company had established its operating headquarters. Armed conflict there would flare intermittently and as late as 1855, long after Baranov's departure.

Dall would say that Baranov exercised "an absolute and despotic sway over the colonies" during his tenure.[9] Regardless of how Baranov's rule is characterized, it was not without significant success: he essentially created Russian America as a business venture based on exploitation of the fur-bearing animal populations; he established a number of settlements, some of which continue into the twenty-first century; and he extended the avenues of trade beyond a reliance on the Mother Country, including significant trade with Americans, who furnished supplies that were difficult to obtain regularly from eastern Russia.[10]

Baranov retired in 1818, and the Russian government took greater control of Russian-American Company operations. Administration was concentrated in the hands of naval officers, who were made governors of the Russian colony in America. Those naval officers were not interested in business affairs and, as it happened, the period of naval rule coincided with a decline in the fur-bearing animal population—marking the passing of the original impetus for Russian expansion in the area. Attention turned to establishing the boundaries of Russian territory; solidifying the Russian-American Company's exclusive fishing, whaling, fur-hunting and other commercial interests; and reaching accommodations with the United States and Great Britain on fishing and trading access along the northwest coast. Conventions that were signed in 1824–1825 formally recognized that Russia owned not only the Aleutian Islands but significant, defined territory on the North American continent.

As the 1800s progressed, the Russian naval governors faced increasing problems over and above the decline of the fur trade. They tried to diversify and make a profit by introducing new ventures, including coal mining, whaling, and the harvesting and sale of ice to California. There was, however, a chronic labor shortage, in many respects attributable to the fact that the primary objective of the Russian-American Company had always been commercial and focused on trade: establishing a permanent Russian population and workforce to draw upon was never a goal, and voluntary Russian immigration to the distant land was minuscule—the Russian population of the colony never exceeded seven hundred.[11] As a result there was a need to develop new policies to deal with the Native populations, and in this the Company was only partially successful: never fully conquering, much less assimilating, the Tlingits, or overcoming the effects of the earlier treatment of the Aleuts and the reduced population of the Aleutian Islands. Despite that treatment, the Aleuts, of all the Native peoples, proved the most receptive to the introduction of Christianity by the Russian Orthodox Church, whose tall churches and missionary schools became features of Sitka and other Alaskan settlements, especially the small towns in the Aleutian chain.

By the middle of the nineteenth century there were many indications that the Russian-American Company was in decline. The fur trade continued to fall off, as did trade in ice, coal, and the harvests of a nascent timber industry. In addition, offshore whaling and fishing operations by other countries proved difficult to control, and American expansion along the Pacific coast and the ocean areas to the north, into what the U.S. saw as a natural sphere of interest, continued to increase. Almost since 1799 when the Russian government first granted the Company a monopoly in Alaska, it had experienced increasing difficulties in meeting the government's expectations for developing the territory, especially in the absence of adequate governmental financial assistance as the Company's own resources and revenues declined. And in Saint Petersburg, as well as in Washington, D.C., the idea of a sale of Russian America to the United States began to be viewed as beneficial to both countries.

As early as the spring of 1853, the governor-general of Eastern Siberia advised Czar Nicholas I that in his opinion it was inevitable that the United States would occupy all of North America, and that Russia would eventually have to cede its possessions on that continent to the Americans. In that same year, the status of those possessions came into even greater focus with the outbreak of the Crimean War, with Russia facing a coalition of European powers, including Great Britain. Russia had many needs related to its eastern borders, most important of which were strengthening its position on the Asian coast and developing strong relations with the U.S. as a counterweight to the English.[12]

The younger brother of Czar Alexander II was apparently the first, in 1857, to propose the sale of Russian America to the U.S.[13] While some initial approaches were made, negotiations were stalled by the outbreak of the U.S. Civil War in 1861. However, in February 1867, Russian diplomat E.A. Stoeckl arrived in New York and contacted Secretary of State William Henry Seward, who was a long-time believer in America's "Manifest Destiny." Negotiations began in March and moved at a rapid pace, with Seward offering a price of $7 million (eventually $7.2 million) in gold, and insisting that the cession was "to be free and unencumbered by any reservations, privileges, franchises, grants or possessions."[14] By March 30 the treaty was signed and sealed; the U.S. Senate approved the treaty by a vote of 73–2 on April 9; and the Russian government ratified the transaction in May. Transfer ceremonies took place in Sitka in October 1867, with the process ending on October 26 when representatives signed the official protocol transferring Russian America to the United States.

⸻ ◆ ⸻

The new U.S. possession was not a "Territory" (it would be the twentieth century before it achieved that status) but a military and customs District which, until 1884, was destined to be governed by, successively, the U.S. Army, the Treasury Department, and the U.S. Navy. The Russians had historically called their North American possession "Bolshaya Zemlya"—the Great Land. "Alaska" as the designation of the territory traced its origin back to the Aleuts, who had called their homeland in the Aleutian Islands "Aláxsxaq," literally meaning "the object toward which the action of the sea is directed."[15] Over time, "Alaska" had gradually grown to be used not just in reference to the Aleutian Islands or the Alaskan Peninsula, but to the entire Russian possession as such. In 1867, Seward and others who had championed the purchase proposed that the newest manifestation of American expansion be officially named "Alaska."[16]

Beginning in 1867, the U.S. Army had a ten-year "tour of duty" governing the new Military District, but the Army had little direction from Washington and only a vague understanding of what it was supposed to accomplish. While the Russian-American Company had ruled supreme and essentially unhindered in its control, its departure created a void in governance: apart from U.S. statutes governing foreign commerce and the collection of customs duties, when the transfer took place no other laws were in force in Alaska, and there were no agencies of civil government, including courts. This situation would obtain, in greater or lesser degree, until almost the turn of the century. Looking back on this period, Dall would write that "a history of conditions in Alaska from 1867 to 1897 is yet to be written, and when written few Americans will be able to read it without indignation," adding that in great part, and for thirty years, Alaska had been "a country where no man could make a legal will, own a homestead or transfer it ... where polygamy and slavery and the lynching of witches prevailed, with no legal authority to stay or punish criminals."[17]

Alaska's population entered a period involving both change in composition and stagnation in numbers. After the transfer, many Russians—as well as people of mixed Russian and Native ancestry—left Alaska: by 1869, former employees of the Russian-American Company who had stayed behind numbered about 375.[18] The departures were replaced by U.S. military and accompanying civilian personnel "probably totaling no more than 900," and the Native population of the subcontinent "probably did not exceed thirty thousand."[19] The inability to homestead; the remoteness of the territory and its perceived weather; the practical absence of a legal system; the lack of employment opportunities on the one hand and, on the other, a sparse, scattered population insufficient to support more than a few small businesses of even the simplest character; and no prospect of improvement in any of those realities, were more conducive to the contraction, rather than the growth, of America's newest possession. There was precious little incentive for Americans to move north.

An early and portending development was the founding of the Alaskan Commercial Company, which purchased most of the Russian-American Company's property including boats, furs, wharves, and facilities in Sitka and elsewhere. In 1870, it bid on and acquired a twenty-year lease from the U.S. government. The lease conveyed the exclusive rights to harvest fur-bearing seals in the Pribilof Islands, and those operations were soon extended to the Aleutians and other areas. The Company became a power in Alaskan affairs—soon dominating shipping and commerce, becoming active politically and socially by providing schools and medical services in a number of communities, and taking some responsibility for maintaining law and order. On the other hand, tied to its dominant interest in the fur trade, it was "adverse to government regulations and the payment of taxes, and it made its voice known whenever there was talk of extending government services to Alaska or organizing it as a territory."[20]

In 1877 the Army prevailed upon the Department of the Treasury to assume control of Alaska. If anything, Treasury was even less able and prepared for its role, especially after almost all the troops left. Sitka remained the largest settlement, but after the troops departed it gave the appearance of being deserted: its scant population included few Americans, Europeans, or Russians.

Just prior to the Army's departure in favor of Treasury, commercial salmon operations began to get a foothold. In 1878 canneries were initially established at Klawock and Sitka, and others followed in locations to the west and north between 1882 and

1884. However, it was mining not canneries that provided the source for Alaska's first population boom. In 1880 placer gold was found in streams near what would become Juneau, and after the placers were exhausted hard rock deposits were discovered that were sufficient to lead to the development of the great Treadwell Mine, known as the "Glory Hole."

In the continuing absence of any government structure, miners in Juneau and other areas moved toward governance of sorts by the "miners' code"—which provided rules for staking claims and a registrar to record those claims, as well as some rules for conduct within the community, a system of fines and other punishments, and a court of miners who sat in judgment.

By mid–1879, the U.S. Navy had succeeded the Treasury Department as in de facto control of Alaska, largely via the rotating presence in Alaskan waters of various war ships. The Navy's stint as the governing body of the District lasted until 1884 when Congress, finally responding to the clamor for action to deal with the absence of law and government in Alaska, passed the Organic Act. While far from comprehensive, this legislation made Alaska a civil and judicial district with Sitka as the capital, and provided for a governor, judge, marshals, and four commissioners who were to function as justices of the peace. The Organic Act also declared that the general laws of Oregon "now in force are hereby declared to be the law in said district, so far as the same may be applicable and not in conflict with the provisions of this act or the laws of the United States."[21] The Act marked a beginning to civil government in Alaska, but it left much to be desired. For example, Alaskans still could not obtain title to land and had no ability to tax themselves to provide the services they needed and which Congress ignored. As a result, the miners' code continued to operate to fill in the gaps and impose some order and some remedies.

Throughout these years, Alaska's total population changed little from what it was after the exodus of the Russian population following the transfer of possession to the United States. Alaska's first census came in 1880, and 33,426 people were counted as residing in the District, with 430 being non–Native. Ten years later, in 1890, the number of non–Natives had increased to 4,298, but the total population had fallen slightly to 32,052. However, in the next decade the population would almost double to nearly 60,000 at the turn of the century, with the overwhelming bulk of that increase occurring in 1897–1899 and being almost exclusively in the non–Native population. In 1900, non–Natives outnumbered Natives by 30,450 to 29,542.[22]

The population boom in the 1890s can be traced to July 17, 1897, when the steamship *Portland* docked in Seattle with news and tangible proof of the gold strike on the Klondike River in Canada's Yukon Territory. "GOLD! GOLD! GOLD! GOLD!" screamed the headline of that afternoon's *Seattle Post-Intelligencer*, with smaller headlines telling of "Sixty-eight Rich Men on the Steamer Portland!" and "STACKS OF YELLOW METAL!" Gold fever quickly affected people from all walks of life: even Seattle's mayor resigned to join the fortune seekers who came from near and far, and who quickly turned Seattle into the provisioning and jumping-off point for those bound for the Klondike and the burgeoning tent city of Dawson. Although no one was keeping or could keep an actual count, "of the 70,000 or so who would leave home for the Klondike, historians estimated only 40,000 actually set out on the Klondike Trail; with nearly thirty thousand reaching Dawson ... 300 found gold in quantities large enough to call themselves rich."[23]

Those who set out for the Klondike had two options. The less arduous but far longer and more expensive journey was by steamer from Seattle to St. Michael on the Bering Sea, and from there by river boat up the Yukon River to the Klondike and Dawson. The Bering Sea and the rivers were treacherous and travel was often delayed for weeks and months by ice flows. The more celebrated route was overland from the Alaska Panhandle across either White Pass or Chilkoot Pass. The latter, with a starting point in the town of Dyea, was shorter but steeper. The White Pass out of Skagway was longer but somewhat wider, and animals—chiefly horses—could be more often used for carrying supplies. Both land routes were treacherous and tortuous, and neither was adequate to handle the demands of the traffic. Harriman Expedition member Edward Curtis had journeyed to Alaska at the height of the Gold Rush, and provided a first-hand account of some of the perils of the prospectors' journey.

> The crush of men and animals on both these trails was terrific, and became the worst feature of the problem. A multitude of horses' hoofs cut the open parts of the trail into rivers of mire.... Horses, overloaded or worn out, fell in their tracks; and so warped had men become in their struggle to get over the summits toward the fairyland of the Klondike that no friendly hand would be lent to help the owner raise the fallen animal. But worse than these delays was the destruction of horses which resulted from the frightful condition of the trails. Many animals died from exhaustion; but by far the greater number were destroyed by falling among boulders, the heavy packs nearly always causing broken limbs.[24]

The White Pass route became known as the "Dead Horse Trail" as hundreds of frequently overloaded horses slid to their deaths. Prospectors without horses made dozens of repetitive journeys up the passes, often carrying 150-pound packs. The danger was high and death stalked men as well as horses: in one case, on April 3, 1898, a tremendous snowslide at Chilkoot Pass took the lives of forty-three people. Once across the passes, the prospectors made their way to Lake Bennett and the headwaters of the Yukon River, where they assembled flat-bottomed boats and waited for the spring thaw, when they could float with their supplies down to Dawson. Most of those who made it that far never found gold, and in fact found few likely places to even prospect, since most of the valuable claims had long been staked-out. The hardships of the prospectors, and their stories of success and failure, became front page news across the country.

In addition to focusing media attention on the human-interest stories and the hardships faced by prospectors and others in Alaska, beginning in 1898 the Gold Rush and the influx of people had the effect of spurring governmental action in a number of areas. Congress appropriated money for the U.S. Geological Survey to begin survey and mapping work in Alaska, and it extended the U.S. coal-mining laws to the District. The legislators also made the first changes to the Organic Act of 1884—including extending the Homestead Act to Alaska, thus giving settlers the right to obtain title to land; authorizing potential railroad builders to obtain a right-of-way; changing some of the criminal provisions of the Act to better address conditions in Alaska; creating two new judicial districts; giving Alaskans a first taste of self-government by providing for the incorporation of towns; and levying and collecting taxes on businesses, with the revenues to support the costs of government in the District. And the U.S. Army, responding in part to the temporary nature of mining camps, reorganized its operations, including establishing a number of new army posts.

By the spring of 1899, when the Harriman Expedition set-out from Seattle, the frenzy of the Klondike Gold Rush had largely run its course, though prospectors continued to work the Dawson area and many streams that ran into the Klondike and Yukon Rivers. Alaska, however, now had its own gold rush. Significant discoveries were made near Nome on the Seward Peninsula in the winter of 1898–1899, and after the ice went out that spring, ships arrived in Seattle with gold from that area. The activity at Nome diverted many of those who had originally gone to St. Michael with the idea of going on to Dawson and the Klondike. And the Peninsula became a preferred gold-seekers destination in the summer of 1899, spurred by the news that gold was literally lying on the beaches at Nome. By October more than three thousand men were working in the area, and by the summer of 1900 Nome's beaches were crowded with a tent city of more than twenty thousand. While Nome was easier to get to than the Klondike, living conditions were difficult: it was a wide-open, lawless town, where numerous instances of claim jumping put nerves and tensions on edge.

═ ◆ ═

As the *George W. Elder* and its passengers steamed north from Seattle, they were on their way to becoming the then latest chapter in the European-American history of Alaska. The "Great Land" had been shaped by that history, and what that Land was like as the nineteenth century drew to a close was a function of a number of influences, actions, events, and results that were a part of that history.

America's presence, after more than thirty years, and despite the inconsistencies and difficulties under Army, Treasury, and Navy rule, was clear: the American influence and contemporary "Americanization" had carried the day in Alaska. Many of the indices and the active memory of the era of the Russian-American Company were long gone. Still, the century and a half of Russian colonization and rule had left its mark in Russian names on the map of Alaska and in the surnames of many residents, particularly in the Aleutian chain. And the Russian heritage was most prominently evidenced by the ongoing vitality of the Russian Orthodox Church, which seemed to fill a spiritual gap: especially in the smaller villages, it was cherished by the Natives and retained a central role under the dedicated nurturing of the clergy and many Native leaders.

As noted above, and driven by the Klondike and Nome Gold Rushes, Alaska's resident population spurted in the last decade of the nineteenth century and would be recorded in the 1900 census at over 63,000. It was, however, widely scattered. Juneau, Sitka, and Nome were among the largest population centers, with Nome's numbers being inflated by the Gold Rush that began in the summer of 1899. Anchorage did not yet exist—it would date from 1915 and the choice of that location (at the time the site of a non-descript collection of rough buildings and tents at the mouth of Ship Creek) as a construction port and headquarters for the recently government-authorized Alaska Railroad, though the city was not incorporated until 1920. As to the nature or character of the population at the turn of the century, and reflecting, save for the Native portion, a still-developing commitment to the land, Henry Gannett would conclude that "at present few people go to Alaska to live; they go to stay until they have made their stakes."[25]

Civil government had begun to take hold after adoption of the Organic Act in 1884, and by 1899 Alaska was on its fifth civil Governor, John Green Brady. Pervasive law and order, however, was still lacking. Nome, in particular, and though by no means completely unique, stood out: "In 1900, the town was filled with pimps, prostitutes, conmen, and gamblers. It had fifty saloons, and that figure soon doubled."[26] In response to the gold discoveries, and perhaps with some regard to the specific situation in Nome, in early 1900 Congress passed additional legislation which expanded both the number of courts of general jurisdiction and the civil code of Alaska. Time would prove that there was still a long way to go in taming the hard-nosed elements of the population in the mining communities.

Except for the continuing harvest of fur-bearing seals in the Pribilofs and other areas, and the essentially short-term life of the Nome Gold Rush, Alaska's natural resources were only beginning to be discovered, much less tapped. Mining had achieved long-term success only at the Treadwell Mine at Juneau. Russian coal-mining activity had never proved profitable, had been abandoned by the Russian-American Company, and had attracted little American interest. Salmon canneries had obtained an early foothold and significant financial success in the early 1880s, and the industry continued to expand northward and westward along the coast, tapping into the salmon runs of Alaska's many rivers. In 1897 Alaska's output of canned salmon amounted to about 1,000,000 cases, with forty-eight one-pound cans to the case.[27] Production would reach 2,500,000 cases by the turn of the century.[28] In the forests, timber cutting—via "clear cutting" in modern parlance—had made its mark, but it was unclear whether the spruce and other native trees that filled the shorelines and mountain slopes could be competitive with the great cedar and Douglas Fir forests of Washington State and the Pacific Northwest.

Tourism was a fledgling business, though by and large it would for decades be confined to the Alexander Archipelago. In the early 1880s, steamers had begun to bring the wealthy and the not-quite-so-wealthy up from Seattle, San Francisco, and other West Coast ports to southeastern Alaska. In the Inside Passage, in the Victorian culture of those who could afford the trip, tourism "was a quiet, comfortable way to touch a fringe of the wilderness, with spectacular mountains, dramatic glaciers, and lush evergreen forests."[29] The Russian Orthodox Churches that towered over the low buildings of the towns and villages were an attraction, and the residents of those towns and villages were beginning to tap into the typical tourist wants and needs of souvenirs, food and drink, and local color. Few if any of the ships ventured any further north than Sitka, but still the *Elder* was not the only passenger steamer in Alaskan waters that summer.

Nineteenth-century exploration, geographic and scientific, of the territory was largely individual, and less frequently organized and systematic. During its tenure, the Russian-American Company was focused on its commercial purposes; its "exploration" activities were narrowly directed toward those ends, including finding suitable coastal sites for settlements to encourage and facilitate fur-sealing and trade opportunities. The search for a route for the proposed telegraph line led to some systematic investigation of the interior and parts of the Bering Sea and its coast beginning in 1865; Dall and others in that party collected data and specimens, with Dall sending many to the Smithsonian Institution when he finally quitted Alaska.

Following the Alaska Purchase and beginning with, roughly, Dall's departure from Alaska in 1868, little exploration was done on an organized basis for the next fifteen years: Reconstruction following the Civil War and other national needs took precedence over government funding and manpower for exploration in a remote and sparsely-populated area. From 1876 through 1886 some more-coordinated efforts were undertaken. One was the work of Edward Nelson, then head of the Army's Signal Service (and later a successor to Merriam as Chief of the Biological Survey), who by 1881 had conducted extensive exploration of the Yukon River delta region, including sending more than 2,000 bird skins to the Smithsonian. Another was headed by Army Lieutenant Henry Allen, who led a small party which explored the Copper, Tanana, and Koyukuk River valleys—charting those three major river systems in a 1,500-mile exploration. Scientific investigation and exploration suffered again in the period from 1886 to 1896, once more reflecting the lack of federal funding from a Congress preoccupied with domestic issues and dealing with economic distress from causes including the financial panic of 1893. Some official exploration by both Canadians and Americans arose out of the need to settle the boundary between the two countries, especially in Alaska's southeast. In 1896, the U.S. Geological Survey began to take a more active interest in Alaska, spurred by Congressional appropriations to study the region's coal and gold resources. The USGS also found a focus for its surveys in prospectors' needs for maps and information, and survey expeditions collected general geographic and topographic data on principal rivers and valleys. The War Department mounted two Alaskan expeditions in the spring of 1898, one of which, the Glenn Expedition including Yellowstone Kelly, explored possible routes of travel from Prince William Sound and Cook Inlet to the interior. And in the spring of 1899, Hart Merriam himself had sent a Biological Survey team out to investigate Lake Bennett and the Upper Yukon.

The result or extent of American exploration in Alaska in the nineteenth century has been summarized by Morgan Sherwood, a historian of Alaskan exploration: "By 1900 the general facts of Alaska's relief and drainage were known, the major rivers had been traced, and the important mountains outlined" as a result of a pace of exploration and progress of discovery which had, since 1865, been "consistent with social attitudes in the United States during the nineteenth century, the remoteness of the territory, the economic interest expressed in the country, and the popular interest as evidenced by the population of the region."[30] Further as to the state of exploration, and perhaps more romantically than Sherwood, another historian, Douglas Brinkley, has concluded, "In the late nineteenth century, Alaska—from southwestern rainforests to Aleutian volcanoes to barrier islands along the Arctic coast to the ice glaciers of the Inside Passage—was a never-never land of unnamed mountains, unnamed rivers, and unnamed species."[31]

For the interests and aims of the particular group aboard the *Elder*, and as far as such a group's interest in *any* part of the United States and its possessions was concerned, there could not have been a more intriguing destination than the land to which they were going.

PART II

On the Beaten Path

FOUR

The Byways of the Inside Passage

"I am actually tired of the constant strain of trying to take things in."
—Charles Keeler

As the *George W. Elder* moved out of Seattle in the early evening, steaming north through the waters of Puget Sound toward the Strait of Juan de Fuca and Vancouver Island, the members of the Expedition party tended to unpacking, visiting with their neighbors in adjoining staterooms, and exploring the ship. On the Upper Deck, they found that an eclectic library of five hundred volumes provided by Mr. and Mrs. Harriman was being arranged in the Social Hall (which would also be variously referred to as the "Lecture Hall," and the "Science Hall," and the "Main Cabin"), and many of the Harriman's guests added books of their own to supplement the collection. "Within reach of all," Merriam would write of this library, "it included most of the important and useful works relating to Alaska and proved of great service." Merriam also noted that soon to be "constantly in use" in the ship's Chart Room was "a complete series of charts of Alaska, provided by Dr. Henry S. Pritchett, Superintendent of the U.S. Coast and Geodetic Survey."[1]

The next morning, they awoke to find the *Elder* docked in Victoria, British Columbia, with a breakfast of "strawberries, oatmeal and cream, fish eggs and corn bread" awaiting them on dining tables festooned with roses.[2] After breakfast, in what Burroughs would poetically characterize as "mist and a warm slow rain,"[3] most of the party boarded trolleys that Harriman had arranged as transportation to the Victoria Museum, which featured exhibits of Native artifacts and indigenous animals of the sort they might encounter in the days ahead. Much as they had been on their cross-country rail journey—and would inevitably be at other times during the trip—they were sightseeing and playing the part of typical tourists. But not everyone visited the Museum. De Alton Saunders was one who went off on his own, collecting seaweed in the harbor; a collection which he then spent much of the rest of the day happily mounting and pressing.[4] And a few stayed back on the ship, including Dr. Nelson, who would duly record that "most of the party went on shore in the rain to see the town, but I did not set foot on this British soil, preferring to read and write."[5] For Nelson, this established something of a pattern: in the coming weeks he would often choose to remain on the ship, happily ensconced in the Social Hall library, while the others were off on various excursions.

Their schedule did not allow for a long visit in Victoria, and the *Elder* was soon making steam and moving out to sea, swinging around the south end of Vancouver Island to pass, via the Strait of Georgia, between the island and the British Columbia

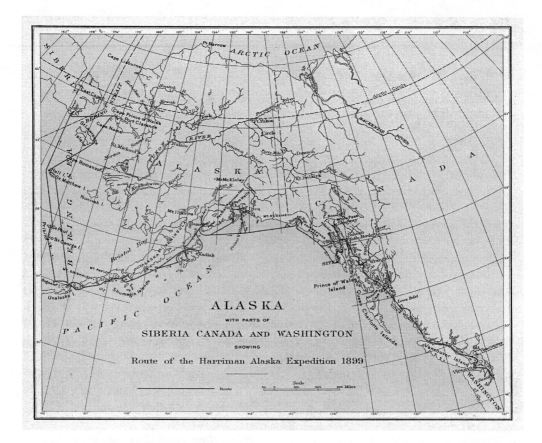

Map showing the route of the Harriman Expedition in 1899. Reduction of the size of the map to accommodate, for the convenience and reference of readers, its inclusion in this book necessarily and unavoidably impacts the clarity of the correspondingly reduced text of place names. University of Washington Libraries, Special Collections [UW 2506].

mainland on the journey north. For the next week and more, the *Elder's* route would be through the Inside Passage, a network of straits, channels, and other waterways that ships use to weave through the islands and along the coastlines of British Columbia and the Alaskan Panhandle. The route provides island buffers and shelter from the weather and the high seas of the open Pacific Ocean off the North American coast.

That evening all gathered in the Social Hall for the first of a regular series of programs organized by the Committee on Lectures and, on occasion, by the Committee on Music and Entertainment. This first installment of the "Alaska Institute" featured a talk by William Healey Dall on the history and general geography of Alaska.[6] The Institute became a staple of life on board ship, with the lectures sometimes held outdoors, weather permitting.

> Nearly every night at eight o'clock, some one of our college professors or government specialists held forth upon the upper deck or in the Social Hall. One night it was Dall upon the history or geography of Alaska; then Gilbert upon the agency of glaciers in shaping the valleys and mountains, or upon the glaciers we had recently visited; then Brewer upon climate and ocean currents, or Coville upon some botanical features of the regions about us, or Ritter upon the shore forms of sea life, or Emerson upon volcanoes and lava beds, or John

Steamer *George W. Elder* sailing the Inside Passage. Photograph by E.H. Harriman. University of Washington Libraries, Special Collections [Harriman 10].

Muir on his experiences on the glaciers and his adventures with his dog Stikine in crossing a huge crevasse on a sliver of ice, or Charles Keeler on the coloration of birds or Fuertes on bird songs, or Grinnell on Indian tribes and Indian characteristics, and so on. On Sunday evenings, Dr. Nelson conducted the Episcopal service and preached a sermon, while at all times books and music and games added to the attraction of the Social Hall.[7]

Grinnell would subsequently tell the readers of *Forest & Stream* magazine that under the circumstances of the Expedition the lectures "had a living interest for all," and were soon accompanied by a late evening routine where, typically, from a lecture's conclusion at around 9:00 p.m. "until 10 the smoking room was crowded; by 10 it had begun to thin out, as the men retired to their staterooms, and before 11 o'clock only the owls were up. Soon after this there would perhaps be an adjournment to the cabin for some supper, and by midnight the lights were out, and all the ship's company, except the officers on watch, were in bed."[8]

The second of June, a Friday, dawned peacefully enough, but in the afternoon the *Elder* passed the northern limit of the shelter of Vancouver Island, became exposed to westerly winds and ocean swells, and "the boat showed us that she could roll with the rollers as well as glide smoothly in smooth waters."[9] In fact, for some years the ship, which possessed a rounded iron hull, had been known as "the old rocking chair" and the "*George W. Roller*."[10] Part of the recent overhaul in Portland involved the installation of "bilge keels" to counteract the rolling, but those were at best partially effective, and, though these swells soon passed, a number of the passengers became squeamish, while a few suffered greater consequences. Palache sadly reported that "I am rather ashamed to say that I was one of the few who felt the effect of the swell and I had to dispose of my lunch before I could eat a little supper."[11] John Burroughs also hurried to his cabin, his sensitive stomach succumbing to the first—but by far not the last—of the bouts of seasickness that would trouble him from time to time in the coming weeks. Nature, however, revived his spirits as the day drew to a close: "The event of the day was the sunset at 8:30 p.m.…. Where the sun went down the horizon was low, and but a slender black line of forest separated the sky from the water. All above was crimson and orange and gold, and all below, to the right and left, purple laid upon purple until the whole body of the air between us and the mountains in the distance seemed turned to color."[12]

The *Elder* returned to calmer seas on Saturday as it moved into the protected waterways off Princess Royal Island, where it dropped anchor near a small salmon cannery situated at the entrance to Lowe Inlet. The stop presented an opportunity, the first of the journey, to go ashore without an arranged tour to take or a specific sight to see, and small groups of the scientists fanned out over the island.

A number visited the cannery, and among its employees saw their first coastal Indians. Burroughs, Dellenbaugh, and Gifford took a small boat and worked their way up the Inlet to the waterfall at its head, where the two artists set up for some quiet sketching. Louis Fuertes went off on his own into the forest along the shore, but found it almost impenetrable: the brush was wet, the fallen logs were slippery, and he took a bad tumble, "but it didn't do any damage beyond a red pancake mark on the slats—and a jolt in the wind." He caught only brief glimpses of warblers and other birds but, was awed by the "great, majestic spruce columns, often eight or even more feet in diameter, and as much as 200 feet high." He also began hearing "curious and loud noises" up in the forest, and was working his way toward them when "they got so queer and human sounding that I thought that Dr. Fisher, who is summate of a jollier, was doing it to get a rise out of me. So, I got proud and turned off." As he worked his way back to the ship, he heard a couple of shots in the distance, and after some time Fisher emerged at the shore with a huge northern raven, one of the first specimens collected by the party. Perhaps exculpating Fisher and offering an explanation for the noises he had heard, Fuertes noted that these particular ravens "are great devilish jokers who give you a jolly and then chuckle, peep, whistle, grunt, croak, bark, cackle, gobble, and everything else about it."[13] Fisher turned the raven over to Fuertes, who was soon at work on a pencil study in his studio above the engine room.

Mrs. Harriman grew to be an admirer of Fuertes sketches, and often borrowed and posted them in the Social Hall. "They look pretty," Fuertes observed in a letter home, "but are of course only rough studies, and not very much like the birds they bluff at."[14]

Fuertes was a naturalist as well as a painter, with an ornithologist's keen eye for detail. His career exhibited an almost unparalleled ability, combining artistic talents with his own extensive field observations, to depict birds in lifelike poses. Unlike other artists of his time who created paintings of birds from stuffed specimens, almost as still life in fabricated settings, he believed that to be accurately painted birds not only had to be observed in natural settings in the wild but that their coloring and other important characteristics were transitory, and could only be carefully and accurately painted from either living or freshly shot birds—in his words, "Almost all water birds, the birds of prey, and many land birds have colors in life, and especially at the breeding season, which cannot in any known way be preserved."[15]

The stop on Princess Royal Island also afforded "photo ops" for many members of the party. In addition to the professional-level equipment wielded by Expedition photographers Curtis and Inverarity, others like Merriam and Keeler had the best readily-available popular cameras of the day, including Kodak box and folding cameras, and the ship had the facilities for processing those pictures. Leaving Lowe Inlet, Keeler would write home that he had already "taken about twenty photographs, some good and a few poor. I developed them today. We have a fine dark room very conveniently fitted up."[16]

⚬

After dinner Saturday evening the members of the Expedition party, some toting after dinner coffee, gathered in the Social Hall. They had left Lowe Inlet and were continuing north on a course that would bring them into Alaskan waters during the night, and then to anchor at Annette Island. The talk that evening was by Dr. Nelson and his subject was the village of Metlakatla,[17] a large Indian Mission settlement on the island. This stop had a special meaning for Dall, who had given the island its name in 1879 in honor of his then fiancée and future wife, Annette Whitney Dall.

Nelson related how William Duncan, a Scottish lay missionary in the Church of England, had come to British Columbia on a mission to Christianize a group of Tsimshian people who had settled in the vicinity of Fort Simpson. Duncan went to live in their village, though he refused to start his missionary and religious conversion work until he had learned the Tsimshian language. That accomplished, he not only succeeded in his teaching of the Christian Gospels, but taught the people how to exist in a world much more mechanically advanced than they had known. He showed them how to build wooden-frame houses, and helped them build sawmills and start a salmon cannery so they could become self-supporting. Duncan increasingly operated independently of the Church: he made up and conducted church services in ways that departed from Church practice, but which he felt were workable in his community. Among other things, he administered communion—though he gave his parishioners only bread and no wine, being fearful that the merest taste of alcohol would start his people down the wrong path. Church authorities, however, were insistent that he administer rituals and ceremonies to the Tsimshians in the orthodox manner.

In response, Duncan and his followers sought to remove themselves from the negative influence of detractors and Church authorities. Initially, they moved to a new location at Metlakatla, B.C., but disagreements between Duncan and the bishop under whom he was supposed to serve continued and intensified. Duncan eventually sought help from the United States, and found a powerful ally in President Grover Cleveland. President Cleveland recognized the right of aboriginal Indians to occupy land within their aboriginal region, and authorized Duncan and the members of his congregation to choose a spot among the Alaskan islands for a new community. They found a suitable location on Annette Island, and in 1887 Duncan and 826 Tsimshians moved and founded what they initially named "New Metlakatla." In 1891 Congress granted recognition to the new community by creating the Annette Islands Reserve, which to this day is the only federal Indian reservation in the State of Alaska.[18]

A large number of Metlakatla's citizens were gathered on the wharf early on Sunday morning when the *Elder* tied-up, "their big round faces and black eyes showing only a quiet respectful curiosity."[19] The party called on Duncan, a short, gray-haired

Indian reservation w/resident missionary

and gray-whiskered man, at his home. After a brief visit, they took a tour through the village, walking along its numerous streets on broad plank walks. They found, Burroughs would write, "a hundred or more comfortable frame houses, some of them two stories, many of them painted, all of them substantial and in good taste, a large and imposing wooden church, a large school house, and a town hall."[20] As they wandered about the village, with its sawmill, salmon cannery, four stores, and the workshops of blacksmiths, shoemakers, tailors, and others, it all seemed to Grinnell "like an old fashioned New England hamlet in its peaceful quiet."[21] Taken with the scene, Grinnell was perhaps wafted from reality into another world: one without ravens. "They were everywhere," said Burroughs, "on the roofs of the houses, and on the stumps and dooryard fences. Six were perched on one of the towers of the church as I approached. Their calls and croakings and jabberings were in the ear at all times."[22]

At eleven o'clock, and probably to the distress of the perching ravens, the pealing of the church bells summoned hundreds, including the Expedition party, for the morning service. Nelson made a brief address and said prayers, Duncan preached a sermon in Tsimshian, and Burroughs averred that "the organ music and the singing were quite equal to what one would hear in any rural church at home."[23]

The community and its "Americanization" under Duncan's leadership impressed the members of the Harriman party. They shared the then prevailing and overwhelmingly accepted contemporary views of the inherent nature of Native populations, and that the best future for those populations lay in assimilation into the broader, white society by learning English, being taught the skills of farming and the trades, acquiring the Protestant work ethic, and adopting the customs, values, dress, and outlook of the more advanced or productive civilization. In that context, Duncan's approach in organizing and supervising the development of his charges won the approval of the party. To Burroughs, Metlakatla was "one of the best object lessons to be found on the coast, showing what can be done with the Alaska Indians."[24] And Grinnell would agree, writing, "It took many years for Mr. Duncan to change these individuals from the wild men that they were when he first met them, to the respectable and civilized people that they are now. Whatever they are today, Mr. Duncan has made them, and he himself and no other is responsible for the change in the individuals that have been born and lived and died, and still live in this colony during the period of his wise and beneficent influence over them."[25]

For his part, Harriman seemed impressed with the inherent industry and intelligence of Duncan's charges, and saw in them a future potential for success independent of the direction and influence exerted by the missionary's stern, guiding hand. Interviewed after the Expedition had concluded, he was of the opinion that if the Native population "could be taught to speak the English language, they could be largely used in the development of the territory."[26]

Metlakatla continued to grow under Duncan's supervision in the years after the Expedition's visit, though he gradually—in part voluntarily, and to an extent under pressure from his charges—shared control and authority over the business and management of the community and its affairs with the Tsimshians. He passed away in 1918, and after his death the town's government evolved under its tribal council and took over management of community, economic, and social affairs.[27]

After the church services, and with pleasant early afternoon weather, everyone had a chance to continue exploring the town and the nearby areas of Annette Island.

View of village of New Metlakahtla. Photograph by Mary Harriman Rumsey. National Museum of the American Indian, Smithsonian Institution [NMAI AC 053_010_000_L00742].

Charles Keeler returned to the *Elder*, took a few turns on the deck and then, alone in the stateroom he shared with Muir, began a letter to Louise, "It is Sunday afternoon and I have been walking up and down the deck thinking of home and my dear ones.... It is very hard to go so long without knowing just how and where you are my dearest, but we must feel it is for the best this time." The separation was not the only thing weighing on his mind. Though they were only in their fourth day out from Seattle, he lamented the stress he already felt, perhaps out of concern for the money he hoped to earn from the articles he might write about the Expedition.

> I am actually tired of the constant strain of trying to take things in ... and hard to know what to put down in my notes and what to leave out. I don't quite see yet what phase of Alaska I can write about when others know it so much more exhaustively than I can ever begin to. Mr. Burroughs has been made the official historian of the expedition, and Mr. Harriman is to have a book published giving an account of the trip and in an appendix the scientific reports. Dr. Merriam has asked me to contribute something to the literary part and intends asking Mr. Muir, but I hardly see what I can write on with Mr. Burroughs as historian. Still all this will no doubt straighten itself out as the expedition advances.[28]

[handwritten margin notes: "Someone left behind", "expedition", "a little", "symbolic"]

While Keeler wrote his letter, Albert Fisher was still on shore. Ambling back from a walk in the woods, and taken with the sights and absorbed in the chirps of Annette Island's birds, he was oblivious to the fact that the afternoon had worn on and all his traveling companions were back on board the *Elder*, which was pulling away from the wharf. Dellenbaugh's diary notation of the incident was succinct: "Fisher, who was photographing up in the town somewhere, came near being left, arriving just as the boat was clearing, and had dropped her hawsers." No one had noticed Fisher's absence until he had come into sight, and it was apparent that something was needed to keep track of those who might leave the ship at future ports and remote anchorages along the way. That evening, Dellenbaugh "painted all the names on a board the carpenter made, with pegs after them, the pegs to be shifted from 'aboard' to 'ashore' by each one as he goes or comes so as to be sure no one is left behind."[29]

As the day drew to a close, Burroughs and others on deck experienced another dazzling sunset, highlighted by colored skies and the sun's rays on the distant mountain peaks. John Muir was below decks and arrived on the scene shortly after the sun had set, leading Burroughs to call to him, "you ought to have been out here fifteen minutes ago." Never one to let a chastising comment pass without a comeback, Muir, one imagines with a little extra emphasis in his Scottish brogue, and targeting his friend's well-known propensity as a homebody, quickly returned the friendly rebuke: "Aye, and you Burroughs, ought to have been up here three years ago instead of slumbering down there on the Hudson!"[30] The exchange highlighted one characteristic of the Muir-Burroughs friendship.

They had first been introduced and met in 1893, but became truly acquainted in June 1896, when Muir visited Burroughs's Slabsides retreat. In his journal, Burroughs would write about that visit and that Muir was "a very interesting man; a little prolix at times. You must not be in a hurry, or have any pressing duty, when you start his famous stream of talk and adventure.... He is a poet, and almost a seer; something ancient and far away in the look of his eyes." And whether with admiration or wonder, and certainly because it was the sort of thing he himself would never do, Burroughs added, "He could not sit down in a corner of the landscape, as Thoreau did; He must have a continent for his playground. He starts off for a walk, after graduation, and walks from Wisconsin to Florida, and is not back home in eighteen years! In California, he starts out one morning for a stroll; his landlady asks him if he will be back for dinner; probably not, he says. He is back in seven days; walks one hundred miles around Mt. Shasta, and goes two and one-half days without food." Yet, Burroughs would say that Muir was "probably the truest lover of Nature, as she appears in woods, mountains, glaciers we have yet had."[31]

While in age and physical appearance, in their dedication to nature and the environment, and in their true underlying philosophies of life, including a preference for being undisturbed and alone, these two men had much in common, they were nonetheless a study in contrasts. Muir was loud, combative, politically astute, constantly on a mission, and unflinchingly self-assured. Burroughs was quiet, mild, introspective, more of a deep thinker and a writer than he was a talker—Muir would prod him to speak out on conservation issues and, as on the deck of the *Elder* that evening outside Metlakatla, chide him for being a "slumbering" homebody. And Burroughs could, in his own genteel and sly way, jab in return, as in his "Narrative of the Expedition" where in describing the accomplishments of various members he wrote, "In

John Muir we had an authority on glaciers, and a thorough one—so thorough that he would not allow the rest of the party to have an opinion on the subject."[32] Their relationship was a mixture of true friendship and combative rivalry, deep and somehow unhindered by the brevity of the various occasions they spent together over 20 years: the Harriman Alaska Expedition brought them into their closest, longest, and perhaps most important contact with each other.[33]

The underlying regard each had for the other was evident when Muir passed away in December 1914. Burroughs wrote sadly in his journal, "News comes of John Muir's death—an event I have been expecting and dreading for more than a year. A unique character—greater as a talker than a writer; loved personal combat, and shone at it ... his talk came easily and showed him at his best. I shall greatly miss him, though I saw him so rarely."[34] One suspects that Muir, if he had been the survivor, would have similarly mourned the loss of Burroughs.

═ ◆ ═

The town of Wrangell was the next destination, and the *Elder* dropped anchor in the harbor late Sunday night. The party was forewarned that while there would be time Monday morning to go ashore, that time would be brief. Accordingly, and along with a number of others, Muir was up by 5:00 a.m. and he was in one of two rowboats full of people who went ashore in the rising water vapor and the early light of dawn.

Muir had been in Wrangell twenty years earlier, in the summer of 1879, when he had found it "a rough place" and "a lawless draggle of wooden huts and houses built in crooked lines, wrangling about the boggy shore of the island for a mile or so in the general form of the letter S."[35] During the Gold Rush of 1898, and because it was on the route to Skagway, Wrangell had exploded to include two sawmills, a cigar factory, a cannery, two blacksmith shops, a shipyard, ten laundries, two breweries, and numerous other businesses. During that brief period of boom, no less a person than the legendary Wyatt Earp had arrived and spent ten days as the town's temporary marshal, declining to stay longer since he was on his way, with his wife Josie, to strike gold in the Klondike—though they soon turned back when they discovered that Josie was pregnant.

The brief boom of 1898 had become more of a bust in 1899, and the shore party found a Wrangell that, though larger, seemed very similar to what Muir experienced in 1879. Burroughs found some interesting totem poles but described it as a "shabby old town," while Keeler characterized it as "a dirty miserable town ... with streets of boards on stilts and gullies below them full of tin cans and old shoes. The totem poles were interesting but invariably close behind the most hideous monstrosities of painted modern houses all dirt and dilapidated." Dellenbaugh noted "a remarkable number of restaurants, beer places and hotels," many of them deserted, while Dall lamented a row of once useful steamers "peacefully decaying on their skids."[36]

Once ashore, the party quickly fanned out across the awakening town and into the surrounding area. Muir walked along the edge of the woods, and at one of the sawmills stopped to measure a log that "straight as an arrow," turned out to be one hundred feet long with a three-foot, eight-inch diameter, and "Age 168 yrs."[37] Saunders took advantage of the early morning low tide to prowl the shoreline for seaweed. Further inland, the ornithologists had their most productive excursion of the journey to date: Fuertes recording that they brought in a raven, a Steller's jay, an Oregon

Wrangell. Photograph by Edward S. Curtis. University of Washington Libraries, Special Collections [Harriman 18].

Junco, a red-throated woodpecker, a lutescent warbler, and a Lincoln's finch.[38] In the misty forest behind the village, Palache scrambled up the hillside on his own, intent not on rocks and minerals but photography. The dense woods were an obstruction; so, he would write to Helen, "Behold me then 'shinning' with mighty labor up a broken tree trunk on whose top, 15 feet from the ground I perched unsteadily while taking a time picture of a fine mountain group. And behold me also exposing the same film again five minutes later for a still longer exposure at another point." Later, after joining some of the others who were headed back to the waterfront, he encountered some early morning Native fishermen and "obtained a first-rate souvenir of the place—a huge wooden fishhook which the Indian willingly took from his line when we showed him our money."[39]

All this at Wrangell was compressed into a few hours: by 8:00 a.m., everyone was pegged back "aboard," breakfast was being served, and the *Elder* weighed anchor.

By ten o'clock, they were threading the intricate waterway of the Wrangell Narrows. The air was brisk, the sky was clear, and a panorama of snow-covered mountains and glaciers reaching to the sea drew most of the party, many armed with cameras, to the outdoor decks. Spouts of water marked whales blowing, "their glistening backs emerging from the water, turning slowly like the periphery of a huge wheel."[40] The ship passed along the coast, with the frozen expanse of the Patterson Glacier soon appearing off to starboard. Muir noted that as fine as Patterson was, many larger glaciers lay ahead, including the Muir Glacier which, he advised, contained in itself

19th c. quality to parse

"more square miles of ice than all the glaciers of Switzerland put together."[41] The sightseers and photographers were joined on deck by the hunters who, Palache noted, "kept up a fusillade, practicing on the sea-fowl and eagles that were within range on either side of the ship."[42]

That afternoon brought the *Elder* to Farragut Bay, where Captain Doran dropped anchor. Merriam hoped to capture some of the area's smaller animal inhabitants, and he led a party shoreward, their boat loaded with traps. It proved to be a fruitless effort: by the end of two hours the traps contained exactly as many specimens as they had when they left the ship, though Merriam did pick up some deer antlers and bones that he ran across while exploring the woods with Dr. Morris.

═ ◆ ═

With Farragut Bay receding astern, the *Elder* continued on, making good time throughout the afternoon and early evening, with many of its passengers remaining on deck to watch the passing scenery. The weather was fine and, with ample light and moderate temperatures, the evening lecture was moved outdoors from the Social Hall to the hurricane deck. Walter Devereux, the Expedition's mining engineer, had recommended that as part of a stop in Juneau the next day they should visit the nearby Treadwell Mine. Since it was his idea and he was the resident expert, he was tapped to speak and provide some background for the visit. Juneau was at times referred to as the buckle on a "gold belt" of mineral-bearing ore in the area, and the Treadwell was a common stop for early cruise ships.[43] Devereux alerted the party to the huge size of the excavations and described how the latest technology was providing for efficient and profitable returns from essentially low-grade ore.

The days were long but even so the light was growing faint when, shortly before eleven o'clock, the ship anchored in Taku Bay. Merriam and Fisher were bound to make another try at setting traps for small animals. Despite the late hour, others including Muir, Curtis, and Palache, crammed into a single rowboat with the two scientists and all the traps and set out for shore, a mile away. It was appreciably darker when they reached the rocky beach, but the two scientists set about getting their traps out. Palache recalled that "the rest of us wandered about the ruins of an Indian Village without finding anything of interest." Muir remembered that twenty years earlier one hundred Indians had lived at Taku, but that tribe was nearly extinct, with only a few fallen-down and overgrown cabins providing evidence of their previous existence. Once the traps were set, the party returned to the ship, with Palache taking one of the oars. Of that experience he wrote, "It is no fun to wield one of those 16 foot instruments. I am afraid I made poor work of it but so did the others, so I was satisfied not to have been knocked out of the boat by it. It was midnight when again we got on board."[44]

Palache, Muir, and Curtis were apparently sawing logs or counting sheep at 4:00 a.m. when Merriam and Fisher settled in with those 16-foot instruments and went out to retrieve their trap line and such animals as they had caught: though accounts vary, it appears that they returned to the *Elder* with perhaps five field mice.

Later that morning they entered Douglas Sound and made for Juneau, the largest town they had encountered since Victoria. Then, as now, the community was on a confining strip of land, sandwiched between the Sound and the towering mountains that rose like a wall to the east. The 1900 census would peg the population at 1,864, and that number probably approximated the size of the population in June 1899. For the party, the stop was brief: Juneau was a place for mailing letters and doing a little shopping in a town that was beginning to reap the economic benefits of tourism. Charlie Palache may have been reflecting the thoughts of many in the party when he characterized Juneau as "an uninteresting town of the typical frontier type—board shanties, pretentious stores, bad streets, innumerable dogs, lots of loafing citizens, and now and then a picturesque Indian."[45] Dellenbaugh was in town long enough to capture a story about a man who was in Juneau, but did not live there, and was asked if it ever stopped raining in Alaska: "How the devil do I know," he answered, "I have only been here two years!"[46] *frontier towns scorned*

After a couple of hours, the *Elder* moved across the sound to Douglas Island and the famed Treadwell Mine. Much of the land around the mine had been clear-cut as operations expanded, and the air above the channel between Juneau and the island was perpetually clouded with haze.[47] But the overriding sensory experience was the tremendous noise, increasingly discernible as the ship approached the island and especially when the party went ashore to explore the operation. Some of the deafening sound was created by blasting; far more by the processing of the rock being mined. Burroughs:

> Nearly 2000 tons of quartz rock are crushed daily at these mills and the roar made by the eight hundred or more stamps, all under one roof, in pulverizing this rock dwarfs all other rackets I have heard. Niagara is a soft hum beside it.... Never before have I been where the air was torn to tatters and the ear so stunned and overwhelmed as in this mill. It was not a grand reverberating sound like the sounds of nature, it was simply the most ear-paralyzing noise ever heard within four walls. Heard, I say, though in truth we did not hear it. To hear a thing there must be some silence; this hubbub was so great and all-pervasive that the auditory nerve was simply bruised into insensibility.[48]

Enough was soon more than enough, and the party scampered back to the ship. The destination was now Skagway, but a return to the dock in Juneau was a first stop in order to leave off a party of six—Ritter, Palache, Saunders, Kearney, Kincaid, and Starks—for some more careful study of the area. Palache in particular relished the chance to examine the mine and mining operations more thoroughly, and looked forward to simply spending the time ashore, noting that "it will be a sudden change from the luxurious table we have on board to a miner's boarding house in Juneau but I do not know but a simpler bill-of-fare will be better for some of us."[49] It was agreed that the main party would return to Juneau to pick up the six scientists on the morning of Thursday the 8th.

As the *Elder* steamed away to Skagway, the shore party went in search of hotel accommodations and, with rooms quickly secured, Palache returned to the docks, boarded a launch bound for Douglas Island, and returned to the mine.

The *Elder* was still easily in sight of Juneau when Harriman noticed that the ship's company had a new member—a small, apparently stray dog was wandering about the deck, making new friends. Told by one crewman that the dog had followed another crew member on board at Juneau, Harriman announced that "as long as this dog remains on board, he is our guest," and then hunted up the dog's new friend among the crew and gave him the responsibility of feeding the animal until they returned to Juneau and could set it back on its home turf.[50]

dog adopted

FIVE

Gold Rush Country

"The Skagway paper gave a list of our party. It has created a great sensation in this country."—Frederick Dellenbaugh

Leaving Juneau, the *Elder*, as carefully noted by the ship's Second Officer, A.W. McIntosh, traveled ninety-two miles up the channel of the Lynn Canal (which is actually a fiord) to Skagway.[1] While fairly accessible, the area was remote, and as an inhabited town, Skagway had an almost "overnight" history, largely compressed into the twenty-four months prior to the arrival of the Harriman Alaska Expedition.

The antecedents or seeds of that history trace to 1887, when William "Billy" Moore was working as a member of a survey party wrestling with the ongoing problem of establishing the boundary between Alaska and British Columbia. In the course of the survey crew's work, Moore made the first recorded reconnaissance of what would become known as White Pass. Attracted to the land, and becoming a believer in the backcountry rumors of signs of gold in the rivers and mountains to the north, with the Pass being the route to those riches, Moore staked a claim to a 160-acre homestead at the mouth of the Skagway River. He put up a log cabin, constructed and operated a sawmill, and built a large wharf. For the next decade he worked and waited.

On July 29, 1897—only twelve days after the coastal steamer *Portland* arrived in Seattle with ample tangible proof of the gold strike on the Klondike River, and just a little less than two years before the arrival of the Harriman Expedition—the steamer *Queen* appeared at Moore's wharf, packed with the first load of erstwhile gold seekers. Other steamers soon followed, unloading thousands of miners-to-be, and Moore was quickly overwhelmed by claim jumpers, who drove him out, stole and divided his land, and sold it to others. The land at the mouth of the Skagway River sprouted stores selling needed, and many unneeded, supplies to miners. Before long more stores, as well as saloons, hotels, offices, brothels, and other places of business sprang-up along hastily staked-out and always muddy streets. A year after the *Queen's* arrival, Skagway had become the largest town in Alaska, with a population of more than 8,000 souls and with thousands of others passing through on the way to the treacherous, back- and spirit-breaking White Pass, and then on to the Klondike via Lake Bennett and the Yukon River.

Skagway was, from the arrival of the *Queen* through 1898, a town beyond the law and a place that quickly fell under the control of Jefferson "Soapy" Smith and his men. They controlled many of the businesses, including the town's newspaper. They also proved to be accomplished con men, who preyed upon many of the transient prospectors. Reminiscent of latter-day Mafia godfathers, Smith also ran what amounted to a local welfare agency; allowing him to gain supporters among a segment of local businesses and citizens who relied on and benefited from his protection and support. Those who resisted faced the consequences of Smith's company of private militia, and a less public group of thieves and other shady characters that he may have controlled.

Soapy Smith's rule in Skagway came to an end on July 8, 1898—a month less than one year before the arrival of the Harriman Expedition—when Frank Reid and Jesse Murphy, leading a group of townspeople vigilantes, confronted Smith on Skagway's Juneau Wharf. In a gunfight vaguely reminiscent of that at Arizona's OK Corral, shots were exchanged, and Smith died instantly. Mortally wounded, Reid died a few days later. Both were buried in the town cemetery.

Two years had passed between the arrival of the *Queen* and the arrival of the *Elder*. In that time Skagway had boomed to the top of a bell curve of growth and activity, and then, as early as the time of the gunfight, had begun sliding on the downside of the curve. The stream of prospectors had slowed to a trickle and was rapidly drying up; businesses of all types had cut back or closed as the demand for supplies and services faded; the con men and thieves had gradually moved on after Smith's death (though the town was, if not completely lawless, still "open"); the population was falling—by the spring of 1899 it stood at a little over 3,000; and thoughts were turning to tourism instead of the road to gold as the economic hope of the town.

⇒ ◆ ⇐

Steaming up the Lynn Canal all afternoon, the *Elder's* passengers marveled at the number of glaciers high up on the mountains on both sides of the waterway. They reached Skagway before sunset and soon tied-up at a long, high pier that was crowded with people. "Such a gathering and such curiosity and alertness we have not before seen," Burroughs observed, "Hotel runners flourish their cards and call out the names of their various hostelries before we have touched the dock. Boys greet us with shouts and comments, women and girls, some of them in bicycle suits, push to the front and gaze intently at the strangers. All seemed to be expecting something, friends or news, or some sensational occurrence."[2] The crowds on shore may have thought, since it was an unscheduled arrival, that the *Elder* was an overdue mail boat, or as evidenced by the presence of the hotel runners, that it was a boatload of early season tourists who might need overnight lodging and other services in town. Somewhat alarmingly, no sooner had the ship tied-up and put down its gangplank than the boys on the pier "swarmed in upon us like ants and began to explore the ship," though they were quickly swept back ashore by Captain Doran and his crew.[3]

After awhile the hubbub died down, the crowd gradually dispersed, and most of those on board ventured out in small groups to explore the town in the fading light of the day. In the business district they found hotels and restaurants: some of these were open, others were boarded up. And they found that it was "the stumpiest town in the country. Many of the houses stand upon stumps; there are stumps in nearly every dooryard," and that, though Skagway was barely two years old, "the people already speak of the 'early times,' three years ago."[4] While others walked about town, John Muir went in search of the Rev. Samuel Hall Young, an old friend who he had first met in Wrangell in 1879 and who had accompanied him to Muir Glacier and on a number of Muir's other forays into the Alaskan coastal wilderness. He located Young, and they "had a good time ... we talked over old times."[5]

Turning in early—aboard the *Elder*, not in any of the hotels whose rooms the runners had so earnestly hawked when the ship arrived—the party woke on Wednesday, June 7 to a chilly, rainy Alaska morning. After breakfast they gathered their things together, armed themselves with umbrellas and rain slickers, and set out to board the narrow-gauge White Pass and Yukon Railway.

so detailed

The first and, at the time, the only railroad in Alaska, the WP&YR's trackage ran from Skagway to White Pass and beyond that another thirty miles to Lake Bennett in the Yukon, though the line was currently operating only so far as the White Pass summit; the first train would not roll into Bennett until July 6. The route to the top of the Pass covered some twenty miles. Initially passing through the settlement and across the flat delta land for two miles, the grade then began to rise rapidly above the Skagway River. For the next eighteen miles, climbing 3,000 feet to the summit, the rail line followed, on a shelf of rock blasted out of the side of the mountain, the narrow route blazed by the prospectors—what had become known as the "Dead Horse Trail," a name derived from the number of loaded pack horses that had met their demise in struggling up to the summit during the deadly winters of 1897 and 1898. Novelist Jack London would memorably write that "the horses died like mosquitoes in the first frost and from Skagway to Bennett they rotted in heaps."[6]

Riding in the relative comfort of the train as it worked its way upward through the drizzle and low clouds that June morning, George Bird Grinnell pictured the miners struggling along the steep grade and noted that, preserved by the cold and snow, "evidences of their passage are still to be seen in the dead horses, rotting fragments of clothing, and rusty utensils—articles abandoned from time to time as the way grew harder and the loads relatively heavier."[7] Horses and prospectors were not the only ones to suffer in White Pass: construction of the railroad had been plagued by accidents, explosions, falling rock, and other misfortunes that had killed thirty-two men—at least those were the admitted deaths.

At a spot known as Glacier Switch, five miles below the summit, the train stopped on a siding to allow a freight train to pass. Looking out the window, Merriam spied the camp of Wilfred Osgood, who Merriam had sent out from Washington in mid–May. Osgood and two associates were on their way, on behalf of the Biological Survey, to Lake Bennett and from there down the Yukon River to Dawson, their mission being to study the animal life of the Klondike and the interior.[8] The Harriman train tarried on the siding long enough for Merriam and others of the party to visit the camp and examine the collection of birds and mammals the Osgood party had gathered to date.[9]

Disembarking at the summit, the party stepped into a cold, damp north wind. Even though it was June, there were still heavy banks of snow, and they passed "the carcasses of two horses all in a heap on a snow bank their heels in the air, and then stopped at a camp of tents or canvass covered shanties."[10] Some of the tents belonged to the railroad's construction crew, while others provided temporary accommodations for the continuing trickle of prospectors making their way to the Klondike—prospectors who, with the rail line not yet open to Lake Bennett, still had to make their way on foot, pulling loaded sleds down to the lake from the summit. Near the tents were two tall flag poles, one bearing a crisp British flag and the other a worn and

Scenic view of White Pass and Yukon Railway. Photograph by Mary Harriman Rumsey. Source: National Museum of the American Indian, Smithsonian Institution [NMAI AC 053_pht_008_P11143].

tattered American flag, marking what was still in many ways a "provisional boundary" between Canadian and American territory.[11] Several Canadian police officers were on duty, interviewing those seeking to push on beyond the summit, into Canada.

The ornithologists, botanists, zoologists, and others fanned out over the summit, but specimen collecting, save for a bird or two and a few hardy plants, was sparse. Gathering again near the idling train, they soon made their way in twos and threes to one of the larger tents where an unexpected, cooked-in-camp lunch had been set up, courtesy of the officials of the White Pass and Yukon: "two long tables groaned under a load of pork and beans, pie, rice, potatoes, cake, coffee, etc."[12]

They were soon back on the train, headed slowly down toward Skagway, in all likelihood not realizing that the summit of White Pass was the farthest inland that the members of the Harriman Expedition would travel on their long journey. On the way back they talked of the miners and their hardships, the stories they had heard or read about, and what Skagway's future might be in the wake of the gold rush. Grinnell may have related the best tale, involving the sort of greed and obsession that might have afflicted many of those who braved White Pass in search of illusory fortune. The story was of a man who started the journey with one coffee pot but collected, hoarded, and protected discarded ones he found along the trail until he had burdened himself with a hundred coffee pots, while at the same time casting away his other more valuable supplies and possessions, along with any chance of realizing on his dreams.[13] Dall

Trestle on the White Pass and Yukon Railway. Library of Congress.

listened to the stories, mused about the end of the gold rush, and in his mind began to see the railroad, not gold miners, as the key to Skagway's development and existence—the new railroad, he reasoned, would lure tourists and make Skagway a "town of the future."[14]

Back in Skagway, which was very much a "town of the present," they found that the local newspaper had published a list of the party, which Dellenbaugh observed "has created a great sensation in this country."[15] With that as a send-off, and with only a few of the local citizenry on the pier to watch their departure, the *Elder* pulled in her lines and steamed away down the Lynn Canal to pick-up the party of scientists that had been left in Juneau.

═ ◆ ═

In Juneau on the evening of June 6, while the main party in Skagway was exploring that town and John Muir was meeting with his old friend Hall Young, Charles Palache took up his pen and wrote to Helen Markham, beginning "Behold me at the Occidental Hotel, writing at the card table after a busy day." After relating the events of the day including the arrival in Juneau, the visit to the Treadwell Mine, and the departure of the main party for Skagway, he confided that "I went back alone to the mine and pounded rocks all day very busily. I go over again tomorrow morning to go underground."[16] The next evening, after experiencing a day-long, pouring, uncomfortable rain, he sat down in his room at the hotel to report to her on his further activities. Those had begun at 9:00 a.m. when the launch had again ferried him to the Treadwell Mine where, with the mine's foreman, he "went down in the cage and then 100 feet of vertical ladders and I collected specimens and information to my heart's content. It was noon by the time I had my stuff packed and then all dirty as I was I went to the superintendent's to lunch. His wife was very cordial and gave us a fine meal."[17]

Later that same evening, the scientists found themselves invited to a smoker and "stag social" given by the Elks Lodge. Not at all sure what to expect, they decided to

more Wild West atmos.

attend. A couple of days later, perhaps after thinking over how he would describe the event to his fiancée, Palache included a summary of the evening in a letter to Helen.

> It was held in "Slim Jim's" Opera House whose hall space we found filled with long rough board tables on which we found clay pipes and smoking tobacco laid out while kegs of beer and piles of sandwiches showed the character of the refreshments. The chairman took the stage and we soon saw where the fun came in. He had full power and none might refuse obedience. Most of his acts of power consisted in the levying of fines on the members for doing or for not doing things of all sorts, for saying or thinking or for not doing so, all sorts of things or for not carrying out with sufficient dispatch the orders of the chair. Two burly policemen hustled culprits to the bar to be fined and a refreshment committee kept the beer circulating. At intervals there was a song or dance or story either by members or by some theatrical variety people who happened to be in town. Among other things the head of our party, Prof. Ritter from Berkeley, was summoned to tell what new animals he had found in Alaska and after a very decent speech he escaped by telling them that they might find out more if they would all come to the Elder at four the next morning when she would be at the dock. We escaped at midnight when the stories were beginning to get unpleasantly coarse.[18]

Ritter and Starks were less circumspect in the few words they each privately committed to their diaries. "An interesting event," Ritter wrote, "but interest of a kind that hardly needs gratifying more than once for a respectable person." Noting that there were perhaps a hundred men present, he wondered, "How do men of so much intelligence enjoy such moral filth?" and referring to the part in all this that was played by the "theatrical variety people" (apparently a group of male and female actors) that Palache had mentioned, Ritter concluded, "And how do people with such obvious talents as these four play people find it possible to put them to such use?"[19] For his part, Starks was more forthcoming in terms of the festivities, including a veiled comment or hint about the ladies of the town. "We were," he wrote, "entertained (?) at the rough theatre with the most indecent show I ever saw, and having lived in Chicago in its widest-open days I am not easily shocked. Perhaps I was not shocked so much, however, as plain disgusted," he continued, "for the acts were wholly without point, being simply the vehicle to put over the sort of thing that would make a good honest cussing mule driver blush. Most of the ladies of the town have a habit of printing on their door plates only their first names, and you see in large letters Maud, Tilly, Maggy, etc."[20]

Escaping the hospitality of the Elks at midnight, the men made their way back through town and returned to the Occidental Hotel—only to be awakened at 2:30 a.m. with the news that the *Elder* had returned ahead of schedule and was waiting at the dock. After much scrambling about in the dead of night, and in Palache's case tracking down some laundry he had sent out, they made their way along the stumpy, unlighted streets to the wharf and went on board, not getting to bed in their staterooms until almost 6:00 a.m. "I was," Palache wrote in concluding his account, "up at 8 with a fine headache and general Katzenjammer as a memorial of the previous night's entertainment and was not good for much of the day."[21]

period slang

Thursday the 8th of June was given over to steaming the one hundred or so miles from Juneau to Glacier Bay—a course that required the *Elder* to retrace part of the route to Skagway before moving on northward through the passages between the offshore islands of the Alaska Panhandle.

The coast region of the mainland that was in sight throughout the day became continuously mountainous. The weather was fine, bringing many on deck, including the geographer Henry Gannett, who would write of the abrupt transition from ocean to mountains, "The land rises from the water almost everywhere at steep angles, without a sign of beach, to altitudes of thousands of feet. It is a fiord coast. The relief features of this region, its mountains and gorges partly filled by the sea, are all of glacial origin, presenting everywhere the familiar handwriting of ice."[22]

It was the sort of day that lent itself to a variety of on-board activities. On sunlit days like this, the hurricane deck became a favorite lounging place. "In the lee of the chart room," Grinnell would remember, "sheltered from the wind and warmed by the sun, a group of idlers usually reclined in steamer chairs, reading, chatting or working.... Often, too, the small children, and some others of greater stature, engaged in riotous games of tag about the saloon deck, and it was a pleasing sight to see men whose beards had been silvered by many years of work, or whose heads, in war time, would have been a distinct disappointment to the conventional North American Indian, racing to and fro, dodging around pillars, and leaping over hatchways and deck beams, in the effort to escape the children who were pursuing them."[23]

For Harriman, afternoon cruising was an ideal time, whether outside or in the smoking room, for his favorite board game—Crokinole. At the time, a relatively new parlor game, Crokinole is like shuffleboard or curling but miniaturized and in the round, with players flicking discs and scoring points by landing them in various scoring regions on the board, while also trying to knock away opposing discs. Either two or four players are involved, and Brewer, Emerson, Merriam, and Muir were among those who played the game with Harriman.

It appears that somewhere in these first few weeks of the Expedition, perhaps on this day's cruise out of Juneau, and maybe even over a game of Crokinole, Muir overcame the initial suspicions and qualms he had had about accepting the invitation to be a member of the Expedition and about Harriman himself. Years later, looking back on the experience, Muir would write, "I soon saw that Mr. Harriman was uncommon. He was taking a trip for rest, and at the same time managing his exploring guests as if we were a grateful, soothing, essential part of his rest-cure, though scientific explorers are not easily managed, and in large mixed lots are rather inflammable and explosive, especially when compressed on a ship." He remembered how, as the trip progressed, Harriman had been true to his word to let his guests decide the itinerary, "putting us ashore wherever we liked ... taking us aboard again at given times, looking after everything to the minutest details; work enough to bring nervous prostration to ordinary mortals instead of rest." And he found that "one of the telling sights" was "Mr. Harriman keeping trot-step with little Roland while helping him drag a toy canoe along the deck with a cotton string."[24] By the time the Expedition was over, Muir and Harriman would become fast friends for the remainder of their lives.

In the afternoon, the *Elder* entered Glacier Bay. Small icebergs and cakes of ice made their appearance. The ice drew the eye of the artist Dellenbaugh: "The color was exquisite. The most tender blue green or green blue, running down sometimes to the color of blue vitriol." And then after lunch, with most of the party on deck, he noted that "the Muir Glacier was plainly in sight, far away at the end of the Bay, a long, massive wall of ice, stretching back into the mountains."[25]

Muir's description
Harriman, coming around
to him

SIX

The Big Ice-Mountain Bay

"The other part goes way beyond my vocabulary, which has gradually become dwindled down to Wow and Gee."—Louis Agassiz Fuertes

The looming ice wall at the head of Glacier Bay that so captured Frederick Dellenbaugh's attention was a familiar sight to John Muir; in fact, some years before, he and the *George W. Elder* had a shared experience in the shadow of that wall. idio.

In the summer of 1890, and on his third extended visit to the Bay, Muir set-up camp and built a simple cabin on the east shore, some short distance from the edge of the Muir Glacier. In the wee hours of the morning of the first of July that summer, he was awakened by the whistle of a steamer. It was the *Elder*, and the ship soon unloaded a party of students, led by Professor Henry Fielding Reid. They were, Muir would note, "well provided with instruments to study the glacier," and soon carried those instruments and the other freight they landed to a camp they pitched beside Muir's. "I am delighted," he wrote, "to have companions so congenial—we now have a village."[1] Reid and his students would spend the summer with Muir; though the latter, as was his want, often traveled off on his own during those months.

Now, on a bright afternoon nine years later, Muir stood at the rail on the hurricane deck as the *Elder* bucked an increasingly strong, cold wind from the north and slowly worked its way up the Bay to a point a mile from the front of the Muir Glacier, and within sight of his cabin. The water was extremely deep, and it was only after repeated soundings that Captain Doran found bottom within reach of the ship's anchor cables. In the near distance, the face of the glacier towered more than 200 feet above the surface of the water. Learning that the glacier's base rested on the deep floor of the bay, and taking into account the depth of the water, Burroughs would record with some awe that "could the inlet have been emptied of its waters for a moment we should have seen before us a palisade of ice nearly 1000 feet higher and over two miles wide, with a turbid river, possibly a half mile wide, boiling up from beneath it."[2] And the visible face of the Muir Glacier was active: writing to his family back in upstate New York, Louis Fuertes described how "every few minutes or seconds a great piece will scale away with a report of a great cannon, strike the water with a roar, and spray sometimes as high as the face of the ice cliff, force up an immense foaming wave which floods across the bay, breaking up in roaring surf a half mile from where it started."[3]

To Muir, it was an almost proprietary scene: he and the missionary Hall Young had discovered Glacier Bay in 1879. Accompanied by four Tlingit guides, they had navigated the Alaskan coastline in canoes using what was still the best available map,

Front of Muir Glacier. Photograph by A.K Fisher. A.K. Fisher Collection, Library of Congress.

the charts developed by the British Captain George Vancouver during his exploration of the coast in 1794. However, in the area that formed the mouth of Glacier Bay, Muir and Young found that "Vancouver's chart, hitherto a faithful guide, failed us altogether"—the chart showed "no trace" of the present Glacier Bay and Vancouver had labeled the area as a single ice mountain.[4]

Vancouver's voyage had occurred toward the end of the Little Ice Age, when the front or terminus of what was to be called the Muir Glacier was at its maximum.[5] At that time, the Muir and other glaciers may have extended so far out into the present bay as to fill it entirely; so that to Vancouver there was no "bay," but only an imposing façade of ice along the coast. A considerable retreat of the ice, and an opening-up of the bay, had occurred by 1879, and Muir would quickly conclude that "this Icy Bay is being still further extended by the recession of the glaciers."[6] In 1880, after his 1879 explorations had been halted by weather, Muir returned to Glacier Bay, hiked up the east side of the Muir Glacier for five or six miles, and after climbing a mountain twenty-five hundred feet high, had a view of the glacier and its principal branches.

> Instead of a stream of ice winding down a mountain-walled valley like the largest of the Swiss glaciers, the Muir looks like a broad undulating prairie streaked with medial moraines and gashed with crevasses, surrounded by numberless mountains from which flow its many tributary glaciers. There are seven main tributaries from ten to twenty miles long and from two to six miles wide where they enter the trunk, each of them fed by many secondary tributaries; so that the whole number of branches, great and small, pouring from the mountain fountains perhaps number upward of two hundred, not counting the

smallest. The area drained by this one grand glacier can hardly be less than seven or eight hundred miles, and probably contains as much ice as all the eleven hundred Swiss glaciers combined. Its length from the frontal wall back to the head of its farthest fountain seemed to be about forty or fifty miles, and the width just below the confluence of the main tributaries about twenty-five miles.[7]

Now, in 1899, and as the Expedition party did its work in the coming days, Muir would find that the glaciers on Glacier Bay were in further retreat: the Muir and the neighboring Hugh Miller Glacier had "receded about two miles in the last twenty years, the Grand Pacific about four," and "by the recession of the Grand Pacific and corresponding extension of Reid Inlet an island two and a half or three miles long, and over a thousand feet high, has been added to the landscape. Only the end of this island was visible in 1879."[8] The natural retreat of the glaciers, accelerated by global warming, would, of course, continue in the twentieth and twenty-first centuries, with one Alaskan historian noting that, as to the Muir Glacier, scientific studies indicated that "between 1914 and 2010, this thirty mile glacier retreated by almost twenty miles."[9]

═══ ◆ ═══

During the Harriman Expedition's voyage up the Bay to the *Elder's* deep water anchorage, Muir "excited the enthusiasm of the hunters," with a tale about the abundance of large game in a narrow valley he called Howling Valley, on the southeast edge of the Muir Glacier and about eighteen miles back from the glacier's front.[10] According to Grinnell, "the glacier's owner" averred that the Valley was "easy to get at" and that "in years past he had seen there the fresh tracks of bears, wolves, caribou, mountain goats and other desirable animals."[11] Harriman promptly decided to go there, notwithstanding the long hike over the ice and snow and the necessity of spending one or more nights on the glacier. Eight packers, carrying tents, blankets, cooking utensils and food, were soon put ashore in the steam launch to go ahead and set-up camp. After dinner, about 8:00 p.m., the hunters—Harriman, Morris, Grinnell, Trudeau, Merriam, and Kelly—went ashore to follow the packers, with plans to camp on the ice that night "and go 12 or 15 miles further tomorrow for a four or five days bear hunt."[12] Looking back on this trek, Merriam would note that "Muir himself declined to go, making the clever excuse that he was no hunter."[13]

The packers and the hunters were not the only groups that the steam launch brought ashore. In the long-lasting light of an Alaskan evening in June, many left the ship to explore the moraine to the side of the glacier. They found plants, small marine life … and long stretches of plank boardwalks, apparently placed there for the convenience of the many that would arrive by steamer in the coming summer tourist season. Burroughs, Gifford, Gannett, and Dellenbaugh worked their way across to Muir's cabin. Dellenbaugh took pictures and went inside, where he found a fireplace with an outside chimney, and some signs the cabin had been used by other travelers. All in all, he found it in good condition, "except a spot in the roof where the shingles have been blown off."[14]

A few stayed back on the ship, including Charles Palache. Perhaps solicitous of Mrs. Harriman and her possible concerns about her husband crossing the treacherous surface of the glacier in the dark, he closed a letter to Helen, "I staid on board and went to bed early after a little game of cribbage with Mrs. Harriman and the Captain of the ship."[15]

After breakfast on Friday, and with the hunters out somewhere on Muir's glacier, several parties braved the morning cold and a brief, hard rain to go ashore, the steam launch depositing them on the moraine.

Many walked along the shoreline to the face of the glacier, and then hiked up an outcrop known as Red Knob for the view. Once there, Muir led a party of three girls—apparently Mary and Cornelia Harriman and Dorothea Draper—on a hike to a small rocky island, what the Eskimos called a "Nunatak" ("hill of stone"), rising out of the glacier three miles from the front.[16]

The girls, Muir would write, were "fine walkers" and "all were impressed with the vast extent of ice, the lovely blue grottoes, shimmering in the light, like fairyland."[17] Such a hike was a special challenge for these young women since, while the crinoline and the bustles of the earlier years of the Victorian era had largely disappeared, standard women's dress of the day involved ankle-length skirts that flared away from a tight waist into a bell shape, blouses with large sleeves and high necklines, and—particularly for outdoor wear—ankle-length laced or buttoned boots with stiff, low heels. Broad hats were customary and, in the climate the members of the Harriman Expedition were experiencing, long and heavy outer coats completed ensembles that made a six-mile round-trip hike a much more confining and challenging experience for the women than for the men in the party. Throughout the Expedition—from the visit to the Treadwell Mine, to explorations like this on glaciers, to stops at

Gannett surveying with theodolite. Photograph by Edward S. Curtis. Library of Congress.

Native villages—Mrs. Harriman and the "Big 4" endured every adventure willingly and with impressive enthusiasm. Mary Harriman, almost 18 years old, was clearly the leader who the younger girls followed. Among other things she was very outgoing: her brother Roland would describe her as "dark, very attractive" and as someone who "loved company, she loved to dance, she loved great fun … and she had a laugh that was most infectious."[18] All the members of the Big 4 showed a genuine interest in benefitting from the unique chance to learn from their distinguished fellow travelers. Muir, who grew to be particularly fond of them all, succinctly summarized the situation in saying, "The girls were so bright and eager to study the wonderful regions we passed through that we were all proud to become their teachers."[19]

While the climbers were making their way up to the Red Knob and beyond, other members of the shore party chose to stay on the moraine. Henry Gannett, perhaps having in mind Muir's story of how the glacier that carried his name had receded in the last twenty years, and to provide an accurate basis for measuring its future movements, set out on his own with his surveying equipment to establish and record the exact location of the present front of the ice. Saunders and Kincaid roamed the waters' edge in their usual quests for seaweeds and insects. Dellenbaugh set up his easels and paints on the beach and worked on a sketch looking toward the face of the glacier. He "found it a difficult experience on account of the cold north wind blowing in my face, straight off the glacier. I was obliged every few minutes to dance around and stopped also to eat my sandwich and two apples."[20] He finished in a cold afternoon rain, was picked-up by the launch, and returned to the ship.

As Dellenbaugh was headed back to the *Elder*, Curtis and Inverarity were venturing out in light canvas canoes, weaving between the icebergs to take close-up photos of the Muir Glacier. They had taken several glass-plate impressions and were paddling in closer when "about a half a mile of the front fell at once."[21] By now Dellenbaugh was back on the ship and the sound of the fall brought him rushing on deck, where he observed that at the face of the glacier, "mass after mass fell away with a tremendous noise and left a sort of plateau somewhat above the water line. This presently began to sink and then fell away. One of the largest bergs—a great mass—shot up out of the water a great dark head, like a mighty whale, and then sank again to finally come to the surface once more…. The spray from this fall splashed higher than the face of the glacier."[22] Muir and the girls were just coming around the end of the moraine on their way back to the ship when this massive discharge began, and he recalled that the large berg referred to by Dellenbaugh "rose a hundred and fifty feet, the water like hair streaming from it, a wave twenty feet high combing and dashing up spray a hundred feet against the bergs and roaring like the ocean."[23] He hurried his little party high up the shore and out of the range of the surging water. For Curtis and Inverarity things were far dicier. The swell came near to upsetting them and they took on a great deal of water, losing some of their plates and equipment as they battled to keep from overturning. Those on the *Elder* watched anxiously as the photographers paddled directly into the waves and rode the high waters to their crests, somehow keeping afloat and eventually making their way back to the ship.[24]

One of the day's longest excursions involved Emerson, Gilbert, and Palache. Taking the steam launch, they started off in the morning for the west side of the glacier but encountered drift ice so thick that they couldn't risk forcing the launch through. They turned back and disembarked on the east side, where the three geologists climbed up some 700 feet to the shoulder of a mountain whose summit was hidden in the heavy clouds. Here they photographed and "hammered at the rocks," with Palache finding his first "gold prospect," though in writing to Helen Markham he advised her it was not such as was "destined to make our fortunes."[25] He would also relate that as he explored among the rocks he came upon a ptarmigan, calmly sitting on a nest of moss, and "I lifted her off and am rather ashamed to say killed her and took her eggs, six in number. It seemed cruel but she was a prize for the bird men and science excused the deed." Early in the afternoon the men ate the lunch they had packed, climbed down to the surface of the glacier and, after setting some traps in an ice cave, started off on a ten-mile "tramp" to a rocky mass rising from the glacial ice in the distance: "The surface of the ice we walked on was very smooth and even ... nearly covered with a thin coating of mud with here and there bands of rocky moraine material. You could almost have ridden a bicycle for miles over the even surface, except that the sharp ice points would soon have cut the tires." After picking their way through a field full of crevasses, they reached their goal, climbed its summit, and had a broad view over the glacier, though the mountains in the distance were shrouded in mist. A few rock specimens were added to their backpacks and the threesome clambered down to the surface and returned by a somewhat longer route to the moraine, getting back to the ship about 8 p.m., "well tired out but delighted with the day's experience." At the very end of his letter to Helen relating the adventures of the day, Palache added, "I forgot to say that soon after lunch we met the hunting party returning footsore, cold and weary—they had found deep soft snow on the summit and had been forced to turn back."

For those hunters, the trek across the glacier to Howling Valley had been far less than a howling success. After coming ashore Thursday evening, they had first spent a couple of hours scrambling over the steep slopes of a long lateral moraine before reaching the smoother surface of the ice and making good time. About eleven o'clock they overtook the packers, "who, instead of having made camp as they had been told to do, were calmly sitting on their packs waiting for orders."[26] Nearby on the glacier's surface was a little lake of ice water, and tents were set up, tea was made, and at midnight blankets were spread on the ice and all were soon asleep; though as the hours passed, the cold penetrated the sleeping bags and the sleepers' joints, and by 3:00 a.m. everyone was up, moving about.

After breakfast, and warmed by hot tea, they decided to push on, and by 4:30 were on their way. Not long afterward it began to rain hard, and the rain soon turned to heavy snow: within less than three hours the still-falling snow was knee-deep. Walking became increasingly difficult and, since the snow was now deep enough to cover any crevasses, the six leading men were roped together and probed the ice ahead of them with poles. The snowfall continued unabated, and the pace was slow. At around 11:00 a.m., the party reached a crest of the ice and the packers were told to wait there—the packers later told Nelson that for the next hour they "ran around the ice in a circle to keep their feet from freezing."[27] The hunters pushed on until they reached a vantage point from which the sought-after valley could be seen opening up in the distance. It was clearly very deep in snow, and Kelly remembered that "it did not appear probable to me that ... there could be any game of any kind within a day's journey in the direction we were bearing even if the way had been safe and feasible."[28] Grinnell would write that the valley "was all white with snow ... and as the prospects for hunting in this snow were poor, and the chance of the packers getting through with their loads was very doubtful, it was determined to give up the trip and turn back."[29]

They reversed their course but, even though the weather slowly improved, the walking on the return trip was laborious, the packers lagged, and the party became widely scattered over the ice, everyone moving at their own pace and arriving, in ones and twos, back on the beach opposite the *Elder* between two and six o'clock in the afternoon. Merriam in particular struggled. He had apparently injured his left knee some years before and, as he slowly trudged on, that knee "became more and more painful until I could barely walk, and the roughness of the ice battered and bruised the hollow of my right foot, so I was quite a cripple when I reached the ship."[30] He was fortunate to meet Cole and Kearney about three miles from the *Elder*, and they took his pack. Shortly afterward he also encountered Muir and the three girls, and they helped him the rest of the way. "On reaching the ship," Merriam wrote, "I went to bed and the trained nurse bandaged my knee."[31] The entire group returned "pretty well fagged out," according to Dellenbaugh,[32] and Burroughs would charitably summarize that "the hunters came straggling in, footsore and weary and innocent of blood—soberer if not sadder, hardier if not wiser men."[33] Most, like Merriam, went to bed as soon as they had something to eat.

The evening talk in the Social Hall was given by Muir, recounting his nine-day crossing of the glacier in 1890. Fittingly, Muir's talk was punctured by an active evening of calving on the face of his namesake: "All this evening the 'Old Man' has been booming and reverberating," wrote Fuertes, "and all through John Muir's lecture after dinner, the boat would suddenly begin to pitch or roll, according to which side of the glacier the ice mass fell from."[34]

⇒ ◆ ⇐

After Friday's rain and snow, dawn on Saturday, June 10 brought clearing skies and the beginning of what Muir, surely a qualified observer, would enthusiastically call "a perfectly glorious time in Glacier Bay—five days of the most splendid weather I ever saw in Alaska."[35]

The scientists were eager to get on land and collect specimens. In the first blush of morning the steam launch took Ritter, Saunders, Coe, Coville, Kincaid, and Trudeau ashore. They immediately split up, most working on the shoreline and in the shallow water searching for marine life. Coville, the botanist, would spend part of the next two days off to the side of the moraine studying an area where the glacier had at one time engulfed and buried groves of trees.

With that shore party on its way on the steam launch that Saturday morning, the *Elder* ran down the Bay to land an ornithological and botanical party of Fernow, Fisher, Ridgway, Kearney, Cole, and Fuertes for a three-day sojourn on Gustavus Peninsula, a long, low, wooded stretch of land twenty miles below the Muir Glacier. Arriving at about noon, the men lost no time in making camp and having lunch in a cove between two rocky and sandy points, with a spruce forest behind them and the long blue bay stretching out in front. They were soon out scouting the area and collecting. That evening, they sat around their campfire listening to Fernow's stories of the Franco-Prussian war, in which he had fought before immigrating to America. Their initial collecting success encouraged them to start out early the next morning, though they were at least temporarily brought-up short by the scene around them. Fuertes tried to capture it in a letter home.

> When we first saw the mountains this a.m. the far ones looked like icebergs, the distant blue of the rocky parts was so light. The blowing and snorting of the whales, the screaming, way out on the bay of gulls and loons, and an occasional goose, and nearby, the licking of the little waves in the pebbles and hum of a big bee, with just a thin "ray" of the hermit's song way over across the bay in the spruces, make the part of the picture that you see with your ears. The other part goes way beyond my vocabulary, which has gradually become dwindled down to Wow and Gee.[36]

Using the small boat that had been landed with them, some of the men were soon out on the water, while others worked their way up through the forest—Fernow studying and taking notes on the trees, the others setting traps, with guns at the ready for any birds that might be seen. Two days of this work resulted in a total collection of 45 small mammals and 25 birds. It was rewarding but tiring work, followed by sleep made restless by an unpleasant introduction to Alaska's legendary mosquitoes, an experience Fuertes was able to describe in one graphic sentence: "The mosquitoes had simply changed the whole topography of our faces during the night, and I had to lift one eyelid with my thumb for about an hour after I got up."[37] They spent a quiet final day collecting their traps, breaking camp, and taking in the scenery before being picked-up late on Monday afternoon by the *Elder.*

Camp at Point Gustavus. Photograph by A.K. Fisher. A.K. Fisher Collection, Library of Congress.

After dropping off the Gustavus Peninsula party on the morning of the 10th, the *Elder* went as far up Glacier Bay as the ice would allow the steamer to proceed, and at 4 p.m. off-loaded a rowboat containing Gilbert, Muir, Palache, and three packers. This group was to explore the head of the Bay and its glaciers, with the expectation that they would be picked-up at a designated point on Tuesday the 13th. After a straight-away row of twelve miles, they reached a sandy cove where the packers set up the tents and prepared supper, while the three scientists set-off to see the nearby Charpentier and Hugh Miller glaciers. These, like others the Expedition encountered, had retreated far back from the point they occupied when Muir first visited them. "Comparison of the present position of the glaciers with their former extent was the chief aim of our trip," Palache wrote in a long letter to his fiancé summarizing [*error*] this excursion. He also related how it was nearly midnight and still light when they turned in, enjoying the luxury of the latest thing—air mattresses inflated with a bicycle pump—and scorning the tents to sleep under the open sky.[38] It was a short night: they were up and about at 3:30 a.m. Sunday morning, spent the hours before noon in the cove studying rocks and the glaciers, and then rowed down the shore some ten miles before setting up another camp, where, tired and despite "broad sunlight," they turned in at 9:00 p.m. *air mattresses a new tech*

On Monday, they were again up early, found a fresh skin of ice on the water, which made rowing hard, and coasted slowly along the shore for a dozen miles toward the Pacific Glacier. In his long letter, Palache said, "we landed on a fine projecting knob of beautiful white marble cut by innumerable dykes of green rock. On reaching the top we were surprised to find just beyond a fine glacier which was unnamed upon the map so we called it the Harriman and spent most of the day surveying and mapping it."[39] Actually, Muir would note, the Pacific Glacier had melted back four miles and changed into three separate glaciers, one of which, previously unnamed and unexplored, he named the Harriman Glacier.[40] The upper portion of Glacier Bay contained a number of huge icebergs: landing on one, Muir paced it off and found it was seven hundred feet long.[41] Camping in a sheltered cove that evening, they found it was already occupied by two Indians, a father and son "making a hearty supper on boiled gulls' eggs, with celery and dried fish while a couple of marmots newly shot indicated what the next meal would be."[42]

The party was fascinated the next morning when the Indians, who were there to hunt seal, started off with their boat "draped in white cloth, white hats on their heads and a big white cloth screen hung in front, all to make the boat look like an ice cake so that they may draw up to the seal and spear him before he takes alarm."[43] Like the Indian seal hunters, the three men and their packers also had to get underway, since they had some distance to go to reach their rendezvous point with the *Elder*. Icebergs slowed their progress and it became clear that they would not meet the ship on time; indeed, shortly before noon they saw her passing by, out of hailing distance. Muir was confident that they would not be abandoned, and was bemused by how his colleagues feared not being found, and were "wild to get on the steamer," including at one point when Gilbert and Palache climbed up an iceberg and "wigwagged from the top."[44] On board the *Elder*, and when the Muir party failed to appear at the appointed place, Harriman became concerned for their safety and sent out two launches in search. "One of these," Merriam recalled, "he placed in my charge, the other he himself operated. We went in different directions through the floating ice, and when at six in the

Steamship *George W. Elder* and launch in Muir Inlet. Photograph by Mary Harriman Rumsey. National Museum of the American Indian, Smithsonian Institution [NMAI AC 053_011_000_L00814].

Harriman pulls his weight

evening I heard four whistles from the steamer I knew that he had found them." It was, Merriam would also note, the first but not the last time that Harriman took a perilous boat journey to gather in absent members of the party.[45]

In recording the story of the Gilbert, Muir, Palache party in his "Narrative" of the Harriman Expedition, John Burroughs drew some wry comparisons with the group that had gone hunting in Howling Valley. "It is much easier in Alaska to bag a glacier than a bear," he said, "hence our glacial party, made up of John Muir, Gilbert, and Palache, who set out to explore the head of Glacier Bay, was more successful than the hunters. They found more glaciers than they were looking for."[46] *good line*

Not all the shore excursions were for collecting purposes. Many others of the ship's party spent the days in Glacier Bay walking, sketching, painting, photographing, and mountain climbing, according to their tastes. On Sunday, the 11th, Henry Gannett wanted to visit two "islands" on the east portion of Muir Glacier, and soon had together a party including Dellenbaugh and Trudeau, along with Mary Harriman, her sister Cornelia, and Elizabeth Averill. After attaining the low summit of the first island, where the girls helped Gannett place his measuring instruments, they descended to a pool of fresh water where they ate lunch, and then covered the mile and a half to the second island, where, after "quite a pull up," they reached its thousand-foot top and enjoyed a "magnificent view" before retracing their steps and reaching the ship at 7:00 p.m.[47]

That same day, Burroughs and Keeler, perhaps feeling somewhat divorced or isolated from the exploring and collecting activities of the others, climbed the mountain behind Muir's cabin, where the two poets soaked up the scenery on a clear afternoon, including a view of the distant Fairweather Range. In the bay below, Keeler thought the *Elder* floated like "a little toy boat ... amid cakes of ice."[48] Dr. Nelson spent Sunday afternoon walking on the hurricane deck. That evening, he was gratified "by hearty singing and responses" at the evening service, where he "distributed 50 prayer books and 50 hymnals which I brought from New York. I made an address on Psalm 104 'He layeth the beams of His chambers in the waters.'"[49]

The evening of Tuesday, June 13 brought most of the traveling party together in the Social Hall, where Gilbert and Muir combined for an impromptu talk about their trip to the ends of Glacier Bay, including the situation with the Pacific Glacier and its split into three separate tidewater glaciers. Muir would record that his announcement that they had named one of those the Harriman Glacier "was received with many hearty cheers," and that "after the lecture, Mr. Harriman came to me and thanked me for the great honor I had done him."[50]

a glacier named,
for Harriman

SEVEN

A Touch of Culture and a Mix of Cultures

"People actually live in Sitka from choice and seem to find life sweet. There are homes of culture and refinement."—John Burroughs

Though the hour was late, the sky still held the colors of fading twilight as the *Elder* weighed anchor and began carefully picking its way through the floating ice. The night owls aboard gathered at the stern rail for a last look at the high wall of the Muir Glacier as it receded from view.

Glacier Bay was soon left behind and the ship steamed south through the woodsy Peril Strait to Sitka, entering the island-studded harbor at ten o'clock on the morning of Wednesday, June 14. Suitable anchorage was found in the bay a short distance offshore, with the party using the launches to reach the town's wharf. It was a wet, drizzly day, with periods of heavier rain. "But still," Palache wrote, "we all went to see the sights of this old Russian town which is the seat of what little government Alaska boasts."[1]

When John Muir first visited Sitka in 1879, he described it as having "a rusty, decaying look—a few stores, a few houses inhabited, many empty and rotting and falling down, a church of imposing size and architecture as if imported entire from Constantinople ... cannon lying in the streets sinking like boulders in the mud; dirty Indians loafing about; everybody of any character away at the mines or out-a-fishing. It was the capital while the country was in the hands of the Russians and a place of considerable trade, but since the purchase it has been practically abandoned."[2]

Coming ashore twenty years later, Muir found a town that not only had a stable population of just under 1,400 people, but which had also evolved considerably since his first visit. Many of the better Russian buildings remained, including the dominating and onion-domed St. Michael's Cathedral, with its soaring spires. Tlingit influences were apparent, including a line of Indian houses close to the beach. And the town had also acquired newer, American-built shops, businesses, and houses, though apparently these did not always show to advantage: Keeler advised Louise that "Sitka is a beautiful and romantic spot, full of historic associations and wonderfully beautiful in its setting, but it is being unmade as rapidly as possible by the hideous architecture of the Americans."[3]

Ashore that morning, the group visited the American Commercial Company's store, which featured Indian-made artifacts and souvenirs that the Company bought and then resold to tourists. Most of the Tlingits—who made up about half of Sitka's

Sunset over Muir Glacier. Photograph by Edward S. Curtis. Library of Congress.

population—lived on the outskirts of the town in an at least partially segregated situation, with separate schools and churches. Dellenbaugh, Keeler, and Ritter wandered off from the main group and went through the Tlingit settlement where, hunting for souvenir baskets, they "were cordially received into the homes of many of the Indians."[4] Muir and others strolled "uptown," visiting curiosity shops. Many also checked for mail at the post office, though most walked away disappointed.

Merriam—with Grinnell and Palache in tow—called on an old acquaintance, Lt. George Thornton Emmons. A naval officer and explorer who had retired to Sitka, Emmons had become a student of Tlingit culture and had succeeded in acquiring quite a number of artifacts and pieces of art, many of which he had donated to New York's American Museum of Natural History. Emmons arranged for the group to see ceremonial artworks that were usually not shown to outsiders.[5]

Doctors Nelson and Morris, ecclesiastic and physician, went off on another mission: visiting the cemetery and the grave of Morris's cousin, Captain Wm. Gouveneur Morris. Captain Morris had served as Collector of Customs in Sitka. His weather-worn gravestone recorded his death on January 31, 1884.[6]

The party's first day in Sitka drew to a close with an early evening tour of St. Michael's, after which they boarded the launches to return to the *Elder*. Harriman had invited a dozen or so of Sitka's notables, including Governor John Green Brady and his wife Elizabeth, to dinner aboard the ship. Brady had started life as an orphaned runaway on the streets of lower Manhattan. Like many other orphans in New York City, he found a benefactor in Theodore Roosevelt, Sr., the father of the

Sitka Trading Company housed in the old Russian barracks. Photograph by Edward S. Curtis. Library of Congress.

future President. Through the elder Roosevelt and the Aid Society he founded and supported, the ten-year-old Brady went west on an orphan train to Indiana, where he became part of the family of Judge John Green. Brady progressed to being a farmer, a schoolteacher, and a distinguished Yale graduate (class of 1874) before going to Alaska in 1878, where he became a popular missionary and then the head of a trading company. President McKinley appointed him Governor of the territory in 1897.[7]

Muir succinctly summarized the dinner as featuring "champagne and a merry, chatty time. Had gramophone songs and speeches at table, then smoke and chat. Following that a lecture on the plants of Glacier Bay and fossil forests by Coville."[8] Late in the evening, all were on deck to see their guests off, and to enjoy some clearing weather.

≡ ◆ ≡

Over dinner, Governor Brady had invited those who might be interested to join him and his wife the following morning for bathing at a hot springs some fifteen miles south of Sitka. Quite a few took him up on the invitation and turned out bright and early the next morning, including a group of hunters less interested in bathing than in getting out into the heavily-timbered country. In fact, along the way a promising spot was found at Biorka Island and a hunting party consisting of Merriam, Morris, Grinnell, Trudeau, Devereaux, Gifford, Kelly, and, auspiciously, Mary Harriman was put ashore. The others proceeded on to the hot springs, where the steam and hot water created a relaxing spa-like experience, marred only in part by the pervasive smell of sulfur.

All, however, was not idyllic. A scene near the springs disgusted Muir: "The keeper of the Hot Springs murdered a mother deer and threw her over the ridgepole of his shanty, then caught her pitiful baby fawn and tied it beneath its dead mother."[9] Muir left the scene in favor of tramping through the woods. Others also found time before lunch to do a bit of exploring and collecting. Saunders and Ritter successfully combed the beaches for starfish, while Palache went off with Gilbert "for a ramble over the boggy moor to a good lookout point over a lonely lake and then back along the shore."[10] And Fuertes was successful in shooting a Stellar's Jay and a Sooty Song Sparrow, while Ridgway got a Harris's Woodpecker.[11]

On the way back from the hot springs that afternoon, a stop was made at Biorka Island to pick-up the hunters, who for all their combined efforts had bagged but one Sitka Deer—though there was some question about who had shot it. Grinnell would relate how, upon being deposited on the island, the hunters had split up, with Miss Harriman and an unnamed "assistant" (who almost certainly was Grinnell) going off to set-up a stand from which they could watch a narrow neck of land which joined two parts of the island. After close to three hours their patience was rewarded when, as Grinnell would later inform the readers of *Forest & Stream*, a deer was seen approaching on the beach.

> She shot at it and missed, and the deer did not heed the report. A second shot caused the deer to raise its head and look about. Then a watcher, stationed southeast of them, fired a shot and the deer turned and ran, quartering toward the girl, who fired again, and the deer dropped to the report. On looking it over it was clear that the animal had been hit only once, the ball breaking its shoulder and killing it instantly. It had been untouched by the previous shots.[12]

While Grinnell concluded that Mary Harriman's last shot was decisive and the only ball to hit the deer, Mary—not an inexperienced hunter, she had hunted and killed deer in the Adirondacks—wasn't so sure that she had hit it, and that perhaps Merriam (apparently the "watcher" in Grinnell's account) had.[13] For his part, Merriam was silent; though diplomatically noting in his diary that while several animals were seen, "only one came our way and Mary Harriman and I killed it."[14]

On returning to Sitka, each member of the party found that they had received an invitation to a reception Governor Brady would host in honor of the Harriman Expedition at 8:45 p.m. on the evening of Friday the 16th at the Executive Mansion.

But that was tomorrow. This Thursday evening, the party gathered in the Social Hall for a talk by Ritter on "the order and method of advance of the marine shore life toward Muir Glacier."[15] The late evening hours also saw the arrival of the steamer *City of Topeka*—bearing tourists who were soon thronging the streets, to the delight of the shopkeepers who were only too happy to stay open to satisfy the eager customers. For the Harriman party, the arrival of the *Topeka*, which had come up the coast from California and through the Inside Passage well behind the *Elder*, held out the promise of mail that could be picked-up the following morning.

⇒ ◆ ⇐

Friday, according to Muir, was a fine day: he did some early shopping, then went to the woods where he found the spruce were in bloom and marveled at the beauty of those flowers, their various colors, and how upright the spruce stood, "as if deter-mined to do so."[16] When he encountered this sort of thing on his solitary excursions into the woods during the course of the Expedition, Muir was likely to be so taken with what he saw that he couldn't resist bringing some of nature's bounty back to the ship. "Our stateroom," his roommate Keeler would recall, "was filled with 'brush'—pine and spruce boughs, with cones or blossoms, and other trophies gathered on shore rambles. 'Look at that little muggins of a fir cone,' he would say to me, lovingly stroking the latest accession with which he littered the room, to the despair of the steward who tried to keep order."[17]

Those who went in search not of trees but of mail that might have come in on the *City of Topeka* had mixed success. Charles Palache was one of those for whom the mail "was a blank." Writing disconsolately to Helen he said "I can only hope that the old saying is true—no news is good news and that you are well and happy on this your last day of school," adding, "I cannot tell you how disappointed I was not to get a let-ter when others were reading theirs." Then, perhaps realizing he was feeling sorry for himself at her expense, he added, "I know it is the fault of the mails and not because you did not write … it was very hard to believe that there was nothing for me."[18]

Keeler, on the other hand, found not one but two letters waiting: an older one forwarded from Juneau, where it had originally been delivered, and another more recently dated June 1. While those were comforting, that comfort was dissipated when on the wharf he ran into friends from Berkeley: Professor and Mrs. Moses, and Professor and Mrs. Beaver. Mrs. Moses carried with her a letter from Ritter's fam-ily, which she asked Keeler to deliver to him. Writing to Louise later that day, Keeler couldn't help but scold, "How I wish you had thought to do likewise for now I must go on with no letter since the 1st, but Mrs. Moses said you were well and I am thankful to have had a personal word about you if not from you." Like Palache, and perhaps with pangs of guilt over what he had just written, he quickly backtracked to assure Louise that he knew she would "try to reach me with letters at other points beyond and I will look at each post office however far out of the world it may be."

Mrs. Beaver gave him worse news—a message from his publisher saying he was going to have to postpone publication of a book Keeler had recently completed "owing to errors in the text." Standing on the Sitka wharf balancing a notepad on his camera, and clearly agitated, he wrote to Louise expressing how "annoyed" he was with this news and giving her instructions about dealing with the publisher, including "I wish you would tell him with my compliments that if it is true he is a fool to spread such a report about the book in advance," that he "was very inclined to withdraw the entire book from them," and that "I thought strongly of returning by this boat but haven't the money to do so."[19]

The *City of Topeka* sailed at 1:00 p.m., beginning its return trip to California and carrying many letters from the Expedition party. The ship's departure, with its tourists, caused most of the shops in Sitka to close up. As the *Topeka* was weighing anchor, it was signaled by the *Elder* and took off the *Elder's* First Officer Thos. Adam-son (disabled by what was generally considered to be rheumatism), and graciously leaving in his place the *Topeka's* own First Officer, Charles McCarty.[20]

That afternoon, Devereaux and Palache undertook a journey via one of the *Elder's* launches to explore a mine at the head of nearby Silver Bay. Others of the sci-entific party went out in the surrounding area in a last effort to supplement what they had collected to date around Sitka. On the whole, according to Burroughs, "it was not a good place for our collectors: there were few birds and they were very wild. Our mammal collectors put out 100 small traps and caught only two mice."[21]

The reception given in honor of the Harriman Expedition at the Governor's home that evening was an eclectic affair, though not necessarily an unusual one for Sitka, which had acquired a reputation for cultural activities, including being home to a civic orchestra and a theatrical association. Keeler would note that for the evening, and as to the men, "we all wore white shirts," though he at least felt "peculiar" in such formal attire.[22]

On arriving, the guests were escorted upstairs to the home's main room where they passed through a receiving line—or as Dellenbaugh would record in his journal, they "ran the gauntlet of the governor and the governor's wife and the ladies receiving with her."[23] Ritter was impressed with the turnout, observing that "most probably all of the white population of the town was present."[24] While that estimate was undoubtedly on the high side, those that were present made, in their conversations over coffee and cake, an impression on Burroughs. In his "Narrative of the Expedition" he would write that "people actually live in Sitka from choice and seem to find life sweet. There are homes of culture and refinement. Governor Brady is a Yale graduate, and his accomplished wife would shine in any society. At a reception given us by the Governor, we met teachers from New England and people who keep in touch with current literature."[25]

And there were other guests at the reception. At dinner aboard the *Elder* on Wednesday evening, conversations about the local Indians, and then discussion about the plans for the Governor's reception, had led Harriman to request that the chief and other members of the Tlingit community be invited. They arrived, also sporting white shirts, and bringing musical instruments. In addition to including the Tlingits in the event, Harriman had a broader plan in mind. Trevor Kincaid would relate that "Mr. Harriman brought up the phonograph and during the evening a number of records were made of Indian songs and speeches. The party of Indians was rather dubious about the machine at first but later entered into the spirit of the occasion and sang and danced and beat their tom toms before the receiver."[26] They were more than a little surprised, and greatly pleased, when the recording was played back and they heard their own voices. *native songs recorded*

The Tlingits were not the only providers of musical entertainment. Dr. Nelson was apparently the only one to record that "Mr. Dudley, Land Commissioner or agent, having arranged fifteen or twenty wine glasses before him on a table produced some very good music 'Way Down Upon the Sewanee River' by rubbing their rims with his finger. He was repeatedly encored."[27] The evening ended, shortly before midnight, with Professor Brewer giving a lecture on "Climate"—he may have been under a half-hour time limit, since Dellenbaugh would specifically note in his diary that "Brewer then gave us a 29-minute lecture on 'Climate' in which he discussed fogs, clouds, etc."[28]

Walking back to the waterfront, the weary celebrants were cheered to find that the *Elder* had tied-up at the wharf, preparatory to taking on supplies and provisions in the morning.

Odd use of hyphenation throughout

Expedition vessel *George W. Elder* at dock, with two small boats loaded with fish in the foreground. Photograph by Edward S. Curtis. Library of Congress.

With departure from Sitka not scheduled until late in the day, most members of the party were left to their own interests and pursuits for much of Saturday, June 17.

Charles Keeler, in a bit of a better mood, took the occasion to write separate letters to Louise and young Merodine, noting in the former that the group had washing done in Sitka and "are in good condition now for six weeks away from the civilized centers," while to Merodine he enclosed "some pretty flowers that Mr. Muir picked in front of his old cabin by the Muir glacier and gave me to send to my little girl."[29]

Muir himself sketched in the forenoon and went off to the woods in the afternoon, following along the Indian River, where he "found hermaphrodite flowers of *Picea sitchensis*" in the spruce boughs.[30] One would assume he brought samples back to the Keeler-Muir stateroom.

An early riser that Saturday morning was Dr. Nelson, who met a local cleric on the wharf and went with him to visit the Sitka jail. He provided a short account in his diary:

> Small cells: 2 bunks, one over the other; very small grated window; air stifling. Sometimes as many as 50 prisoners brought from all parts of Alaska. Most of those charged with grave crimes such as murder. Prisoners wait sometimes 6 or 8 months before they can get a trial—they're sent to Juneau or Skagway for trial—if condemned for imprisonment longer than a year sent east to someplace in State of Washington.[31]

Grinnell and Palache paid a return visit to Lt. Emmons, who took them into the Tlingit village where he asked the chief whether "the guests might be shown some of

Russian blockhouse in Sitka. Photograph by Edward S. Curtis. Library of Congress.

the ancient and sacred articles in his possession, and soon there were brought out a number of ceremonial hats and headdresses, which have in some degree a sacred character, and which are not commonly shown.... One of these headdresses was of wood, and represented a killer whale. It was manifestly very old, paint worn off in some places and the wood polished by much handling."[32] Later in the day, Palache would write to Helen that "Emmons has been friendship itself and sent me away a little while ago with several charming souvenirs of Sitka, one of them a wedding present for you."[33]

In that same letter, Palache told of a "funny sight at the Gov's house this afternoon." Harriman was sitting on the porch with Brady and had set up the graphophone for the benefit of an audience of Tlingits, who "gathered around in crowds and their amusement was great when they heard their songs of the night before sung out to them."[34]

Although the weather during the day had been good, a light evening rain began to fall as the stragglers onshore responded to the *Elder's* whistle, signaling that departure was imminent. It was half past seven when the ship weighed anchor, came about, and began to work its way out of the harbor, serenaded by the Tlingit band, which assembled on the wharf to play a farewell with their rendition of "Yankee Doodle."

≡ ◆ ≡

The usual Alaskan steamship excursion ended at Sitka—tourists seldom went beyond the former Russian town and current American government center. As a place within range of the wilderness and sights of Glacier Bay, Sitka was a natural terminus for the tourist business, featuring a sparkling harbor, dotted with islands; a backdrop of high snow-capped mountains; the streets with their remaining Russian buildings and new curiosity shops; the mixed American and Native citizenry; the opportunity to shop for Tlingit-made souvenirs; and a choice of hiking, boating, and other activities in and around the town. There was nothing like it farther north, and no reason for tourists to proceed beyond Sitka.

The Harriman Expedition was, however, not the usual excursion: Burroughs would observe that unlike the typical tourist itinerary "ours was now only fairly begun," and that "after four warm humid days in Sitka we turned our faces for the first time toward the open ocean, our objective point being Yakutat Bay, a day's run further north."[35]

Sitka visit ends

end of tourist-friendly Alaska

PART III

The Route Less Traveled

Eight

Yakutat Bay and Enchantment

"The Queen of Night keeps her whitest robes for display in the northern latitudes."—William Brewer

The cruising distance to Yakutat Bay was 225 miles; requiring long hours of travel and with the distance itself emphasizing that they were leaving the beaten path behind and traveling where few, apart from Alaskan Native peoples and whaling ships, went with any regularity. Coming out of Sitka's harbor in the night, they also confronted the beginnings of extended travel on the open ocean—something that was certainly on the minds of those who had experienced and feared seasickness. John Burroughs was clearly a member of the "experienced and feared" group, and was undoubtedly relieved and delighted to record that upon leaving the more sheltered waters "the Pacific was very good to us and used us as gently as an inland lake, there being only a long low sleepy swell that did not disturb the most sensitive."[1]

The night sky was clear, filled with bright moonlight. William Brewer had often observed what seemed to him to be the "peculiar clearness" of the Alaskan air because of the lack of dust and smoke, and the consequent whiteness of the moon. It was surely this Saturday night, with its half-moon, that he recalled and had in mind when he wrote that "one evening on the way up, the half-moon when rising seemed poised, as it were, on the very summit of a low peak which was but a short distance inland. The dark crags of the peak were sharply cut on the intensely white face of the planet, which by the contrast, seemed even brighter than when in mid-sky…. The Queen of Night keeps her whitest robes for display in the northern latitudes."[2]

Sunday the 18th was mild and gentle, and they steamed north, in sight of land, though well offshore. While looking out to sea, those on deck could see blue sky and sunshine; the view toward land on the starboard side, however, was obscured by a blanket of clouds, blotting out the peaks of the Fairweather Range—"we saw them," Burroughs observed, "only from the waist down as it were."[3] Monday's planned stop at Yakutat was much anticipated, as was the fact that they would spend at least three days in the area and various parties would be put ashore. Groups of men drew chairs together on deck and in the Smoking Room, planning these shore parties. Others used the time to circle the deck in conversation, including Burroughs and Muir. The young, not quite eight-year-old Averell Harriman would remember occasions such as this when these two men "would walk together and stop and talk to us in a kindly manner. This kindness tended to offset their rather terrifying appearance with their long gray beards."[4]

As the afternoon wore on, they entered an area where heavy spruce forests lined

Fairweather Range and La Perouse Glacier. Photograph by Edward S. Curtis. University of Washington Libraries, Special Collections [Harriman 197].

the coast, with here and there a glacier cutting through and reaching the ocean. One of these glaciers, the La Perouse, not only ran down to the sea with a front a mile or more long, but also featured an enormous amount of moraine material, and along its north side the ice had cut into the forest "and shoved and piled up the trees as a heavy vehicle shoves and folds up the turf."[5] All this caught Harriman's attention and stirred his curiosity; so that when the *Elder* was within a couple of miles of La Perouse's front, he and a number of others set out in one of the larger boats, towing a small skiff. It was not a well-destined trip. After landing and spending an hour or two exploring the margin of the glacier, the party made its way back to the beach, intent on returning to the ship. The sea by now was rising, with whitecaps and rolling breakers. As Grinnell would tell the story:

> It was determined that three men should go off in the skiff, to lighten the load of the ship's boat. The surf was passed without difficulty, but before the skiff had gone far it was seen that she leaked so that the men must return to the shore or sink. All had prepared for a swim by removing their boots, but the beach was reached before the boat sank. Just as all were about to spring out and run the boat up beyond the waves, a breaker broke beneath the stern, lifted it high, struck the boat's nose into the sand, and unceremoniously dumped out the passengers. The large boat was then launched with no more serious disaster than shipping a few barrels of water.[6]

While maneuvering the large boat through the heavy surf and back to the *Elder*, Harriman gashed his hand on a nail and spent the trip back using his other hand to bind the cuts and stop the bleeding.

That all proved to be enough excitement for the day. In the evening there was dinner, a service and sermon in the Social Hall, and early "Good Nights" all round.

⇒ ◆ ⇐

The next morning, the early risers found that during the night their ship had anchored in front of Yakutat Village, at the entrance to Yakutat Bay. The village sat on a wooded point on the southern side of the broad entrance to the bay, and was comprised of eight or ten frame houses (a few of two and even three stories), a store, and a sometimes post office. There were, they found out, upwards of a hundred people in the immediate area, mostly Tlingit Indians, many of whom were off seal hunting. The village residents included two Swedish missionaries, one of whom had a wife. After visiting with her, Keeler would dutifully write home to Louise that "she told me that she had not seen a white woman for a year, so you see we are quite out of the world here."[7]

Time in the village was short, and the *Elder* was soon weighing anchor and moving up the bay. While many in the party—Harriman, Burroughs, Elliott, Emerson, Gifford, and Brewer among them—would stay with the ship and make short day trips, the plan was to make a number of stops to put off hunting and collecting parties who would make camp at various points and be picked-up later in the week.

From the village they ran up the bay on the northwest side to the great Malaspina Glacier, a vast plateau or plain of ice that Muir estimated was twenty miles long and sixty-five or seventy miles wide.[8] Running from the St. Elias Mountain Range from which it was fed, the Malaspina did not reach tidewater, but was at that time separated from the sea by a girdle of forested moraines five or six miles wide. More than a dozen men were landed on this rocky shore. Six of these were hunters, and they soon split into two groups: Morris, Grinnell, and Devereux went off to cross the moraine and work the edge of the glacier, while Yellowstone Kelly, William Averell, and Trudeau chose to go in the opposite direction along the rock-strewn beach. The collecting, as opposed to hunting, party was comprised of Merriam, Coville, Fisher, Fernow, Palache, Curtis, and a cook, all of whom were soon employed in putting up tents and making camp in a sheltered corner behind some sand dunes. "A lovely place," Palache informed his fiancé, "but for the mosquitoes which soon swarmed out of the swamps and woods. But on went our mosquito nets—black affairs which hang down from our broad brim hats and keep the hungry pests at bay."[9] Notwithstanding the mosquitoes, lunch was made and eaten, and the party was soon engaged in setting out trap lines.　　*Mosquitos big annoyance*

Leaving the Malaspina's moraine, the *Elder* steamed back across the bay to a small inlet directly opposite the far distant Mt. St. Elias, and soon found an open sand flat where it put Ridgway, Ritter, Saunders, Keeler, Starks, Cole, and a packer to serve as cook, ashore. The sand flat, surrounded by a dense forest of spruce and hemlock, made an excellent campsite.

While these stops were being made, another party consisting of Gilbert, Gannett, Kearney, and Muir waited with their gear on deck; their goal was to be taken as far up Yakutat Bay as possible before being put ashore. It was 4 p.m. when the ship cleared away after disembarking the Ridgway party and made full steam up the bay. The four men expected to, at best, be let off well below Haenke Island—but a strip of unexpected open water allowed the ship to steam farther toward the Island and into the narrow reaches of Disenchantment Bay, though they were soon brought to a halt by thick, moving ice floes that at least temporarily blocked the way. Disenchantment Bay had acquired its name from the Spanish explorer Alejandro Malaspina, who had explored the area in 1791 in search of the elusive Northwest Passage.

Traveling beyond the north end of Yakutat Bay, he had entered what appeared to be a long, extended valley stretching northward into the mountains, but a blank wall of ice (what was then the front of the Hubbard Glacier) had blocked his passage. Thwarted and disappointed in his quest for the Northwest Passage, Malaspina christened the narrow inlet that he was prevented from exploring "Disenchantment Bay." Years later, William Healey Dall had named the Malaspina Glacier in honor of the explorer.

As the *Elder* waited for an opportune time to push forward through the blocking ice, a group of Tlingits paddled out from the shore, holding up skins and furs they hoped to sell to the visitors. Harriman invited them aboard, and as the bartering went on he struck up a conversation with one of the Indians named James: who drew attention from all, and cut quite a figure, with his red eye patch and a weathered, broad-brimmed felt hat. Impressed by the newcomer's obvious knowledge of the area, Harriman invited him to stay on as an adviser to the pilot, an invitation that James quickly accepted.

The moving ice soon shifted enough for the *Elder* to find an opening up the east side, and the ship was able to steam past Haenke Island all the way to the head of Disenchantment Bay. There the water was exceptionally deep, and a good deal of time was spent in taking soundings in search of a bottom to provide anchorage. They were ultimately successful when "Indian Jim," as he had been dubbed, calmly suggested a place where the anchor quickly took hold, near the confluence or junction of Disenchantment Bay and Russell Fiord. That junction was in the form of a near right angle elbow: Disenchantment Bay ran northeast past Haenke Island to the front of the Hubbard Glacier, and at that point the Russell Fiord cut sharply off to the south-southeast. Over dinner that evening Captain Doran informed the party that the *Elder* was the first large ship ever to successfully enter Disenchantment Bay and Russell Fiord.[10]

Disenchantment Bay proved to be an alluring place: the original plans were changed, and the *Elder* remained there—putting off parties at various points as it moved about—for two more days. "The scenery," Muir wrote, "was wild and enchanting ... the slopes of the mountains are mostly low and green and yellow and purple with grass, willows, alders, and cottonwood and hundreds of species of charming flowers and mosses.... Egg Island, joined to the mainland at extreme low tide, is the floweriest of all, and we could easily detect the fragrance a half-mile off." In such a scene, he added that "all agreed to leave off the 'Dis' from the name."[11] In their minds, they were now in "Enchantment Bay."

Muir, Gilbert, and Gannett spent Tuesday, June 20 in the Hidden Glacier and Nunatak Glacier inlets off Russell Fiord. In the morning they were given two hours at Hidden Glacier, and Muir spent his time in leisurely sketching. The two surveyors, however, took five hours, "much to the Captain's disgust, who wanted to take on water further down." In the afternoon, those three, with Dall, Dellenbaugh, Cornelia Harriman, and Elizabeth Averell took one of the steam launches and traveled twelve miles up the Nunatak Glacier inlet. Gannett and Dall set about mapping the moraine and ice for the reference of future researchers, with the two girls helping to carry instruments and set surveyor's stakes, all the while gathering-up their long skirts to hike across the rocks and ice.[12]

That same day rumors of bear tracks filtered back to the ship, and a hunting party led by Harriman quickly set out along Russell Fiord: they "climbed and threaded the snow-covered mountains nearly all day in quest of bears, but came back as empty-handed as when they set out."[13] Burroughs's "diversion" that afternoon was to climb one of the nearby mountains. Along the way up he encountered and watched nesting titlarks, four or five species of songbirds, and a solitary barn swallow "skimming along as one might have seen it at home—no barns within hundreds of miles." At 2,500 feet, "I thought to reach the peak of the mountain up a broad and very steep bank of snow, but I looked back once too often. The descent to the sea was too easy and too fearful for my imagination, so I cautiously turned back."[14]

On Wednesday, Muir, Gilbert, Gannett, and Kearney made up a foursome that embarked on a two-day exploration of Hubbard Glacier and Egg Island. From around their campfire on the mainland on their second night out, they could see across to where four Indians who had been seal hunting had made a shoreline camp on Egg Island and were skinning the seals they had killed, as well as hunting others that came by throughout the night—"We heard them shooting and heard the seals barking or half howling, in a strange, earnest voice," Muir would write in his journal.[15] On Friday the 23rd the Muir group arrived at a larger Indian summer sealing village and boarded the *Elder,* which had come around after picking up the hunting and collecting parties that had been left off on Monday. Most of the Tlingits at this summer campsite had come from Yakutat Village, but some had traveled from as far away as Sitka and had set up bark huts and tents for the annual hunt that provided them with food, skins, and oil for their winter needs. Burroughs assayed the situation:

> The encampment we visited was upon the beach of a broad gravelly delta flanked by high mountains. It was redolent of seal oil. The dead carcasses of the seals lay in rows upon the pebbles in front of the tents and huts. The women and girls were skinning them and cutting out the blubber and trying it out in pots over smoldering fires, while the crack of the Winchesters of the men could be heard out amid the ice.... The Indian women frowned upon our photographers and were very averse to having the cameras pointed at them. It took a good deal of watching and maneuvering to get a good shot. The artists with their brushes and canvas were regarded with less suspicion.[16]

There were three such camps on Yakutat Bay that June, and while getting an exact count on the number of seals killed by the Indians was impossible, Grinnell would note that more than 500 skins were counted in this camp, and that from that it would seem that a thousand seals would not be too large a number to be credited to the combined efforts of the three camps.[17]

=⇒ ◆ ⇐=

When the *Elder* picked-up the parties that had been put ashore earlier in the week, it developed that they had experienced mixed success. The hunters that were put off at the Malaspina Glacier fared no better than those who had gone out in search of game in Howling Valley and Russell Fiord. "No large game was secured by our hunters in Yakutat Bay," Burroughs would duly record, "though Captain Kelly declared he was at one time so near a bear that he could smell him. The bear undoubtedly got a first smell of the Captain."[18] Grinnell, who was among the returning hunters, would confide to his *Forest & Stream* readers that "when the hunters reached the ship they were received with the usual shouts of derision for their non-success, and many jests, not very witty to their minds, but greatly enjoyed by those who uttered them, were made at their expense. To this, however, they were now becoming accustomed."[19]

The Ridgway, Ritter, Saunders, Keeler, Starks, and Cole collecting party had a

Tlingit Indian sealers' camp with canoe in foreground, Yakutat Bay. Photograph by E.H. Harriman. University of Washington Libraries, Special Collections [NA 2100].

productive three days in their camp on the sand flat. For Keeler it was a first camping trip, and he seemed to revel in it and was proud of withstanding the elements. To Louise he wrote, "Imagine me sitting by the camp fire [*sic*], dear love, listening to a dwarf hermit and thinking of home ... we have had a very good time of it in spite of mosquitoes and a drizzling rain every now and then." In that same letter he related to her how, on their first night in camp, an elderly Indian had appeared with some trinkets to sell, "and I hired his canoe for ten cents and paddled over to the village. It was a wonderful experience, with the dark clouds overhead and the dark water rocking my little dugout as I paddled along, with the base of Mt. St. Elias opposite me, a thrush singing in the solemn pine woods and a wilderness all about."[20] At least for a time he had put aside his worries about articles he might write, commissions he might earn, and the situation with his publisher.

Getting all the parties back on board was not without its issues, and once again Harriman took a perilous boat journey to gather in a group of his charges. This involved Merriam and his collecting party of Coville, Fisher, Fernow, Palache, and Curtis, all of whom had been landed on the 19th at the moraine of the Malaspina Glacier. They had been highly successful in collecting plants and small animals: in the evening of just the first day their traps had collected twenty-two rodents. They had also become blockaded by ice. After the party had been ashore for three days and was ready to be picked-up, they saw that the ice was preventing the *Elder* from reaching them. On the fourth day they again saw the steamer's smoke as it approached, but the ship came only to the edge of the ice drift and stopped.

For a long time we watched and waited, but could see nothing. Finally someone called out and looking westerly close to the land we were thrilled by the sight of two small boats. Slowly and laboriously they came, picking their way among the loose ice in the narrow space between shore and the line of grounded bergs which kept the heavy drift from pressing in. It was a dangerous undertaking, and when they were near enough to distinguish persons, we were not surprised to see Mr. Harriman standing in the bow of the first boat, directing her course. We and our camp outfits were taken aboard, and on the return trip to the ship took the more direct but still hazardous route through the pack ice, which in the ocean swell constantly threatened to smash our frail craft.[21]

With these groups on board, and after the stop at the fishing encampment to pick up Muir and his three companions, the *Elder* returned to Yakutat Village on the evening of Thursday, June 22. Among other things, this stop provided the opportunity to drop letters off at the post office. For Palache, it was an important stop, since he was able to send on their way (though with no idea of when they would leave Yakutat, much less be delivered) a number of letters he had written to Helen Markham, including one dated June 21. That was their originally intended wedding date, and he was careful to begin that letter, "You see I have not forgotten that this is our day and that I was to write to you on this date if on no other."[22] He also assured her, in a letter dated the 23rd, that he was well, and that as to the chilly weather that evening in Yakutat, "here my winter wear is none too heavy and I find plenty of use for my sweater and the hideous but warm clothes I purchased in Seattle."[23]

The *Elder* weighed anchor in the awakening light of dawn the next morning and returned up the bay to the Tlingit fishing encampment, so that the trappers could check and collect their traps and Harriman could buy canoes from the Indians. Palache "spent the time in a splendid scramble with two of the girls whom I piloted across several rushing mountain streams which they waded in their rubber boots while I jumped as well as I could." They collected bunches of flowers and "got back to the shore just as the whistle called us aboard, so instead of wading the streams again we hailed some Indian canoes near at hand" and were paddled out to the ship.[24]

With everyone back and accounted for, the *Elder* quickly made its way back down Yakutat Bay toward the open ocean and its next destination—the town of Orca, at the mouth of Prince William Sound. Low clouds and fog hid the St. Elias range but the great Malaspina Glacier was clear and visible across the way, and the conditions that morning allowed those on deck to make out the "discharge of roily water" from beneath it, "so great," Burroughs would marvel, "that it colors the sea over an area equal to its own; 'glacier milk' someone called it, and the Pacific had a milky tinge for thirty miles offshore."[25]

In addition to waxing eloquent about glacier milk, Burroughs would also observe that at this point "our party had now been a month together and had assumed the features of a large and happy family on a summer holiday cruise. We were of diverse interests and types of character, yet one in the spirit of true comradeship. This fortunate condition," he concluded, "was largely due to the truly democratic and manly character of the head of the expedition, Mr. Harriman, and to the equally cheerful and obliging temper of Captain Doran. The ship was equally at the service of men who wanted to catch mice or collect a new bird, as to those who wanted to survey a glacier or shoot a bear."[26]

NINE

Prince William Sound and Discovery

"The work assumed more the character of exploration, as the region is little known to the chart or to scientific literature."—Henry Gannett

By mid-morning on Friday the twenty-third of June, the *Elder* had left Yakutat Bay well behind and was headed north along the coast of the Gulf of Alaska, steaming through low clouds and fog that obscured the view of those who ventured on deck. The limited visibility, combined with the poorly-charted waters and the hazards they might conceal, convinced Captain Doran to travel at reduced speed and on a course that kept the ship some distance from the shore. They were proceeding cautiously when something occurred that undoubtedly brought to the minds of many of those standing at the ship's rail some well-known lines from Samuel Taylor Coleridge's monumental poem, *The Rime of the Ancient Mariner*:

> At length did cross an Albatross,
> Through the fog it came;
> As if it had been a Christian soul,
> We hailed it in God's name.

A large, majestic black-footed albatross had found them out, and it followed the *Elder* for hours, much to the fascination of John Burroughs, who would describe the bird "wheeling about us close to the water, coming and going, now on one side, now on the other, slanting and curving, and all on straight unbending wing. Its toilless, effortless flight and its air of absolute leisure were very curious, strange, solitary, weird—it seemed like the spirit of the deep taking visible form and seeking to weave some spell upon us or lure us away to destruction."[1] Burroughs's ominous view or interpretation of the presence of the albatross may have been colored by the eeriness of the fog, or by his personal duel with the ocean swells that slowly rocked the ship. The fact that an albatross followed a ship—as these birds often did—was not commonly viewed as necessarily either bad luck or good luck, though many nineteenth-century seafarers spoke of the birds as the souls of lost sailors.

The *Elder's* route, dictated in large part by the uncharted shallows and the danger posed by any reefs and rocks that might be lurking in those waters, took it first on a long leg west to Middletown Island, and from there back sharply northward on a direct course for the town of Orca. The total distance was 317 miles, necessitating over thirty hours of travel time, including steaming through the night. Saturday morning dawned with the absence of the albatross, but with the continuing presence of a decidedly thick, dampening fog that swallowed up everything more than a few yards from the ship, requiring it to stop frequently for soundings.

The *Elder* reached Middletown Island around eleven o'clock and reset its course northward.[2]

As the afternoon passed by, the fog lifted into scattered floating wisps, the sun burned through, and before long they reached the approaches to Orca Inlet and Prince William Sound. For Muir it was simply "the place above all others I have long wished to see,"[3] while Palache described "mountains that rose up as we entered the bay in a great snowy wall ahead of us and the nearer slopes were all dark green with forest," and thankfully "the swell ceased as soon as we got into the bay, and we all lay around on the upper deck basking in unwonted sunshine and enjoying the view," though the sunshine reverie was disturbed later in the afternoon by a fire drill, "all appearing with life preservers on the upper deck and the boats being manned."[4]

At 8:00 p.m. they arrived at Orca, anchoring between a small island and the mainland, and most of the party went ashore. They found a compact little town, consisting of a store, a post office, and a salmon cannery operated by the Pacific Steam Whaling Company. Despite the lateness of the hour, the cannery was in full operation: about half of the annual catch had already been processed, and a ship lay at anchor nearby ready to take it away.

The cannery gave Orca its reason for existence and its character—Merriam would describe the town as "a foul smelling place and the water up and down for miles is oily and dotted with salmon heads and debris."[5] The cannery employed Chinese laborers, brought up from California and working long hours in blood-soaked conditions for low wages, leading Muir to write in his journal that "men in this business are themselves canned."[6] The conditions and long working hours here, and at

Social consciousness/
reform attitude

Members of the Expedition taking part in a lifeboat drill. Left to right: Edwin C. Starks, John Burroughs, W.B. Devereaux, Mrs. Averell, Averell Harriman, Edward H. Harriman, Roland Harriman, Elizabeth Averell, Cornelia Harriman. Photograph by William H. Averell. University of Washington Libraries, Special Collections [Harriman 87].

other canneries they encountered in their travels on the coast, would lead Grinnell to observe that competition between the canning companies was so great that the goal of each of the cannery managers seemed to be to put up more fish than his competitors, without regard to the rate of the harvest or the workers' welfare, and thinking nothing of the future. "Their motto," he wrote, "seems to be, 'If I do not take all I can get somebody else will get something.'"[7]

The atmosphere at the Orca cannery quickly began to repel the visitors, and in the long twilight many of them climbed to the top of 2,500-foot Eyak Mountain behind the town. Curtis was in that group, toting his six-by-eight camera, a tripod, and glass plates. At the summit, he found he had the light to take pictures until almost eleven o'clock.

Others of the party, including Burroughs, wandered down the beach to where groups of prospectors, just out from the Copper River a short distance from Orca, had camped. They were waiting for a ship to take them home, or for funds from friends to enable them to leave. In conversation with these miners over their campfires, the Harriman party heard stories of the 3,000 men who, on the basis of vague rumors of fabulous strikes, had gone into the Copper River region a year or more before in search of gold; of how they fought cold, snow, glacial ice, and swollen rivers; of hardship and deprivation; of an outbreak of scurvy that had killed many, and lamed and disabled others; and of finally abandoning everything but their lives, and coming out destitute and without one cent's worth of gold. In this group, Burroughs found two men, a father and son, who were particularly noticeable.

> The father, a man probably of sixty-five years, had nearly died with scurvy and was still very lame, and the tenderness and solicitude of the son towards him warmed my heart. Homely, slow, deliberate men but evidently made of the real stuff. These stranded men were penniless and were depending upon the charity, or the willingness to trust, of the steamboat company to take them home to San Francisco. I was glad when I saw them depart on the steamer the next day.[8]

Nearing midnight, sobered by their conversations with the disappointed and destitute miners, the party returned to the *Elder*. Many went to the Smoking Room, where they shared the miners' stories with the others who were keeping late hours.

═ ◇ ═

On the morning of Sunday, the twenty-fifth, Charlie Palache was up at 5:00 a.m. and was soon off mountain climbing through forests, patches of snow, and alpine meadows, finally reaching a height of 2,000 feet. There he lingered, enjoying the view "while the morning light was still soft and delicate on the distant mountains," before descending "for a second breakfast and a lazy morning on deck stretched in the hot sunshine."[9]

Frederick Dellenbaugh was among a few who went ashore a bit later in the morning, when it became clear that the *Elder* wouldn't be leaving immediately. He set up his easel on the beach to paint, and soon had company in the person of a young miner who wandered up from his campsite to watch. Unlike those who Burroughs had encountered the night before, this never-say-die prospector was waiting for money from home to finance another try at his luck in the Klondike.[10] Their conversation was cut short by a blast from the *Elder's* whistle, calling those ashore back to the ship.

Two new guests, invited by Harriman to accompany the party in its journey through Prince William Sound, had come on board that morning. One was Captain Omar J. Humphrey of the Pacific Steam Whaling Company, who was knowledgeable about Prince William Sound and its poorly-charted coast. The other was M.L. Washburn, an official with the Alaska Commercial Company and one of the founders and principal owners of the Semidi Propagating Company, which was engaged in blue fox farming at various locations in the coastal islands.

With all aboard, at about noon, and under clear blue skies with temperatures pushing above 50° F., the *Elder* steamed out of Orca Inlet and into the broad waters of Prince William Sound—an enormous expanse which Burroughs would succinctly describe as "shaped like a giant spider, an open irregular body of water eighty miles or more across, with inlets that reach far in amid the mountains."[11] In fact, Burroughs's "giant spider" has over three thousand miles of coastline, dotted with fiords, bays, and inlets, all in the shadow of the Chugach Mountains. The region they were entering was sparsely populated, had been little explored, and was not yet a tourist destination. Writing in the fall of 1899 after returning to the United States, Henry Gannett would observe that in Prince William Sound "the work assumed more the character of exploration, as the region is little known to the chart or to scientific literature. The coast was found incorrectly mapped in many places ... here also were found fiords, extending many miles inland, whose existence was unknown even to people living in the neighborhood." He concluded that "altogether, no locality visited by the expedition afforded as much new material to science as Prince William Sound."[12]

From Orca, the *Elder* plowed northward some forty-eight miles to Port Valdez, a long, deep channel situated at the northeast corner of the Sound and stretching more than thirty miles into the mountains to—near its furthest point inland—the site of the future oil pipeline port of Valdez. They came to a halt before a huge and stunning uncharted glacier, rivaling anything in Glacier Bay, on the west side of the Port Valdez channel. Its front was two hundred fifty to three hundred feet high and four miles long. Enormous falls of ice were descending from the front of the glacier, though Grinnell would point out that these "were not in great masses holding together, but when a huge piece falls it seems at once to break up into small pieces, so that it looks almost like an avalanche, or a great torrent of falling water streaming down over the glacier's front."[13] As a result, there were no great icebergs, but there was a choking flood of ice floes. The *Elder's* crew made repeated soundings half a mile from the front of the glacier, and found the water was about six hundred feet deep.[14] They named this the Columbia Glacier, after Columbia University. On a wooded island at the front of the glacier they landed an exploring and collecting party of Gilbert, Palache, Coville, and Curtis, together with a cook and an oarsman. This group quickly dubbed their temporary home "Heather Island," and set-up their "Camp Perfecto" on a high gravel beach a mile from the glacier.[15]

With that group ashore, and with the understanding that the *Elder* would return Tuesday evening to pick them up, the ship sailed back down the channel to a bay, variously called Gladhough Bay or Virgin Bay, which was just south of the entrance to Port Valdez and separated from it by a mountainous neck of land. Dropping anchor in this bay at about 8:00 p.m., they found two or three small, rough houses scattered along the shore, the homes of copper prospectors. A boat full of campers went ashore. Once tents had been set up as a base for exploring, the campers split off in various pursuits: Devereaux went off to visit the nascent copper mines; Kincaid,

Saunders, Trelease and others of the botanists went collecting; Harriman and Indian Jim climbed the mountain behind the bay in search of game. John Muir ascended the same mountain to walk in the woods, where he found a spruce tree three hundred eighty years old and four feet in diameter.[16] It was also in this bay that the party had a brief encounter with its first Eskimo: "He came paddling toward our ship in a double kayak and as our naphtha launch circled about him he had an amused childish look."[17]

After the Sunday evening church service, at about 10:00 p.m., when "the sun was still glowing upon the distant white peaks," another dozen or so of the party, including Burroughs and the ladies, left the *Elder* and went ashore for "a walk in the long twilight." Near the camp that Kincaid and others had set up earlier in the evening, they visited the cabin of a Norwegian-born prospector. He had been there for a year, "and as our ladies were the first who had ever visited his camp, he took off his hat, and with his hand upon his heart, made a gallant bow to them in acknowledgment." He had done well in his copper mining, and revealed that he planned to travel halfway around the world to France and the 1900 Paris Exposition: Burroughs concluded that "life seemed to offer him many bright outlooks."[18] *19th c. gallantry*

As midnight approached, those among the shore parties who were not spending the night at the campsite began working their way back to the ship. The last to arrive, at just about 12:00 o'clock, were the hunters, Harriman and Indian Jim—empty-handed.

⇒ ◆ ⇐

On Monday morning, with the campers back on board, the *Elder* made its way west to Port Wells which, like Port Valdez, is a long fiord or channel extending into the interior, in this case at the northwest corner of Prince William Sound. Such exploration as may have been done of Port Wells in the past had led to very little recorded information, and what information there was probably reflected times when it was closed-off by glaciers that had since retreated: Gannett would write that it was "represented on the charts as a shallow bay ... in fact it penetrates the land northward to a distance of 40 miles."[19]

The *Elder* traveled up Port Wells, following the long and narrowing arm of its channel as it angled off to the northeast. Turning out for breakfast, the party found the weather fair, the sea air cold, and that they were, in Burroughs's words, in "a great ice chest—glaciers to right of us, glaciers to left of us, glaciers in front of us, volleyed and thundered; the mountains were ribbed with them, and the head of the bay was walled with them. At one time, we could see five, separated by intervals of a few miles, cascading down from the heights, while the chief of the flock was booming at the head of the valley incessantly."[20]

The discharges of the glaciers had filled the channel with ice, and as the ship cautiously continued north, it was finally blocked off and forced to anchor some twenty miles from the head of the valley. The launches were put out, and managed to get about ten miles closer, where they put parties ashore in the bright sun of the morning. Dellenbaugh and Gifford set up on the shore and, sitting on the rocks, made sketches looking toward the head of the bay; Gannett and Muir commenced surveying and mapping; the ornithologists and botanists went hunting birds in the bushes and along the shore, exploring the moraine for gull and tern eggs, and searching for whatever plants and insects they could discover; and Harriman went ashore with the younger children, Carol and Roland—who by now had been christened the "Little Two" by Muir—to play in the sand and gather flowers.[21]

With the various shore parties occupied, the ship watered, in what Grinnell described as "primitive fashion," by towing one of the boats to shore, filling it with water from a mountain brook, and then towing it back to the ship, where the water was pumped out and into the storage tanks below deck. Later, ice was also taken on board, with crew members working to maneuver a large net under blocks of floating ice weighing upwards of five hundred pounds, then using the ship's winch to hoist the blocks on deck, where they were chopped into manageable cakes and taken to the refrigerators deep in the bowels of the ship.[22] Throughout the morning, "the thundering of the great ice Niagara was in our ears every moment; but we could not get near it; it beat us off with its ice avalanches."[23]

At the far head of this northerly extension of Port Wells were two great, hitherto unidentified glaciers, including "the chief of the flock" that Burroughs had identified as "booming" and "thundering" incessantly. The party would reach a quick consensus—continuing the academic christening begun the day before at Port Valdez with the naming of the Columbia Glacier—to name the eastern great glacier Yale and the western, "the chief," Harvard. The five steep, cascading glaciers on the west shore of the fiord, which Gannett surmised had once been tributaries of the Harvard before it receded, were named Radcliffe, Smith, Bryn Mawr, Vassar, and Wellesley. And a large glacier on the east side, south of the Yale, was named Amherst. The entire location was, logically enough, denominated College Fiord.[24] *Ivy League mindset/ orientation*

Midday brought the ship's whistle, calling the boats and shore parties back to the *Elder*. Once on board, the returning parties found that a new, twenty-foot-long pennant had been run up on the topmost mast.[25] Dark blue with a white border, the pennant featured two white stars on either end of three large, white block letters, "H A E," and was apparently designed by Frederick Dellenbaugh.[26] With that new insignia of the Harriman Alaska Expedition flying high in the light breeze, the *Elder* began to work its way back down College Fiord and into the main body of Port Wells. Somewhere along the ship's route in these waters, John Burroughs was struck by the scale and vast expanse of Alaska.

> Two things constantly baffle and mislead the eye in these Alaska waters—size and distance. Things are on a new scale. The standard one brings with him will not hold. The eye says it is three miles to such a point and it turns out six; or that the front of yonder glacier is a hundred feet high and it is two hundred or more. For my part I never succeeded in bringing my eye up to the Alaska scale. Many a point, many a height, which I marked for my own, from the deck of the ship, seemed to recede from me when I turned my steps toward it. The wonderfully clear air probably had something to do with the illusion. Forms were so distinct that one fancied them near at hand when they were not.[27]

Through the late afternoon the *Elder* steamed south through Port Wells, at length arriving, on the west or starboard side of the ship, at a small inlet running up to the imposing and blocking high wall of the Barry Glacier. As they approached the face of this glacier, they caught sight of a school of four or five killer whales, with the characteristic white patches on their backs, and "they rose to blow, very deliberately, the tail fin appearing first, and then the shoulders and back."[28]

According to the U.S. Coastal Survey maps, the Barry Glacier marked the western boundary or end of the navigable waters of Prince William Sound. That seemed

College Fiord. Left to right: Wellesley, Vassar, Bryn Mawr, Smith, Radcliffe, and Harvard glaciers. Photograph by A.K. Fisher. A.K. Fisher Collection, Library of Congress.

to be confirmed by Yellowstone Kelly, who was apparently the only one onboard who had ever been in this part of Prince William Sound or come close to the Barry Glacier. In April 1898, only a little more than a year earlier, he had traveled with the Glenn Expedition up what was now College Fiord and seen the twin glaciers that had just been named Harvard and Yale. The Glenn party had come down past the Barry, which Kelly said was found to mark the end of the bay.[29] That, however, was not the case on the evening of June 26, 1899.

As the *Elder* moved closer to the front of the Barry Glacier to get a better angle for photographs, those crowding the deck could see that the front of the glacier did not reach all the way to the high, steep mountainside wall to the south. Instead, there was a narrow opening or channel which seemed to extend into what appeared to be open water beyond the face of the glacier. It was possible that this opening had existed for some time, though escaping notice by the Glenn Expedition, or that it had opened just within the last year, as some event in the recession of the glacier caused it to lose its attachment to the mountain wall. In any event, "but few years have passed," Gannett would reason, since the glacier "bridged or dammed the fiord at its bend, closing it to all access except by land journey."[30]

Proceeding to within a half mile of the opening, the ship turned slowly until it reached and faced the mouth of this narrow channel. Whether to go further in these unknown waters, through that narrow channel, was an issue. Captain Humphrey, the local pilot and Prince William Sound veteran, balked, telling Captain Doran, "Here, take your ship. I am not going to be responsible for her if she is to be run into every

hint of danger

unsounded, uncharted channel and frog marsh."[31] Doran also was hesitant about proceeding in these uncharted and unsounded waters, particularly against Humphrey's advice. Harriman, however, was more than a little intrigued at the prospects. He assured Doran that he would assume the risk and would take full responsibility, and ordered the captain to "go ahead and try to pass between the ice-wall and headland."[32] Keeler would write that "slowly and cautiously we advanced, casting the lead all the time, until the great blocks of ice thundered off from the glacier into the sea close beside us."[33] The sounding lead showed the water was deep, finding no bottom at ten fathoms, and Harriman ordered "full speed ahead." The passage, Muir wrote, was "dangerously narrow and threatening, but gradually opened into a magnificent icy fiord about twelve miles long, stretching away to the southward."[34] An excited Harriman declared, "We will discover a new Northwest Passage!"[35]

It was not the long sought-after Northwest Passage, but it was a stunning, hitherto unknown world. Though the evening was well-advanced, the skies were still bright, excitement ran high, and as they steamed up the fiord they had just discovered they saw that it was rimmed by glaciers large and small, flowing out of the surrounding mountain sides. Some of the glaciers, Daniel Elliott said, "looked like the stretched skins of huge polar bears."[36] Names were soon attached to many of the largest glaciers. Some had characteristics or features that quickly suggested the names they were soon to carry, including the Serpentine, "by reason of its winding course down from the hidden sources in the mountains ... a great white serpent with its jaws set with glittering fangs at the sea," and the Stairway, featuring giant terraces or benches such that "a Colossus of Rhodes with seven-league boots would have been an appropriate figure upon it."[37]

At the head of this newly-found waterway was a massive glacier, the true end of navigation. This fiord was fittingly named Harriman Fiord and the glacier at its head was christened the Harriman Glacier—a decision that was the subject of some necessary discussion, since scarcely two weeks earlier, in Glacier Bay, Muir had bestowed the "Harriman Glacier" name on an eleven-mile long split-off of the Pacific Glacier. Clearly, the Harriman name was more appropriate as the designation and identification of this large glacier at the head of the newly-discovered Harriman Fiord, and the decision was eventually made, one might guess at Muir's suggestion, to rename the earlier find the Reid Glacier in honor of Henry Fielding Reid—the geophysicist and seismologist who had brought his group of students ashore at Muir's cabin on Glacier Bay in 1890.[38]

As to the evolution of this area, Gannett concluded that "from all indications, it is certain that within the century the four great glaciers which now drop bergs into the waters of Harriman Fiord were united in one, which occupied the fiord from its present head to its mouth."[39] Burroughs, less the scientist and more the "dreamer" by his own characterization, would say, "The various ice sheets united in one body, in no very distant past, which filled the inlet to the mountain's brim—a vast ice monster. Now the body of the monster is gone and his limbs lie upon the mountains on either side, while his tail and rump are at the head of the valley."[40]

The euphoria of the discovery notwithstanding, the hour was growing late: while the light was still relatively good, they were in completely uncharted waters and some decisions had to be made. Further exploration of the area was clearly in order, but it also developed that the ship was in need of repair: a propeller blade had been

Harriman Glacier, Harriman Fiord. Photograph by E.H. Harriman. University of Washington Libraries, Special Collections [Harriman 121].

damaged when it struck a submerged cake of ice, which had the effect of "making our craft limp a little."[41] It was agreed that a party headed by Gannett should be left to map the new fiord and the glaciers, while the *Elder* returned to Orca to make repairs. In addition to Gannett, the shore party included Muir, Kelly, Inverarity, Indian Jim, and two packers; they set out in one of the ship's boats, also taking a canoe with them.[42] This party left the ship at 9:30 p.m. and made camp three miles from the head of the fiord, fifty or sixty feet above the water. In his element, at an unexpected point of discovery, in that part of Alaska "above all others I have long wished to see," Muir would record that after supper at 11 p.m. they "went to bed at 2 a.m., after a grand exhilarating evening, pitying them on the ship."[43]

Those on the ship were also up late as the *Elder* worked its way back toward the Barry Glacier, and their passage out into the main body of Port Wells. As they steamed back down Harriman Fiord, enjoying a late evening dinner of Welsh rarebit, a snowstorm set in, for a time whiting out the mountains. Brewer, Merriam, and others remained up into the late, after-dinner hours, watching from on deck as the ship approached the narrow opening—due to be christened Doran Strait—that they had discovered and navigated earlier in the evening. As they turned the point at the front of the Barry Glacier, the incoming tide caught the ship and swung it toward the ice-wall; the rudder was put over hard but the ship was sluggish, responding slowly after a few moments and clearing the space into the larger waters of Port Wells just when those on deck thought the vessel would be crushed against the ice.[44]

⇒ ◆ ⇐

In the fog and rain of Tuesday, the *Elder* steamed back across Prince William Sound for Orca, where its main objective was to repair the broken propeller. There was no dry dock at Orca, but it did have a long and deep "shelving beach" and extreme tides. When the ship arrived in the evening at high tide, Captain Doran brought it in as far as possible and the low tide that night left it sitting in shallow water on the beach. The Wednesday morning high tide pushed the ship still further onto the beach and, when the tide again went out, scaffolding was quickly built around the stern and work on replacing the propeller got under way.

On arriving at Orca, the party discovered that the steamer *Excelsior* was anchored there, not far from where the *Elder* was run aground. Dr. Nelson awakened at 1:45 a.m. on Wednesday morning "to readjust my mosquito net." Orca, he would note, was the only place where mosquitoes invaded the ship. Despite the hour, it was "light as day" and Nelson would record a scene of men lounging about the *Excelsior*, the pervading odor in the air from the cannery, and that he was kept awake by the screams of circling sea gulls and the constant whining of a dog chained on the *Excelsior's* deck. Though deprived of sleep, he "had the satisfaction of knowing that the mosquito that had broken my repose ... was himself broken upon the wheel of retribution."[45]

Later in the morning, the down-time occasioned by the propeller repair gave Burroughs, Brewer, and others who had not visited the cannery on Saturday, the chance to view the canning process. Burroughs was fascinated by the skill of the Chinese workers, especially those at the first stage of the process where the workers, each wielding two knives with long, thin, and razor-sharp blades, cut off the fins, severed the tail and head, and disemboweled the fish with "lighting-like rapidity" before funneling them along for washing, scraping, cutting, and packing into one-pound cans. Still, Burroughs found that "for some reason the looker-on soon loses his taste for salmon—there is such a world of it. It is as common as chips; it is kicked around under foot; it lies in great sweltering heaps; many of the fish are pecked and bruised by gulls and ravens while lying upon the beach before they are brought in; the air is redolent of an odor far different from that of roses or new-mown hay."[46] Small wonder that, like Muir on the previous Saturday evening, Burroughs was soon turning away to walk in the woods. *industrial cannery process*

Although repairs on the propeller were progressing nicely, it was evident the work would take more time than anticipated, and then the ship would need to await the next ultra-high tide to be floated and able to move off the beach. A picnic was organized, and soon the two launches and other smaller boats were ferrying a party of thirty, along with packers and stewards, to Bom Point, some eight or ten miles distant. This turned-out to be an idyllic spot, with a crescent-shaped beach half a mile long at the head of a shallow bay, surrounded by woods, natural meadows, and profusions of wildflowers. It was a large family picnic.

> When the point was reached two tents were put up, fires were built, and luncheon cooked. The party scattered out through the spruce forest, and over a wide bog which lay at the head of the little bay, and gathered plants. Some of the bird collectors took specimens, among which was a spruce partridge. Many salmon were jumping in the little bay, into which the tide water estuary flowed. It was a pleasant stopping place, and the children and young girls had great times frying bacon over the fire and cooking flapjacks.[47]

Toward 4 o'clock the steamer's whistle was heard, and by the time camp was broken, fires put out, tents packed-up, and the small boats launched, the repaired *Elder* had come around to meet them. The course from Bom Point took the party to a small landlocked bay for a brief early evening stop at a copper mine, where the vein was found high up in the face of a steep, sheer cliff. Devereaux would observe that it seemed at first glance that the vein could only be reached "with a pack train of bald eagles."[48] From there the ship steamed north to Port Valdez and the area of the Columbia Glacier to pick up the party that had been left there on Sunday. Closing his diary that evening, Nelson would note that Captain Doran's left arm was "giving him no little trouble." The Captain's elbow was swollen and "the arm from shoulder to wrist is streaked with black—probably he has struck the elbow against something but he has no recollection of having done so and now has his arm in a sling—but he continues on duty."[49]

At about midnight, and some short distance off the Columbia Glacier and Heather Island, the *Elder's* whistle signaled the denizens of "Camp Perfecto" that their transportation had arrived.

⇒ ◆ ⇐

After setting up that camp on Sunday evening, Gilbert, Palache, Coville, and Curtis had climbed the heights of Heather Island. Though the elevation was only 400 feet, it gave them a good view of the ice field atop the Columbia Glacier and enabled them to plan its exploration.

Apparently anxious to get going, they were up at 2:30 a.m., and as a consequence Palache would wryly observe that "Monday was what one may fairly call a long day." They rowed some three miles to an angle of the glacier's front. Gilbert remained there to work on his map, while Palache, Coville, and Curtis started off across the ice to climb an island peak arising from the glacial flow five or six miles away. After a short distance they encountered some geese, one of whom "fell a victim to the skillful aim of Coville's rock, so that we had a famous goose stew for lunch next day." Their destination turned-out to be a mass of rock with a 2,000-foot peak. Working their way up, they encountered a large, white mountain goat, who eyed them for a while before calmly picking its way up and over a cliff that they dared not attempt to climb. Reaching the summit, they lunched, photographed, and studied the sources and flow of the glacier. In the late afternoon they headed back, found Gilbert, and returned to Heather Island.

On Tuesday they worked the front of the glacier as a group, spending most of the day in a cold rain; Palache would confide to Helen that on returning to camp around 8:00 p.m., and "as a heroic means of getting warm," he stripped and "took a plunge bath in the bay among the floating ice cakes and came out shivering enough but soon was warm and happy." They were all, however, concerned—being unaware of the *Elder's* propeller problems—when the steamer, which was to have picked them up that evening, failed to appear. That concern grew on Wednesday as they again explored the glacier, keeping an eye out for the ship, and beginning to worry about their food supply. That evening, around a half past ten o'clock, a cold rain drove the six of them into their ten-foot by fourteen-foot tent, where they gathered around their small sheet iron stove. While most had found at least restless sleep by midnight, they were happy to be aroused from their slumbers by the *Elder's* whistle, echoing off the wall of the Columbia Glacier. They quickly packed their gear, manned their boat, and were soon on board for a late dinner.[50]

While they ate, the ship turned west and south, making full steam through the night to pick-up the surveying party that had been at Harriman Fiord. That group had spent most of Tuesday exploring the shore of the fiord, all the way up to the Harriman Glacier. Gannett's task was surveying and mapping, with the others helping with chains and stakes, taking photographs, and, in Muir's case, making notes on the trees and plants they encountered. Ptarmigan were abundant, and Kelly hunted day and night, crossing bear tracks at one point and embarking on a solitary hunt, during which he would occasionally catch glimpses of a pair of brown bears but never getting a clear shot.[51] On Wednesday, and hoping the steamer would *not* show up for another day, they moved their camp seven miles, to get better surveying angles on other glaciers in the fiord, and extending their work into the late evening. As the night and the wee hours of the morning wore on, the repaired *Elder* worked its way, without incident, across the Sound, through the narrow channel at the Barry Glacier and into the fiord. Awakened by the ship's whistle at 6:00 a.m. Thursday morning, the shore party abandoned the breakfast their cook was preparing in the rain, folded their tents, loaded their boats, and were soon breakfasting on the ship.[52] Muir's delight with the discovery of Harriman Fiord was neither momentary nor short lived: in the coming months he would remember and describe it as "full of glaciers of every description, waterfalls, gardens and grand old forests—nature's best and choicest alpine treasures purely wild—a place after my own heart."[53]

Steaming out of the fiord, in the cold and clear early morning of Thursday, June 29, the *Elder* turned her bow back to the open ocean, leaving Prince William Sound and its discoveries and wonders behind. Years later, several peaks in the mountains above Harriman Fiord were named to commemorate and honor the members of the Expedition—including Mounts Gilbert, Curtis, Muir, Gannett, and Emerson for the scientists, and Mount Doran for the ship's captain.

Harriman "Fiord"

TEN

Kodiak Island and Celebration

"Thus stands our country with the great
Where other lands have often stood;
Yet hard! To hold this envious place,
As well as great, we must be good"
—Frederick Dellenbaugh & Carol Harriman

"Life on board the *Elder,*" Grinnell would recall, "was never monotonous." The days were filled with activities, many centered or originating in the Smoking Room, which was a favorite haunt for all—including the Harriman ladies—and a place for lounging, reading, conversation and debate, planning shore excursions, writing letters, smoking, and storytelling. Many members of the party were well-traveled and had stories from all parts of the world. One of the chief story tellers was John Muir, and Grinnell would relate that it was in the Smoking Room that Muir told the story of his "perilous passage across a wide crevasse in a glacier by means of a narrow comb of ice which joined the two sides," including "the feelings and actions of the little Indian dog which accompanied him."[1]

As was to be expected, the Smoking Room was heavily frequented by smokers; who could often be found buried in a book in some corner, contentedly puffing away on a pipe or a cigar, obscured by a mushrooming haze of blue and gray smoke. The non-smokers who visited the area sometimes found the air so thick that in simply moving through the room they parted the smoke in rolling waves, leading them to quickly open doors and windows in search of breathable air. "This seemed to the smokers," according to Grinnell, who was one of them, "a little hard, but they bore it shivering."[2]

The Smoking Room's established uses and character notwithstanding, on the morning of Thursday, June 29, as the *Elder* steamed out of Prince William Sound, it also became a literary center, chiefly in terms of an ongoing outpouring of poetry.

The party's first poetic effort was actually penned some weeks earlier by Mrs. Harriman, either before the Expedition left New York or perhaps on the train as it headed west. In verse titled "A Receipt for a Trip to Alaska," she wrote of ingredients including "a tired Papa," and "bitters and sweets or both if you will" made up of "kids who are anxious a grizzly to kill," together with a "Biology Chief" as "a riser," and a dressing "of great scientists, geologists, botanists and artists," all placed in the mold of a "Pacific coast ship" where the whole would be dished up "as a bully good trip."[3]

Mrs. Harriman's effort was, however, but a precursor to the torrent of verse that was unleashed when the anonymously-written "Song of the Glacier" appeared tacked to the wall in the Smoking Room on that Thursday morning in June.

Who wouldn't be a glacier
Descending to the sea
With Muir at hand to praise me
Most multifariously?
With Muir at hand to praise me
And Gannett to survey,
Who wouldn't be a glacier
Ascending from the bay?

Who wouldn't be a glacier
With pinnacles at play,
A-dropping little icebergs
On Indians in the bay?
I open cheerful fissures,
And several kinds of splits,
And frighten little Indian dogs
Out of their seven wits.

Who wouldn't be a glacier
Receding from the shore?

My lovers come in boat-loads
Determined to explore
In open admiration,
Unnumbered ladies throng
And wave their kerchiefs from the rail
Till the steward beats the gong.

Who wouldn't be a glacier
An influenza cure?
My benefits afforded
For rich as well as poor;
Spontaneously provided,
According to John Muir.

To lie upon the glacier
Free from all bronchial pain
And think upon the family
One ne'er shall see again
Oh! This beats all the castles
Erected in old Spain![14]

In the succeeding weeks, throughout the remainder of the voyage, more than thirty poems and poetical essays would be produced, with almost all making their debut on the Smoking Room wall. News that a new poem had appeared would spread quickly through the ship, and a crowd would gather in the Smoking Room to read and, since most of the poems were at least initially unsigned, to speculate as to the probable author, especially if the verses contained good-natured satire aimed at some member of the party. A new poem would sometimes draw a reply or a parody: "Often," Grinnell noted, such a reply would be "written by some individual who fancied that he saw in the original poem a reference to himself, and who took this method of getting even, in kind, with the supposed author of the attack."[5] In fact, that was the case with "Song of the Glacier," which most quickly recognized as the work of William Healey Dall, who was often found in the Smoking Room enveloped in a cloud of smoke.

As it happened, that same day, the 29th, the Smoking Room was enlarged by removing partitions and taking over space formerly occupied by two staterooms, with the relocation of the former occupants of those rooms.[6] And that circumstance played into a quick, anonymous response to Dall—thought by some to be the handiwork of Muir, while others suspected Burroughs, and a few pointed fingers at Brewer and Gannett—titled "The Song of the Smoker."

Who would not be a smoker
And with the Smokers sit
With heels in air
Or thrust on chair
Regaled with smoke and wit?

Who would not be a smoker,
And have the walls pushed back
To make more room
For smoke and fume
And space for jokes to crack?

Poor Gifford had to pack and run
And Saunders had to skip
To push the bounds
Of the smoking grounds
And make more work for "Chip."

Expansion is the word, my lads
On ship board as on ground,
Pull down the walls,
Enlarge your halls,
Let smoke and jest abound.[7]

In writing in *Forest & Stream* about the entire body of ship-board poetry, Grinnell hastened to advise his readers that it was all "in the nature of the most good-natured chaff, and that nothing ever appeared with the slightest intention of being taken in the least seriously."[8]

lack of tension & interpersonal conflict, at least avowedly

The *Elder*'s course from Harriman Fiord took it first to Latouche Island at the southwest entrance to Prince William Sound. Rich copper deposits had been discovered on this long, narrow island a few years earlier, and Harriman and Devereaux were interested in both the infrastructure and the actual mining operations that were just getting underway. The two men went ashore, but they were soon back on board—none the less for wear nor the more for knowledge—and the ship set out on a 185-mile journey to Cook Inlet and the town of Homer. While still near Latouche Island, the party watched as an enormous and apparently curious whale approached the ship. Merriam estimated it as at least eighty feet long, perhaps indicating that it was a humpback. Other whales joined the first as the *Elder* steamed along, putting on a show, including a number who "standing up like huge stumps" in the water, twisted in the air and slapped the surface with their tails before diving for the deep.[9]

The long hours at sea provided ample reading and letter-writing time, and as usual Keeler was among those who put pen to paper. Writing to his wife, who may have been doing some traveling of her own, he admonished her to "be sure to be in Berkeley by the first of August," since "it would be a dreadful disappointment to arrive there and not find you awaiting me." And financial matters continued to weigh on his mind: he regretted again giving his bird book to the troublesome publishers, and was worried that "even if they get it out in time I will not make a cent out of it." His discouragement was fueled by conversations with Burroughs and Muir, who both reported that even with their books selling well, those publications did not themselves provide the income to fully support their families. Keeler clearly wished for better for his family, telling Louise that "if only I could make enough from my writing to take off the constant strain and worry about the future and to enable you to have enough help to go on with your work how happy we would be!"[10]

They reached Cook Inlet in bright sunshine on Friday morning, the last day of June, and dropped anchor off the town of Homer. Situated on a low sand spit jutting out into Kachemak Bay, Homer was then only about three years old, and was made up of five or six buildings, including a post office. Though Burroughs would find that "there was nothing Homeric in the look of the place," he and others were impressed by the sight of the Iliamna and Redoubt volcanoes across the inlet to the west.[11] Their stay in the area was brief, though they had time for a stop at the former Russian settlement at Seldovia, southwest of Homer.

There they came upon the campsite of Mr. and Mrs. Dall DeWees, an American couple from Canyon City, Colorado, who were hunting in the area. One reason for going to Cook Inlet had been to investigate its hunting possibilities. Those were good, according to DeWees, but the hunting ground was some distance away: at least four days travel to where sheep could be found, with moose at "perhaps half that distance." He also reported—to no recorded reaction from the so far largely unsuccessful Harriman hunters—that the petite Mrs. DeWees had recently killed two sheep and a bear.[12] Though the prospects seemed promising, it was clearly impracticable to

lack of success of exp. hunters

keep the ship and its company at this point for upwards of a week to allow the hunters the time needed to get into the interior and back. However, the news seemed to make Harriman all the more anxious to get to Kodiak Island in pursuit of its famous bears. So, for one of the few times when he directed or ordered the course to be followed, he scrapped further exploration of Cook Inlet in favor of proceeding to Kodiak Island. The *Elder* left Homer that afternoon.

While determined to get on with the big game hunting that had played a large part in selecting Alaska as the destination for the family vacation turned expedition, Harriman did not lose sight of the scientific purposes of the trip. A group of the biologists and ornithologists, disappointed by the early exodus from Cook Inlet, wanted additional time on the mainland before the ship followed its planned course up the waters of the Alaskan Peninsula and the Aleutian Islands. Accordingly, from Homer the ship set out for Kukak Bay, a promising, wild area in what is now Katmai National Park. It was a hundred-mile journey that started under clear, sunlit skies; but when they arrived off the entrance to the bay it was late at night and the far shoreline was all but invisible from the ship. Still, for whatever reason, it was decided to send the party off in the ever-deepening darkness, rather than waiting until morning. Ridgway, Saunders, Kearney, Fisher, Kincaid, and two packers were put off in one of the larger boats.

Although a number of similar parties had been put ashore and left isolated at other stops in Yakutat Bay and Prince William Sound, the eerie remoteness of the area, the late hour, the distance the shore party would have to travel to cross the largely uncharted bay to an unknown landing place, as well as the pending lack of any means of communication between them and the ship for a truly extended period of time, all seemed to hit home with the watchers on deck. "It looked like a perilous bit of business," Burroughs would write of his worries as the men rowed away into the darkness, "in an open boat on an unknown coast many miles from shore. Might they not miss the bay? Might they not find the surf running too high to land, or might not some other mishap befall them?"[13]

Nonetheless, the *Elder* steamed away, and when those aboard woke up on the morning of Saturday, the first of July, they found themselves anchored in Uyak Bay on the north side of Kodiak Island. Two salmon canneries were visible on the shore, and a boat soon left the dock, bound for the *Elder* with a quantity of fresh salmon. The stop here, however, was not for visiting the canneries or collecting specimens. Burroughs was again on deck to watch as another party, in a naphtha launch, departed the ship "heavily armed, bent on finding and killing the great Kadiak bear—the largest species of bear in the world, as big as an ox." These hunters, he continued, "had been making up their mouths for this monster bear all the way, and now they were at last close to his haunts. In two or three days we were to return and pick them up and hoist their game aboard with the giant derrick."[14] The party—conspicuously not including Harriman—was made up of Morris, Devereaux, Grinnell, Trudeau, Harriman's brother-in-law William Averell, the hunter Charles Fredell, and three packers. This group, Muir wryly observed, was "gun-laden for war."[15]

About 8:00 a.m. the ship's whistle announced its departure. Uyak Bay is located off Shelikof Strait on the northern coast of Kodiak Island, more than seventy miles sailing around the island to their now primary destination of Kodiak village, on the eastern, Gulf of Alaska side of the island. As they plied the waters off the island, they

hunting of "Kadiak" ~~hout~~ bear

encountered a dramatic change of scenery. In writing his "Narrative of the Expedition" some months after the completion of the trip, Burroughs would reflect that at this point in their travels, off Kodiak Island, "we were now about to turn over a new leaf, or indeed to open a new book, and to enter upon an entirely different type of scenery—the treeless type. Up to this point, or for nearly 2,000 miles, we had seen the mountains and valleys covered with unbroken spruce forests. Now we were to have 2,000 miles without a tree, the valleys and mountains as green as a lawn and to the eye as smooth." And later he would add that Kodiak Island "is treeless, except upon the east end, which faces toward the great Alaska forests from which the tree infection may have come."[16]

Bernhard Fernow, the consummate forester and "student of forest distribution," was also watching this change of scenery. The true forest, he would observe, was found only along Alaska's southern coast, on the islands of the Alexander Archipelago, and in the panhandle that separated British possessions from the ocean, and that forest was but the northward extension of the great Douglas Fir and cedar forests of Washington and British Columbia. As this forest pushed north, however, its character changed: the firs, cedars and pines disappeared, and the growth became largely hemlock and spruce, and even that came to "an abrupt termination on the north shore of Kadiak Island." Assessing what he saw as the value of these Alaskan timber resources—that is, the vast stands of mostly hemlock and spruce—under existing economic conditions, Fernow concluded that "in addition to the small value of these woods, and their comparatively unsatisfactory development, the conditions under which lumbering on the rugged slopes would have to be carried on are extremely difficult; add to these distractions the distance from market, and we may readily see the reason why this resource will, for an indefinite period, be left untouched except for local use." He would, however, add that the value of Alaska's timber resources could well increase "with the development of the country and with the increase of local needs."[17]

⇒ ◆ ⇐

The approach to the village of Kodiak—which during their occupation the Russians had called St. Paul—involved a passage so narrow that to Dellenbaugh "It seemed as if we could not get so large a ship in and one could almost pick flowers from the left bank as we passed."[18] They reached the wharf sometime after three o'clock Saturday afternoon, and Burroughs was exultant with the warm weather: "How welcome the warmth! ...the mercury near the seventies, and our spirits rose accordingly. How we swarmed out of the ship, like boys out of school, longing for a taste of grass and of the rural seclusion and sweetness!"[19] He estimated the population at "seven or eight hundred" (though in truth it was more likely a couple of hundred less than that), comprised of Native peoples, some Russians, "half breeds," and a number of Americans, all living in "comfortable frame cottages," and engaged in fishing, hunting, and working for the Alaska Commercial Company. There were no horses or wheeled vehicles, and the streets were but grassy lanes. "Such a rural Arcadian air I have never before seen pervading a town upon American soil," Burroughs would enthuse, adding that "the only incongruous thing I saw was a building with a big sign on the ridge board, 'Chicago Store.'"[20]

Ashore, Keeler and Ritter made a beeline for the post office, where they were

Kodiak, Kodiak Island. Photograph by Edward S. Curtis. University of Washington Libraries, Special Collections [Harriman 133].

initially disappointed, but drew encouragement from the anticipated arrival of a mail steamer early in the following week when, it seemed, the *Elder* would still be there, since her boilers needed cleaning and the ship's compass was to undergo repair. Ritter would also note that as to pronunciation of the name of the Island and the Village, "the people here say 'Kodiak.'"[21] Many others in the party also made their way ashore, spending the afternoon in the village or, as might be expected from the likes of Muir and Burroughs, wandering out into the meadows and the fields of wild flowers. In the village, Harriman soon struck up a conversation with an elderly Russian villager, Stepan Kandarkoff, a reputed expert bear hunter, and one of the major goals of the entire Expedition immediately rose again to the fore. *remnants of Russian period*

After supper Saturday evening, Ritter and others went to the Russian church service, though most of the party spent a quiet evening on the ship. Conversation included speculation about rumors that the trip would be extended on to the coast of Siberia, "and so get within the Arctic Circle and see the midnight sun."[22]

Harriman, however, was busy with other, more immediate plans. Much as he had done in impulsively setting out for Howling Valley in Glacier Bay, he decided not to wait until the next morning and quickly launched his hunt for the great Kodiak bear. Shortly after 8 p.m., he and Merriam, accompanied by Mary Harriman and her cousin Elizabeth Averell, both of whom longed for the camping adventure, set off in the steam launch for Eagle Bay, some eight miles distant, where they set up camp in the last light of the evening. The camp party was augmented early Sunday morning by the arrival of Coville, Kandarkoff, and Kelly, with the latter two almost immediately setting off on the hunt with Harriman. They wandered far up into the hills, established a bare-bones camp on a high ridge, and set off on a long day of hunting. This produced no game, "but when they returned to their camp at night they found close to the tent the tracks of an enormous bear," who had apparently wandered by in their absence.[23]

That same morning, back in Kodiak, and as he would report in a letter to Helen Markham, Mrs. Harriman asked Charlie Palache to join the hunting camp "where the girls were to have their first taste of outdoor life," and he, Cornelia Harriman, and Dorothea Draper went up to the Eagle Bay camp in the launch, "arriving in time for luncheon, eaten among many mosquitoes." They went for a walk after lunch and, befitting the location of their camp, discovered an eagle's nest, with Palache climbing the tree and bringing back "the funny downy young one" he found there. The evening meal "was a lively one for each girl was bound to cook their own bacon and flapjacks," and afterwards Palache and all four girls "escaped the flies by going out in the boat," with the girls rowing and Palache "trying to tell stories." By the time they returned to camp the mosquitoes had mysteriously disappeared and they all slept on the ground, "under the stars in perfect comfort."[24]

Back in Kodiak Village that Sunday, Muir watched when Kandarkoff and Kelly departed for Harriman's camp, and again later as others of his companions headed off on their own hunting forays, toting their rifles and "sauntering as if it were the best day for the ruthless business." Muir, Trelease, and Gifford climbed the mountains east of the village, to spend the day hunting and collecting plants, not game.[25]

Monday dawned warm and clear. At the Eagle Bay camp, Coville and Palache went off to climb a 3,000-foot peak, carefully collecting flowers all along the way, and returned at 4:00 p.m. to find Merriam and the girls breaking camp and preparing to return to the ship.[26] Merriam would subsequently return to Eagle Bay with the launch to wait for Harriman, Kandarkoff, and Kelly. As to those three hunters, they had made an early morning start from their high camp. It wasn't long before, at a distance of two miles, they saw a large bear but after taking a long, circular approach they lost the trail.[27]

As the afternoon wore on, things improved—dramatically. With the party trailing behind Kandarkoff as they worked through the woods, Kelly would recall that "suddenly he stopped and pointed to our left, and sure enough there was a bear moving around with her head down, showing first one side and then the other." The bear was some 300 yards away, but they maneuvered to close the range by 50 yards, and "Mr. Harriman raising his rifle took deliberate aim and, as the bear turned its side, fired and the bear fell at the shot." It was the only shot that was needed, though immediately a smaller bear came into view, charging at the hunters and being met with a fusillade "and the poor fellow gave up the ghost in a nearby hollow."[28] Harriman was elated, and after they had taken pictures and carefully marked the location, they headed back to Eagle Bay, where Merriam was maintaining a solitary vigil. They were soon on the launch and on their way back to the ship in the growing darkness.

In the meantime, and back at Kodiak, Monday's good weather led Mrs. Harriman to organize a picnic on nearby Wood Island, where the American Commercial Company had its headquarters. A large group left mid-morning and returned at 3:00 p.m. On Wood Island, Muir found part of an old forest and "got good approximate ages of 10 spruces: one nearly 5 feet in diameter and perhaps 300 years old."[29] Keeler and Burroughs "heard or fancied we heard voices calling us from out of the depths of the woods," so they packed a lunch and wandered off on their own, "listening to the birds and ravens, and noting the wood flowers and moss-draped trees."[30]

Kodiak Bear shot by E.H. Harriman. Photograph by E.H. Harriman. University of Washington Libraries, Special Collections [Harriman 136].

While Burroughs took an after lunch nap "upon a bed of moss in the shade of a great old spruce tree," Keeler took advantage of the time to catch up and have a written "little talk" with Louise.[31] Their experience on Wood Island would soon lead Burroughs to wax poetic about the birds of Kodiak, resulting in a contribution to the Smoking Room's poetry wall titled "To the Oregon Robin in Alaska."

Shortly after the picnicking group returned to the ship, the Eagle Bay party including Palache and the four girls also made their return, and finally, as midnight approached, Harriman and his hunting companions came in and clambered aboard with news of the day's hunt. "It seemed, even to the most eager bear hunter of the ship's company," Grinnell would write in retrospect, "a peculiarly satisfactory thing that Mr. Harriman, who is himself an enthusiastic hunter and a hard worker, should have been the one to kill the first—and as it afterward proved, the only—specimen of this very desirable game."[32] *"dramatic climax" under hotel*

That "desirable game," however, was still out there, in the woods. Fuertes and Cole, the taxidermist, quickly volunteered to bring the trophies back to the ship; accompanied by Kandarkoff, they set out on that mission at 3:00 a.m. the next morning—which happened to be the 4th of July.

≈ ◆ ≈

The holiday dawned bright, fair and warm, very fitting, Ritter thought, for "the day we love and don't forget, even when far from home."[33] The celebration began in the morning on the hurricane deck, where the crew manned the ship's brass cannon and fired a salute of ten rounds at five-minute intervals. High above, two dozen flags floated in the rigging, and Dr. Nelson would approvingly record that "at breakfast Mrs. Harriman gave each member of our party a little U.S. flag and it is needless to say we all wore our emblem all day."[34]

Shortly after breakfast, the Committee on Music and Entertainment (Fernow, Dellenbaugh, Gifford, and Draper, but sans Fuertes, who was off bear-fetching) met to review their work on a program of songs, recitations, readings, and music to commemorate the day. Nine-year-old Carol Harriman had lobbied to be part of the program, and the Committee thought to have her recite something appropriate—though they were struggling to find anything, the ship's vast library notwithstanding, that filled the bill. Their deliberations were interrupted by the departure of the ship's launches for Wood Island, where the party was to take in what was apparently an annual baseball game between Kodiak and Wood Island teams. In the launch, Dellenbaugh put pen to paper "to write something as suitable to the occasion as I could, for Carol had her heart set on the appearance," and proceeded to write a four stanza poem titled "Our Banner," though "in order to avoid criticism and comment" he wrote a line at the bottom attributing the work to "John Hay, Fourth of July Banquet July 4, 1898."[35]

The ballgame on Wood Island lasted most of the morning. The Reverend Nelson was in the crowd along the sidelines and found the quality of play consistently irregular, in part occasioned by "all the players being decided novices and among them smoking cigars while making runs from base to base."[36] *early baseball game*

Back on the ship and after lunch, a crowd, including the American citizens of Kodiak, gathered on the Upper Deck for the patriotic exercises orchestrated by the Committee on Music and Entertainment. Harriman's graphophone launched the festivities with John Phillip Sousa's "Stars and Stripes Forever," Dr. Nelson gave an opening prayer, and William Brewer—not only a noted orator, but also the party's senior member—delivered the major speech: focusing on revolutionary principles, freedoms Americans have and observe, the strengths of the country, and that "when we bought Alaska it carried the flag as far west as there is a west, so far that it becomes east."[37] Dellenbaugh found Brewer's speech "appropriate and well-delivered," but he and a number of the other members of the party were less than pleased with a presentation by Charles Keeler: "Keeler read an original poem the first portion of which on Alaska was good but then he branched off into an impassioned denunciation of the government's policy in Manila which was decidedly out of place."[38] Little Carol Harriman was, however, a hit. Haltingly but firmly and with a child's charm, she read "Our Banner," the poem Dellenbaugh had written for her.

social protest appears & is seen as inappropriate

From tropic seas to midnight days
Our banner flies, a promise clear;
From East to West, the sun always,
Follows the flag that knows no fear.

Our navy's guns awake the world
And crush the tyrant's evil power.
Oppression's flag is quickly furled
Where Columbia rises to the hour.

Thus stands our country with the great,
Where other lands have often stood;
Yet hard! To hold this envious place,
As well as great, we must be good.

Then fling our emblem far and near,
In every clime and every sun;
But let us all remember here,
That greatness, goodness are as one.[39]

"Carol read the poem nicely," Dellenbaugh concluded, and she beamed at the applause that followed. The "Grand Finale" was listed in the Program as simply

"Messrs. Ritter, Gifford and Fernow," and turned out to be Fernow and Ritter "dancing a jig to Gifford's fiddling."[40]

The afternoon's activities concluded with local boat races involving dugout canoes, rowboats and other vessels of various descriptions, accompanied by hilarious mishaps, occasional sinkings, and predictably disputed results. Harriman turned-in a second-place finish in a close race in a four-man canoe against a naphtha launch, for which effort he was cheered on by the members of his Expedition. And as they returned to the *Elder*, they found that Fuertes and Cole had brought in the two bears—leading to more cheers for Harriman and the success of his hunt. Success aside, in the final analysis the adult bear was actually but a small representative of the species: Muir would note that "the hind foot was only eight inches long; some tracks seen were five inches longer"—still, Merriam was sure it was the first Kodiak bear ever measured and photographed in the flesh.[41]

Years later, in his tribute to Harriman following the latter's untimely death, Muir would relate a story with a setting "one evening when the Alaskan Expedition was at Kodiak"—which probably meant the evening of July 4, since of all the nights the party spent there, this was perhaps the only one when both men were on the ship at the time of day when the story played out. On that evening, "the scientists, assembled on the forecastle awaiting the dinner bell, began to talk of the blessed ministry of wealth, especially in Mr. Harriman's case, now that some of it was being devoted to science." Standing nearby, Muir teasingly interrupted that "I don't think Mr. Harriman is very rich. He has not as much money as I have. I have all I want and Mr. Harriman has not." This comment apparently found its way to Harriman and after dinner, finding a seat beside Muir, he said: "I never cared for money except as power for work. I was always lucky and my friends and neighbors, observing my luck, brought their money to me to invest, and in this way I have come to handle large sums. What I most enjoy is the power of creation, getting into partnership with Nature in doing good, helping to feed man and beast, and making everybody and everything a little better and happier." Recalling this conversation, which undoubtedly played its part in the fast-growing friendship between the two men, Muir would conclude in his tribute that "this has proved true. He earned the means and inherited the courage to do and dare as his great head and heart directed."[42]

As Independence Day drew to a close and the evening wore on, the organized group activities of the day gave way to individual pursuits. Muir was visited by a mountaineer who had seen the *Elder* docked in the harbor and being advised that Muir, who he had heard of, was aboard, wanted to make his acquaintance. The man was familiar with much of the coast from Wrangel northward, and Muir noted in his journal, "He said he was just like me, liked to go on glaciers and mountains alone. Was chased by wolves, had crossed many glaciers … and lived in a cabin near the head of Cook Inlet."[43]

With Muir occupied in visiting, Keeler had their shared stateroom to himself and took the occasion to write to his wife Louise about the day's activities and his part in the program. He also recorded a hint of despair, since "all day long I have been watching the harbor's entrance for the arrival of the Dora with mail. She was due today but now I fear she will not arrive and my last hope of word from my loved one will be gone, as we are to sail early tomorrow."[44] And Charley Palache was also writing home, advising Helen that he had "bought a bearskin here which I hope will make a handsome rug for some place in our Room."[45]

Harriman had his own bearskins, but he was also in the market for other pelts, and he had something to trade. The span of horses that had been loaded onboard in Seattle, and which were to have been used "to transport the hunters and their traps inland and to pack out the big game," had, in Burroughs words, "proven to be a superfluity." Though occasionally taken off the ship for exercise, the terrain and the hunting opportunities had not been suitable for their use. But horses were scarce in Kodiak Village, and before leaving Harriman traded them for "two choice pelts of the rare and coveted black fox."[46] In addition to the horses, two of the packers were not traded but were left behind at Kodiak, because, it was Dellenbaugh's understanding, "Mr. H. was not satisfied with them."[47]

Midnight approached. The crew of the *Elder* was busy feeding the boilers and building steam, securing the deck, and making ready to weigh anchor as the ship prepared to leave Kodiak and again turn its bow northward. One can imagine a restless Burroughs on deck, perhaps with thoughts that he would eventually commit to writing—"Kadiak I think won a place in the hearts of all of us. Our spirits probably touched the highest point here. If we had other days that were epic, these days were lyric."[48]

ELEVEN

Into the Snarling Bering Sea

"A horrible raking blow from some source made the ship tremble from stem to stern; then another and another, still more severe."—John Burroughs

The *Elder's* exit from Kodiak harbor did not quite go according to plan. At the time of departure the tide was out—perhaps lower than normal—and the steamer was soon aground. Muir succinctly recorded that "the ship, lying over on a gravel bar, nearly rolled us out of bed."[1] Palache would be a bit more descriptive, noting that "instead of going off last night as intended the steamer stuck in the mud near the wharf and this morning we got up to find her decks sloping at an angle of about 20 degrees so that locomotion was difficult and it looked as if we were all a little worse for the 4th."[2] However, by ten o'clock, with the morning high tide working its way in, the ship was righting itself, and near noon they were finally underway in fine, quiet weather under a cloudless sky.

The delay was in at least one way fortunate since, shortly after leaving Kodiak, they met the long-expected mail steamer *Dora*. Keeler caught sight of the approaching ship and "I ran to the captain on the bridge and told him I knew there was mail for me aboard the Dora, and he whistled for her to stop. As she came alongside her captain called out that he had one letter for our party. I supposed," he wrote to Louise, "it must be from Mrs. Ritter mailed in Sitka, but when the skiff was lowered and Mr. Harriman was rowed over to the Dora they gave him your letter to me mailed to Homer. It was the only letter for the entire expedition and you may be sure I was indeed happy to hear from my loved ones."[3] *letters a rare commodity for exp mbrs*

The afternoon was warm, and most of the party spent the time on deck, watching the passing scenery as the ship retraced its steps northward to pick up the parties that had been put ashore five days earlier. It was not as quiet and pastoral below decks, where some members of the crew were engaged in the activities necessary to support and feed the large traveling party. Nelson was reading in his stateroom when "I heard the piteous bellowing of a wounded steer and the butcher's pistol shots" and, though no vegetarian, complained to his diary and posterity that "if we must take animals along to eat, we might at least give them a quick and easy exit from this world where 'big fish eat of the little ones.'"[4]

The plan was to first return to the mainland to pick up Ridgway, Saunders and the others who had been put ashore, amid much worry by Burroughs, in the darkness at Kukak Bay on the night of June 30. Steaming all day, the *Elder* entered the Bay shortly before 6:30 p.m., and in the strong late afternoon light those on board quickly had any lingering concerns alleviated when they saw the group gathered at their camp

mosquitos major irritant

on shore. They came on board "in good spirits," enthused about "a fine collecting trip but rather a poor camp owing to <u>many mosquitoes</u>," and "they brought many birds and plants and a fine lot of fossil plants from some Tertiary beds near the shore."[5] Fuertes was particularly taken with Ridgway's collection, including "a Western double crested cormorant and ... an eagle with a spread of 7' 5½", and in almost perfect plumage."[6] That evening, as the ship headed toward the north end of Kodiak Island, Saunders gave a short talk on the results of the trip.

Just before midnight they reached Uyak Bay to pick up the hunting party. In contrast to the Kukak Bay group, the hunters "came in looking tired and disgusted, no game, much disgruntled from flies and mosquitoes, hard walking through alder country, poor camps and packers," according to Palache.[7] Among other things, it appears that the "careless packers" had left "a coat, a gun case and a gun belonging to different members of the party" on the beach, where—though subsequently recovered—they had been immersed in the tide and rendered useless.[8] The hunting had been totally fruitless, to the extent that no fresh signs of bear, much less bears themselves, had been seen at any time. The insects were another story. "At no point visited were the flies so bad as at Uyak Bay," Grinnell asserted. "They flew against the face in great clouds ... their numbers were so great that it was difficult to keep them out of eyes, nose and mouth." Efforts to fight the flies were unavailing—"various preparations of grease, used by some members of the party, did prevent the flies from biting, but did not keep them from flying against the face, where they got caught in the oily mixture and crawled about," to the extent that one of the party "compared the face of one of his companions to 'a large pudding with currants in it.'"[9] The overall experience had been disappointing—and the comments and reports about the "poor packers" were the apparent cause for the three of them being discharged before the *Elder* returned to sea.[10]

⇒ ◆ ⇐

From Uyak Bay on Thursday, July 6, the Harriman Expedition set its course west by southwest through the open waters of the Pacific on a 177-mile cruise to the Shumagin Islands. The weather was conducive to the activity of the inveterate deck walkers. Chief among those was John Muir, who apparently found circling the deck an acceptable, if confined, substitute for his endless woodland wanderings on land. Though often found in the company of Burroughs, by far his most frequent companion on these elliptical tramps around the deck of the *Elder* was Henry Gannett. The friendship that developed between these two men stemmed, Muir would explain, from how impressed he was, when he first saw Gannett, by what he called the "preternatural solemnity" of his expression. "This," Merriam would recall, "convinced him that Gannett, like himself, was fond of humor, and he was not long in learning that Gannett, though not a Scotchman, also loved an argument. The result was that the two were always happy together."[11]

For others, a good deal of time that day was spent, at least according to Palache, in "reading and loafing," though after lunch he himself pitched-in to help with the packing of the many fossil plants that had been collected by the Kukak Bay party.[12] And there was considerable discussion on and below decks about the now near certainty that Mrs. Harriman's wish to visit Russian territory on the Siberian Coast would come true, in which case they were in for a long pull across the Bering Sea.

out of normal travelers' domain

Even apart from that added jaunt, they had long ago left behind those ports of call frequented by tourist steamers, and as they left the vicinity of Kodiak Island's north coast they were also passing the limits of most other ocean traffic—the waters ahead were generally frequented only by Native boats, the whaling fleet, a few small trading ships that irregularly serviced the canneries and scattered settlements, and the occasional U.S. Navy vessel.

When the party turned out early Friday morning, they found the ship at anchor in a cove at Sand Point on Popof Island. At one time in its history, Sand Point had been a rendezvous for ships of the seal poaching fleet. Later its role had reversed, and it became a government station in the effort to restrict sealing. It had also functioned both as a supply point for cod fishing ships working the grounds off the Russian coast and as a general trading post. In those various "heydays" a number of buildings had been put up, including some small hotels, but they were now largely crumbling and deserted. Muir provided a one sentence description: "A few houses are here, a trading post, and a deserted, wrecked schooner on the beach."[13]

Nonetheless, it was a sylvan and promising setting, and a party had been organized to remain at Sand Point for exploration and collecting while the *Elder* went on to the Bering Sea, the Pribilof Islands, and Siberia. This was a significant undertaking and would involve the longest separation from the ship of any of the Expedition's shore parties: the *Elder* would travel to a destination a thousand miles away and would not return to Sand Point for at least ten days. Initially, the shore party was to consist of the botanists and zoologists Ritter, Saunders, and Kincaid, but that morning Kelly was added to the roster and when Palache returned from a productive hike ashore collecting lava samples, he also hurriedly determined to join the group in order to study the island's volcanic formations in greater depth.[14] And before long the party had grown further to include the *Elder*'s pilot, J.K. Jordan, as well as the hunter Charles Fredell, a cook, and two of the remaining packers. By mid-morning, the steam launch *Manila* had been outfitted and loaded with a small boat and a canoe, food stuffs, and other needed supplies, and with the party of ten crowding its decks, it headed off for Sand Point.

Shortly after the shore party departed, and the peg board had been checked to be sure everyone else was on board, the *Elder* began maneuvering away from Sand Point. It was not an uneventful departure. From literally out of nowhere, a small boat carrying "two drunken prospectors" approached, its occupants tried to board the ship, and when prevented they became enraged and for a time "floated about yelling at us and singing."[15]

rare humor

The ship soon outdistanced the chorus, and those on deck settled in to watch the passing scenery. Merriam was among that group, though somewhat off to himself, when Burroughs approached, bearing a fox sparrow's nest and four eggs he had collected ashore early that morning; something more than a little out of character for Burroughs, since he had at times quietly complained about the bird hunting and collecting activities of the ornithologists. He wanted to effect a "swap"—the nest and eggs for the brightly and variously-colored skin of a Golden-Crowned Sparrow that Merriam had shot earlier and which Burroughs apparently admired.[16] Merriam would record the incident in his diary, without indicating how he responded, and Burroughs himself was silent about the whole business. Thomas Kearney, however, was present and years later would recall that Merriam quickly announced Burroughs's proposal to the other scientists on deck, who proceeded to tease Burroughs good-naturedly but still "unmercifully."[17]

⇒ ◆ ⇐

The immediate destination was Unalaska Bay and Dutch Harbor, where they arrived early on Saturday, July 8. Describing the trip that led to this destination in a letter to "Wanda and Helen and Mama," Muir would tell his wife and daughters that "we arrived here this cloudy, rainy, foggy morning after a glorious sail from Sand Harbor all the way along the volcano-dotted coast of the Alaska Peninsula and Unimak Island. The volcanoes are about as thick as haycocks on our alfalfa field in a wet year, and the highest of them are smoking and steaming in grand style."[18]

The primary purpose of the stop was to take advantage of the fact that the North American Commercial Company maintained a supply depot at Dutch Harbor, where Captain Doran could fill the ship's water barrels and pick up extra coal for the long miles ahead. It was planned that the *Elder* would be back at sea by mid-afternoon, but despite the few hours involved, the day was productive and eventful. Shortly after breakfast, with the ship tied-up at the Commercial Company's dock, a launch put off to take a number of the scientists and artists across the bay. Fuertes and Fisher were among those who "piled ashore to hunt," and they soon were elated to discover that some "of the loveliest birds, whose names had become familiar, but which had in themselves become myths, were found to be very common, and easily obtainable."[19] Merriam would make note of similar success by Ridgway and Starks when they left to collect birds and mammals.[20] In fact, those two were so successful, and felt that in the few hours ashore they had just scratched the surface, that they determined to stay behind while the *Elder* went north to Siberia.

Dellenbaugh found Unalaska "uninteresting" with "nothing picturesque" about it. But back at the docks he heard of a steamer that had recently come in from St. Michael with three hundred passengers from the Yukon, "most of them with nothing but others with a goodly weight of gold dust." One man on that ship reportedly had $60,000 worth of gold dust, while another, it was said, "had sent to San Francisco for two armed men to guard his gold every minute and several had a stateroom together with gold in it, each guarding it in turn." Dellenbaugh talked with many of the miners who were idling and killing time on the waterfront, most of whom were tired, dispirited and "had had enough of it and said about 95 out of every hundred had made nothing." Still, the rumors were that another ship, the *Roanoke*, was "expected today or tomorrow with 'several millions' in gold," and that "news" seemed to excite even the weariest of the gathered miners.[21]

On the *Elder*, as it provisioned and coaled that morning, Charles Keeler wrote a lengthy letter, responding to the one he had been so excited to receive when they were leaving Kodiak and had hailed the *Dora*. His initial mood in reporting about that excitement gave way to brooding, advising Louise that "I find we are to be made to pay for this trip with a vengeance. I am expected to send all my photographs to Mr. Harriman and he is to take his pick from them with all the others, for his book," and that as he understood it, "we are not supposed to be allowed to publish the results of our observations in magazine articles or newspapers lest it take from the originality of the book or books they expect to publish, so here I am with my hands tied and nothing to show for these two months."[22] It was neither the first nor the last time when Keeler

[handwritten: approaching Bering Strait]

expected the worst, misinterpreted plans, or worried at the slightest supposed threat to his publication and financial endeavors. Finishing his letter, Keeler went ashore with Muir to take a walk about the village while waiting for the ship to depart.

John Burroughs—unlike Dellenbaugh—found that Unalaska as a whole "looked quite as interesting as Kadiak," and he longed "to spend some days here in the privacy of its green solitudes, following its limpid torrent streams, climbing its lofty peaks, and listening to the music of the larkspur."[23] Those longings bred and hatched a plan to jump ship: motivated, it seems, in part by the bucolic scene, in part by the chance to spend time alone in solitary surroundings similar to those of his farm, and, last but probably not least, in part because of his fear of the roiling waters of the Bering Sea that they were about to challenge. Toting a small bag he had packed, he was walking down the gangplank when he encountered Keeler and Muir returning to the ship. As Keeler would later tell the story, a suspicious Muir demanded "Where are you going with that grip, Johnny?" Burroughs tried to be evasive but finally confessed, according to Keeler, that "he had found a nice old lady ashore who had fresh eggs for breakfast and he was going to board there and wait for us while we went up to Behring [*sic*] Sea. He didn't like to go into those tempestuous waters." Muir would have none of it: "Why, Johnny!" he exclaimed, "Behring [*sic*] Sea in summer is like a mill pond. The best part of our trip is up there.... Come along! You can't miss it!" Burroughs, Keeler concluded, "could not withstand Mr. Muir's scorn. He weakened a bit and was lost." Keeler took the grip and he and Muir conducted Burroughs back to the steamer.[24]

Although there were others on board the *Elder* that afternoon who witnessed Burroughs's departure and return, there is scant mention of the event in diaries and letters—perhaps in deference to Burroughs and the teasing he had endured barely a day earlier for the proposed nest-and-eggs for bird skin trade with Merriam. Muir himself noted in his journal only that "we kept John Burroughs on the ship."[25] In his "Narrative of the Expedition" Burroughs passed the incident with no reference to his aborted plans and only a vague mention of how "content" he would have been to "only have a few days" of intimacy with nature in this location, "but in the afternoon the ship was off into the Bering Sea headed for the Seal Islands, and I was aboard her, with wistful and reverted eyes."[26] He would, however, soon provide a shipboard sequel to the story, and hurl a barb or two at Muir, when the Bering Sea's rough weather gave life to his worst fears.

[handwritten: good-natured(?) teasing closest thing to conflict/drama]

The *Elder* set its course for Bogoslof, the then dual-summit of a submarine stratovolcano set some forty miles west of the northern tip of Unalaska Island in the southern reaches of the Bering Sea. At the time of the Harriman Expedition's visit, Bogoslof consisted of two islands—"Old Bogoslof" was created by an underwater eruption in 1796, while its companion "New Bogoslof" appeared via an eruption that began in the summer of 1883. Initially the two summits were connected by a spit, though by 1899 the connection had become a submerged sandbar. Dall had visited the area in 1873 and 1895, while Merriam had been there in 1891, and they knew it as a breeding ground for sea lions and murres, a penguin-like bird in the auk family.[27]

In approaching the Bogoslofs, though still twenty-five or thirty miles away, the *Elder* was passed by flocks of murres on their way to the islands: "As we neared the islands," Merriam would write, "their numbers increased until the air was full of them,

The Bogoslofs, Old and New (erupting). Photograph by A.K. Fisher. A.K. Fisher Collection, Library of Congress.

coming from different directions and all moving in straight courses to the cliffs."[28] At 7 p.m., in a heavy fog that obscured the summits of the volcanoes, the ship dropped anchor two miles offshore and put off a boat with a half-dozen explorers including Merriam, Harriman, Fisher, Coville, and Curtis. Making their way to Old Bogoslof, they found that the water was dotted with murres and the cliffs were swarming with them. Once ashore, Fisher quickly set about collecting, a simple task since any shot into the air was likely to hit a target. The number of murres was astounding and when Fisher fired his gun "the multitudes that shot out into the air and circled around the island formed a dense cloud which cut off the light and made a roaring noise so loud that it drowned even the bellowing of the sea lions. And yet, after their departure, the cliffs seemed as completely peopled as before—so inconceivably great were their numbers."[29] From among the millions on the cliffs and in the air, Fisher quickly had all the specimens he could use in hand.

As astounding and overwhelming in their numbers as the murres were, the sea-lions were far more conspicuous and imposing ... and became restless and alarmed as the ship's boat approached. Forced to land at a place where a number of large bulls were congregated, the party found that they had picked a spot that Merriam later discerned was in the animals' "customary runway to the sea," and a number of the bulls charged down the runway "bellowing fearfully and moving in a clumsy ambling lope" toward the men and their boat, only veering off at the last minute and plunging into the sea. Another group of bulls further off "stared at us and roared, swinging their massive heads from side to side" and as Merriam ran toward them with his camera, "most took fright and made off ... but a few old giants, when I was within about 20 feet of them, made a stand. I did not dispute the ground with them, but waited till they moved slowly off." Apart from the bulls, the shore party found an absorbing scene out in the icy waters offshore.

> Dozens of adults, apparently cows and middle-aged males, were sporting like porpoises in the breakers, moving side by side in schools of six or eight and shooting completely out of the water. These small squads behaved like well drilled soldiers, keeping abreast, breaking water simultaneously, making their flying leap in the air side by side, and taking the next

56

Old Bogoslof. Photograph by A.K. Fisher. A.K. Fisher Collection, Library of Congress.

wave together. This they repeated again and again, evidently finding it great sport. It was a marvelous sight and one to be long remembered.[30]

In the lowering, misty weather and growing darkness, Fisher gathered up his birds and some murre eggs, Coville packed away the few beach plants he had been able to find, and the party rounded up two small sea lions to take back to the ship. The arrival of the latter on board the *Elder* attracted far more attention than Fisher's dead birds, though to Muir's way of thinking these "handsome little fellows had been stolen from their mothers," and Nelson sorrowfully predicted that "there is little chance of their surviving."[31] *animal welfare concerns nascent*

The after-dinner talk or lecture that evening was delivered by Merriam, covering his experience on the Bering Sea Commission, seals and the sealing industry, and what they might expect to find the next day when they visited the Pribilof Islands.

=== ◆ ===

The morning of Sunday the 9th of July brought anything but a day of rest. In what was actually a measured bit of understatement, Dellenbaugh would record that they experienced "very bad, rolling weather; many feeling ill." That included the artist, whose stomach was rolling along with the weather, the seas, and the ship. His thoughts turned to the morning of the day when the Harriman train left New York for the west coast and the stop he had made at the Century Club, where a friend had given him a small bottle of coca leaf extract that was a supposed cure for seasickness. Rummaging through his belongings, Dellenbaugh found the bottle and thought to mix its contents with a little whiskey as a way of settling his stomach—the combination proved to have a dramatically opposite effect, and he was soon bolting for the ship's railing to pay his "respects" to the rough waters.

Many others were not at breakfast that morning, while a number of those who did eat soon repaired to their staterooms and were not seen or heard from again until much later in the day. That included Burroughs, who would advise Dellenbaugh that "he felt fairly well as long as he remained in bed."[32] Down the hall, Keeler—faring better than most in the heavy weather, and apparently with some prodding from a concerned Muir—set out to look in on Burroughs, and wound up pulling up a chair to sit by his bunk: "Mr. Burroughs lay in his berth and groaned while I attempted to atone for my share in persuading him to venture into those stormy waters by sitting beside him and reading Wordsworth to him."[33] *v. 19th c. —> Wdswth for heavy sea*

The seas had calmed, at least relatively, by the afternoon, when they reached the Pribilofs and dropped anchor off St. Paul Island, 210 miles by the ship's log from the Bogoslofs. Before long a boat, "pulled by a half-dozen Aleuts," left the shore and the *Elder* was boarded by three Americans, two of whom were Treasury agents, while the other was a representative of the North American Commercial Company, which held the license for "harvesting" seals in the Pribilofs. Landing on the seal islands was prohibited by Treasury Department regulations, but a special permit had been obtained from the Secretary of the Treasury to allow the Harriman party to visit the islands.[34] In short order, the naphtha launches and the lifeboats were lowered, and most members of the ship's company were soon making their way down the ladders to find places in the boats. "Only one or two of the party were left on board," Grinnell reported, "for all were anxious to see what is one of the most interesting congregations of animal life in all the world, and now quite unique."[35]

Burroughs had bestirred himself to join the shore party (perhaps out of a combination of interest and a more basic desire to feel firm, unmoving ground underfoot), and recorded that the Treasury agents "conducted us a mile or more through wild meadows starred with flowers and covered with grass nearly knee high, to the boulder-paved shore where the seals were congregated."[36] In his typical, cryptic journal style, Muir described "thousands of seal on the black lava rocks, one big watchful, defiant male to 10 to 20 to 30 females. A rough place to lie on to say nothing of taking care of young." The males, with their long necks and fighting, roaring demeanor caught his attention, especially when they "rushed at photographers with surprising speed in 2 or 3 jumps when they approached too near, shaking their heads and snapping their jaws, showing their teeth, through fierce long-bristled whiskers. The general cry of the multitude like the ba-a-ing of sheep."[37]

While the thousands of seals impressed the first-time visitors, Merriam was stunned and dismayed: since his visit with the international commission in 1891, the seal population had declined to what he believed was less than twenty percent of what it had been.[38] *declining seal pop.*

The regulations that Merriam had played a role in developing had gone into effect but not before the toll had been taken, and those regulations continued to be weak in their control of pelagic or open ocean sealing, in which the sealing vessels, gathering offshore, would follow the herds in the months they spent at sea. Sealing on land, as at St. Paul Island, could be observed and controlled, but the open ocean presented a vastly different situation. Of the seals taken at sea, Grinnell would later explain to his *Forest & Stream* readers, "two-thirds are females, either carrying young or nursing new-born pups. In the legitimate land-killing on the islands, only males are killed, while in pelagic sealing for one male taken there are five [females] destroyed." Once the seals have reached their breeding places on the islands, he continued, the females have greater protection, "the sealers hover about them a good distance from land," and the females were safe except when they went far out to feed.[39] As the shore party watched the seals and discussed the decline in the population, Dellenbaugh would note that the *Elder's* pilot, Mr. Jordan, suggested that if the government would brand the females, disfiguring their pelts, it would "render the skins valueless" and discourage the pelagic sealers.[40]

The seals were the show, but St. Paul Island also had yellow poppies and other wild flowers scattered in the grasses; Lapland longspurs and snow buntings in song; and "noisy waterbirds, mostly little auks called 'choochkies' by the natives."[41] The party wandered about the meadows and watched the activities of the seals throughout the afternoon before making their way back to their small boats. With fog rolling in, they reboarded the *Elder* at 7:30 in the evening and were soon summoned by the dinner bell. As they were seated, the ship got underway, its whistle saluting the Treasury agents and others on shore.

They had been steaming at full speed for perhaps an hour, with after-dinner conversation winding-up and some already leaving the table, when "a horrible raking blow from some source made the ship tremble from stem to stern; then another and another, still more severe."[42] The ship had struck a reef. Harriman calmly went on deck, followed by almost everyone else, despite the dining room steward's plea to remain seated.[43] Thoughts of shipwreck crossed many minds, and someone suggested that Harriman be taken off in one of the boats—he refused and, privately and incredulously, asked Merriam, "Can you conceive of such a suggestion? What would a man want to live for if his family were drowned?"[44] A sail was hoisted to catch a favorable wind, the engines were reversed, and in about fifteen minutes the ship was off the reef, without damage. Muir noted that the episode had "set free lots of kelp," and that as the ship came about and reset its course for St. Matthew Island, they "gave the shore a rather wide berth."[45]

"Some of us," according to Burroughs, "hoped the incident would cause Mr. Harriman to turn back…. But our host was a man not easy to turn back; in five minutes he was romping with his children again as if nothing had happened." They plunged on through "the fog and obscurity with our 'ferocious whistle,' as Professor Emerson characterized it, tearing the silence, and with it our sleep, to tatters."[46]

═ ◇ ═

The Pribilofs and others of the islands in the Bering Sea are, literally, in the middle of nowhere. Finding any one of them could in itself be an issue: as Henry Gannett would observe, "It is not uncommon experience for vessels bound for the Pribilofs to miss the islands in the fog and to spend days searching for them, as for needles in a haystack. They are a small target to shoot a vessel at … and once missed, they are not easily found in this great foggy waste."[47] And so it was the next day, July 10, when—hundreds of miles north of the Pribilofs in grim gray fog, rough seas, and rain—the *Elder* passed their "target" of the day, St. Matthew Island, without anyone catching even a glimpse of it. Captain Doran determined that under the conditions searching for the island was too hazardous, so they went on, steaming northward.

The rough seas continued. Dellenbaugh recorded that "there was a great swell and the ship rolled badly from side to side so that moving about was difficult," and there was an eeriness in the air, magnified as throughout the ship "doors left open slammed and banged."[48] The eerie feeling was heightened as large numbers of murres flew about the ship, "as if curious to see it."[49] Intermittent rain combined with the swell kept many in their staterooms and berths. That confinement found Burroughs ruing his aborted escape at Unalaska and nibbling at his pen: soon a new poem, "On Bering Sea," appeared on the wall in the Smoking Room, lamenting and excoriating the "Snapping, Snarling, Spiteful" sea and its effects, and concluding:

Barren Sea!
Only murres abide with thee!
Had not John Muir put in his lip
Thou had'st not found me in this ship,
Groaning in my narrow bed,

Heaping curses on thy head,
Wishing he were here instead.
On green hills my feet would be,
Beyond the reach of Muir and thee.[50]

By evening on the 10th a temporary lull in the weather brought a good crowd to the Social Hall to hear a talk by Captain Humphrey, of the Pacific Steam Whaling Company, on the Bering Sea and Arctic Ocean whale fisheries. Humphrey provided a number of insights, including how when whalers would reach Alaska they would recruit a secondary crew of Eskimos and their dogs. These would accompany the vessel throughout its cruise, living on deck, serving as scouts and hunters, and, on occasions when the ship found itself surrounded by ice, scattering across the ice pack to search for open water.[51]

The late hours of the evening after Humphrey's talk might well have been one of those times Grinnell had in mind some months later when he wrote of a new-found cure for seasickness. Even those so afflicted, he would observe, were not so ill that they couldn't be coaxed out of their staterooms by "the smell of a Welsh rarebit at 11 or 12 o'clock at night." In the eyes of some, he continued, it was much like catching rabbits.

> One eminent man—not himself a biologist, but interested in all science—propounded to one of the mammal men a new and infallible method by which rabbits might be captured. He said "All you have to do is to hide behind a rock and make a noise like a turnip, and the rabbit will at once come straight up to you." This was paraphrased by the chairman of the Big Game Committee, who declared that he had at last discovered a certain remedy for seasickness. This was to go into the ship's cabin and make noise like a Welsh rarebit, when all the seasick men would come directly to him, cured.[52]

The Chairman of the Big Game Committee happened to be the ship's physician, Dr. Lewis Morris.

TWELVE

The Farthest Points

"Beyond the sea, to the east," they said, "there was a great land inhabited by people who had tusks growing out of their cheeks and had tails like dogs."—George Bird Grinnell

John Muir would note in his journal that at about 2:00 a.m. on the morning of Tuesday, July 11, high head winds and heavy seas had the *George W. Elder* pitching so much that "the screw [was] out of the water at times," necessitating that speed be cut to no more than four to seven miles an hour.[1] The heavy seas forced abandonment of a planned stop at St. Lawrence Island. Instead, the ship passed to the west of that island, bound for Plover Bay at the southern end of the Chukchi Peninsula on the coast of Siberia. The rough seas began to abate in the morning, but fog set-in and continued until nearly noon, when clear air and sunshine not only lifted spirits but allowed the *Elder* to resume steaming speed.

The Siberian coast soon came into view, and within a few hours they were approaching Plover Bay, one of a number of sheltered anchorages within the larger Providence Bay. A neighboring bay, called Telegraph Harbor on the English maps, was named for the Western Union Telegraph Expedition of 1866–1867. Dall had been a part of that expedition, and he was one of two members of the Harriman party who had been to Siberia. The other was Muir, who was on board the Treasury Department steamer *Thomas Corwin* in the summer of 1881, searching the Bering Sea and the Arctic Ocean for signs of the converted yacht *Jeannette*, which had sailed north in the summer of 1879 on an exploratory voyage to the North Pole. The *Corwin's* search grew to encompass looking for the *Mount Wollaston* and the *Vigilant*, two whaling ships that failed to return from Arctic waters in the autumn of 1879. The *Corwin* made at least three separate stops in Plover Bay to interview villagers as to their knowledge of any of the missing ships and, as recorded by Muir, "to fill our coal-bunkers from a pile belonging to His Majesty, the Czar of Russia."[2]

The entrance to Plover Bay failed to impress Dellenbaugh, who concluded that "a more barren, god-forsaken place cannot exist anywhere on the face of the earth ... not a vestige of vegetation or life of any kind could be discovered. A cold wind swept down from the icy north and penetrated to our bones."[3] At six o'clock the *Elder* dropped anchor behind a long, crescent-shaped sand spit; home to an Eskimo village of a dozen skin-covered houses. The ship's arrival caused a burst of activity in the village, and in a few minutes, boats, made of walrus skin stretched over a wooden frame, were launched from shore and made their way out to the ship. There were three women and nine men in the boats. One of the men, wearing "a cloak of reddish gray fur," was standing in the bow and Burroughs observed that "he had a thin black beard and regular clear-cut features and looked as one fancies an old Roman of his age might have looked." Burroughs would also surmise that the boats had come out through a combination of curiosity and the hope of gifts of tobacco and whiskey: "The tobacco was freely showered upon them by Mr. Harriman, and was as eagerly seized, but the whiskey was not forthcoming."[4]

The *Elder's* own boats were soon lowered, and the party quickly made its way to shore. While they had encountered and mixed with Tlingits and Aleuts in the settled towns and villages of Alaska during the past six weeks, and had come ashore to isolated fishing encampments in places like Yakutat Bay and Prince William Sound, this was the first truly permanent indigenous village of any size, populated only by Native people, that they had visited. Grinnell estimated the village population as perhaps twenty-five or thirty people: comprised of eight or ten men, roughly as many women, and some children. As to the men, he would note that they all "had scanty beards and mustaches, and all had the crown of the head shaved, the hair being cut short in a tonsure all about," while "The women are very short. One by whom I stood came about up to my chest." Observing that on the whole "the people seem well-formed and strong," Grinnell also recorded that "all were dressed in reindeer skin clothing; the men in parkas or shirts, usually with collars of bear fur ... the men wear tightly-fitting knee breeches and leggings; the women very large baggy knickerbockers."[5]

Wandering about onshore and inspecting the village, the party bought sealskin

Eskimos in Umiaks alongside the *Elder*, Plover Bay, Siberia. Photograph by C. Hart Merriam. University of Washington Libraries, Special Collections [NA 2107].

boots, ivory hooks, and assorted items from the villagers, who preferred payment in knives, tools, tobacco, or other useful articles, rather than silver dollars. "They were not shy of our cameras," Burroughs found, "and freely admitted us to the greasy and smoky interiors of their dwellings. As the Eskimos stood regarding us they would draw their hands into their sleeves, after the manner of children on a cold morning."[6] There is no record, of course, of how the Eskimos viewed this group of visitors. They were not unused to whalers stopping by—Burroughs would note that some of the villagers showed a strain of white or European blood, and others bore the scars of chronic syphilis—but they probably had had little chance to observe anything like the Harriman women in their Victorian dresses, coats, boots, and hats. And the village dogs were clearly nonplussed: "As we came in one end of the encampment most of the dogs went out at the other end. They had never seen such looking creatures, and they fled off toward the mountain, where they sat down and howled their mournful protest."[7]

To Grinnell, the surroundings showed that the village had existed for a long time: "The moldering bones of many whales lay about it ... there were old pits surrounded by whale skulls and other bones, in which blubber is stored until it can be tried out. These were practically refrigerators, though it is doubtful how far refrigerators are needed here." He would also relate to his *Forest & Stream* readers that "the Eskimos say that they have lived here for a long time, but that their fathers came from the American side a great many years ago."[8] And Burroughs would find, in wandering a little further down the sand spit, "the ruins of an older or earlier village, the

Village, Plover Bay, Siberia. Photograph by Edward S. Curtis. Library of Congress.

foundations of whale bones partly overgrown by the turf."[9] Also at some greater distance was a burial ground, though of a sort that the members of the Harriman Alaska Expedition were not familiar with.

> About a mile from the village, under the high bluff which seems too steep to be climbed by man, is the village burying ground. Soon after dissolution the dead are carried to the gravelly beach at the foot of this bluff, where, dressed in their ordinary clothing, they are laid on the ground and left. The dogs of the village soon devour them, all except the skulls, which roll about until destroyed by the weather.[10]

Muir would marvel that in spite of the hardscrabble existence, Plover Bay's inhabitants "make a living in this seemingly desolate land of frost and barren stone."[11] And Burroughs would find beauty in the barren surroundings, coming across blooming yellow poppies, "a large patch of ground covered with a small low pink primrose," and "a low forget-me-not, scarcely an inch high, of deep ultramarine blue—the deepest, most intense blue I ever saw in a wild flower."[12]

Mrs. Harriman's wish to set foot on Russian and Siberian soil had been granted, and the bone-chilling winds of evening were upon the party as they clambered aboard the *Elder*. They were soon underway, headed for Indian Point, a larger village to the north. On arriving they found heavy surf breaking on the beach, making any landing impossible—they sailed instead for Port Clarence on the Alaskan shore. The evening, however, was not lost. They were nearing the land of the midnight sun: an orange and purple sunset at 10:45 p.m. was followed by the sun rising again at 1:45 a.m. On deck in the unending twilight, "it was possible to read ordinary type all through the night, and several members of the party sat up reading and writing letters at the darkest hours."[13]

[handwritten: farthest pt. reached by expd'n.]

Port Clarence, just south of Alaska's Cape Prince of Wales, was the northernmost point reached by the Harriman Expedition. Arriving at midday on the 12th, the *Elder* dropped anchor behind the ten-mile long, sickle-shaped sand spit that curved out from the southern headland, terminating in Point Spencer. Ten whaling vessels, many belonging to Captain Omar Humphrey's Pacific Steam Whaling Company, were anchored in the huge basin behind the spit: outfitting, taking on coal, and generally making ready to enter the Arctic Ocean. The presence of these ships and the possibility of trade and barter with the whalers had drawn hundreds of Eskimos to the sand bar, with their camp stretching along the beach for over a mile.[14] Many of those campers soon took to their canoes, racing out to the *Elder*.

There were about fifteen walrus and sealskin canoes, filled with men, women, children, dogs, and provisions. According to a count "by the mathematician of the ship," more than 175 persons were soon alongside.[15] In Muir's view they were "a merry gypsy crowd," soon involved in "lively trading at big competitive prices: $3 for a pair of walrus tusks, 4 for deer hides, 2 for boots, 1 for a bit of carved ivory."[16] It was an animated and picturesque scene, drawing the attention of the cameras of Curtis and Inverarity, as well as the amateur photographers on board. As to these Inuit Eskimos, Burroughs concluded that "in dress they presented a much more trim and shapely appearance than the people we had just left in Siberia, though much the same in other respects."[17] Grinnell would ascertain that, drawn by the whalers, some of the Eskimos

[handwritten: meet up w/ whalers & trading Inuit]

Members of the Expedition bartering with the Eskimos, Plover Bay, Siberia—"a doubtful bargain." Expedition members left to right: Dr. George F. Nelson, Captain Peter Doran, Dr. Lewis Rutherford Morris, Daniel G. Elliot. Photograph by Edward S. Curtis. University of Washington Libraries, Special Collections [NA 2116].

had come from Cape Prince of Wales, others from Cape Nome, and still others from the St. Michael area.[18]

While the Inuits traded from their boats, a half dozen of the whaling ship captains came on board the *Elder*, impressing Burroughs as "large, powerful, resolute looking men, quite equal, one would say, to the task before them."[19] They visited for a time in the Captain's cabin, and advised Doran to procure potable water from a stream that ran into the bay something over a dozen miles to the south. After lunch, Merriam, Grinnell, and Keeler went onshore at the spit to visit among the Eskimos in their village, while a second group of Harriman, Morris, Devereaux, Curtis, and others took one of the launches and went on a tour of the whaling fleet, returning some of the captains to their ships. In the meantime, the *Elder* weighed anchor and with the rest of the party headed for the recommended watering source.

In the Eskimo encampment, Merriam, Grinnell, and Keeler roamed about, inspecting implements and tools, eying the profusion of wolf-like but largely good-natured dogs, noting the construction of the village huts or "topeks," and examining baskets and carved figures. Grinnell, true to his concern for and study of indigenous and native peoples, had his eye caught by two Eskimo men who were each "wearing a wolf or dog tail hanging down" from a belt behind them. He was reminded of a story dating back nearly two hundred years when the Russian explorers coming to the Chukchi Peninsula were told that "beyond the sea, to the east, there was a great land inhabited by people who had tusks growing put of their cheeks, and had tails like

Eskimo children dressed in hair seal or reindeer skin parkas, Port Clarence, Alaska. Photograph by Edward S. Curtis. University of Washington Libraries, Special Collections [NA 2120].

dogs." Grinnell had seen an old man at Plover Bay with labrets in his cheeks, recalled that the Eskimos there had spoken of "their fathers" coming from the American side "many years ago," and concluded that the pieces of the old Russian story and his current observations fit together.[20]

The *Elder* proceeded to the mouth of the stream recommended by the whaling captains. While the ship took on water, Burroughs, Muir, and a number of others including Mrs. Harriman, the Big Four, and the smaller children, went ashore to explore the perpetually frozen tundra. Fascinated by the novelty, Burroughs would recount, "How eagerly we set foot upon it; how quickly we dispersed in all directions; lured on by the strangeness." The ground proved wet and boggy in places, but the party scattered in the usual search for wildflowers, birds and insects.[21] Fisher and Fuertes went up the stream, and in the course of a couple of hours saw sixteen different birds including Lapland Longspurs, Golden Plovers, Sandpipers, and three different types of sparrows. Fuertes described their luck in making a special catch:

> Dr. F. and I, while separated by quite a distance, saw at the same time a long tailed Jaeger, sitting on a moss tuft way off on a distant hill; and unbeknownst to it and to us, he became the apex of a triangle, where F. & I were doomed to meet. Our sneak became interesting as we neared each other, & became aware of our position. The bird however, relieved us of our responsibility, and let us both out in a sportsmanlike manner by catching sight of me

first, and rising with a scream which I took for alarm at first, but when he repeated it came squealing straight at me, I saw that it was defiance, and there was nothing to do but wait for him to get the right distance and shoot in self-defense.[22]

The afternoon wore on and at about half-past six in the early evening, and back at the Eskimo encampment on the spit, Harriman showed-up with the launch to pick up Merriam, Grinnell, and Keeler and take them back to the steamer. That proved to be an adventure. The *Elder* was some fourteen miles away, and the supply of gasoline aboard the launch was running low.

> Meanwhile the wind had increased to a gale, driving the water in such big waves that to lose headway meant the capsizing of the launch and, doubtless, the loss of all on board. But luck was in our favor. The gasoline held out and Mr. Harriman was at the wheel. On coming alongside, the sea was so high that we would have been dashed to pieces against the vessel had we attempted to run in close. By means of pike-poles we were kept from striking, and with the aid of a rope-ladder and the out-stretched hands of the sailors most of us scrambled on board.[23]

One of those who did not scramble on board was Harriman: with the launch bobbing in the water he learned that a number of Expedition members—including some of his family—were still ashore, out on the tundra near the watering place. He took on a new supply of gasoline from the *Elder* and struck out again.

As to that party, the shore landing earlier in the day had been difficult, and since that time conditions had progressively worsened. Getting back into the rowboats that had brought them to shore was a trial. While some of the Big Four hiked up their long skirts and splashed through the knee-deep water to the boats, others of the ladies and children had to be carried through the surf: creating, all in all and according to Muir, "a sight to see, demolishment of dignity and neat propriety."[24] Rowing against the wind and heavy waves was difficult, but Harriman soon appeared with the launch and towed the rowboats to the ship—where they encountered the same boarding problems Merriam's group had faced, all finally climbing up the rope-ladder despite the instability of the small boats in the churning waters. Merriam would put a simple finis to the day, and to Harriman's labors, in noting that "it was nine in the evening when he returned with the last boat-load and we had supper."[25]

═ ◆ ═

Aboard the *Elder* that night, William Healey Dall would draw on not only that day's visit to the village of the Inuit Eskimos but also his lengthy previous experience in Alaska and with these Native people, to reflect and compose a poem encapsulating much of Inuit (or "Innuit" as he spelled it) life as he knew it.

The Song of the Innuit

Oh we are the Innuit people,
Who scatter about the floe,
And watch for the puff of the breathing seal
While the whistling breezes blow.
With a silent stroke the ice is broke
And the struggling prey below,
With the crimson flood of its spouting blood,
Reddens the level snow.

Oh we are the Innuit people,
Who flock to the broken rim
Of the Arctic floe, where the walrus lies,
In the Polar twilight dim.
Far from the shore their surly roar
Rises above the whirl
Of the eager waves, as the Innuit braves
Their flying lances hurl.

use of Invit (spelled differently) to refer to specific Native ppl

Oh we are the Innuit people
Who lie in the topek warm
While the northern blast flies strong and
    fast
And fiercely roars the storm.
Recounting the ancient legends
Of fighting, hunting, and play
When our forbears came from the southland
To the glorious Arctic day.

There is one sits by in silence
With terror in her eyes;
For she hears in dreams the piteous screams
Of her cast-out babe that dies.
Dies in the snow, while the keen winds blow
And the shrieking northers come,
Of the dreadful day when she starving lay
Alone in her empty home.

Oh we are the Innuit people
And we lie secure and warm
Where the ghostly folk of the Nunatak
Can never do us harm.
Under the well-stretched walrus hide
Where, at the evening meal,
The well-filled bowl cheers every soul,
Heaped up with steaming seal.

The awful folk of the Nunatak
Come down in the hail and snow;
They slash the skin of the kayak thin
To work the hunter woe.
They steal the fish from the next day's dish

And rot the walrus lines,
But they fade away with the dawning day,
As the light of summer shines.

Oh we are the Innuit people,
Of the long, bright Arctic day,
When the whalers come and the poppies
    bloom
And the ice floe shrinks away.
Afar, in the buoyant umiak
We feather our paddle blades
And laugh in the light of the sunshine bright
Where the white man's schooner trades.

Oh we are the Innuit people
Rosy and brown and gay,
And we shout as we sing, at the wrestling
    ring,
Or toss the ball in play.
In frolic chase we oft embrace
The waist of a giggling maid,
As she runs on the sand of the Arctic strand,
Where the ice-bear's bones are laid.

Oh we are the Innuit people,
Content in our northern home,
As the kayak's prow cuts the curling brow
Of the breaker's snowy foam;
Oh merry Innuit people
Of the cold, grey Arctic sea,
Where the breaching whale, the Aurora
    pale,
And the snow-white foxes be![26]

While Dall wrote contemporaneously aboard ship, tacking his handwritten poem to the Smoking Room wall, George Bird Grinnell would contemplate the future of the Native populations at a later date, after the Harriman Expedition had returned home and in light of events that those aboard the *Elder* had not been fully aware of until their return. When they left Seattle in May, they had no knowledge of the gold strikes made in Nome during the winter of 1898–1899. It was only after the ice went out in the spring of 1899, and after the Expedition had left Seattle, that ships arrived in that city with gold from the Seward Peninsula. When the party visited Port Clarence in July, and despite being only fifty miles from Nome, they were unaware of the "fame of the gold fields" that were so near.[27] By the fall of 1899, Nome had become a new boomtown, with upwards of 3,000 inhabitants. These developments, and the probable impact of other incursions by the white man, caused Grinnell—with his wealth of knowledge of Native populations and their fate in the United States—to feel that the Eskimos faced a gloomy future. "Hitherto," he wrote in early 1900, "they have been cut off from civilization, meeting only the whalers, who are few in number and are under a certain rude discipline." The rush to the gold fields, however, was bringing hordes of miners concerned only for themselves, "devoid of all feeling for others," and without any controlling law or government, who were overwhelming the Eskimo.

Concern for Inuit

White men, he had learned, were taking away Eskimo women, debauching the men with liquor, and introducing diseases the Eskimos had never previously been exposed to. "In a very short time," he sorrowfully predicted, "they will ruin and disperse the wholesome, hearty, merry people whom we saw at Port Clarence and at Plover Bay."[28]

≡ ◆ ≡

Early on the morning of Thursday the 13th, the *Elder* worked its way out of Port Clarence and for the first time turned its bow to the south, hoping to make landfall at St. Lawrence Island, which the expedition had been forced to pass when making its way north through the Bering Sea to Plover Bay. Situated some 125 miles west-southwest of Nome, and less than 40 miles from Siberia's Chukchi Peninsula, St. Lawrence is the largest island in the Bering Sea, covering close to 1,800 square miles.

As when they had previously passed the island going north, the weather in the area was again unfavorable, with stiff winds and intermittent rain. Wary but undaunted, they dropped anchor off the island's east shore near nightfall, and put off two boatloads of botanists, birders, and others, including Harriman and the Big 4. In the wind and surf, the small boats struggled: it took fifty minutes, "after a hard pull," to reach land.[29] Once ashore, and with their stay restricted to a few hours, the landing party split up into smaller groups and fanned out. Merriam, shotgun in hand, and accompanied by the Harriman sisters, Mary and Cornelia, set out in search of ducks.

Among other things, it was known that in the spring the ice floes from the north sometimes stranded polar bears on the island. So, it was not a surprise to Merriam when, as they penetrated the island in a light fog, the girls, who had been some distance ahead, came running back, gasping "Bears! Bears!" Taken to the ridge where the animals had been spotted, Merriam would record how "looking ahead over the tundra I saw two white bears in the distance." Having only his 20-gauge shotgun, loaded for shooting small birds, Merriam found some more suitable buckshot cartridges in his pockets, but thought to send the girls running back for reinforcements in the shape of hunters armed with rifles. "I set out over the tundra alone," Merriam wrote, "and walked and walked and walked for about two miles. The polar bears were down in a slough and every now and then the white back of one of them would appear above the bank." Carefully hugging the ground, Merriam could see the very top of one of the bear's heads, and was working his way "nearer and nearer when suddenly he raised his head, saw me, and gave a hoarse creaking call, whereupon his mate raised his head also. Instead of polar bears they were swans!"[30] Grinnell, while not identifying the erstwhile bear hunter by name, would relate the details of Merriam's adventure to his *Forest & Stream* readers, and add that "it was comforting to the members of the Big Game Committee to listen to the shouts of laughter which hailed the shining light of science when he returned to the ship and told his story. The only polar bears seen on the trip were those he had hunted."[31] Swans mistaken for bears

The ship's whistle called everyone back to the *Elder*, and the anchor was pulled up shortly after 8:00 p.m. The after-dinner talk was by Fuertes, who spoke on the songs of the Alaskan birds they had "met with," complete with imitations of those songs.[32]

≡ ◆ ≡

Hall and St. Matthew Islands are among the world's remotest places. Situated in the middle of the Bering Sea, 200 miles from St. Lawrence Island to the north, 230

St. Matthew Island. Photograph by A.K. Fisher. A.K. Fisher Collection, Library of Congress.

miles from the Pribilofs to the south, and some 375 miles southwest of Nome, they have never been permanently settled and have been rarely inhabited for even short periods of time. Historically, the Bering Sea winter ice pack reached and surrounded these islands and extended far beyond them. Their isolation even today is enhanced by consistently rough weather; sheer bluffs and steep precipices to the sea; capes and points of land that are bold and jagged; and rugged shorelines that make access difficult if not impossible in most places.

Though not conducive to human settlement, the treeless islands had, even in the fairly recent past, supported a significant year-round polar bear population. The naturalist Henry Wood Elliott visited St. Matthew in 1874, and estimated that over the expanse of the 32-mile-long island he and his party saw no less than 250 to 300 bears during the nine days they were there; and in 1891 a shore party from the U.S. Revenue Service cutter *Corwin* shot 16 bears.[33] For the naturalist collectors and bear hunters, St. Matthew in particular was a stop of interest.

The *Elder* reached these forbidding island outposts, made all the more so by dark skies, rolling seas, and rain showers, at 6 p.m. on Friday, the 14th. At Hall Island, a party of twenty was put ashore, and the ship then traversed the Sarichef Strait to St. Matthew, where another group was landed. The Hall Island party reached land at a beach "covered with driftwood in which were many pieces of wreckage."[34] For the "bird men," Hall Island would prove to be even better than St. Paul Island with its masses of Murres. From the ship they had seen many seabirds around the island. On arriving, they found that the cliffs were densely populated with nine or ten different species of birds. For Fuertes it was "truly the most wonderful sight I've ever seen. Thousands and thousands of birds—tame to stupidity, seated on every ledge or projection—from the size of sandpipers up to a great white gull that spreads five feet—all the time coming and going, croaking, peeping, chuckling, with constant movement of countless heads—all where you can reach over the cliff and catch the birds from the top in your hands."[35] Keeler was in this party and identified Horned Puffins, Murres, Harlequin Ducks, Fulmars, Auks, Cormorants, and various gulls.[36] Perhaps their greatest find involved specimens of Arctic Snowflakes, "so called from the beautiful white plumage of the birds. Complete collections, nests and eggs, were made of these birds, which are regarded as extremely rare, only being known to science by a few imperfect specimens."[37] *rare bird species spotted*

As the evening wore on, the collectors returned to the shore of Hall Island, where they huddled and built a driftwood fire. At eleven o'clock, seeing the approach of the *Elder*, they gathered up their collections and left the beach, "the fire of the driftwood on the shore still glowing through the mist as we rowed away."[38]

From Hall Island, the ship returned to St. Matthew to pick-up Albert Fisher, Frederick Coville, and the others who had been put ashore with only a couple of hours to explore and set traps, and soon all were enjoying a late dinner before adjourning to the Smoking Room. There, the remoteness of their location and the eeriness of the surroundings were magnified by tales of tragedy on St. Matthew almost a hundred

Frederick V. Coville and Professor William Brewer, probably on St. Matthew Island. Photograph by Edward S. Curtis. University of Washington Libraries, Special Collections [Harriman 184].

"The Two Johnnies"—John Burroughs and John Muir on St. Matthew Island. Photograph by Edward S. Curtis. University of Washington Libraries, Special Collections [Harriman, 186].

[handwritten annotation: dramatic or & tragic stories related more so than main narr.]

years earlier. Henry Elliott had recorded the story of an ill-fated party of Russians and Aleuts who had wintered on the islands in 1810–1811 to hunt polar bears; all but one of the Russians died, reportedly of scurvy, and the rest of the party barely escaped alive.[39] To the audience gathered in the dimly-lit Smoking Room in the late and lonely hours, Dall spun another version of the story, building to a conclusion in which the surviving Russian told his rescuers that his companions had ventured out into the Bering Sea on ice floes and never returned—though legend had it that cannibalism was involved, and the lone survivor had eaten his fellow hunters. Dall's audience was spellbound, and had no problem in finding the story plausible.[40]

At 4 a.m. the next morning, Fisher, Kearney, and Fuertes were up, manning a rowboat and headed to St. Matthew Island to take up the traps Fisher had set the night before. On the way to shore, Fuertes, sitting "at watch" in the bow as they moved through the fog, saw a couple of large birds, which he casually identified as Bonaparte Gulls. Fisher took a quick look and immediately disagreed: "Pot it," he said, "It's a Sabine." Fuertes dispatched the bird with a single shot from his rifle, and upon collecting it confirmed that Fisher was correct: it was a rare Sabine's gull, with white plumage, slaty-black hood, a mantle of slaty-blue, and a forked tail. It was, Fuertes concluded, "the finest bird the trip had yet produced."[41]

The early morning hunters and trap-retrievers scrambled back to the *Elder* just before the ship moved down to the south end of the island, where a large group of hunters and collectors went ashore in launches and boats, in search of plants, birds, and animals. They had a remarkably successful morning, and they returned to the ship at noon loaded with the trophies of the day. Muir, who understood and accepted the scientific purposes of the hunting but still regretted the taking of life, mournfully observed that "a fine pure-white Point Barrow gull was shot, also a snowy owl, and two young blue foxes and one old one, the mother; the pitiful things were laid out on the wet deck. Nests were robbed of their young and eggs, and the parents killed. Many little birds were left to starve."[42]

bear-hunt failures

    Burroughs, who had spent most of his time ashore collecting and recording flowers, and reveling in "nature's tapestry," eyed the display on deck and found the local foxes "a sorry apology" for the species, their drab summer appearance suggesting to him that they "might have been singed or else skinned once and this was the second growth of fur." He also noted that "the polar bears which our sportsmen had hoped for were not found." The continuing misadventures and frustrations of the bear hunters led to some Burroughsian analysis that "nothing is plainer than that one cannot go to Alaska or probably to any other country and say: 'Come, now, we will kill a bear,' and kill it, except as a rare streak of luck. It is a game at which two can play, and the bear plays his part extremely well."[43]

Muir has more modern attitudes twd — animal welfare

PART IV

Homeward Bound

THIRTEEN

Familiar Territory

[handwritten: More vivid - if flowery - prose by travelers]

"A charming night, purple and gold, with a full moon, and fish splashing silvery. Everybody sad and glad that the end of the glorious trip is near."
—John Muir

The *Elder's* Chart Room had been given over as a work room for the bird and mammal men, and with what the collectors had gathered on St. Lawrence, Hall, and St. Matthew islands it was a busy place, filled with scientists and taxidermists, as the ship headed south toward Unalaska on the afternoon of Sunday, July 16. "Dull weather," Muir wrote, not hesitating to add, "Burroughs sick."[1]

They arrived and tied-up at Dutch Harbor at 4:30 the next morning. The weather had gone from "dull" to balmy and many went ashore, finding various ways to pass the morning hours: the inveterate collectors prowling the shore and others, including Kearney and Fernow, climbing the 1800-foot "mountain" near the wharf.[2]

A primary and necessary reason for returning to Dutch Harbor was to retrieve Robert Ridgway and Edwin Starks, who had elected to stay there to pursue collecting on the island while the *Elder* had gone on to the Bering Sea and Siberia. The two men had taken up residence at the Baranof Inn: "A small hotel," Starks would note, "which for good reason I pronounced bare enough. It was, however, as comfortable as one had any right to expect in Alaska." Ridgway recorded little about the time the two spent in Unalaska. Starks, however, would write of going on collecting hikes virtually every day, and that he spent much of his time setting and taking-up traps for small mammals. They also found four University of California men "batching in an old Russian house." These four, Starks noted, were "Profs. Setchel, Jepson, and Lawson, who are botanizing, and a civil engineer name of Hunt, who apparently came for the good time." He also recorded that they had some excitement on the night of July 14 in the form of an earthquake: "The house rocked and shook for some time…. I found myself in the hall in my nightie with all the other guests similarly dressed." The house/hotel escaped serious damage, and the guests soon returned to their rooms. Throughout their stay they experienced beautiful weather—"even too warm when the sun shines, and when we are in the house it is warm enough to enjoy keeping the windows open."[3]

Another reason for the stop at Dutch Harbor was to take on water and coal. In addition, Unalaska served as a point of departure for Captain Humphrey, who left to board another ship, the *Excelsior*, that was in the harbor and would carry him to Bristol Bay.

That same morning, Joseph Stanley-Brown of the North American Commercial Company's office in Dutch Harbor accepted an invitation from Harriman to

[handwritten: idio. hyphenation]

return with the party to Seattle.[4] It seems unlikely that this invitation came about on the spur of the moment; more probably it was discussed and arrangements concluded when the *Elder* made its first, outbound stop in Dutch Harbor. Stanley-Brown had once done secretarial work for John Wesley Powell, and through that association had gone on to be private secretary to James Garfield, including—as but a twenty-three-year-old—during Garfield's Presidency. After the President's assassination in 1881, he stayed on to organize Garfield's papers and prepare them for binding. Thereafter he completed his formal education, married Garfield's daughter Mollie, and pursued a career in private business.[5] Stanley-Brown traveled with the Expedition party not just to Seattle but on to New York, where he served as Harriman's secretary for a number of years.

The ship left Dutch Harbor that afternoon, crossing through waters just outside the bay that were "black" with floating birds, which turned out to be Fulmars; at one point "they encircled the ship for a distance of 800 yards or more."[6] As they cleared the floating aviary under a graying sky, a presumably happy Burroughs would note that "for the first time, our good ship pointed eastward and toward home."[7]

The evening "talk" was by Charles Keeler, whose Fourth of July oration criticizing United States intervention in the Philippines had been found "out of place" by many. In this presentation, Keeler chose to use his subject, the coloration of Alaskan birds, to advance his interpretation or variation of Darwin's still relatively new ideas on evolution and natural selection. Again, though not politically charged like his Independence Day speech, Keeler's talk here raised some disapproving eyebrows.

Even as Keeler spoke, the *Elder*'s course that Monday evening was once again slowed by reduced visibility, and at 10:00 p.m., in the midst of an especially heavy area of fog, an uncomfortable Captain Doran dropped anchor. The ship remained in place, periodically sounding its whistle, until 3:00 a.m. on Tuesday morning, when the fog began to loosen its grip and they were able to proceed through steadily improving weather. The immediate destination was Sand Point on Popof Island, to pick up the party of ten that had been left there on July 7.

Darwinism still controversial w/conservative mbrs.

The party that had been put off at Sand Point included Palache, Ritter, Saunders, Kincaid, the hunters Kelly and Fredell, the *Elder*'s pilot, J.K. Jordan, and a cook and two of the remaining packers. Undoubtedly in recognition of the fact that after leaving Kodiak there was going to be a long interval where there was no place to post letters, Palache temporarily suspended his almost daily correspondence to Helen Markham. However, consciously or unconsciously, he expanded his daily journal entries, and those provide a wealth of information on his activities in this part of the Shumagin Islands, though he would spend much of his time separated from the other scientists.

After the party had landed, and paused for a few minutes to watch the *Elder* turn-about and head away northward, Palache, Ritter, and Saunders did a brief reconnaissance of the island and the prospects for collecting—which they quickly concluded were promising. The remainder of the party, led by Kincaid and Kelly, looked for a place to set up a base camp. They found that Sand Point was a collection of abandoned buildings, with a current permanent population consisting of but one man, who kept a store and supervised seasonal cod and salmon fisheries, though there were no canneries in the immediate area. Whether at his suggestion or otherwise, the party installed itself "in a big empty hotel erected for the Lord knows what" when Sand Point was a port of call for sealers and whalers. Later in the afternoon, Palache, Kelly, and Jordan took the launch fifteen miles down the coast to Unga, a tiny settlement located at the site of a gold mine, where they visited with the Superintendent and his wife before returning to Sand Point around midnight.[8]

The next day, a Saturday, Palache, Kelly, Fredell, and Jordan commandeered the launch to travel, in "cloudy squally weather," some thirty miles to Chicago Bay. They landed that evening, in the midst of a heavy rain, at the entrance to a little creek, where they set up "Camp Chicago" on a sheltered gravel bar. They brought with them one of the packers and a "half breed Russian" named Ivan, a hunter who they had met that morning in Sand Point and who seemed "to know the land and waters of the region well."[9]

For the next several days most of this small group hunted, with limited success, while Palache worked in the tertiary shales and sandstones near camp, finding and collecting a number of fossils. He and Fredell also found ptarmigan and a porcupine, which they killed for Merriam's collection. The creek in front of their camp proved to be alive with spawning salmon, a number of which were caught and their roe provided spectacular bait for trout: Jordan "caught them as fast as he could throw his hook until he had 99," providing the main entrée for a supper of "stewed hare, fried trout, boiled potatoes, stewed peaches and tea."[10] On Monday, Palache found a "rich haul of fossils in the cliff near camp," and then went off on what proved to be a fruitless search for Ivan, who had disappeared on Sunday. The next day, in the midst of heavy rain, Jordan and the packer departed in the launch to return to Sand Point, leaving behind Palache, Kelly, and Fredell—who had a late breakfast "and then a bully smoke in the tent," watching the rain while "Kelly told stories of his adventures as a scout in Montana in the 60 and 70'ties."[11] *v. idio. pd. spelling*

For the remainder of the week, Kelly and Fredell hunted while Palache continued his exploration for fossils and minerals. The hunters had scant success: finding many fresh bear tracks but—fitting the Expedition's hunting pattern—no bear. Kelly averred that he "had been near enough to the bear to smell him and found his feeding place but not him." Palache had greater success, both in collecting and in terms of game: he shot and skinned some ground squirrels for Merriam, and also caught 75 trout and a ten-pound salmon for the group's larder. On returning to camp on Friday, he found that Ivan had come for his boat, having had a successful hunt on his own somewhere, though not to the benefit of the party who had brought him along as a guide. The big day for Palache was Sunday, the 16th, which he spent climbing "as far as the crumbling pinnacle peaks would allow, then scrambled by dangerous ledges around the talus slopes to a snow slope that led to a notch in the ridge," where he "found the wished-for key to the geological structure of the region in the intrusive rocks filling a big area behind the peak."[12]

During these same days Ritter, Saunders, and Kincaid enjoyed significant collecting success back in the Sand Point area. Kincaid discovered several remarkable cases of mimicry, including that of stingless flies mimicking yellow-tailed bumblebees.[13] The Sand Point party also had some unexpected excitement when they had "a double earthquake shock one night," with "the first one preceded by a roaring sound."[14] This was probably the same earthquake that shook Dutch Harbor, and rousted Ridgway, Starks, and the other guests at the Baranof Inn.

In the early afternoon of Tuesday, July 18 the *Elder* arrived at Sand Point, and after picking-up the main party moved on to retrieve Palache, Kelly, and Fredell at Chicago Bay. It happened to be Palache's thirtieth birthday, and after lunch he had wandered up the stream with his fishing rod. Having caught a dozen large fish, he was headed back when he was "aroused by a call" and was surprised when he "looked up to see Merriam and Miss Mary Harriman across the stream.... Hastening back I find the tents already struck and soon everything is in the boats. Those who have come in on the launch are fooling with the salmon in the creek or shooting at the eagles on the cliff. Kelly comes in just as we are about to depart without him and Camp Chicago is at an end."[15]

On board the ship that evening—after a late dinner featuring some of Palache's freshly caught trout—Ritter, Saunders, and Kincaid took the floor in the Social Hall to report on the insects, plants, and marine life they had collected.[16] Kincaid stole the show, with Dellenbaugh noting that "Kincaid is thoroughly absorbed in his work and his talk was specially interesting."[17] Muir was even more, and uncharacteristically, effusive: "Young Kincaid's address on insects far the best of the 3, and was one of the very best of the trip. He has genius and will be heard of later, I hope."[18] While Palache did not share the podium that night, the young geologist was proud to note in his journal that he had accomplished a good bit of geologic work and "Dall declares my fossils to belong to a period not before found in Alaska, so I have a good feeling."[19]

Fuertes, like Palache, was feeling good about his artistic accomplishments and satisfaction with the overall experience of the Expedition. In a letter he wrote that evening, he confided that "I begin to feel as if my face were turned homeward, and it's not a bad feeling, though I've had good luck and a bully time. I've got ninety-five skins put up, and a portfolio of studies, and suppose that about a dozen more of each will about conclude this trip's work."[20]

Teddy Roosevelt term

══ ◆ ══

From Sand Point the steamer headed for a return visit to Kodiak Island to replenish its supplies of water and coal. It was a long run, of some 250 miles, interrupted by a late afternoon stop at Sturgeon Bay, on the northwest corner of the island. Harriman had the last vestiges of interest in pursuing the bears that made the island home, and the hunters were put out to scout—they reported a few bear and reindeer tracks but nothing fresh and no glimpses of the animals. Those who had gone on shore with the scouts scattered in their usual collecting pursuits, before gathering and building "a grand driftwood fire" while waiting for the boat to take them off.[21]

After dinner that night, there was "a general meeting" to discuss the long-rumored, proposed publication that would memorialize and provide the results of the trip. The consensus seemed to be in favor of a two-volume work, one providing a narrative and the other the scientific results—though the latter would first be published in bulletins by the Washington Academy of Sciences.[22] A grouchy John Muir—perhaps affected by a headache he had been nursing all day, and perhaps just being John Muir—would record the discussion as "a long talk on book-making, with much twaddle about a grand scientific monument of this trip," and "much ado about little.... Game-hunting, the chief aim, has been unsuccessful. The rest of the story would be mere reconnaissance."[23] He would prove to be, as one historian has noted, "spectacularly wrong."[24]

John Muir dissatisfied w/ trip?

In connection with the books, Harriman asked that prior to publication, and so that advance publicity wouldn't adversely affect those two volumes, no articles about the Expedition be written without his approval. It seems likely that in addition to protecting the official account, he was also mindful of being obliged to the Washington Academy of Sciences, who had endorsed the Expedition, for some publication priority. As a practical matter, time would show that independent publication and writing opportunities by members of the Expedition were little affected, and as the two-volume publication grew to thirteen volumes, many of them would also write significant chapters for those books. *Harriman asserting some control over expdtn metic*

They reached Kodiak Village early in the morning on Thursday the 20th. Their time there revolved around two events. *charming moment, but not milked*

It happened to be Cornelia Harriman's fifteenth birthday and, apparently with a bug in the ear from Mrs. Harriman, as distinguished and renowned a group of flower gatherers as any fifteen year old has ever had was soon out in the early sunshine, acquiring "great bunches" of the wild briar roses that had bloomed since the Expedition's first visit almost three weeks earlier. Led by Emerson, Muir, and Palache, they returned mid-morning with armloads of flowers that were destined to decorate the tables at lunch.[25] The tables were also decorated with fifteen candles and small round cakes. In some of those cakes the baker had hidden coins, including the grand prize, a two-and-a-half-dollar gold piece; which became the property of the party's youngest member, Roland Harriman, when he bit into that cake.[26]

After lunch, some went walking about the village and nearby hills, while a larger group, guided by M.L. Washburn, went to nearby Long Island, about an hour's boat ride away, to visit the fox farm operated by Washburn's Semidi Propagating Company. Although the party had previously encountered fox-farming operations on a small scale, nothing compared to Long Island, which housed 800 to 1,000 blue foxes. In an explanation he provided to the visitors and later expanded in the Expedition publication that Harriman sponsored, Washburn noted that commercial farming had started some fifteen years previously with a small stock of twenty animals taken from St. Paul Island in the Pribilofs; that farms now existed on approximately thirty islands; and that the value of the blue fox skins ranged, depending on quality, from $5 to $50, with $20 being a fair average. He also provided an explanation of how the fox were harvested each year in rather minimal quantities, and with care to preserve a balance between breeding males and a greater number of females. And he noted that the foxes learned to recognize their keepers but were shy of strangers.[27] As to the latter point, Grinnell would relate that "we saw three adults and two puppies, bright, woolly little creatures, which were suspicious yet curious. The struggle between their fears and their inquisitiveness was amusing. While we were watching the young, which had retreated under a building, an old fox approached quite close to the party and hid behind a rock, occasionally peeping over to see what was going on."[28]

The group returned from Long Island at about 5:00 p.m. and the *Elder* was soon underway. Champagne was served at dinner in further honor of Cornelia's birthday, and after dinner Palache got his chance to talk about what he had found at Chicago Bay. Afterwards he confided to his journal that he thought he had done "fairly well, only Muir says I stopped altogether too soon."[29]

Traveling through the night, the *Elder* steamed into Cook Inlet and at 5:00 a.m. Friday put Kincaid and Ridgway off at Seldovia. Later in the morning a second party made up of Gilbert, Palache, Coville, and Dall took the steam launch and went ashore at Homer. The plan was for these parties to spend two days ashore while the *Elder* continued northward to the far reaches of the Inlet. However, after the ship had traveled some fifty miles, they turned back, "discouraged with the shortness of time, and for want of arrangements as to getting a smaller steamer for the shoals and rivers at the head of the bay."[30] They reached Homer at 7:00 p.m., surprising that party and taking them back on board. It was 1:00 a.m. Saturday morning before they were able to find Kincaid and Ridgway near Seldovia and get them back on the ship—Harriman once again manning the launch to go ashore to collect these two, who were not expecting to be picked up for two days and were sound asleep.

In transit that evening and between picking up the shore parties at Homer and Seldovia, the evening dinner and lecture on board ship took place as usual, with Dellenbaugh handling the lecture assignment. This presented those who had given talks during the earlier days of the trip a chance to band together for some role reversal. At the behest of Mrs. Harriman and "partly for information, partly to break the dead silence that settled down" when a talk finished, Dellenbaugh had frequently taken the lead in posing questions at the close of lectures. This evening, he had not launched far into his talk before he discovered that "there was a regular conspiracy to flood me with questions and they came regularly." Coville and Gannett were especially active in interrupting the speaker. "When I spoke of the wind blowing toward me," Dellenbaugh wrote, "Gannett asked if wind always blew toward me, and so it kept up." In good humor, he added "This added interest and amusement to the occasion and didn't hurt me and I did not mind it. When I got through, I realized I had run the gauntlet fairly well and we had a good deal of fun with it."[31]

After retrieving Kincaid and Ridgeway in the wee hours of Saturday morning, the *Elder* undertook a long run to Yakutat Bay. They were at sea and out of sight of land all day, with the waters quite rough in the early morning—so much so that "spray and rain" were driven in the window of the Muir-Keeler stateroom, wetting their clothing.[32] The weather and the seas had calmed down considerably by evening, when a champagne dinner celebrated Mrs. Harriman's birthday, including a heartfelt toast by the Harriman's old family friend, Dr. Morris, followed by music and speeches and "fancy dancing," concluding with Morris and the Big Four proceeding to the ship's galley and, "with much hilarity," preparing Welsh rarebit for all.[33] Many stayed up late, playing euchre in the smoking room—the card players probably hearing, as was often the case when shore activities were limited and exercise was needed by the ship's company, "the steady tramp on the hurricane deck of some who were walking back and forth, back and forth, as a matter of serious duty."[34]

⇒ ◆ ⇐

The late night activities did not discourage early risers—in fact, Swain Gifford was up at two o'clock Sunday morning, and coming on deck to find the summits of the distant St. Elias Mountains "just smitten with the rising sun, he painted till his hands were too cold to hold the brush."[35] William Brewer was also up before most, taking care to record the 7:30 a.m. temperature (it was 57° F that morning) and barometric pressure in his field journal, a task he carefully performed at that hour every day from June 2 to July 30.[36]

At about noon they steamed past Icy Cape and, with the clouds slowly lifting, coasted along the Malaspina Glacier, with the panorama of the St. Elias range coming into spectacular view off to port. Harriman and his wife were sitting on the deck on the starboard side and Merriam ran to fetch them to see "the most glorious scenery of the whole trip." Harriman was unimpressed, and apparently already "checking out" of his vacation: he waved Merriam off with "I don't care a dam [*sic*] if I never see any more scenery!"[37]

Yakutat Bay was reached in the late afternoon. The primary reason for this stop was to return Indian Jim to his family and home village. As the steamer came up the bay and within sight of the village, many boats put off from shore and were soon alongside, bringing with them baskets of "excellent" Yakutat strawberries.[38] Celebration over Jim's return mixed with trade opportunities and "for an hour there was a lively scene."[39] After a time, Indian Jim said his good-byes and the boats returned to shore—one would imagine to a late night in the village, with many crowded around to listen to the stories Jim had to tell of the month he had spent with the Expedition on its journey to the lands far to the north.

In the meantime, the *Elder* moved up the bay, intending to put a party, headed by Harriman, ashore for a last bear hunt. However, their attempts to land were thwarted by a high surf and they soon returned to the ship, "baffled and disgusted," according to Muir, who would close his journal for the day with a bit of doggerel: "No bears, no bears, O Lord! No bears shot! What have thy servants done?"[40]

Monday July 24 was clear and warm, and the *Elder* steamed all day in view of the Fairweather Range. Many spent the day on deck, some, including Palache, settling into deck chairs, others finding a comfortable observation post in one of the ship's boats. Dellenbaugh spent much of the day painting, and noted that what seemed to be the only disturbing aspect of the day was when an unexpected lurch by the ship "caused one of the ship's engineers to lose his balance and fall down a hatchway," sustaining three or four broken ribs that were tended to by Dr. Morris.[41] The "lurch" which occasioned the engineer's fall may well have resulted from an earthquake, one of many tremors—probably including the ones which the shore party at Sand Point had felt the previous week—in Southeast Alaska preliminary to a series of much more significant earthquakes later that summer.[42] As the light failed toward evening, they left the open water and began to thread the channels of the Inland Passage at Cross Sound.

After dinner that evening, and though, as Muir observed "nothing stronger than Apollinaris was served," lightheartedness took over.[43] According to Palache, "something started us to giving college yells and once the ball was set rolling we kept up a lively jig the rest of the hour. A yell was immediately invented, adopted and practiced:

"Who are we? Who are we?
We are! We are! H.A.E.!!"[44]

That did not end things. "Everyone who knew how was called upon to dance and Ritter, Burroughs, Fuertes, Coville and Fernow followed in succession."[45] Muir, as Coville put it, "did a neat double-shuffle, immediately followed by [the 63-year-old] Burroughs, who stepped forward ... and gave an admirable clog dance ... an astonishing exhibition of agility in an old man with white hair and beard."[46]

The dancing, joking, and cutting-up gave way as time for the evening talk approached. The speaker was Daniel Elliott; and, somewhat oddly, he chose to lecture on a collecting trip he had taken to Somaliland. When he concluded, and "to his astonishment," according to Muir, "he was cheered and greeted with cries of 'What's the matter with Elliott? He's all right! Who's all right?' etc."[47]

Traveling through the night as had been the custom throughout the Expedition, the party arrived in Juneau at 4:00 a.m. on Tuesday. The town that morning was quiet, Muir dryly recording "the miners all away getting gold or trying to get it, mostly for poor or vicious uses."[48] He went off into the nearby hills for exercise, while others, later in the morning, once the stores had opened, went shopping in the business district. Palache, Emerson, and Trudeau went walking up Gold Creek behind the town, and on their way back encountered and stopped to visit with Navy Lt. George Thornton Emmons, who they had first met in mid–June in Sitka.[49] At noon the ship's whistle called everyone from town and, after a stop at Douglas for coal, the *Elder* resumed its homeward course. That evening, closing his journal entry for the day, Muir showed a romantic and melancholy strain: "A charming night, purple and gold, with a full moon, and fish splashing silvery. Everybody sad and glad that the end of the glorious trip is near."[50]

ship heading back

FOURTEEN

A Village Silent as the Tomb

"The village bore the appearance of having long been abandoned. There was no evidence that people had been there for years."—George Bird Grinnell

At the time of the Harriman Alaska Expedition's first, northward-bound visit to Kodiak in early July, Frederick Dellenbaugh was one of those who joined the party Mrs. Harriman organized for an outing on nearby Wood Island. The American Commercial Company had its headquarters there, and on the Company's dock Dellenbaugh met a prospector who introduced himself as George Howe. Listening to Dellenbaugh's explanation of the purposes and travels of the Expedition, Howe told him of a "deserted Indian village full of totem poles opposite St. Mary Island," and gave him a rough sketch showing the village's location.[1] The site proved to be well to the south, near Annette Island and the village of New Metlakatla, which the party had visited the first weekend in June.

Dellenbaugh had mentioned this all to Harriman at the time, and now, in the waning days of July, as they passed through the Wrangel Narrows on their way south, the two compared Howe's sketch with the ship's charts, found what Howe had labeled "Foggy Bay," and also located a place on the chart that was marked "Cape Fox Village."[2] This proved to be at the end of a mainland peninsula, slightly southeast of Annette Island, north of Port Rupert, and in what is today Misty Fjords National Monument.

They arrived at the cape the afternoon of Wednesday, July 26, and as the ship came to anchor those on board could see a row of a dozen or more houses, fronted by a number of tall totem poles, some distance back from a low sand beach. Coming ashore, they found "the houses were only 50 or 100 feet from high water mark and all in front of them the sand was overgrown with tall rank bushes" through which the party forced its way.[3] "The village," Grinnell would tell the readers of his *Forest & Stream* magazine, "bore the appearance of having long been abandoned. There was no evidence that people had been there for years." Describing the "dense thicket of weeds and brush" that made getting from their landing place on the beach to the houses difficult, he continued that upon cutting through the brush and reaching the houses they found that "within, the scene was the same. Weeds grew up through the crevices ... thick branches of elders had made their way through holes in the walls, and were now flourishing all over."[4]

Some of the houses had decayed, while others were in comparatively better shape. "In the houses," Dellenbaugh found that "boxes and other receptacles lay about the floors, and had evidently been rifled by earlier visitors," while the Reverend

Totem Pole, deserted Tlingit Village, Cape Fox. Photograph by Edward S. Curtis. University of Washington Libraries, Special Collections [NA 2134].

Nelson wrote of finding "strong hardwood chests; shelves on walls; a few very decent looking wooden bedsteads; a few small iron stoves; painted images, masks, etc.," and that, to his disgust, "whiskey bottles were lying here and there among the rubbish."[5]

There was no question in the minds of all but that the site had not been occupied for many years. They pondered why "the village had been so completely deserted and apparently all at once, and suddenly" and speculated that "it may have been small-pox or other disease. Certainly something that had caused a panic as it seemed that the owners had never returned, though it is possible that they moved for some more rational cause."[6]

Interior roof-post totem pole representing a bear, Cape Fox village. Photograph by Edward S. Curtis. University of Washington Libraries, Special Collections [NA 2136].

Exactly why the native Tlingit had left Cape Fox Village (or Gaash, as they called it) was a question whose answer may lie in local Tlingit lore, but which was otherwise buried in the larger vacuum of any recorded history of the village. In the late twentieth century, Alaska's modern-day Cape Fox Corporation published the booklet *A Time Remembered: Cape Fox Village 1899*, which states that the earliest known written documentation of the village was in fact that provided by the Harriman Expedition, who "discovered the village to be abandoned."[7] And the speculation by members of the Expedition that smallpox may have played some role in the abandonment finds support in later-discovered evidence that the village was struck with a smallpox epidemic in approximately 1892, and that the "villagers thought they had been subject to a witchcraft spell, and they immediately left the village to protect the relatives still alive."[8]

They would ultimately establish, and relocate to, the village of Saxman, situated north of Cape Fox and about three miles south of Ketchikan. The history of the founding of Saxman, the Cape Fox Corporation publication notes, "has only been passed along by word of mouth." Apparently, sometime in the 1880s the villagers had agreed to accept a new site so that a church and school could be provided for them by the Presbyterian Church and the U.S. government. In 1886, Professor Samuel Saxman and others from the church led a party which set out by canoe to find a new location; they never returned and were presumed lost at sea. In 1894, and together with members of the Tongass Tlingit, the former Gaash villagers selected the site south of Ketchikan as a new, permanent home, and named their new village in memory of Professor Saxman.[9]

discover abandoned
native vill.

That history, brief as it is, including the very existence of Saxman Village, was unknown to the Harriman party. What they knew in July 1899 was that they had encountered a deserted village, clearly unoccupied for a long period of time, with all the visible signs of having been abandoned by its former inhabitants. Also apparently abandoned—since having not been removed by those inhabitants at the time of their original departure or in what seemed from the overgrowth and other signs to be a number of intervening years—were the eighteen or nineteen tall totem poles that fronted the houses, together with other items, large and small, scattered on the ground and in the houses, that hadn't been carried-off by those who had chanced across the site in the years after the villagers had left.

After they had been ashore for some time, the Expedition members gathered to discuss what they had found. Their diaries are replete with indications of "much discussion" and "much consideration" of the situation.[10] William Healey Dall, America's then undisputed foremost expert on Alaska, and George Bird Grinnell, an early ethnographer and anthropologist with a growing storehouse of knowledge on the Indian populations of the United States, were participants in that discussion. And among other things the Expedition members may have reflected on—and seen some parallels in—what they had learned of earlier in their travels involving the mass relocation of the Tsimshian village from "Old" Metlakatla to "New" Metlakatla on nearby Annette Island, including that in leaving their former village the Tsimshian had abandoned all the property they had accumulated there.[11]

Ultimately, as William Ritter would record, it was decided "that a portion of this material shall be taken aboard and distributed among the various institutions represented by the expedition. No promiscuous plundering is to be done."[12] The decision to remove even "a portion" of the material did not meet with universal approval. John Muir disapproved, consistent with his reaction to the taking down of a totem pole, by an "archeological doctor," that he had witnessed, and characterized as "sacrilege," in an abandoned village in 1879.[13] However, on this occasion at Cape Fox, Muir had little to say, at least in his diary, beyond noting that "in taking down a totem pole a nest of Douglas squirrels was found ... and of course made into specimens."[14]

The decision in place, collected "masks and other paraphernalia" were brought to the beach and photographed before being put on board the *Elder*, and "Curtis took a very large negative of the whole party with a totem pole background."[15] The "whole party" was not quite accurate: Curtis, of course, was not in the picture, and neither was Muir—perhaps as a sign of silent protest.

After dinner, Dellenbaugh would write, "a gang started to take down some of the totem poles and as they were 20 to 40 feet high, and three feet more in diameter at base this was no light task. There was of course seven or eight feet in the ground also."[16] There is some uncertainty about the number of totem poles that were removed; counts vary and in addition to the large poles described by Dellenbaugh, smaller "totems" found lying on the ground were "counted" by some and not by others. Nelson believed there were fourteen totem poles in all, but that it was "thought advisable to pull down only five of them, together with four smaller totems from the interiors of the houses."[17] It appears that after Nelson made his record another totem pole was added, bringing the number to ten. The work on these totem poles, the "gang" of workers being comprised of many of the ship's crew and the younger members of the scientific party, consumed the evening of the 26th and much of the

Expedition party on the beach at Cape Fox village. *Front left, seated:* **Wesley Coe, Trevor Kincaid, B.K. Emerson, Robert Ridgway (fifth, looking to right), William Ritter (black derby), Alton Saunders (bearded), unidentified man, Thomas Kearney (in cap, behind 3-year-old Roland Harriman), W. Averell Harriman (boy in white hat) on lap of G.K. Gilbert, Henry Gannett, three Harriman daughters and their guests, Mrs. E.H. Harriman on log, C. Hart Merriam (white Stetson).** *Middle row, kneeling:* **Charles Palache (holding arrow), A.K. Fisher.** *Rear, standing:* **Charles Keeler (third from left), William H. Brewer (fifth), Frederick V. Coville (tall), B.E. Fernow, Frederick S. Dellenbaugh, two unidentified women guests, George F. Nelson (chaplain), tall unidentified man, John Burroughs, Louis Agassiz Fuertes, Edward H. Harriman (behind wife), Lewis R. Morris (physician), William Trelease, George Bird Grinnell, Daniel G. Elliot, William H. Dall. John Muir was along but is not shown here, nor is the photographer E.S. Curtis. Identification of those in the picture from Alton A. Lindsey, "The Harriman Alaska Expedition of 1899, Including the Identities of Those in the Staff Picture," *Bioscience*, Vol. 28, No. 6 (June 1978). University of Washington Libraries, Special Collections [NA 2130].**

following day. In addition to their length, some of the poles weighed, in Luther Kelly's opinion, "more than a ton," yet he noted they were successfully "floated to the ship and hauled aboard."[18] One observer of this work was the young Averell Harriman, who years later would recall that while watching "he was afraid that the Indians would come back as suddenly as they had left years before, catch the intruders," and, perhaps associating in his mind images of stories Kelly had told about the American Indian wars, "slaughter all of them."[19]

The totem poles, large and small, were designated for various institutions,

Chief's painted house with totem pole, Cape Fox village. Photograph by Edward S. Curtis. University of Washington Libraries, Special Collections [NA 2132].

though as the years passed they were sometimes relocated. Two were to go to the California Academy of Sciences, two to the Field Museum in Chicago, one to the Burke Museum at the University of Washington, one to the University of Michigan (it would subsequently go to the University of Washington), two to the Peabody Museum of Archeology and Ethnology at Harvard, one to Cornell University, and at least one to the New York Zoological Society (which later donated it to the Smithsonian's Museum of the American Indian).[20] Similar distributions were made of the scattering of smaller artifacts collected from the grounds and houses of the village.

The Expedition members were not personal souvenir hunters or scavengers. Throughout their travels they had bought and traded for goods and artifacts with indigenous peoples, settlers, prospectors, and others. Their focus at Cape Fox was on institutional acquisitions, but a few items were taken for personal collections: specifically noted was Harriman taking a pair of wooden carved bears, and Merriam a "moldering" blanket that he found in a state of "fair preservation."[21]

When all was said and done, and their time at Gaash/Cape Fox Village was ended, Trevor Kincaid was moved to write a poem, *The Vanished Tribe*, grounded in the apparent cause of the village's abandonment being the introduction of smallpox into the small and quiet community. The final verse of that poem speaks to a wrenching flight from home, the villager's fear of the illness, and the scene after their departure:

The people fled with sickened hearts
To 'scape the awful doom
And left the village as it stood
As silent as the tomb.[22]

[handwritten annotation: first person plural used for auth's vc]

From a vantage point more than a century removed from the days of the Harriman party's visit to Cape Fox, and applying the American societal and cultural context and standards of *today* as to which of their actions and conduct are on the one hand understandable and justified, and on the other hand which are subject to criticism or even condemnation, one can certainly question, criticize, and fault the removal of the totem poles and other items from Cape Fox Village.

Still, in judging—if we think we must—the members of the Expedition we should consider and give due regard to the state of knowledge and the standards and practices of *their time*: the world they lived in and were a part of academically, scientifically, socially, and popularly. Perception, like beauty, lies in the eye of the beholder—and at any particular point in time the eye of the beholder is affected by the knowledge he or she possesses and by the goals, values, and a myriad of other considerations and factors that prevail in the society they are a part of at that point in time.

As was noted in the Introduction to this book, the end of the nineteenth century was a part of a second great age of discovery, which was to a degree involved in exploring unknown areas but was as much, if not more, concerned with advancing scientific and popular knowledge through such things as mapping, naming, and describing the land and its inhabitants, flora, and fauna in detail. Very importantly it involved collecting and preserving specimens for study and, in many cases, to place in the museums of natural history that were coming into their own across the country and were vehicles of public education. The turn of the century was also marked by concern, at least within a number of scientific and academic communities, that native cultures in America were fast disappearing with "the march of progress," and that preservation of the languages, traditions, beliefs, art, and artifacts of those cultures, in the face of what was generally considered to be their inevitable submersion or demise, was the best that could be done and was a responsibility of the dominant culture. The value of preserving the material culture of Native Americans for posterity was a prevalent idea in many of those communities.

In that context and historical perspective, one writer has observed that "to the Expedition participants, collecting artifacts was analogous to collecting animal specimens to bring back to scientific institutions for study."[23] In American culture of the time, this—"right" or "wrong" by today's measures—was not viewed as dishonorable, nor was it uncommon. In fact, little more than a month later, a delegation from the Seattle Chamber of Commerce visited the Tlingit village of Tongass and removed a totem pole that they believed to have been abandoned: that pole became a fixture in Seattle's Pioneer Square. And, in 1903, Alaska Governor John Brady collected about twenty totem poles from Tlingit and Haida villages, which were then shipped to St. Louis and became part of the Alaska Exhibit at the Louisiana Purchase Centennial Exposition.

It is also the case that societies and legal systems differ in how they recognize

[handwritten annotation: Considers the exp.'s taking of totem poles & other artifacts fr empty village]

property ownership, including abandoned or apparently abandoned property. For the Saanya Kwaan Tlingit who had inhabited Cape Fox Village it was simple: "abandoned property," unlike its recognition in American jurisdictions under common and statutory law, was not a concept then or now under Tlingit law, and it has been plausibly asserted that the Tlingit "never doubted that they retained ownership of their property when they left Cape Fox—under traditional Tlingit law the ownership of clan property remains with the clan, absent or not."[24] And what Harriman and company perceived as property that has been abandoned or deserted "is described by modern Tlingit historians as 'temporarily uninhabited.'"[25]

Hindsight as to what someone else should have done, particularly when considered at a later, far-removed point in time, is often 20–20. One can only speculate what course of action the members of the Harriman Expedition would have followed, at the time they were deciding what to do, had they known of Tlingit beliefs and traditional Tlingit law. Clearly, and sadly from a twenty-first-century point of view, they lacked that knowledge; though there is much in the lives and character of those in Mr. Harriman's party to support the thought that possession of that knowledge could well have led to a different course of action.

⸻ ◆ ⸻

On July 23, 2001—but three days short of the 102nd anniversary of the July morning in 1899 when the *George W. Elder* anchored off Cape Fox—another ship, the *Clipper Odyssey*, found a similar anchorage facing the same crescent-shaped beach that ran up some hundred yards from the water's low-tide line to the high-tide or wrack line. When the *Elder* arrived, the passengers on deck had a fairly clear, though brush-obstructed, view of the old village, fronted by its row of tall totem poles. For those aboard the *Clipper Odyssey*, the view was quite different: over the years a spruce forest had grown up, advanced seaward, and now "consumed the old village site that arriving boats would have easily seen a century ago."[26] As Kincaid had observed a hundred and two years earlier, the barely discernable remnants of the village behind the brush and trees lay "silent as the tomb."

The *Clipper Odyssey* boasted a cadre of scientists, artists, writers, and other scholars who were in the early days of another expedition: "The Harriman Expedition Retraced"—a journey of some thirty days, sailing from Prince Rupert, British Columbia, and ending in Nome, Alaska. Retracing a goodly portion of the route followed by Harriman and his guests, this expedition had many goals and purposes, including significant interaction with the communities along the way, analysis of many of the observations and findings of the original expedition, and, in basically all respects, looking for answers to the question "What has changed with the passage of a century?"[27]

On this morning, however, the spotlight was on the repatriation of many of the objects—including totem poles—which had left the area 102 years earlier and were being returned after residing in the custody of the Field Museum in Chicago, Cornell University, Harvard's Peabody Museum, the Smithsonian Institution's National Museum of the American Indian, and the Burke Museum of Natural History and Culture at the University of Washington. Repatriation claims had been submitted to those institutions by the Saanya Kwaan Tlingits through their village corporation, the Cape Fox Corporation, under the Native American Graves Protection and

Repatriation Act of 1990. The Harriman Expedition Retraced provided an immensely appropriate vehicle for the physical return of these sacred objects to the Tlingit.

Repatriation had many aspects. At Cape Fox, both on board the *Clipper Odyssey* and in a subsequent and important ceremony on the beach, Saanya Kwaan representatives met with the entire ship's party—and most importantly with E.H. Harriman's great-great-granddaughter, Margaret Northrop Friedman, her husband, and their four-month-old son, Ned Northrop Friedman, who had journeyed to Alaska for this purpose. The presence of Margaret and Ned, direct Harriman descendants, together with the Tlingit descendants of the last Gaash villagers, provided a necessary tie between the original Expedition and the Tlingit ancestors, and a form of potlatch for settling disputes. After the ceremony on the beach, all returned to the *Clipper Odyssey*, which made its way north to Ketchikan for offloading of the clan objects, which had now been brought on deck. From the docks, the totem poles made their way in a long procession through Ketchikan to Saxman, which had continued as the home of the Saanya Kwan Tlingits since they left Cape Fox in 1893. Additional ceremonies there included remarks by Margaret Northrop Friedman, who spoke on behalf of the Harriman family and noted "the importance of the day and of her family's happiness that the clan's property was returning home." She also presented to the Saanya Kwaan leadership a quilt that had been in the family since 1895 ... a gift of reconciliation and friendship.[28]

repatriation of "looted" artifacts

FIFTEEN

Never to Be Assembled Again

"No doubt every one of the favored happy band feels, as I do, that this was the grandest trip of his life."—John Muir

The loading of the totem poles was completed on the late afternoon of Thursday the 27th, but the *Elder* remained at anchor in order to avoid passing through the rough water of Dixon Entrance[1] during the course of a dinner-hour celebration in Harriman's honor.

The dinner featured a number of speeches, all thanking Harriman for his largesse and hospitality, with Keeler contributing a poem—"To Mr. Harriman"—in which he thanked a "man of power" who "chose to enjoy the wilds with men most keen to read in nature's book, of rock and flower, of bird and worm."[2] Harriman acknowledged the cheers, and noting that some of the speakers had advocated formation of a "club" among the Expedition participants, expressed the hope that if such a group were organized it "would take at least one dinner each year with him at his expense, either at Arden or in New York."[3]

The following morning they embarked on their final run, down the Inside Passage to Seattle. The weather was clear, with a mild breeze and early morning temperatures in the low 70s F. A good deal of their time over the next three days was spent labeling specimens, packing, writing-up field notes, and attending meetings of the various committees. Harriman named Merriam to be the chairman and editor of a new Committee on Publications, a post that Merriam accepted with "much regret as it means a large amount of additional vexatious work."[4] That committee would grow to twelve members, including Keeler, Palache, and Dellenbaugh. Gilbert also had a new position as chairman of a Committee on Photos, and he promptly distributed a carbon copy letter to all HAE members in which it was noted that "as soon as a set of prints representing the best work of each camera has been assembled it will be forwarded in rotation and pictures could be ordered from the list, to be paid for individually," and that photos taken by Curtis could be purchased directly from him.[5]

At 8:30 of the evening of Friday, June 28, the *Elder* anchored in a sheltered cove for an evening of dinner and entertainment in honor of Captain Doran. Drinks on the top deck were followed by the rendition of a Sioux war dance by Yellowstone Kelly, and a poem by Keeler dedicated to the Captain. As it grew dark, everyone adjourned to the Social Hall for more speeches, poems, and songs. "The speech of the evening," according to Palache, "was by Emerson who was quite up to his high standard."[6] Members of the crew were also involved, and Muir would note that the sailors' songs featured one crew member who had a "good voice and is a good actor."[7] Cards and resolutions were presented, and the evening program closed with the singing of "A Farewell," written for the occasion by Dorothea Draper and Mary Harriman, and sung to the tune of the then popular song "There's a Tavern in the Town."[8] Beer, cheese, crackers, and conversation ended what Palache reminisced was "Altogether the most successful and jolly evening we have had."[9]

Saturday was bright and clear, but, Palache would write, "a restless day—everybody packing or idling about, not knowing how to pass the time this last day of the trip."[10] Burroughs detected a film of smoke in the air, which increased as they moved south and neared an area of active forest fires; by the time they approached Puget Sound "this smoke had so increased that all the great mountains were hidden by it as effectually as they were by the clouds when we entered upon the voyage."[11] The smoke made for a spectacular sunset, and Palache would wistfully and perhaps romantically record the last evening on the ship, one which its passengers seemed not to want to let go.

> Glorious sunset with the reddest of suns owing to the smoky air. A school of whales sporting about, throwing their great bodies clear of the water to come down with a tremendous splash. After dark some modest fireworks on the upper deck—then whist till late—beer and crackers and again a little whist before bed at midnight. The lights of Victoria visible in the night.[12]

return to Seattle

When the party awoke Sunday morning they found they were tied to the wharf in Seattle, and dock workers were already swarming in the *Elder's* hold, beginning to deal with the stacks of crates, trunks, and boxes full of collected Native artifacts, birds, fossils, rocks, plants, insects, mammals, and mollusks, as well as the specially-crated paintings and drawings produced by the Expedition's artists. Burroughs took it all in, and some months later, reflecting on that morning and the end of the journey, would close his official "Narrative of the Expedition" with a few simple sentences.

> We had three tons of coal left in our bunkers, but of our little stock farm down below only the milch cow remained. She had been to Siberia and back and had given milk all the way. No voyagers were ever more fortunate than we. No storms, no winds, no delays or accidents to speak of, no illness. We had gone far and fared well.[13]

⇒ ◆ ⇐

But still, they were not—save for Kincaid, Starks, Curtis, and Inverarity—home. And there was some at least temporary confusion as to what was to happen next, including whether the *Elder* would go on to Portland or if it would be necessary for everyone to disembark in Seattle. With time to kill, Dellenbaugh and a number of others visited Curtis's gallery to pick up mail that was being held there, and to see some of the photographer's work.[14] Others went walking and sightseeing, and at one o'clock all met at the Hotel Butler for lunch hosted by Harriman.

By afternoon, word of their arrival was out to the Seattle press, and Muir would note, "Had to submit to interview for the *Examiner. Post-Intelligencer* got interviews from Gannett, Fernow, Merriam, Grinnell & others."[15] An article in the next day's edition of the *Post Intelligencer* covered Gannett's comments on the gradual retreat of many of the Alaskan glaciers, including, and presaging the global warming concerns of a century in the future, that the retreat "is due, he thinks, to climactic changes."[16]

global warming theorized

Late in the day, it was decided that the majority of the party would remain aboard the *Elder* and go on to Portland, while Harriman, his family group, and a few others would take the waiting special train and meet the ship in that Oregon city. Most spent Sunday night on the *Elder*, which, presumably to avoid the curious, left the dock and anchored out in Elliott Bay.

The party began to split-up on Monday morning. In addition to Kincaid, Starks, Curtis, and Inverarity, Grinnell stayed in Seattle to attend to personal business. Gilbert—aided by a railroad pass provided by Harriman—also opted to leave the party at this point and set out for western Washington, where he would spend some weeks studying the Columbia and Snake River systems. And "Seaweed" Saunders made his farewells and began preparing for a trip with Kincaid to collect marine algae on Whidbey Island, north of Seattle. The Harriman family, together with Burroughs, Devereaux, Muir, Gannett, and others, went ashore to take the special train to Portland.[17] Notably, while the rest of the Harrimans took the train, daughter Mary elected to extend the adventure, stay on board, and make the trip down the coast on the *Elder*.[18]

That trip passed uneventfully, and late on the afternoon of Tuesday, August 1 they arrived in Portland, where they were met at the dock by Harriman and many of the others who had arrived earlier on the train. For some the stay was brief: Muir, Ritter, and Keeler said their good-byes at the railroad station, and took the evening train for San Francisco. And the following morning Dall and Merriam also departed for California—Merriam noting that "it was a reluctant farewell we took of the Alaska party after the glorious voyage we have had together."[19]

The remainder of the party boarded the special train late Wednesday morning, bound for New York. The special had been augmented by the arrival of Harriman's new private car, the "Arden 1900," which was attached to the end of the train for its baptismal use by the Harriman family.[20] Harriman himself, however, was not on board; his "rest and relaxation" came to an abrupt and official end as he elected to stay in Portland for a few days on railroad business.[21]

The special rolled through Oregon, Idaho, and Utah, reaching Salt Lake City on the evening of Thursday, August 3. After attending a choral concert at the Mormon Tabernacle, the party returned to the train for a near-midnight departure. At breakfast Friday morning they found themselves delayed and sitting on a siding at Helpers, Utah. "The delay," Dellenbaugh would record, "was caused by a washout 80 miles ahead by which a freight train was wrecked and the engineer and fireman killed."[22] That delay continued throughout the day and night, and it was Saturday morning before they got underway. Upon arriving at the still chaotic and crowded scene of the wreck, the special was again required to halt, and it was nearing two o'clock that afternoon when the tracks were finally cleared, the washed-out bridge was stabilized, and they were able to proceed.

The accident finally behind them, the special proceeded cross country without further incident. Saturday night in Glenwood, Colorado, Devereux's wife and three boys met the train, and Devereaux went through the cars, bidding his farewells. Further down the line, at Grand Junction, Mrs. Harriman and her five children disembarked, "intending to remain at the hotel until Mr. Harriman can join them some days later—the private car 'Arden' being sent back to Portland to bring him."[23]

Speeds were slower as the special worked its way through the heartland, arriving in Chicago on the morning of Tuesday, August 8. Elliott and Trudeau left the train there. And Dr. Nelson, that careful recorder of all things related to the special train, duly noted that "on account of our diminishing numbers one of our sleepers—the Horatio—was left in Chicago. We now have only 3 cars—the sleeper Borachio, the dining car Gilsey, and the combination smoker, baggage and barber car Utopia."[24] The party was further diminished late that night at the brightly-lit station in Rochester, New York, where many gathered to say good-bye to the Averell family, Fernow, Coville, and Fuertes.

The end of the trip for those still on the train took place at Grand Central Station at 9:00 a.m. on Wednesday, August 9, 1899.

⇒ ◆ ⇐

The impetus or inspiration for the Harriman Alaska Expedition lay in rest and relaxation, reconnaissance of the territory, and the gathering and distribution of information and knowledge for the benefit of others. Those factors or considerations were also the primary measures of success and results, but the Expedition also created a powerful continuing bond among those who shared in what Merriam had accurately foretold would be "the event of a lifetime." In the waning days of August in Northern California and the early stages of Indian Summer in the Adirondacks, "the Two Johnnies," Muir and Burroughs, both of whom had expressed doubts and reservations about accepting Harriman's invitation, would each reflect on the lasting and personal aspects of the experience.

Muir had been skeptical and uncomfortable about accepting the largesse of a railroad mogul, as well as being concerned about somehow becoming indebted to a man he did not know and may, perhaps, have inherently distrusted because of that man's wealth and position. And, used to wandering and tramping alone, with the minimum necessities of life, he recoiled at traveling with a large party, on a confining vessel, and without total control of what he would do from day to day. He quickly overcame his distrust of Harriman and reveled in the experience of the Expedition. Much is revealed in correspondence he had with the "Big Four" in the weeks following the return to Seattle. *Muir's overall happiness*

That correspondence began when the homeward-bound train was delayed in Utah by the freight train wreck on the tracks ahead. Waiting out the long delay, Mary Harriman started what turned into a "compound" letter to Muir, each of the four girls in turn adding a few paragraphs. Mary alluded to how they all wished for "the coolness of a Muir glacier, and for your refreshing sayings," and the others added memories and their best wishes. By the time the letter circulated to Dorothea Draper it was August 6 and they were in Omaha. Having "the last whack" at the letter, she closed it, saying, "The 'big four' will always look back with pleasure on the happy times we spent with 'cold storage' and be mighty happy that he and we were members of the H.A.E." Muir's long response to the young ladies who he had grown so close to summed up his feelings, and his evaluation of the journey they had shared, as reflected in these excerpts: *Muir corresponding w/ young girls on exp.*

Dear Girls:

I received your kind compound letter from the railroad washout with great pleasure, for it showed, as I fondly thought, that no wreck, washout, or crevasse of any sort will be likely to break or wash out the memories of our grand trip, or abate the friendliness that sprung up on the Elder among the wild scenery of Alaska during these last two memorable months. No doubt every one of the favored happy band feels, as I do, that this was the grandest trip of his life. To me it was peculiarly grateful and interesting because nearly all my life I have wandered and studied alone. On the Elder, I found not only the fields I liked best to study, but a hotel, a club, and a home, together with a floating University in which I enjoyed the instruction and companionship of a lot of the best fellows imaginable....

It is not easy to stop writing under the exhilaration of such an excursion, so much pure wilderness with so much fine company. It is a pity so rare a company shall have to be broken, never to be assembled again....

Kill as few of your fellow beings as possible and pursue some branch of natural history at least far enough to see Nature's harmony. Don't forget me. God bless you. Good-bye.

Ever your friend
John Muir[25]

For his part, Burroughs had agonized over the invitation and the idea of departing from the quiet life at his Slabsides retreat in the Adirondacks: even as the train left Grand Central Station in late May, he had written of being sad and wondered whether he had made a mistake in signing-on for such a long trip. In early August he made a very different and upbeat concluding journal entry: "Returned from the Alaskan trip today," he wrote, "in much better condition in every way, in both body and mind, than when I left...."[26] And the pleasure he felt in the company he had kept for two months would be reflected a few weeks later in a letter to Albert Fisher, where he enthused "What a tie the trip furnished. What a peculiar interest we are likely always to have in each other!"[27]

That interest had been anticipated and articulated before the party scattered to the winds. Writing home when the *Elder* returned to Seattle on the last day of July, Louis Agassiz Fuertes happily reported, "The H.A.E. (termed in full Ham and Eggs) has resolved itself into the Ham and Eggs Club, with Mr. H President." The club, he continued, was "to meet in full as possible once a year in New York and as often as it wants in 2's and 3's and anywhere."[28]

And they would. Barely a month after Fuertes posted his letter, John Muir advised the Big Four that "already I have had two trips with Merriam to the Sierra Sequoias and Coast Redwoods.... A few days after I got home, Captain Doran paid me a visit, most of which was spent in a hearty review of the trip. And last week Gannett came up and spent a couple of days, during which we went over all our enjoyments, science and fun, mountain ranges, glaciers, etc."[29] At his home in Martinez, Muir would continue to host Expedition members who were traveling in northern California. The same role was filled on the East Coast by Burroughs, back to "rusticating" north of New York City at his main home of Riverby and at Slabsides, and by Merriam, at his spacious Lafayette Square home near the White House. So too, places like the Cosmos Club in the nation's capital and the Century Club in New York City continued, for years, to be gathering places for many Expedition members, who now had the memories of their lengthy voyage together to share in the quiet lounges and drawing rooms of those clubs.

One early gathering took place in late November 1899 when all the Harrimans (save for young Roland), together with Dorothea Draper, Elizabeth Averell, and Ned Trudeau, traveled to Washington for Thanksgiving at the Merriams.[30] And what was perhaps the largest "reunion," and the one most fitting of Fuertes's description of a "Ham and Eggs Club" meeting, took place in New York City on May 23, 1900—a year to the day since the special train had departed for Seattle from Grand Central Station. Nineteen Expedition members gathered for dinner at the Harriman home at 1 East 55th Street. "Matters had been so carefully arranged," Merriam would record, "that the affair was a complete surprise to Mr. H., to whom we presented a handsome punch bowl of hammered steel, with a walrus head at each end."[31]

Ham and Eggs Club gp of exp. alumnae

PART V

In the Wake of the Expedition

SIXTEEN

For the Benefit of Others

Harriman becomes famous (?) thru Exp coverage

"We saw what we had eyes to see. Our point of view was the measure of our perception and appreciation."—Grove Karl Gilbert

The Harriman Alaska Expedition may have departed from Seattle to relatively little fanfare, but its return occasioned an outpouring of attention, publicity, and praise in the nation's press.

The telegraph wires were soon carrying the initial reports from the Seattle papers, forming the basis for stories in newspapers across the country, with the Union Pacific office in Omaha apparently having a hand in being sure the details reached the press in the territory served by the railroad.[1] The coverage of the Expedition brought its leader and benefactor into the public spotlight he had long avoided. Returning to New York in August, Harriman agreed to be interviewed by the *New York Times*, which introduced him to its readers as "the New York financier who is now one of the powers in the railroad affairs of this country," and highlighted his position as President of the Chicago and Alton Railroad, as well as Chairman of the Executive Committee of the Union Pacific.[2] The reporting in the *Times* and other papers also identified many of the party's members, with the mere mention of well-known names like Muir and Burroughs helping to establish the early credibility of the Expedition in the collective mind's eye of the public.

And the anticipated results of the Expedition, the "useful information" gathered and to be distributed, as Harriman had hoped from the outset, "for the benefit of others,"[3] drew quick and uniform praise, even though those results were not yet known in any detail. The early accolades flowed from the magnitude and variety of the collections brought back on the *Elder*, the thousands of photographs of a territory so little known to the general public, the acknowledged expertise of the members of the Expedition party, and the promise of the scholarly writings which were to be generated by those men. The *New York Daily Tribune* cited the photographs, the studies of the Eskimos, and the mapping of existing glaciers and the discovery of new ones, as among the accomplishments which made the journey "an entire success."[4]

And as the members of the party returned home, they, like Harriman, were sought out for interviews that kept the Expedition in the news. As one example, Yale Professor William Brewer was interviewed by the *Boston Evening Transcript* on his return to New Haven, and was quoted extensively in describing the activities and collections of the party; in stating that he was "certain that the results to science of the expedition would be many and valuable"; and in characterizing the trip as a whole as "a great success, both socially and scientifically." The article's author termed the

Exp collection described

Harriman Expedition "in many respects the most important in recent scientific history," involving "the most unique party of students of science which this country has yet seen."[5]

The early enthusiasm of the press and the public would prove to be well-founded. In terms of tangible items for research and study, the *George W. Elder* returned with over one hundred carefully packed trunks, many devoted to containing the vast collection of animal and plant specimens accumulated on the trip. Just as to insects there were over 8,000, including 344 species previously unknown to science.[6] The collections also included thousands of shellfish, birds, small mammals, and even a few large mammal specimens. Among the "bird men," Fuertes alone returned from the journey with over one hundred bird skins and a portfolio of sketches and watercolors.[7] The collection of marine invertebrates—sponges, snails, crabs, worms, and others— was singularly impressive, reflecting hours spent by the likes of Coe, Kincaid, and Ritter, who could easily be imagined standing "in cold, shifting waters, bent over at the waist, staring down into the ebb and flow, foraging in the sand, poking around and under rocks, looking for small, spineless creatures."[8]

These vast collections could not be organized, processed, and studied by just the small cadre of scientists who had spent two months on the Expedition. Ultimately, fifty specialists and research assistants would be recruited: they and members of the Expedition party would spend nearly a decade in studying and cataloging the collections, and then writing, editing, and publishing the thirteen volumes that would eventually make-up the *Harriman Alaska Series*—a far larger project than the two-volume work that Harriman and the party had discussed the night before their return visit to Kodiak, and which Muir had characterized as "much ado about little." Hart Merriam, as editor, and chair of the Committee on Publications, would devote much of the next twelve years of his life to ensuring that the collections were placed in the right hands for study, as well as continuously monitoring and prodding that work, selecting photographs, commissioning illustrations, and directing the publication of the results— including being personally involved in details such as typography, paper, and format.

Although it would be the authoritative, encyclopedic work on the discoveries and many of the legacies of the Expedition, the *Harriman Alaska Series* had a long gestation period, and the first reports of the scientific results actually appeared under the auspices of the Washington Academy of Sciences, in recognition of its endorsement of the Expedition. Merriam, one of the Academy's founders, was especially devoted to the organization's magazine, the *Proceedings of the Washington Academy of Sciences*.[9] In March 1900, his 27-page article entitled "Description of Twenty-six New Mammals from Alaska and British North America" was the first in a series of thirty "Papers from the Harriman Alaska Expedition"—with a heavy focus on the insect, invertebrate, and plant discoveries—that ran in the *Proceedings* over a three-year period. These articles, a number penned by the likes of Ritter, Coville, and Kincaid, as well as others written by researchers working on discrete parts of the collections, were directed to an audience largely confined to the Academy's members and other subscribers.[10]

In addition, while Harriman had asked, in order to avoid adversely affecting or "scooping" the official publication when it came out (as well, perhaps, as in deference to the perceived obligation to the Washington Academy of Sciences), that members of the party not publish articles about the Expedition without his approval, that

13-vol Exp. history written over nearly a decade

approval—whether by Harriman or on his behalf by Merriam—was granted relatively freely. One of the first pieces to reach publication was an overview article by Dall that appeared in *The Nation* in August 1899, and by year's end Henry Gannett had written for both *The National Geographic Magazine* and the *Journal of the American Geographical Society*.[11] And in February 1900, Grinnell launched a fifteen-part, non-scientific "Harriman Alaska Expedition" series in his *Forest & Stream* magazine, thus reaching a wide, public reading audience. It seems that Harriman and Merriam quickly realized that with the long timelines involved in production of the *Harriman Alaska Series* (it would be two years before the first volumes appeared) articles such as those by Gannett and Dall would not only help sustain interest in the Expedition, but would assist the scientists in meeting the expectations and publishing obligations of their professions.

With all those "preliminaries," the *Harriman Alaska Series* made its debut in 1901. In his "Introduction" to Volumes I and II, Merriam noted that "the first and second volumes contain the narrative of the Expedition and a few papers on subjects believed to be of general interest," whereas "The technical matter, in the fields of geology, paleontology, zoology and botany will follow in a series of illustrated volumes."[12] Thus, the first two volumes were aimed at the general public, and upon their publication they quickly achieved a level of popularity, enhanced by the choice of topics and by the fact that the first authors to be published—Burroughs, Muir, and Grinnell in Volume I—were all well-known, with their own substantial followings.

Burroughs had been designated to write the "Narrative" history of the Expedition, and it appeared as the lead chapter or article, written in his familiar style, recording his observations and impressions, and adding anecdotes, stories, and three of the poems he composed during the journey, all, as in "To the Lapland Longspur," focusing on birds he had observed. He was diplomatic in avoiding commentary on points of difference among his fellow travelers—such as Keeler's Fourth of July speech that many had found "decidedly out of place." And he said little about the experiences and adventures of the shore parties that were sometimes out for days, simply because he was not a part of those groups and lacked first-hand knowledge. His approach was clear and conversational, appealing to many reading audiences and providing a personalized view from the perspectives of a naturalist and of a first-time Alaskan tourist.

[handwritten annotation: disagreements elided in contmp. accounts]

Muir authored a piece in Volume I on the "Pacific Coast Glaciers," describing the appearance of the major glaciers, differentiating between tidewater glaciers that discharged icebergs and others that failed to reach the sea, discussing the discoveries in Harriman Fiord, and reporting on what he had observed in terms of the recession of glaciers, particularly the Muir Glacier. The word pictures of Glacier Bay and Prince William Sound that Burroughs and Muir painted probably excited the wanderlust and interest of many would-be tourists.

George Bird Grinnell contributed the final pages of Volume I with his essay on "The Natives of the Alaska Coast Region." Grinnell described, often in detail not previously available about the Native populations, his observations on the Tsimshian and Tlingits of the Southeast, the Aleuts the party encountered in Kodiak and Unalaska, and the Eskimos of Plover Bay and Port Clarence. He was direct in pointing out the adverse influences and effects of the white man on these populations, and his fears for their future.

The Burroughs, Muir, and Grinnell pieces were heavily illustrated with full-page photographs by Curtis and others, and by sketches, many drawn by Charles Keeler's wife Louise, an accomplished artist who was hired by Merriam and who worked from photographs taken on the Expedition to produce smaller, detailed drawings that were interspersed throughout the text. It was Louise's artwork, more so than her husband's writing, that resulted in the financial return to the Keeler family that he had fretted about during the voyage.

As with the first volume, Volume II continued the theme of providing information on Alaska and the Expedition for the popular audience, beginning with a brief survey of Alaska's history written by the country's acknowledged Alaska expert, William Healey Dall. For his part, Keeler, who had worried so much about whether he would be allowed to write about the trip and, if so, what he would write about, contributed a piece, complete with illustrations by Fuertes, on "Days Among Alaska Birds." Henry Gannett authored a substantial piece on "General Geography." Giving the topic a wide interpretation, Gannett ranged across subjects from climate to population to a discussion of mineral resources, including the abundance of gold, copper, and coal, before turning to what he saw as "one of the chief assets of Alaska, if not the greatest."

> This is the scenery. There are glaciers, mountains, and fiords elsewhere, but nowhere else on earth is there such abundance and magnificence of mountain, fiord, and glacier scenery. For thousands of miles the coast is a continuous panorama.... The Alaska coast is to become the show-place of the earth, and pilgrims, not only from the United States, but from far beyond the seas, will throng in endless procession to see it. Its grandeur is more valuable than the gold or the fish or the timber, for it will never be exhausted. This value, measured by direct returns in money received from tourists, will be enormous; measured by health and pleasure it will be incalculable.
>
> There is one word of advice and caution to be given those intending to visit Alaska for pleasure, for sight-seeing. If you are old, go by all means; but if you are young, wait. The scenery of Alaska is much grander than anything else of the kind in the world, and it is not well to dull one's capacity for enjoyment by seeing the finest first.[13]

Gannett's predictions about the scenery and tourism would, of course, come true. In 1999, a hundred years after the HAE, 1.4 million visitors contributed $800 million to Alaska's economy—and three out of four of those visitors said that the main reason for their visit was to sightsee and view wildlife.[14]

Among the other essays in Volume II were one by Fernow on the "Forests of Alaska," including his prediction that the existing spruce forests were not destined to be a great source of timber and profit; an interesting exploration of "Bogoslof, Our Newest Volcano," written by Merriam; and a second Grinnell essay, this one on "The Salmon Industry," including his observations on working conditions, waste, impact on Native populations and subsistence, and what he saw as the unending and ruthless competition among the various operators and companies. Grinnell also sounded an alarm about depletion of the salmon fishery—noting that while those connected with the industry argued that the supply was inexhaustible, this was the same language that "was heard in past years with regard to the abundance of wild pigeons, or of the buffalo, or of the fur-seals of Bering Sea."[15] Looking into the future, Grinnell prophesied that "numerous as they have been and in some places still are, [salmon] are being destroyed at so wholesale a rate that before long the canning industry must cease to be profitable"—though while warning that industry about what he saw as its self-inflicted economic future, he seemed to soften the alarm by concluding that "notwithstanding the wholesale destruction which is going on, the salmon of Alaska are not in danger of actual extermination."[16]

Grove Karl Gilbert was the sole author of Volume III, *Glaciers and Glaciation*, which appeared in 1904. This was something of a transition volume: while it marked a shift in focus for the *Series* to writings which were directed more to the scientific community, it still, and to an extent because of the subject and Gilbert's approach, had appeal to the general public.

Gilbert recognized the influence of personal point of view as playing a key role in any observer's understanding and reporting on what they saw. In later writings he would relate a story of individual point of view in telling of how, in exploring and mapping unknown country, he had once been riding on a high plateau in Utah with an army officer, a veteran topographer, and a young assistant whose primary responsibility was to carry the party's instruments. The prairie they were riding on suddenly ended, and a long cliff fell away at their feet. Below them stretched an expanse of sandstone desert, "filled with cañons, buttes, and cliffs, all so bare that the brilliant colors of their rocks shown forth, which to most of us was a superior vision of beauty and grandeur as well as desolation, a scene for which we were inadequate and we stood spellbound." Their silence, Gilbert went on, was at last broken by the assistant, who exclaimed "Well, we're nicely caught!"—all he could see was an obstacle to their progress. Gilbert told this story as a parable of perception: the relation and impact of a traveler's point of view to his appreciation of what he sees. He would reason that as to each of the four men gathered on that plateau in Utah, "we saw what we had eyes to see. Our point of view was the measure of our perception and appreciation."[17] In Volume III of the *Harriman Alaska Series* he would restate this, noting that when viewing a complex phenomenon an observer's attention "is naturally directed to the peculiar features which his previous training enables him to appreciate; he sees what he has eyes to see, and the difference of eyes makes the work of independently trained observers more or less complimentary."[18]

Gilbert broke *Glaciers and Glaciation* into three chapters: "Existing Glaciers," "Pleistocene Glaciation," and "General Considerations as to Glaciers." That said, within those chapters he concentrated—though not to the exclusion of other topics—on glacial climate, glacial topography, and glacial motion. It is difficult to adequately summarize the substantial contributions to science encompassed by Gilbert's work, but a condensed version of some of his key observations, findings, and analysis in two areas is illustrative.

As to glacial climate, he believed that overall changes in the Alaskan climate were the result of changes not in air temperature but in the temperature of the ocean.[19] While significant climactic changes had occurred, Gilbert found that each glacier was uniquely affected by those changes: so that cooling or warming trends could have opposite and unexpected effects on particular glaciers, meaning that the behavior of glaciers might not be subject to a single explanation or theory. "The combination of a climactic change of a general character with local conditions of varied character, may," he reasoned, "result in local glacier variations which are not only unequal but opposite."[20] With regard to glacial motion, Gilbert deduced that the main factor was velocity, which in turn was determined mostly by gravity, but also by other factors including rock resistance and friction.[21] Gilbert also proved, as a result of experimentation, that rather than simply displacing their weight in seawater, glaciers rest on a thin cushion of water and continue to flow upon the ocean floor.[22] The sum effect of Gilbert's many observations, findings, and his clear reasoning from his particular point of view—and as presented in *Glaciers and Glaciation*—was a significant contribution to the study of glaciers and their geology.

Volume III was followed in quick succession during 1904 and 1905 by Volume IV, *Geology and Paleontology*; Volume V, *Cryptogamic Botany* (of which William Trelease served as co-editor); Volume VIII, *Insects, Part I* and Volume IX, *Insects, Part II*; Volume X, *Crustaceans*; Volume XI, *Nemerteans and Bryozoans*; Volume XII, *Enchytraeids and Tubicolous Annelids*; and Volume XIII, *Land and Fresh Water Mollusks*. At that point, things seemed to break down: over a span of nine years, 1905 to 1914, no new volume was published. Finally, in 1914, Volume XIV, *Shallow Water Star Fishes of the North Pacific Coast*, was published. Missing, not just in this listing but to the end and literally for all time, were Volumes VI and VII. In the grand publication scheme, probably devised by Merriam, these were set aside to cover and describe Alaska's mammals and were to be written by Merriam himself; who apparently just didn't get around to it, despite the considerable data he had amassed.[23]

The botanical, zoological, and biological volumes (Volumes V–XIV) contained compilations, lists, and classifications of the thousands of plants, insects, and invertebrates that comprised the Harriman Expedition's extensive collections. New species and new genera were highlighted, and the geographic distribution of all the species and genera in those collections was charted, with one primary purpose being to create a guide to the collections. The long working time on the subjects of these volumes afforded the opportunity to also include the findings and discoveries of others up to and roughly including the publication date of each volume, so that they became comprehensive, up-to-date standard reference works against which future discoveries and collections could be compared. In essence, these volumes created an unprecedented baseline picture of many of the plant and animal species that were common to Alaska's coastal regions in 1899.

= • =

Among the fruits and legacies of the Harriman Alaska Expedition, the surveying and mapping work of Henry Gannett and Grove Karl Gilbert revealed much about the rugged Alaska coastline, and resulted in important corrections and changes—and filled in many blanks—in what were the best maps of the day, some of which dated back to Captain George Vancouver's voyages along the coast. Gannett had the additional rare honor of surveying and mapping the previously unknown Harriman Fiord on Prince William Sound. The two men, at times together but often operating alone, mapped dozens of glaciers, many of which were to that point little-known, with Gilbert adopting a "documentary approach" in which he sought to map and measure as many glaciers as possible, in order to furnish future surveys with benchmarks by which to assess glacial movement.[24] That work would be invaluable for years to come, especially in terms of climate change and measuring the receding movements of glaciers in the 20th and 21st centuries.

Although the Expedition's purpose had never specifically included what we would today call anthropological or ethnological studies, among its results it did

useful if not rigorous data on Native life

create a general, if not perfect picture of Alaskan Native life at the close of the nineteenth century. That included not only Grinnell's focused writing in the *Harriman Alaska Series* and in his *Forest and Stream* articles, but also the observations of diarists such as Burroughs, Dellenbaugh, Muir, and others, as well as the party's interactions with the Native populations from Metlakatla and Sitka to Yakutat Bay and Port Clarence. They produced the first known-recording of Tlingit songs. Curtis's photographs and portraits put the faces, pursuits, and Native way of life into a focus beyond that of words. And Grinnell sounded early alarms about the less than salutary impact of western civilization on the Native populations.

In thousands of pictures—a stunning number considering both the short life of the Expedition and the photographic equipment, methods, and processes of the day—Edward Curtis created a remarkable record of the voyage. Alaska emerged in the faces of its people, and the features of the areas the Expedition visited. And Curtis was able to capture the Expedition and life on board ship in ways that helped to tell the story of the journey beyond what words could convey. The over 5,000 pictures taken by Curtis, Inverarity and others (especially the devoted amateur shutterbugs Harriman, Merriam, and Fisher) represented what was undoubtedly the then largest photographic record by any expedition to anywhere. And in the *Harriman Alaska Series* those photographs were used to great advantage, along with the paintings of the Expedition's three artists and the drawings by Louise Keeler and others, as the graphic means of bringing the story of Alaska, at least those parts that the Harriman party visited, to the mind's eye of the American audience: the first two volumes of the *Harriman Alaska Series* alone contained thirty-nine colored plates, eighty-five photogravure plates, two hundred forty drawings in the text, and five maps.

The trunks in the hold of the *George W. Elder* also contained the "treasures" that the Expedition had collected in its journey, many of which were destined to be exhibited and shared with the public as they became the basis of Alaskan natural history collections at leading institutions including the Smithsonian, Chicago's Field Museum, and the Burke Museum at the University of Washington. These included not only exhibits of flora and fauna and the items from Cape Fox Village, but other Native artifacts, art works, and everyday items, many purchased by Expedition members or received by them as gifts at various stops along the way, and which they subsequently donated to these institutions. Those collections were enhanced with the work of the taxidermists and with photographic displays. As these museum collections were opened to the public, they added to the growing trove of public knowledge about Alaska.

Additions to that trove of knowledge were also made by the members of the Harriman Expedition who found themselves invited to speak about the journey and their impressions of Alaska. Many of those occasions fell to those—among them Emerson at Amherst College, Brewer at Yale University, and Kincaid at the University of Washington—who had ties to academic institutions, and ready on-campus and community audiences. Others found opportunities through their professional associations, including Merriam, Gannett, Gilbert, Coville, and Dall who shared the stage at a Washington Academy of Sciences "Conversazione" on the Expedition in late December 1899.[25] These lectures and presentations were often accompanied by lantern slides: such as a talk by Mrs. Harriman in New York City on Christmas Eve 1899, using slides shipped to her by Merriam.[26]

All of these activities, together with the *Harriman Alaska Series* and the papers, articles, and other writings, contributed to a significant role for the Expedition in helping to bring an identity to what, even as the party was being recruited, the *New York Herald* had called a "Little Known Territory."[27]

[handwritten:] Exp. helped = • = acquaint US w/ Alaska

The influence and legacy of the Harriman Alaska Expedition would ultimately extend far beyond the considerable scientific results, the literary production, the record in the collections of artifacts and photographs, and the awakening of interest in and knowledge of Alaska.

In some cases, pieces of that legacy involved direct action related to the Alaskan territory, growing out of what the party encountered and experienced on its journey. One example involves the survival of the northern fur seals. When the Expedition landed on St. Paul Island in the Pribilofs in July 1899, Merriam was stunned to find that the population of the fur-seal rookery had diminished to less than twenty percent of what he had observed when he visited the island in 1891.[28] Clearly, the herds were being hunted, on land and sea, in excess of what the regulations allowed. Back in Washington, he tracked down the Treasury officials responsible for the Pribilofs to express his concern, beginning a campaign to stave off what seemed to be an inevitable path to extermination.

He was not alone: the outspoken and very public voice of George Bird Grinnell, who had been at Merriam's side on St. Paul Island, was soon heard. In the May 19, 1900, issue of *Forest & Stream* he penned an editorial/article on "Destruction of the Fur Seals," as part of his series on the Harriman Alaska Expedition. The reason for the decline in fur seals was, to Grinnell, traceable to the same impetus he had found with the salmon cannery operators: greed. Exclusive rights to fur harvesting on the Pribilof Islands belonged to the North American Commercial Company, which had not only exceeded its quotas but had further decimated the herds through the indiscriminate harvesting of breeding members of the seal colony. Further, significant damage had been done by unregulated Japanese, Russian, and Canadian sealers, whose pelagic or open-ocean harvesting took many young females, including pregnant and nursing mothers. Grinnell predicted extermination of the species within four years in the absence of immediate steps to limit the number and sex of animals killed. Though nature conservation was a factor to Grinnell, as it had been in his campaigns to save the buffalo, he also appealed to economic considerations; reasoning that sound policy required protecting the seals so that in the future there would be sufficient numbers to restore a sustainable fur harvest, which he asserted had been the one thing of real, measurable value in Alaska at the time of its purchase by the United States. He called on the United States and Great Britain to address the problem: squarely advising his readers that "it rests with the two great English-speaking nations of the world to say whether this herd shall increase or whether it shall be exterminated."

It would be 1912 before the campaign would pay off when the United States, Canada, Japan, and Russia signed the first international agreement to protect wildlife, a treaty imposing limits on seal hunting. In time, this might have happened without the Harriman Alaska Expedition, but its visit in July 1899 brought the matter to the attention of someone, Merriam, who not only had the previous experience to recognize what was happening to the fur seal population in the Pribilofs, but the standing and persistence to make his voice heard. And the Expedition marshaled the pen of Grinnell as an important tool in bringing public attention to the plight and victimization of the fur seals.

In other instances the legacy exerted its influence in realms far distant from Alaska, involving collaborations and achievements that drew upon the relationships and alliances formed in two months aboard the *George W. Elder.* That includes the result of the relationship which developed between E.H. Harriman and John Muir. But for the Expedition, these two would likely have never met; and Muir had initially approached his participation with doubt and suspicion. They would become lifelong friends, and Harriman would soon play an important role in Muir's battles for the wilderness in the American west, especially with regard to Yosemite National Park.

When that Park was first created in 1890, the State of California retained control of Yosemite Valley and the Mariposa Grove. Muir and the Sierra Club he led were relentless in lobbying the national government to take control of the Valley and the Grove, and to put them under federal protection as part of the National Park. Muir's famous 1903 camping trip in Yosemite with President Theodore Roosevelt resulted in the President's support, but the battle was not won until February 1905 when the legislation was passed by Congress and signed by Roosevelt. Muir promptly wrote to his good friend Robert Underwood Johnson, Editor of *Century Magazine*:

> I wish I could have seen you last night when you received my news of the Yosemite victory, which for so many years, as commanding general, you have bravely and incessantly fought for.
>
> About two years ago, public opinion, which had long been on our side, began to rise into effective action. On the way to Yosemite [in 1903] both the President and our Governor [President Theodore Roosevelt and Governor George C. Pardee] were won to our side, and since then the movement was like Yosemite avalanches. But though almost everybody was with us, so active was the opposition of those pecuniarily and politically interested, we might have failed to get the bill through the Senate but for the help of Mr. H— [Harriman] though of course, his name or his company were never in sight through all the fight. About the beginning of January I wrote to Mr. H— [Harriman]. He promptly telegraphed a favorable reply.[29]

With his known love of the outdoors, Harriman played what Muir obviously felt was a critical role in lobbying for the "completion" of Yosemite National Park. And it was not the only instance of his supporting Muir. That sort of collaborative effort among many of the members of the Harriman Alaska Expedition was to continue long after the *George W. Elder* returned to Seattle.

≡ ◆ ≡

In terms of the role of E.H. Harriman, the purposes and results of the Expedition he organized, and that Expedition's lasting impact, the naturalist, writer, and historian Robert McCracken Peck has cogently observed that we cannot know "what he hoped to achieve by inviting such an extraordinary roster of guests on his family vacation. Whatever his intent, by assembling many of the greatest scientific minds of his day for an intense period of thoughtful exchange, Harriman played a pivotal role in advancing the cause of science and conservation at a critical time in history."[30]

[handwritten note:] Harriman's overall goal still a bit mysterious

Seventeen

The Guests:
Accomplishments and Legacies

"There was a wide field as yet unworked...."—George Bird Grinnell

For some of its members, the Harriman Alaska Expedition provided a "last hurrah" of sorts to distinguished careers that begin to wind down or, in one or two cases, came to a premature halt in the early years of the twentieth century.

The Expedition's oldest member, 72-year-old William Brewer, returned to Yale, where he retired in 1903 after holding the Norton Chair in the Sheffield Scientific School for 39 years. In 1899–1900 Benjamin Emerson served as President of the Geological Society of America, and also resumed his teaching career at Amherst College, where he remained until retirement in 1917. Daniel Elliot continued as Director of Zoology at Chicago's Field Museum, remained an active member of many scientific societies, and was honored by the National Academy of Sciences when it created its prestigious Daniel Giraud Elliot Prize and Medal to recognize meritorious work in zoology and paleontology. De Alton Saunders, forever after happily carrying the "Seaweed Saunders" moniker that John Muir bestowed upon him, moved to Texas in 1901, where he served as a Farm Extension Agent and was one of the founders of the U.S. Government's Cotton Seed Breeding Station.

William Trelease returned to St. Louis and his position as Director of the Missouri Botanical Garden, remaining there until 1912 when he resigned to become head of the Department of Botany at the University of Illinois, a position he held until his retirement in 1926. Wesley Coe taught biology and comparative anatomy at Yale until assuming emeritus status in 1938; he then moved to California where he became associated with the Scripps Institution of Oceanography and continued, almost until his death in 1960, to publish articles on the biology and taxonomy of ribbon worms. Walter Devereaux continued to split his time between New York City and Glenwood Springs, Colorado, where he had previously been involved in the building of the prestigious Hotel Colorado and in starting the First National Bank of Glenwood Springs. While attending a polo match in 1905, Devereaux suffered a stroke, leading to permanent partial paralysis and ending his mining and business career.

As for most of the others, whether younger members with full careers still ahead of them or more experienced men with ongoing professional lives, the years after the Harriman Expedition featured a mixture of continuing professional accomplishments, new and unexpected directions, and capstone achievements.

C. Hart Merriam was one whose career and life found those new and unexpected directions. He returned to Washington and his full-time duties at the Biological Survey, while spending much of his spare time throughout the first decade of the new century in editing and publishing the *Harriman Alaska Series*. He also developed a great interest in California: building a second home in the redwoods of Marin County, exploring the nooks and crannies of the state, and making personal, extended contacts with many of California's small and dwindling tribes of Indians. He continued to be highly regarded for his knowledge of and interest in mammals, leading many of his friends to look for a way to have his research endowed, with the idea that he would then be free to leave the Biological Survey and write the comprehensive work on the mammals of North America. The ultimate benefactor proved to be Harriman's widow, Mary: in 1910 she established a trust administered by the Smithsonian Institution and providing Merriam with lifetime support for his research.[1] The terms of the trust were liberal, and Merriam was basically free to do as he pleased—which he did, devoting himself almost entirely to field studies of California Indians. As with the two volumes of the *Harriman Alaska Series* that he never got around to writing, mammals were neglected, except for a long-term study of American brown and grizzly bears, begun many years before and which at the time of completion encompassed over 1,800 specimens. He passed away in California in 1942, at age 87.

Of all the members of the Harriman Alaska Expedition, the name of John Muir rings the loudest in general public recognition more than a century later. Politically and environmentally active in preserving Yosemite, Mt. Shasta, and Kings Canyon among other places, he also had a taste of defeat in the controversy over damming California's Hetch Hetchy Valley to supply water and power to the Bay Area. His life and career were marked by the influence he exerted on the likes of Presidents Theodore Roosevelt and William Howard Taft, and in the awareness of nature and the environment, as well as the value of national parks, that he fostered in generations of Americans. Although John Burroughs had teasingly decried the extent or quantity of Muir's writings, during his lifetime he published over 300 articles and 12 books. Many of these appeared after the Expedition, including, in 1901, *Our National Parks*, perhaps the seminal American preservationist essay, and, later, *Travels in Alaska* and *The Cruise of the Corwin*, books dealing with his Alaskan trips prior to the Harriman Expedition. In the summer of 1908, he joined the Harriman family at their lodge on Klamath Lake in Southern Oregon. There, under Harriman's prodding and with the services of the financier's private secretary, Muir undertook to dictate an outline of his life and the beginnings of his memoirs. He found working with a stenographer "rather awkward at first, but in a couple of months a sort of foundation for more than one volume was laid."[2] That would include so much of Muir's autobiography, encompassing the story of his childhood and youth, that he had written before he died. He served as the Sierra Club's first president for 22 years, until his death in December 1914. In a special *Sierra Club Bulletin* "John Muir Memorial" edition, Robert Underwood Johnson, himself an influential environmentalist and the Editor of *Century Magazine*, would write that Muir's "countrymen owe him gratitude as the pioneer of our national parks.... To this many persons and organizations contributed, but Muir's writings and enthusiasm were the chief forces that inspired the movement. All the other torches were lighted from his."[3]

In the Harriman Expedition, Grove Karl Gilbert found a diversion and some solace after the death of his wife in March 1899, and after returning to Washington

[handwritten margin note: Muir voca'd w/ Harrimans]

he found an anchor in taking lodging with the Merriams—initially for a short stay but eventually as a permanent guest, boarding with them, for the remainder of his life, in a suite of upstairs rooms during the six months or so of each year when he was in Washington.[4] The rest of the year was typically spent in the West, particularly in California, where he continued his brilliant career of geological fieldwork and groundbreaking writings that were to serve as standards in the field, in many cases to this day. In 1904, he stepped in as President of the National Geographic Society when the then President resigned. He would later become the only person who was both a founder of the Society and its President to also receive the Society's Hubbard Medal, its highest award for geographic achievement. Gilbert was in Berkeley in 1906 at the time of the great San Francisco earthquake and immediately devoted himself to studying the geological phenomena, particularly the horizontal displacements along the trace of the fault on which the earthquake originated. Appointed to serve on both a special U.S. Geological Survey team and the California Earthquake Commission, he published his observations in 1907, including photographs of the San Andreas Fault that became staples in geology texts for decades. In his report, and in urging studies regarding the safer construction of buildings and, in essence, the need to face up to the geological facts and make preparations for an inevitable and similar future event, he observed that "the destiny of San Francisco depends on the capacity and security of its harbor, on the wealth of the country behind it, and on its geographic relation to the commerce of the Pacific. Whatever the earthquake danger may be, it is a thing to be dealt with on the ground by skillful engineering, not avoided by flight, and the proper basis for all protective measures is the fullest possible information as to the extent and character of the danger."[5]

As a result of his experiences on the Harriman Expedition, George Bird Grinnell would become a consistent voice of concern for Alaska's Native peoples, its fur seals, and the territory's salmon fishery. These were natural outgrowths of his broader, continuing interests in the environment and in the culture and welfare of Native Americans, especially the Blackfeet and Cheyenne Indians of northwestern Montana. For over thirty years he made at least annual, extended visits to their reservations, acquiring an unequaled wealth of first-hand knowledge about those tribes. Among other things he became determined to tell the story of the Cheyennes from their perspective and point of view: resulting, after years of experience and research, in his publication of two massive and sensitive works, *The Fighting Cheyennes* and the two-volume *The Cheyenne Indians: Their History and Ways of Life*—thorough and unprecedented studies of an American Indian tribe. The time he spent exploring in Montana also fostered a renewed vision of preservation, specifically built around a national park in the land he loved. Using his writings in *Forest and Stream*, lobbying by the Boone & Crockett Club, contacts and alliances with members of Congress, the influence he exerted on Theodore Roosevelt, and the support he worked to build among the citizens of Montana, he was largely responsible for the legislation which President Taft signed in 1910 creating Glacier National Park. In presenting Grinnell with the Theodore Roosevelt Distinguished Service Medal in 1925, President Calvin Coolidge recognized that role, stating that "few men have done so much as you, none has done more to preserve the vast areas of picturesque wilderness for the eyes of posterity in the simple majesty which you and your fellow pioneers first beheld them.... The Glacier National Park is peculiarly your monument."[6] That same year, Grinnell became president of the National Parks Association, another of his almost innumerable leadership roles in the American conservation movement in the late nineteenth and early twentieth centuries. Upon his death in 1938 at the age of 88, the *New York Times* obituary reflected the thinking of many in calling Grinnell "the father of American conservation."[7]

For Edward Curtis, the Harriman Alaska Expedition would be the launching point for what from the outset was destined to be the most comprehensive photographic project in American history, but which quickly evolved beyond even that into one of the most far-ranging publications ever undertaken and accomplished by, essentially, one man. At the time of the Expedition, Curtis had already achieved recognition for his photographs of Indians in the Puget Sound area. On board the *Elder* he was often found in conversation with Grinnell, who had spent twenty summer seasons with Montana's Blackfeet and Cheyenne tribes. As the ship made its way back to Seattle in July 1899, Grinnell invited Curtis to join him the next summer to witness the Sun Dance ceremony in Montana. There, as they mingled with thousands of Indians, watching what would be one of the last performances of this ceremony, Grinnell advised Curtis to "take a good look. We're not going to see this kind of thing much longer. It already belongs to the past."[8] Later, Grinnell would record that as Curtis took pictures that summer, "the idea dawned on him that there was a wide field as yet unworked; here was a great country in which still live hundreds of tribes and remnants of tribes, some of which still retain many of their primitive customs and their ancient beliefs. Would it not be a worthy work from the points of view of art and science and history, to represent them all by photography?"[9] Ten days after returning from Montana, Curtis was in Arizona, hard at work among the Hopi Indians, as the first step in a comprehensive plan to complete a photographic record of the American Indian west of the Mississippi; a project driven by the urgency of making that record before those peoples followed so many of the eastern tribes who had either disappeared or been so assimilated into the white man's culture that their unique identity was lost. Above all else, Curtis was committed that "none of these pictures would admit anything that betokened civilization.... These pictures were to be transcriptions for future generations that they might behold the Indian as nearly lifelike as possible as he moved about before he ever saw a paleface or knew there was anything human or in nature other than what he himself had seen."[10]

For the next thirty years, Curtis devoted his life to the project. He found support and patronage in individuals, most notably J.P. Morgan, who supplied underwriting for many project expenses under conditions that included specifying that the work would involve not just pictures but text, which Morgan insisted be written by Curtis himself. Curtis further expanded the project to capture the language and music of the Indians through the use of a wax cylinder recorder, similar to that used by Harriman in recording the Tlingits in Sitka in 1899. During the course of the project, Curtis took well over 40,000 pictures (most on glass plates) covering 80 tribes from the Mexican border to Alaska; recorded 10,000 songs; wrote vocabularies and pronunciation guides for 75 languages; and recorded oral histories and stories. The publication project was enhanced by Morgan's further insistence on the best leather binding, hand-set letter press text, and the highest quality imported papers available. When completed in 1930, Curtis's *The North American Indian* was a twenty-volume set, with each book involving approximately seventy-five original photogravures and two hundred pages of text. Each volume was accompanied by a bound portfolio containing an average of thirty-six oversize gravures.[11] The project came at a high personal cost: Morgan's underwriting paid only actual project expenses and no salary for Curtis, who had to find other ways and means to make ends meet; his health suffered off and on throughout the work; and by 1910 his marriage was broken, and in the divorce proceedings he lost his house and portrait studio in Seattle, including all of the pictures in inventory in the studio. Despite a list of subscribers (at under $4,000 for the entire set) that included academic institutions and individuals such as Theodore Roosevelt (who wrote the Introduction to Volume 1), Andrew Carnegie, Alexander Graham Bell, and King George of England, the publication was not of any financial benefit to Curtis—though some eighty years later, a single set sold at auction for just shy of $2.9 million.[12] Serendipitously, Curtis's last research trip, for the material on Eskimos that would appear in Volume Twenty, was to Alaska, and one of the final stops on that trip was at the town of Teller, located on the sandspit at Port Clarence that he had visited as a member of the Harriman Expedition in 1899.

Curtis spent the final decades of his life in pursuing a new passion for gold, researching and writing a book tentatively to be titled *The Lure of Gold*, and doing photographic work for others, including the movie director and producer Cecil B. DeMille. He passed away at his daughter's home in Los Angeles in October 1952 at age 83. *Curtis later worked for De Mille*

John Burroughs maintained his position as the best-known and most widely read wildlife and nature writer in America; his sentimental essays on nature commanding a large reading audience. While continuing to feel most at home in New York State cultivating table grapes at his Riverby estate and writing at his Slabsides retreat, Burroughs became a much more frequent traveler after returning from Alaska. This included a series of four-man camping trips in the Adirondacks and the Great Smoky Mountains, where his companions were Thomas Edison, Harvey Firestone, and Henry Ford; a three-month trip west in 1909 where, with John Muir and others, he visited the Petrified Forest, the Grand Canyon, and Yosemite; and a well-publicized trip to Yellowstone with Theodore Roosevelt in 1903. The Yellowstone experience and other outings with Roosevelt were memorialized in Burroughs's book *Camping and Tramping with Roosevelt*. Burroughs and Roosevelt also partnered in a campaign against the "nature fakers," which Burroughs launched with a March 1903 article in *Atlantic Monthly*, accusing named writers of distorting their experiences with nature and inventing stories to corroborate their theories of animal behavior.[13] Roosevelt would consistently back Burroughs in this campaign, beginning with a 1905 dedicatory letter or preface in the former President's book *Outdoor Pastimes of an American Hunter*, in which he congratulated Burroughs on his "warfare against the sham nature writers," and praised him for illustrating "what can be done by the lover of nature who has trained himself to keen observation, who describes accurately what is thus observed, and who, finally, possesses the additional gift of writing with charm and interest."[14]

Late in life, Burroughs took to wintering in southern California. In February of 1921 he was hospitalized there for a month, but though still weak insisted on heading back east at the end of March. He died on the train somewhere in Ohio, before he could reach his beloved Hudson Valley. The traveling bug that he acquired later in life did not diminish his essential character as a dedicated homebody: his friend and literary executor, Dr. Clara Barrus, would record that "characteristic of one of the deepest attachments of his life, the last word on the lips of John Burroughs was the word 'home'—a few minutes before the Silence—'How far are we from home?'"[15]

Among the younger members of the Expedition, Charles Palache and his ever-patient fiancée and correspondent, Helen Markham, were married in Cambridge soon after his return in the summer of 1899, and he resumed his teaching and research duties at Harvard. He would remain there, as Professor of Mineralogy, until his retirement in 1940. During his long career he earned recognition as an eminent crystallographer and mineralogist; helped develop Harvard's Mineralogical Museum into one of the leading mineral research institutions in the world, and built its mineral collection to an elevated status; was one of the organizers of the Mineralogical Society of America; and in 1936 was elected and served as president of the Geological Society of America.

Trevor Kincaid returned to the University of Washington to pick up his diploma, and immediately resumed the teaching career he had started while still an undergraduate. Concurrently, he began working toward and, in 1901, earning his Master's, at which time he became a full Professor in the Department of Biology. He later was named the first chair of the newly-created Department of Zoology. He held that position until 1937; continued teaching and researching until 1943; and remained in service to the University in various capacities until his death (at age 98) in 1970—a remarkable 75-year tenure at one academic institution. While his initial career interest was largely focused on insects, he would later be responsible for bringing Japanese oysters to Washington State and became famous as the "father of the Washington oyster industry."[16] He also established the University's marine research center and laboratory at Friday Harbor in the San Juan Islands, and later played a role in creating the University's College of Fisheries. In 1938, Kincaid became the first person to be designated by the University of Washington as "Alumnus Summa Laude Dignatus" (Alumnus Worthy of the Highest Praise), the highest honor bestowed by the University ... and he still had over 30 years of service to that institution ahead of him.

In his undergraduate years at Stanford University, Edwin Starks was a budding zoology student who traveled with Stanford President David Starr Jordan on a collecting expedition to Mazatlán, later was part of another expedition to Panama, and in 1895 participated in the first systematic dredging exploration of Puget Sound. After graduation he was working as a field assistant at the Biological Survey when Merriam tapped him to be a part of the Harriman Alaska Expedition. For Starks, with a position at the University of Washington waiting for him in the fall, the timing couldn't have been better, and on board the *Elder*, whether by design or by luck, he wound up sharing a cabin with Trevor Kincaid. At the conclusion of the Expedition, Starks remained in Seattle and began his career at the University: initially he served as a museum curator and later became an Assistant Professor in the new Department of Zoology chaired by Kincaid. In 1901, he returned to Stanford to teach and serve as Curator in Zoology. Professor Starks stayed in service to Stanford until retiring to emeritus status in 1932. During his career he became an authority in the osteology of fishes, and earned a reputation as a gifted, patient, and enthusiastic teacher.[17]

Like Starks, twenty-three-year-old Leon Cole had served as a taxidermist on the Expedition. After completing his undergraduate education at the University of Michigan in 1901, he went on to earn a Ph.D. in Zoology at Harvard, and then taught zoology at Yale. In 1910 he moved to the University of Wisconsin, where he initiated the Department of Experimental Breeding for plant and animal improvement, a forerunner of that institution's Department of Genetics. Perhaps because of his exposure to Ridgway, Fisher, Fuertes, and the other ornithologists on the *George W. Elder*, he developed a strong interest in birds and saw the possibilities of using leg bands for identification in studying bird migration, movement, and behavior. He published his first and classic article on the subject in 1901, providing a comprehensive way for following the movement of individual birds without harming or interfering with them. As the practice gained stature in the next decade, Cole became recognized as the "father" of American bird banding and, not surprisingly, served as the first president of the American Bird Banding Association. The principles which he first applied to birds would subsequently be applied throughout the world to banding and tagging other animals for study. Cole held a position as Professor of Genetics at Wisconsin from 1918 to 1947, making significant contributions in that discipline and, near the end of his career, serving as president of the Genetics Society of America.[18]

A couple of years older than Cole at the time of the Harriman Expedition, the botanist Thomas Kearney was then five years into what would be a 50-year career with the U.S. Department of Agriculture. In the early years of the twentieth century he traveled extensively in North Africa and Sicily, studying crops that grew in alkali soils in hot climates with cool nights. In Egypt, he focused on cotton, and upon returning to the United States began work with the Pima Indians in Arizona, breeding and cultivating cotton hybrids. These efforts resulted in a plant that grew well in that desert climate and soil, produced long fibers for a soft and dense cloth, and which came to be known and renowned as Pima Cotton when it was released into the market. He continued to work in Arizona, co-authoring a comprehensive work on the flowering plants and ferns of that state, until he retired from the Department of Agriculture in 1944. He concluded his career as a research associate at the California Academy of Sciences in San Francisco.

Charles Keeler was yet another member of the Harriman party who was in the early stages of his career. Reunited with his wife and young daughter, the family lived in a trend-setting house designed by the architect Bernard Maybeck on Highland Place, near the UC Berkeley campus—a neighborhood which, with the active support of the Keelers, became known for its concentration of Maybeck homes. Keeler continued his career at the California Academy of Sciences, and with his family voyaged to the South Pacific in 1900–1901. He was in the Bay Area at the time of the 1906 earthquake, and after securing the safety of his family in Berkeley, he went over to San Francisco and spent many days in relief and recovery work—later graphically describing the earthquake, the terror of the resulting fire, and his own experiences in his book *San Francisco Through Earthquake and Fire*. Keeler made a worldwide poetry reading tour in 1911–1912 and then settled in New York for a few years, where he presented poetry readings accompanied by music and dance. Returning to Berkeley in 1917, he produced theater parties for soldiers on leave from World War I and was hired as managing director of the Berkeley Chamber of Commerce, specifically working to develop the city as a literary and artistic center. A lifelong spiritual seeker, he eventually developed the idea of forming a new religion and founded the First Berkeley Cosmic Society in 1925, and in that year published a book outlining a new

Keeler later founds New Age-type group

"Cosmic Religion" based on common bonds shared by all religions. He passed away in his Berkeley studio in 1937.

Frederick Coville had joined the Department of Agriculture in 1888, and like other members of the Harriman Expedition would be a career government employee until his death in 1937. Over the course of his life he published some 170 papers and books, helped establish the Carnegie Institution's Desert Botanical Laboratory, and led the efforts that resulted in the founding of the United States National Arboretum in 1927, with Coville as its first director. Beginning in 1920 and until his death at age 70, he served as chair of the National Geographic Society's Research Committee; in his seventeen-year tenure in that position he played an influential role in deciding the areas of exploration supported by the Society.

After the Harriman Expedition returned to Seattle, William Healey Dall—*the* acknowledged authority on Alaska—journeyed to San Francisco, and somewhat improbably traveled on from there to Honolulu to accept appointment as the Honorary Curator of Mollusks at the Bernice P. Bishop Museum. He would hold that position for sixteen years, though the Smithsonian Institution would continue to be his headquarters and primary place of work until his death in 1927. In the last decades of his life he made the mollusks of Alaskan and Pacific Coast waters his particular province, writing hundreds of treatises and studies, and having his name attached to dozens of species and subspecies of mollusks.

Henry Gannett continued, until his death in 1914, to chair the Board of Geographic Names and to play an active role in many organizations. Like Merriam, Dall, and Gilbert, he had been one of the founders of the National Geographic Society and would remain active in the organization's leadership—serving as its first secretary, then treasurer, then vice-president, and finally as president from 1910 to 1914. Gannett was also an active leader of the NGS in the field, organizing Society expeditions to the West Indies, trips to the Polar Seas, and excursions to Alaska and Peru. In 1904, he was one of the founders of the American Association of Geographers.

When he received the invitation to join the Harriman Alaska Expedition, Robert Ridgway had been reluctant to leave his work as Curator of Birds at the Smithsonian, confessing that he had "little love for the North."[19] Not surprisingly, he was delighted to return to life at the Smithsonian Castle, where he was soon immersed in the major projects and works of his career. A descriptive taxonomist who used his own paintings and drawings to complement his writing, the pinnacle of Ridgway's career was reached with publication (between 1901 and 1919) of his 6,000-page, multi-volume *The Birds of North and Middle America*—for which he received the National Academy of Sciences Daniel Girard Elliot Medal, named for the same Elliot who was his companion on the Harriman Expedition.[20] He also was the author (1912) of *Color Standards and Color Nomenclature,* an expansion of his earlier book entitled *A Nomenclature of Color for Naturalists* (1886). In *Color Standards and Color Nomenclature*, Ridgway systematized, standardized, and named 1,115 colors to be used by ornithologists in describing birds. The colors were illustrated with color swatches on 53 plates, with special care taken to maintain the consistency of the reproduction of the colors throughout the book. In many cases involving fine differentiations in shading, Ridgway had to devise names for the colors. He articulated the purpose of the work as providing standardization, "so that naturalists or others who may have occasion to write or speak of colors may do so with the certainty that there need be no question as to what particular tint, shade, or degree of grayness, of any color or hue is meant."[21] Ridgway served as the Smithsonian's Curator of Birds for 43 years until passing away in 1929.

What Ridgway was to birds at the Smithsonian, Albert Fisher was as the leading ornithologist at the Biological Survey, where he stayed and worked until his retirement in 1931. In addition to the Death Valley Expedition of 1891 and the Harriman Expedition, Fisher was a member of the 1929 Pinchot South Seas Expedition, and a significant result of his collecting activities on these major expeditions was the addition of thousands of bird skins to the research collections of the National Museum. Among other accomplishments, he and Merriam played leading roles in the organized studies of bird migration and geographic distribution that evolved under the sponsorship of the American Ornithologists Union.

William Ritter resumed his career at the University of California, Berkeley, and soon became chair of the University's Zoology Department. In 1903 he traveled to San Diego, where he met the wealthy newspaper publisher Edward W. Scripps, and his sister, Ellen Browning Scripps. The three of them soon formed the Marine Biological Association of San Diego and began plans for a permanent biological laboratory and station at La Jolla. Miss Scripps eventually provided the endowment which assured the project's future, and in 1909 E.W. Scripps persuaded Ritter to relocate to La Jolla to oversee operations. In 1912, as completion of construction on the La Jolla campus (including a cottage for the Ritters) neared, E.W. Scripps and the University of California completed negotiations and Ritter was named the first scientific director of the newly-named Scripps Institution of Oceanography. He would serve in that position, leading the Scripps Institution to its early prominence and prestige, until his retirement in 1922.

Bernhard Fernow returned to Cornell University and his position as Dean of the fledgling New York State College of Forestry—only to see that program closed in 1903 when state appropriations were cut-off. He would become a consulting forester (perhaps the country's first) before returning to academia in 1907 as Professor of Forestry at Pennsylvania State University. His tenure at Penn State was fairly short: he soon left that school to become the head of the Faculty of Forestry at the University of Toronto, Canada's first university-level school devoted to forestry. The curriculums he put in place at Cornell and Toronto served as models for many of the university forestry programs that were subsequently established in the United States and Canada. While at Cornell, Fernow had started one of the predecessors of what became the *Journal of Forestry*, and he served as the publication's editor-in-chief until his death in 1923. Fernow Hall on the Cornell campus is named in his honor.

The post–Expedition careers of its three artists were in some ways tied to their varying stages of life. At 60 years of age, R. Swain Gifford's status as one of America's most talented landscape painters was assured. After returning from Alaska, he continued to be a popular teacher at the Cooper Union School in New York City until his untimely death in 1905.

The middle-aged Frederick Dellenbaugh continued his varied artistic career—his paintings sold well and were frequently used as illustrations in natural history books. In his lifetime he traveled widely from Iceland and Norway to South America and the West Indies, and throughout the American West, keeping detailed diaries and journals as he had done on the Harriman Expedition. He lectured and published extensively on Western exploration, particularly the Colorado River Basin. His most famous work was *A Canyon Voyage*, published in 1908, reconstructing John Wesley Powell's second Colorado River expedition in 1871–1873 from the diaries that Dellenbaugh and others kept on that epic journey; in 1932 the book and its author received the John Burroughs Memorial Association Medal as a distinguished work of natural history. Among other activities he served as librarian to the National Geographic Society, and in 1904 was one of the founders of the prestigious Explorer's Club and was the designer of its signature flag. Dellenbaugh passed away in 1935 at the age of 82.

[handwritten note: Dellenbaugh designed Explorers Club flag ✓]

Louis Agassiz Fuertes was twenty years younger than Dellenbaugh, and at the turn of the century was in the early stages of a career that would mark him, for nearly thirty years, as the leading bird artist in the country, in a rank shared only with John James Audubon.[22] The publication of his Harriman Expedition full-color drawings and paintings created a demand for his services: he would become the illustrator of virtually every important book of birds that was published during the rest of his life. He traveled across the United States and in many foreign countries in search of birds. One of those trips, a Chicago Field Museum Abyssinian Expedition in 1926–27 was led by Wilfred Osgood, the Merriam assistant at the U.S. Biological Survey whom the Harriman party had encountered along the railroad tracks at White Pass in 1899. It was shortly after the Abyssinian Expedition, as Fuertes was driving home to Ithaca, New York, that he was killed when his car was struck at a railroad crossing where a farmer's load of hay had concealed the oncoming train from view.[23]

In August 1899, Luther Kelly returned to Washington, D.C. By November, he had been commissioned a Captain in the 40th U.S Volunteers, and was soon traveling with his regiment to Manila for service in the Philippine-American War. His military service ended in May 1901 when, under the Islands' new civil Governor, William Howard Taft, he was sent to the Province of Surigao to serve as Provincial Treasurer, a position he held for the next two years. Upon returning to the United States in 1903, he was appointed by President Theodore Roosevelt to the post of Indian Agent at the San Carlos Agency and Reservation in Arizona. He served in that position from 1904 to 1909, his job including reconciling the various (and at times feuding) Apache tribes west of the Rio Grande River, and seeing that the Apache at San Carlos received the benefits due to them. With the approaching end of the Roosevelt administration, he relinquished his post on the reservation in early January 1909. Kelly had been a long-time member of Roosevelt's famous "tennis cabinet," and as the end of the President's term of office drew near, Kelly traveled to Washington where he and thirty-two other members of that group attended a farewell luncheon at the White House.[24] The Kellys then moved to Southwest Nevada, where he engaged in prospecting and mining, and in 1915 they bought a ranch north of Sacramento, California, where Kelly settled in as a rancher and orchardist. He passed away in December 1928 and the following spring, under the auspices of the Montana Historical Society and the Billings Commercial Club, was buried on the rim above Billings in an area known as Kelly Mountain. In 1958, Warner Brothers released the film *Yellowstone Kelly*, based on a novel of the same name written by Clay Fisher. "The strength of Fisher's novel," Kelly's biographer Jerry Keenan would write, "lay not in its particular fidelity to history—or to Kelly's life, for that matter—but in the author's ability to write an engaging novel that captured the flavor of the Montana frontier, while introducing readers to

[handwritten note: Kelly subj. of WB biopic]

an unusual figure from those distant days. The Warner Bros. film … managed to stray even further from the truth."[25]

Society doctor

Dr. Lewis Rutherfurd Morris returned to his medical practice in New York City, where his list of patients included members of most of the city's prominent families. In May 1900 he married Katherine Clark, whose father, William Clark, was a controversial U.S. Senator from Montana and one of that state's so-called "copper kings." The wedding, in New York City and with an invitation list of over 4,000, was a notable and well-publicized society event, with its share of gate-crashers and curiosity seekers: the *New York Times* reported that a squad of police was kept busy "in driving back hordes of importunate women seeking admittance to the church on various pretexts."[26] Morris would have a long and prosperous career in medicine, was an ardent hunter and wildlife enthusiast, and helped found the New York Zoological Society. He and his wife also became important philanthropists, supporting causes and projects in Oneota and Morris, New York, as well as in New York City. He passed away of a cerebral hemorrhage in 1936, at age 74.

Edward "Ned" Trudeau, Morris's assistant and "doctor to be" on the Harriman Expedition, graduated from medical school in 1900 but his career was tragically short: after a bout with acute pneumonia, he died suddenly of a "heart clot" in 1901.[27]

Captain Peter Doran continued his career on various steamships plying the waters of the Pacific Coast until July 1907, when his ship, the *Columbia*, collided with the steam schooner *San Pedro* off Shelter Cove, California. The *Columbia* sank, killing 88 people, including Captain Doran. Ironically, the *George W. Elder* arrived on the scene shortly after the disaster, assisted in transporting the survivors, and towed the damaged *San Pedro* to shore.

And as for the *Elder* itself? Immediately after the Harriman Expedition it served under charter to the U.S. government as a troop transport in the later stages of the Spanish-American War. Thereafter, the steamer returned to commercial cruising along the Pacific Coast, serving ports from Alaska to Panama, until 1919 when it was sold to a Chilean company, renamed the *American*, and converted into a motorized barge. In 1935 it was involved in a collision off the coast of Chile, and was towed to Valparaiso where, at age 61, it was dismantled.[28]

"Elder" used in Sp-Am War

Eighteen

The Harrimans:
Notoriety and Achievement

"I need my time and energy to do things."—Edward Henry Harriman

[handwritten: Harriman becomes far more famous, and ~notorious, after war]

For E.H. Harriman, the ten years following the Alaska Expedition would be the most tumultuous and contentious, as well as the last, decade of his life. These were years involving an overwhelming diversity of activities, conflicts, and accomplishments. They were also marked by a barrage of criticism, and an at least partially self-inflicted notoriety stemming from a variety of factors, including his business and investment policies; a number of bitter, well-publicized—if not always accurately—struggles that served to blacken his name and put him into the headlines as never before; and a personal disregard of that publicity as not worth countering, coupled with a lack of appreciation for what that disregard itself conveyed and fostered.

When he returned from Alaska, Harriman's attention was initially focused on the ongoing reconstruction of the Union Pacific and on expansion to the California coast from the UP's existing terminus at Ogden, Utah, where the road connected to the Central Pacific, which carried traffic to San Francisco. The Central Pacific was now part of the vast Southern Pacific system, controlled by Collis Huntington, one of the original "Big Four" (with Mark Hopkins, Charles Crocker, and Leland Stanford) who had built the Central in the 1860s. Huntington was in no mood to sell the Central, but when he passed away in the summer of 1900 the situation changed dramatically. Using the proceeds of a special $100,000,000 Union Pacific bond issue, Harriman purchased a controlling interest in the Southern Pacific from the Huntington estate and other sources. At the time, in early 1901, the Southern was perhaps the most extensive transportation system in the world: in addition to the Central Pacific and two or three wholly-owned steamship lines, it included some 9,000 miles of continuous track extending from Portland down through California to the Imperial Valley and then east to New Orleans. Harriman immediately set about improving not only the Central, so its freight-carrying capacity would match that of the Union Pacific, but in upgrading the Southern Pacific railroad to Union Pacific standards.[1]

Soon after acquiring the Southern Pacific, Harriman and the Union Pacific entered into a struggle for control of the Chicago, Burlington & Quincy Railroad: their adversaries were James J. Hill and his Great Northern Railway, and J. Pierpont Morgan, who controlled the Northern Pacific. Neither of those two railroads, each stretching to the Pacific Northwest, had an outlet in Chicago. The Burlington, however, had its eastern terminus in the Windy City, from which it ran west to Denver, competing for business in the Great Plains with the Union Pacific route through Omaha and Ogden. The Burlington was attractive to all three of the contestants because of its Chicago connection. When the Burlington's board of directors rebuffed Harriman's direct offers, he tried, unsuccessfully, to purchase enough of its stock to prevent anyone else from acquiring control. In the meantime, Hill began negotiations with the Burlington's board to buy the road outright for the joint use of the Great Northern and the Northern Pacific. On Harriman's behalf, Jacob Schiff of Kuhn, Loeb & Co. approached Hill and Morgan about acquiring a one-third interest in the purchase, but they declined. In April 1901 the Great Northern and the Northern Pacific completed their acquisition of the Burlington.

Undaunted, Harriman then decided to seize control of the Northern Pacific by buying a majority of its capital stock; in which case he would not only control that company but also the half interest it had just acquired in the Burlington. On his behalf, Kuhn Loeb quietly began acquiring Northern Pacific stock. No one suspected that the purchases were for the Union Pacific. As Kuhn Loeb continued to buy the stock, the price of Northern Pacific shares climbed, to the point that "even the Northern Pacific Company, tempted by the high prices, sold its own stock."[2] By early May, Kuhn Loeb lacked no more than 40,000 shares of Northern Pacific common stock to acquire a majority position and control of the company. At this point Morgan and Hill figured out what was happening, and Morgan's firm went into the market on May 5 under orders to acquire 150,000 shares of Northern Pacific at "any price"— which eventually drove the market price to a high of $1,000 a share.[3] The steady stream of purchases, especially as the Morgan firm sought to stop Kuhn Loeb, spurred widespread activity in shares of Northern Pacific: scores of speculators sold them "short," expecting to be able to buy them, at much lower prices, for delivery a few days later. However, when the shorts were called upon to deliver, they found that it was almost impossible to buy or borrow shares to meet their needs and obligations. As a result, "nearly half the brokerage houses in Wall Street were technically insolvent, simply because they could neither buy nor borrow the Northern Pacific shares they had sold short."[4] On May 9, the panic was quieted when Harriman and Morgan (who between them now held virtually all the Northern Pacific stock) agreed that the shorts could settle with the Kuhn Loeb and Morgan firms at $150 a share for all the Northern Pacific common they had sold to those firms but could not deliver.[5]

As this all took place, the behind-the-scenes cause of the market turbulence unfolded, leading to newspaper headlines such as "GIANTS OF WALL STREET IN FIERCE BATTLE FOR MASTERY, PRECIPITATE CRASH THAT BRINGS RUIN TO HORDES OF PYGMIES."[6] In what has been called "perhaps the most controversial takeover fight in American history,"[7] the Wall Street "Giant" who attracted by far the most negative attention and blame was E.H. Harriman.

And the quieting of the market was not the end of the story. Something had to be done about the relationship between the Great Northern and the Northern Pacific, competitors who were now joint owners of the Burlington. James J. Hill came up with the idea of forming the Northern Securities Company: a holding company that would acquire the stock of the two railroads (including their interests in the Burlington) and in lieu thereof issue stock certificates of its own. Under that plan, Harriman and the Union Pacific received over $82 million worth of Northern Securities stock in exchange for their shares of Northern Pacific, and Harriman was given a seat on the

Northern Securities board of directors. Almost immediately the new company came under attack, and early in 1902 the Roosevelt administration brought suit against Northern Securities for violating the Sherman Antitrust Act. It would take two years, but in March 1904 the U.S. Supreme Court ordered Northern Securities dissolved as an illegal combination with the power to restrain trade.

How to take Northern Securities apart then became an issue between Harriman and Hill. Harriman wanted each Northern Securities shareholder to receive the same amount of stock in Northern Pacific and Great Northern that he had originally exchanged, while Hill argued that the assets of Northern Securities should be distributed on a pro rata basis, regardless of which stocks each holder had turned in when Northern Securities was formed. More litigation ensued, and it was not until March 1905 that the Supreme Court ruled in Hill's favor. When the pro rata distribution was implemented later that year, Harriman was left with a substantial minority interest in each of the two railroads. He would sell nearly all of his shares in both companies during the bull market of late 1905 and early 1906, yielding the Union Pacific a net profit variously estimated at between $58,000,000 and $80,000,000—which one writer characterized as unprecedented "pecuniary compensation for a series of failures and defeats."[8]

Harriman aiming at monopoly

Over the course of the next year, and for the Union Pacific, Harriman invested $130,000,000—representing that profit plus the return of his underlying initial investment in Northern Pacific—in the securities of nine different railway companies whose lines stretched from the Atlantic to the Pacific and from the Great Lakes to the Gulf of Mexico. As to the wisdom of this policy, apart from its long-term and substantial financial benefit to the Union Pacific, Otto Kahn, a close associate of Harriman, characterized these purchases as "the one serious mistake in his management of Union Pacific affairs," because of "the effect which they were likely to have and actually did have on public opinion." To Kahn, "it lent color to the impression that Mr. Harriman was aiming at a gigantic illegal monopoly of the railroad industry."[9] That impression of ubiquitous power and control found further support in the press through articles such as one in the *Wall Street Journal* that revealed Harriman served on the boards of directors of forty-nine companies—including about thirty railroads, half a dozen steamship lines, banks, trust companies, and a variety of other businesses in which he had a personal interest.[10]

Harriman found his reputation and his name further sullied between 1903 and 1907 by a series of widely-publicized struggles which added further fuel to the fire of public perception. One involved the high-profile battle for control of the Equitable Life Insurance Company after the death of its president, Henry Hyde. Hyde's controlling interest in the Equitable passed to his son James, with the intention that he would assume the presidency at the age of 30, in early 1906. In the interim, the senior Hyde's associate, James Alexander, filled the presidency as a caretaker. As the time for turning things over to young Hyde approached, Alexander became reluctant to do so, and sought to wrest the stock and presidency from Hyde. He also proposed changing the system for electing directors, and advocated mutualizing Equitable. Harriman, who had become a member of the board of directors in 1904, was named to a committee to study Alexander's proposals. As this committee was working, Alexander incurred the wrath of its members, particularly Harriman, by leaking news of the internal struggle to the press. Subsequently, the board appointed another committee, chaired by Henry Clay Frick and including Harriman, to conduct a broad investigation of the management of the company.

As that committee went about its work, the accusations in the newspapers mounted, with Harriman accused of controlling James Hyde and seeking to acquire the Equitable. The *New York Sun* asserted that public opinion would never "tolerate a Harriman in control of such a public institution as the Equitable Life."[11] At the end of May 1905, the Frick Committee presented its report, condemning both Hyde and Alexander and calling for a reorganization of the company's management. With both of their positions threatened, Hyde and Alexander combined to attack the committee, and Harriman in particular, "pausing in their internal fight with each other to pour their fire of abuse and innuendo upon him."[12] The board of directors ultimately rejected the Frick Committee report, but requested that Hyde step aside and sell his stock. He eventually sold it to Thomas Fortune Ryan, a commanding and mysterious force on Wall Street, whose ownership of such a position disturbed Harriman to the extent that, even though he had resigned from the board of directors, he effectively became Equitable's self-appointed guardian. After an initial dust-up with Ryan, Harriman made his future cooperation contingent upon Ryan selling him half his shares. Ryan refused, and would later testify before a New York State legislative committee investigating the insurance industry that Harriman had threatened to use all his influence against him if the stock was not shared.[13] *Harriman didn't defend himself*

As the Equitable Life story unfolded, Harriman seemed to be oblivious to how his actions and motives were being painted in the press. Otto Kahn would say that of all "the campaigns of vituperation" of which Harriman was the object, "none succeeded so well in poisoning the public mind against him" as that growing out of the Equitable Life struggle, and which Harriman refused to defend himself against in public.[14] And Harriman biographer George Kennan would observe that "when a man's character and motives are assailed and he does not defend himself in public, the public is apt to assume that he is unable to do so, and that the charges against him are probably true. But Mr. Harriman almost invariably remained silent, even when he had a perfect defense in an absolutely impregnable case."[15] It seems that to Harriman the effort needed to defend himself was a waste of time he could put to better, more productive use. He would tell Kahn that it wasn't worth striking back at the critics, since "for immediate effect they have the advantage, because they will tell lies about me," and he had faith that "the people always find out what's what, in the end, and I can wait," while in the meantime "I need my time and energy to *do* things."[16]

No less public and damaging to Harriman than the Equitable Life struggle was a battle with longtime friend Stuyvesant Fish over the Illinois Central. Contemporary reporting viewed this as a clash of interests stemming from a 1905 contract in which Fish, as President of the Illinois Central, provided another railroad with the right to run its trains into New Orleans over the Central's tracks; Harriman's reaction that this deal with a rival of the Southern Pacific was "treacherous" to both Harriman and the Southern; Fish's rejoinder that he was trying to run the Central for its shareholders and not for Harriman; and the wide-spread belief that Harriman was determined to acquire the Central.[17] In truth, the reporters had only scratched the surface. The unseen story pivoted on Fish's personal conduct.[18] To an extent this involved his own finances, which were, in part, heavily strained by the extravagant lifestyle of his wife, who vied to succeed Caroline Astor as the grand dame of New York City society.

Whether related to that or not, his handling of Illinois Central funds beginning in 1903 raised alarms with the company's directors. An initial concern involved Fish depositing, without consulting the directors, more than a half million dollars of Central money in a small, weak bank of which he was a trustee. The directors who became aware of this transaction questioned its propriety and advised Harriman, who chaired the Finance Committee. When Harriman tried to withdraw the funds, he was told by the bank's officers that a withdrawal of all the money would force the bank into bankruptcy, and he had to settle for withdrawing the money gradually over time. Later, while Harriman was traveling in Europe, Fish again deposited a large sum of Illinois Central money in the same bank, withdrew it, and then deposited it again a third time, apparently to aid the bank in its troubles.

At about the same time, Fish loaned $1.5 million of Illinois Central funds to himself, secured by collateral which seemed wholly inadequate. The board wanted to demand Fish's resignation, but Harriman demurred—realizing that once the matter officially went before the board it would become public, damaging the reputations of Fish and the Illinois Central. He made a confidential, personal loan of $1,200,000 to Fish to clean up his personal and business obligations. Six months after receiving this loan, Fish again drew upon the Illinois Central treasury to increase the deposits of another bank in which he had an interest. This action preceded an increasingly acrimonious series of events that unfolded over the next two years including conflicts over filling vacancies on the Central board; Fish interjecting himself into the affairs of the Mutual Life Insurance company by publicly demanding an investigation of its affairs and its President, Charles Peabody (who sat on the boards of both the Union Pacific and the Illinois Central); and Peabody's response asking Fish to explain his personal handling of Illinois Central funds. Rumors also began circulating that Harriman allies were accumulating Illinois Central stock, and Fish publicly advanced himself as the champion of the stockholders against this presumed takeover—a position that found ample support in the press. All things came to a head in November 1906 when a special meeting of the board removed Fish and elected a new President. The newspapers flocked to Fish's support—with headlines such as that in the *New York World* averring "FISH PUNISHED FOR HIS HONESTY IN MUTUAL LIFE."[19] All in all, Harriman biographer Maury Klein would note, "The deposing of Fish sent the Harriman legend into orbit.... Harriman emerged as the 'Colossus of Roads' and the 'Man of Mystery.' Editors tumbled over one another in their eagerness to blast this naked display of power and ambition."[20]

Even as the struggles involving Equitable Life on the one hand and Stuyvesant Fish and the Illinois Central on the other made headlines, public perceptions of Harriman were further colored by a string of other high visibility events. At the forefront was the disintegration of his friendship with fellow Republican and fellow New Yorker Theodore Roosevelt—traceable to a myriad of circumstances including party politics in New York; the President's trust-busting program and the Northern Securities litigation; a broken promise regarding the appointment of an ambassador to France; and Roosevelt distancing himself from Harriman's public persona as the President sought election to a second term in office.[21]

Another incident that added fuel to the fire, and illustrated how the public mind and opinion had come to view Harriman, occurred in the summer of 1906. At a Union Pacific board meeting on August 15, the directors adopted a Harriman recommendation that the dividend on the company's stock be raised to ten percent. Several key directors had missed the meeting, so instead of making an immediate public announcement about the dividend increase it was agreed that the executive committee, which was meeting the next morning, would release the news once the absent directors had been notified. However, the executive committee meeting was postponed until the afternoon because of a funeral that morning, and by the time the committee convened the New York Stock Exchange was closed; as a result, the news of the dividend increase was not released until the morning of August 17. That news was applauded, and then quickly drowned out by accusations that the announcement had been delayed for two days so that Harriman and others could buy Union Pacific stock and profit from both the dividend and the spike in the per share price of the stock that news of the dividend brought. An August 18, 1906, *New York Times* headline charged that "THE INSIDERS MADE MILLIONS," and criticism was rampant—though no one produced any evidence that any director had bought stock between the 15th and the 17th.[22]

In the midst of all these struggles, public criticism, and hyperactivity in his business dealings, Harriman entered into a period of almost consistently poor health. The first serious occurrence took place in May 1903 when he was in the middle of Wyoming and was diagnosed with appendicitis. With stops in Omaha and Chicago for further diagnosis, and delays by his insistence on attempting to keep to a schedule of business appointments, it was May 16 before Harriman arrived in New York City for the needed surgery, though he didn't finally submit to that until May 20.[23] The appendectomy seemed to spawn a physical decline, born of a series of other ailments that in time necessitated a string of at least a half dozen surgeries, some of which had their own complications. Lower back problems and the onset of rheumatism added to the burden.

Harriman was at home, ill, on the morning of April 18, 1906, when the San Francisco earthquake struck, and soon engulfed that city in marauding walls of flames. On hearing the news, and recognizing that because of its control of the city's transportation arteries the Southern Pacific was critical to relief efforts, he immediately made arrangements to head to the West Coast by special train. As he traveled, he blistered the wires with telegraphed instructions to company officials to divert trains and give priority to bringing supplies into the city, and to make company facilities available to local authorities. On arriving in the Southern's Oakland yards on the 22nd, Harriman set up headquarters in his private car and remained on the scene for nearly three weeks. During that time, the Southern coordinated the accumulation of food, blankets, tents, and medical supplies in nearby towns, and the movement of carloads of those supplies to San Francisco. Company ferries carried refugees to Oakland, and the railroad evacuated thousands of people at no charge: in the week following the quake, and as the fires raged, the Southern carried more than 200,000 refugees out of San Francisco to safety and shelter, with connecting lines also providing free tickets to whatever final destination the riders chose. The company hospital in San Francisco treated victims of the quake—the staff, patients, and equipment had to move twice as flames reached the hospital and, later, when they descended on the rail car barns that had been set up as a temporary site. Refugees who found shelter in boxcars that were opened for their use in the Oakland yards. often encountered Harriman late at night as he walked through, offering encouragement. He also launched public and

Harriman admired for combatting SF fire

private appeals for funds to help in the relief effort, and quickly set an example with $200,000 in cash contributions from his railroads. Among business leaders, Harriman alone went to the scene—and even his critics had to applaud.[24]

By January 1907, and reflecting the cumulative impact of the struggles and events, including those outlined above, in the little more than seven years since the Harriman Expedition had returned to Seattle, an article in a leading magazine could accurately state that "the cynosure of the moment, beyond doubt, is Mr. Harriman."[25] And the attention continued as the public followed the reports of an Interstate Commerce Commission investigation of western railroads, which focused on the practices of the Union Pacific and Harriman himself—including the massive purchases of stock in other railroads following the Northern Securities distribution, and the circumstances of the UP's ten percent dividend payment in 1906. The same article delved again into Harriman's public persona, noting his "baffling personality ... impatience of contradiction, his abrupt manners, his very dominating ways" and that "his exterior indifference has led people to say of him that he cares nothing for public opinion."[26] Those perceptions and characterizations, however, began to change in the spring of the year. To an extent the change resulted from greater public awareness of the facts of some of the battles, such as those involving the Equitable and Stuyvesant Fish, which previously had been unknown. As one critic admitted that spring "most of the sweeping indictments brought against Harriman in the press are rather flimsy in their nature."[27] So too, the Interstate Commerce Commission would report to the President that while it deplored the spread of Harriman's control and influence, "no violation of law by Mr. Harriman had been discovered" and that legal proceedings would not be expedient.[28]

Harriman domineering but not corrupt

The rehabilitation of Harriman's public image was particularly aided by his single-handed rescue of the Erie Railroad from bankruptcy in 1908; a bankruptcy which many on Wall Street feared might trigger a complete market collapse and a recession. The railroad was in danger of defaulting on $5.5 million in notes due to mature on April 8, 1908. The Erie was a "Morgan road," though Harriman was a director and member of its Executive Committee. An Executive Committee meeting on the eve of the maturity date failed to reach any solution on how to meet the debt, with Morgan partners (Morgan himself was in Europe) refusing to provide the funds, despite the fact they had been the Erie's bankers for years. Harriman offered to lend the Erie half the needed money if the other directors, including the Morgan partners, would provide the other half. After a long consultation, the other directors declined to put up any of the money. Harriman then offered to personally lend the Erie the entire amount himself if the other directors would lend him an equivalent amount—effectively substituting his personal debt to them for the corporate debt of the Erie. When that proposal was rebuffed, Harriman disgustedly went to his own bankers and obtained a loan for the entire amount, which he immediately loaned to the Erie. Harriman had little to say about the situation, telling reporters only that it "speaks for itself." Once the word got out, the newspapers did the speaking for him— the *New York Times* headline on April 9 pronouncing that "HARRIMAN SAVES THE ERIE," and "Morgan Plan a Failure" was typical. And the *Financial World* said "Harriman's rescue of the Erie, when its own bankers had apparently deserted it, will long be remembered as a master stroke of courage and resourcefulness, which saved not only the Erie, but the general financial situation, from serious embarrassment."[29]

Harriman's biographers agree as to the impact the rescue of the Erie had on Harriman's public persona. Klein would state that this "did more than any other single act to cleanse his [Harriman's] tarnished image in the public mind," while George Kennan would write that, as to Harriman's public image, the saving of the Erie "changed all this in a single day. It seemed to throw a flash of revealing light upon all his misunderstood activities in the past, and made thousands of businessmen doubt whether they had ever known the real Harriman at all."[30]

Harriman had precious little time to enjoy his rebounding image and status. His health continued to decline at an alarming rate. The real problem now seemed to center in his digestive track; he lost weight and had little energy or appetite. A trip to Europe in the summer of 1909 in search of "the cure," led to visits with specialists in Vienna and Bad Gastein—and a diagnosis that he had cancer: a carcinoma of the stomach, too advanced to be operable. He headed home in August, returning in a weak, frail, and emaciated condition to Arden, where work was continuing on his new home on the heights of the estate.

In his last days, Harriman sent a message to J.P. Morgan—urgent and persuasive enough for Morgan to drop everything and board a special train for Arden and a final meeting between arguably the two most powerful men in American business. They met alone on an outdoor loggia, with Harriman in a steamer chair, a blanket draped over his knees and an overcoat around his shoulders. They talked for over an hour about their long-time differences and seemed to put those all to rest. "Of the meeting," biographer Klein would write, "Morgan said only that he was happy for the chance to clear the air of old antagonisms, but thereafter he referred to Harriman as if he were an old and intimate friend."[31]

E. H. Harriman passed away at Arden on September 9, 1909, little more than ten years after returning to Seattle with the Harriman Alaska Expedition.

⇒ ◆ ⇐

In a simple, less than 100-word will, Harriman left everything he owned, all of his property, "of every kind and nature," to his widow as sole beneficiary.[32] That estate was conservatively worth $80 million in 1909 dollars (approaching $3 billion in 2020 dollars), making Mary Williamson Harriman perhaps the wealthiest woman in the country at that time. In addition to completing the raising and education of her children, finishing the construction of the hill-top home at Arden, managing the households at Arden and in New York City, and looking after the multitude of investments and business interests she inherited, over the course of the next twenty-three years, until her death in 1932, she built a record of public service and private philanthropy spread across a myriad of areas including better government, public health, social welfare, education, and the arts.

In 1910, carrying out plans her husband had initiated, she completed a gift of over 10,000 acres—nearly half of the Arden estate lands—together with $1 million in development funds to the State of New York for what became Harriman State Park.[33] She also cancelled the $113,000 mortgage on the Boys Club's new building in New York City, and began a program of annually contributing a sum equal to 50 percent of the total raised for the Club from other sources.[34] In 1913 she was one of the original incorporators of the American Red Cross, helping to establish its endowment fund and subsequently being a major donor toward construction of not only its national headquarters building but also the Red Cross hospital in Paris. During World War I she was a member of the National Women's Advisory Council, set-up to coordinate women's activities during the war. She was also active in work for retarded children through Letchworth Village, a state institution near her home at Arden, and served on its Board of Managers (later the Board of Visitors) from 1913 until her death.

In addition to supporting the work of Expedition members C. Hart Merriam and John Muir, Mrs. Harriman combined with Dr. Lewis Rutherfurd Morris to create the Harriman Research Laboratory at New York's Roosevelt Hospital: Morris constructing the Laboratory's building and Mrs. Harriman financing the Harriman Fund for Medical Research. She was active in the New York Philharmonic Society, supporting its children's programs and serving as its first woman director. Out of an initial concern for the advanced training of the graduates of various musical schools and their ability to compete with European-trained talent for positions with professional orchestras, she founded the American Orchestral Society in 1920, and became its president, chief benefactor, and chief advocate for aspiring musicians.[35]

In 1927 Mrs. Harriman received an honorary Master of Letters degree from New York University. In conferring that degree, the University's Chancellor said of her, "You have yourself, in these later years, carried weighty responsibilities which you have discharged with fidelity to your own high sense of stewardship; patron of sciences in fields most closely related to the betterment of human life, patron of art and music and religion, friend of boys, friend of artisans, friend of those in need of friends."[36] She passed away in November 1932.

Mary Harriman founds Junior League

Of the Harriman's first-born, Mary, the *New York Times* would write that as a result of the "close companionship" with her father, she "developed a breadth and intensity of interest in large affairs, and a desire to accomplish valuable things herself."[37]

That manifested itself soon after returning from Alaska when, at age 18, she began volunteering at the College Settlement House in the immigrant enclave of New York City's Lower East Side. That work, and perhaps her father's example with the Boys Club, inspired her as a student at Bernard College where, in 1901, and as she prepared for her "coming out," she organized a group of 80 debutantes from New York's most prominent families to form a new organization to move beyond a "debutante life" into more purposeful activity in working with the needy. That organization, initially known as the Junior League for the Promotion of Settlements Movements, soon evolved into simply the Junior League. The idea and the League grew, soon spreading to other cities across the country and remaining an active force that continues to pursue its original idea of enriching members' lives by improving the living conditions of their cities' poorest neighborhoods.[38]

In 1910 Mary married the sculptor and polo enthusiast Charles Rumsey, and settled in to raising the three children of that marriage, while continuing her role with the Junior League and serving (beginning in 1911 and until her death) on the Board of Trustees of Bernard College. She also joined the board of the Maternity Center Association, an organization that worked to provide post-natal care and instruction in an effort to reduce infant mortality in poorer neighborhoods. Her husband died in 1922, and, as her children grew older, Mary began to devote her attention to politics and consumer advocacy. With friends Eleanor Roosevelt and Frances Perkins, she campaigned for Democratic candidates, including Franklin Roosevelt in 1932. When Roosevelt won, and appointed Perkins as Secretary of Labor, Mary moved to Washington. There, she and her brother Averell were among the founders of *Today* magazine—which after her death merged with *News Week*, creating the twentieth-century's *Newsweek* magazine. In 1932, President Roosevelt appointed her to chair the Consumer Advocacy Board of the National Recovery Administration (NRA), which was charged with seeing that, with the Great Depression in full swing, the retail price of goods did not increase proportionally more than wages.

One of her last endeavors, and one of the most lasting, was her work with Frances Perkins as one of the primary authors of the Social Security Act. Mary Harriman passed away in December 1934 from complications following an accident on November 17 of that year when—celebrating her 54th birthday—she suffered multiple injuries while riding when her horse fell and rolled over on her. She was buried at Arden, next to her parents. Her achievements have been recognized by organizations such as the National Women's History Museum, and by her election to the National Women's Hall of Fame in 2015.[39]

Cornelia Harriman was given in marriage by her father to Robert Livingston Gerry in 1908. Gerry came from a distinguished and wealthy family whose lineage traced to a signer of the Declaration of Independence. Cornelia, an accomplished horsewoman and racing stable owner, was a strong supporter of the Boys Club of New York founded by her father. That interest would continue in the Gerry-Harriman family line into the twenty-first century: her son, Elbridge T. Gerry, and her grandson, Elbridge T. Gerry, Jr., both serving on the Boys Club board. The Club's second Clubhouse, located in East Harlem, bears the Gerry name.

The third Harriman daughter, Carol, she of the Dellenbaugh-composed reading at the Fourth of July celebration when the Expedition was in Kodiak, was twice married, first to Richard Penn Smith, who died in 1920 after they had been married but three years, and then to W. Plunket Stewart. She died in 1948 at the age of 59.

≡ ◆ ≡

W. Averell Harriman would have an impressive, varied, and not easily summarized career in business, politics, and diplomatic service. His early business career, at the end of World War I and in the postwar years, included shipbuilding and manganese mining interests. Much like their father, he and his brother Roland also went into banking. In 1931 they merged the family interests with Brown Brothers, creating Brown Brothers Harriman, which remains to this day as an active private banking house.

When E.H. Harriman died, his long-time friend and lawyer, Judge Robert S. Lovett, succeeded him as chairman of the Union Pacific. When Judge Lovett passed away in 1932, he was in turn succeeded by Averell Harriman. During his tenure as chair, Averell led modernization of the road's passenger service and conversion to diesel locomotives. He was also responsible for development of the Sun Valley resort in Idaho, providing a new destination for UP passenger service and helping to open up skiing in the western U.S. In addition to being an accomplished skier, Averell was at various times an elite polo player, a racing stable owner, a breeder of champion Labrador retrievers, and a master croquet player and member of the Croquet Hall of Fame.

Although he would remain chairman of the UP until 1943, beginning in 1941 New Deal politics and the Roosevelt administration increasingly called him to Washington, where for the next dozen years he served in a series of positions, initially as "expeditor" of President Roosevelt's lend-lease program, in which he developed a special working relationship with British Prime Minister Winston Churchill. He was wartime Ambassador to Russia from 1943 to 1946; in that capacity serving as the chief ongoing United States contact with Premier Josef Stalin. After the war, and a stint as U.S. Secretary of Commerce under President Truman, he served, also in the Truman Administration, as one of the creators and implementers of the U.S. Marshall Plan for European recovery after World War II. He was an unsuccessful candidate for the Democratic Presidential nomination in 1952 but prevailed in a later campaign for Governor of New York in 1954, serving one term in that office. During the Kennedy administration he initially served as Ambassador-At-Large, then as Assistant Secretary of State for Far Eastern Affairs, and then Undersecretary of State for Political Affairs. He would later serve as Ambassador-At-Large under President Lyndon Johnson.

Averell also spearhead the transfer of additional land at Arden to expand Harriman State Park, and in 1951 he led the family in a gift of the hilltop main house and 1,000 acres of land to Columbia University, where it became the seat of Columbia's American Assembly and the site of many prestigious conferences and meetings. In 1982, his gift of $10 million led to the establishment of Columbia's Harriman Institute for Advanced Study of the Soviet Union.

Averell Harriman passed away in July 1986; two months shy of his 95th birthday. He was the last surviving member of the Harriman Alaska Expedition.

⚍ ◆ ⚌

Roland, the youngest of E.H. and Mary Harriman's children, passed away at age 82. He had been an active partner in Brown Brothers Harriman until his death, though he was also engaged in many other activities.

In 1920, just three years after graduating from Yale, he was elected to the Union Pacific board of directors. Beginning in 1941, he minded the family's railroad interests while his brother Averell, nominally the chairman, was occupied near full-time with government service. Roland officially became chairman of the board in 1946 and held that spot until 1953 when he stepped aside, though continuing as a director until his death in 1978.

He was a patron of harness racing—he himself held a number of trotting records and his wife Gladys was also a championship racer—and served as Chairman of the United States Trotting Association. He was elected to the board of trustees of the Boys Club in 1921 and became President in 1929—he would continue to support and be involved in the organization for many years. Along with his brother Averell, he served on the Palisades Interstate Park Commission, and in connection with Harriman State Park led a group which financed erection of the Bear Mountain Bridge across the Hudson River to "make the park more accessible to motorists from the East."[40] Undoubtedly spurred by his mother's founding role, Roland was for years a leading volunteer figure in the American Red Cross; President Truman appointed him its President in 1950, succeeding General George Marshall, and he held that position in an uninterrupted tenure under successive appointments by U.S. Presidents Eisenhower, Kennedy, Johnson, and Nixon until 1973.

completely flat conclusion

APPENDIX

Expedition Members and Committees

MEMBERS OF THE HARRIMAN ALASKA EXPEDITION

(As recorded in C. Hart Merriam, ed., *Harriman Alaska Series*, Vol. 1, xxxiii–xxxv)

CLASSIFIED SUMMARY

Harriman family and servants	14
Scientific party	25
Artists	3
Photographers	2
Stenographers	2
Surgeon and assistant	2
Trained nurse	1
Chaplain	1
Hunters, packers, and camp hands	11
Officers and crew	65
	126

The Harriman Family

EDWARD H. HARRIMAN, patron of the expedition, Arden, N.Y.
Mrs. E. H. HARRIMAN
Miss MARY HARRIMAN
Miss CORNELIA HARRIMAN
CAROL HARRIMAN
AVERELL HARRIMAN
ROLAND HARRIMAN
W. H. AVERELL, Rochester, New York
Mrs. W. H. AVERELL
Miss ELIZABETH AVERELL
Miss DOROTHEA DRAPER, New York City

The Scientific Party

Prof. WILLIAM H. BREWER, Sheffield Scientific School, Yale University, New Haven, Connecticut
JOHN BURROUGHS, Ornithologist and Author, West Park, New York
WESLEY R. COE, Ph.D., Assistant Professor of Comparative Anatomy, Yale University, New Haven, Connecticut

FREDERICK V. COVILLE, Curator of the National Herbarium and Botanist of the U.S. Department of Agriculture, Washington, D.C.

Dr. WILLIAM H. DALL, Paleontologist of the U.S. Geological Survey, and Honorary Curator of Mollusks, U.S. National Museum, Washington, D.C.

W. B. DEVEREUX, Mining Engineer, Glenwood Springs, Colorado

DANIEL G. ELLIOT, Curator of Zoology, Field Columbian Museum, Chicago, Illinois

Prof. BENJAMIN K. EMERSON, Professor of Geology, Amherst College, Amherst, Massachusetts

Prof. B. E. FERNOW, Dean of the School of Forestry, Cornell University, Ithaca, New York

Dr. A. K. FISHER, Ornithologist, Biological Survey, U.S. Department of Agriculture, Washington, D.C.

HENRY GANNETT, Chief Geographer, U.S. Geological Survey, Washington, D.C.

G. K. GILBERT, Geologist, U.S. Geological Survey, Washington, D.C.

Dr. GEORGE BIRD GRINNELL, Editor, *Forest and Stream,* New York City

THOMAS H. KEARNEY, JR., Assistant Botanist, U.S. Department of Agriculture, Washington, D.C.

CHARLES A. KEELER, Director of the Museum of the California Academy of Sciences, San Francisco, California

Prof. TREVOR KINCAID, Professor of Zoology, University of Washington, Seattle, State of Washington

Dr. C. HART MERRIAM, Chief of the Biological Survey, U.S. Department of Agriculture, Washington, D.C.

JOHN MUIR, Author and Student of Glaciers, Martinez, California

Dr. CHARLES PALACHE, Mineralogist, Harvard University, Cambridge, Massachusetts

ROBERT RIDGWAY, Curator of Birds, U.S. National Museum, Washington. D.C.

Prof. WILLIAM E. RITTER, President of the California Academy of Sciences and Professor of Zoology, University of California, Berkeley, California

DE ALTON SAUNDERS, Botanist, South Dakota Experiment Station, Brookings, South Dakota

Dr. WILLIAM TRELEASE, Director of the Missouri Botanical Garden, St. Louis, Missouri

Artists

R. SWAIN GIFFORD, New York City
FRED S. DELLENBAUGH, New York City

Bird Artist

LOUIS AGASSIZ FUERTES, Ithaca, New York

Physicians

Dr. LEWIS RUTHERFORD MORRIS, New York City
Dr. EDWARD L. TRUDEAU, JR., Saranac Lake, New York

Taxidermists and Preparators

LEON J. COLE, Ann Arbor, Michigan
EDWIN C. STARKS, Biological Survey, Washington, D.C.

Photographers

EDWARD S. CURTIS, Seattle, Washington
D.G. INVERARITY, Seattle, Washington

Chaplain

Dr. GEORGE F. NELSON, New York City

Stenographers

LOUIS F. TIMMERMAN, New York City
JULIAN L. JOHNS, Washington, D.C.

Ship's Officers

Captain, PETER DORAN
First Officer, CHARLES McCARTY
Pilot, J.F. JORDAN
Chief Engineer, J.A. SCANDRETT
Steward, JOSEPH V. KNIGHTS

At Orca, Prince William Sound, Capt. Omar J. Humphrey of the Pacific Steam Whaling Company joined the ship and accompanied the party to Bering Strait and back to Unalaska. His detailed knowledge of the coast proved of much value in navigating the ship. Mr. M.L. Washburn of the Alaska Commercial Company also joined the Expedition at Orca and went with it to Kadiak. On the return voyage Mr. J. Stanley-Brown of the North American Commercial Company came aboard at Dutch Harbor, Unalaska, and accompanied the party on the homeward voyage and the overland journey.

Author's Notes

The listing above includes titles as of the time of publication of Volume I in 1901—thus Kincaid is listed as Professor and Trudeau as Doctor, though those positions and qualifications were not attained until after the Expedition was completed.

The private post–Expedition publication *The Harriman Alaska Expedition: Chronicles and Souvenirs—May to August 1899*, identifies the Harriman family servants as Mr. Harriman's valet "Stevens" and three maids, Augusta Larson, Mrs. H.D. Budd, and Adelaide Mangold. If all four of these servants are added to the eleven people listed in the roster as "The Harriman Family," the total for the "Harriman family and servants" in the "Classified Summary" would be 15, not 14. In addition to being identified in *Chronicles and Souvenirs*, the three maids are also mentioned by name in various diaries and journals: see Merriam's expedition diary/journal, entry for June 2, 1899, Merriam Papers, Library of Congress, and Ritter's diary (undated loose sheet), Ritter Papers, Bancroft Library, University of California—Berkeley. Apart from his inclusion in the *Chronicles and Souvenirs* listing, no other reference to Stevens has been found in any of the diaries, journals, letters, or other written records of the Expedition.

The *Chronicles and Souvenirs* publication also contains a listing of hunters and packers, including Luther Kelly and Charles Fredell.

Thos. Adamson was the Elder's original First Officer, but when he became disabled by rheumatism he was succeeded, in Sitka, by Charles McCarty, as recorded in Dr. Nelson's diary for June 16, 1899.

In addition to Humphrey, Washburn, and Stanley-Brown, another temporary passenger was the Tlingit "Indian Jim," who joined the outbound Expedition at Yakutat Bay and disembarked at that same point on the return trip.

COMMITTEES

(As recorded in C. Hart Merriam, ed., *Harriman Alaska Expedition*, Vol. 1, xxxvi–xxxvii)

On the westward journey across the continent an organization was perfected, and the various activities of the Expedition were assigned to special committees, as follows:

Executive Committee

E.H. Harriman, *Chairman*	Bernhard E. Fernow
C. Hart Merriam, *Secretary*	Henry Gannett
Frederick V. Coville	G. K. Gilbert
Edward S. Curtis	George Bird Grinnell
Wm. H. Dall	Lewis R. Morris
W.B. Devereux	John Muir

Committee on Route and Plans

E.H. Harriman, *Chairman*	Captain Peter Doran
C. Hart Merriam, *Secretary*	Henry Gannett
Frederick V. Coville	G.K. Gilbert
Wm. H. Dall	Lewis R. Morris
W.B. Devereux	

Committee on Zoology

Wm. H. Dall, *Chairman*	Robert Ridgway
Daniel G. Elliot	Wm. E. Ritter
C. Hart Merriam	

Committee on Botany

F.V. Coville, *Chairman*	Wm. Trelease
Wm. H. Brewer	

Committee on Geology

G.K. Gilbert, *Chairman*	John Muir
B.K. Emerson	

Committee on Mining

W.B. Devereux, *Chairman*	Charles Palache

Committee on Geography and Geographic Names

Henry Gannett, *Chairman*	G.K. Gilbert
Wm. H. Dall	John Muir
B.K. Emerson	

Committee on Big Game

Lewis R. Morris, *Chairman*	George Bird Grinnell
Daniel G. Elliot	Miss Mary Harriman

Committee on Lectures

HENRY GANNETT, *Chairman*	G.K. GILBERT
WM. H. BREWER	GEORGE F. NELSON
FREDERICK V. COVILLE	

Committee on Library

MRS. AVERELL, *Chairman*	MISS DRAPER
MISS MARY HARRIMAN, *Secretary*	MISS CORNELIA HARRIMAN
FREDERICK V. COVILLE	E.L. TRUDEAU

Committee on Literature and Art

MRS. HARRIMAN, *Chairman*	LOUIS A. FUERTES
G.F. NELSON, *Secretary*	R. SWAIN GIFFORD
JOHN BURROUGHS, *Historian*	MISS CORNELIA HARRIMAN
MISS AVERELL	JOHN MUIR
FRED S. DELLENBAUGH	

Committee on Music and Entertainment

B.E. FERNOW, *Chairman*	LOUIS A. FUERTES
MISS DRAPER, *Secretary*	R. SWAIN GIFFORD
FRED S. DELLENBAUGH	

Source Notes

INTRODUCTION

1. Harriman, "Preface" to Merriam, ed., *Harriman Alaska Series*, Vol. I, xxi–xxii.

2. Klein, *The Life and Legend of E. H. Harriman*, 184.

3. Gannett, "The Harriman Alaska Expedition," *National Geographic Magazine*, December 1899, 507.

4. Palache to Helen Markham, May 31, 1899, Palache Papers, Bancroft Library, University of California, Berkeley.

5. Muir to the Big Four, August 30, 1899, Muir Papers, Special Collections, Holt-Atherton Center for Pacific Studies, University of the Pacific. Copyright 1984 Muir-Hanna Trust.

PROLOGUE

The comprehensive Harriman biographies are *E. H. Harriman* by George Kennan (1922) and Maury Klein's superb *The Life and Legend of E. H. Harriman* (2000). Both have been invaluable in presenting an encapsulated narrative of Harriman's life and career up to the time of the Expedition. Kennan's two-volume work benefitted from access to many of his subject's contemporaries, including the Harriman family, in the six years immediately prior to publication. His work was both sponsored and reviewed by the family and its advisers, lending—together with Kennan's own proclivities—a certain discreteness to his treatment of Harriman's life and, at times, to an arguably "partisan" view of some of the controversial aspects of Harriman's later career. Klein, an accomplished historian and biographer, had independence and detachment, together with extensive and developed expertise in critical areas, including nineteenth century railroading in general and the Union Pacific in particular. He was able to draw upon much of Kennan's archived research work, assiduously mined contemporary and subsequent reporting and opinion, and developed access to additional historical sources. Klein's lengthy Prologue, "Mr. Kennan Writes a Biography," is an unusual and critically appreciative look by one biographer at the life of another and his work on the subject of their mutual interest.

1. Emma Lazarus penned the sonnet "The New Colossus" in 1883 in connection with the fundraising for the pedestal of the Statue of Liberty, though another twenty years would pass before the poem was engraved and mounted on the pedestal's inner wall. Today, that plaque is on display in the Statue of Liberty Exhibit in the pedestal.

2. The reference to William as "the rich Englishman" is cited in Kennan, *E. H. Harriman*, Vol. I, 1, and in Klein, *The Life and Legend of E. H. Harriman*, 27.

3. Kennan, *E. H. Harriman*, Vol. I, 1–3; Klein, *The Life and Legend of E. H. Harriman*, 27.

4. Klein, *The Life and Legend of E. H. Harriman*, 28.

5. *Ibid.*, 29.

6. *Ibid.*, 29–30.

7. Keys, "Harriman: The Man in the Making—His Early Life and Start," *The World's Work*, January 1907, 8460.

8. Moody and Turner, "Masters of Capital in America," *McClure's Magazine*, January 1911, 335.

9. Kennan, *E. H. Harriman*, Vol. 1, 11–12.

10. Klein, *The Life and Legend of E. H. Harriman*, 33.

11. Kennan, *E. H. Harriman*, Vol. 1, 14–15. Kennan describes Oliver as a "wealthy merchant." Harriman went into business with James Livingston, scion of one of New York's oldest families, who he met while working for Hayes, but he soon dissolved the partnership with Livingston and reformed E. H. Harriman & Co. with his brother William. Moody and Turner, "Masters of Capital in America," *McClure's Magazine*, January 1911, 335.

12. Klein, *The Life and Legend of E. H. Harriman*, 36–37.

13. Moody and Turner, "Masters of Capital in America," *McClure's Magazine*, January 1911, 335.

14. Klein, *The Life and Legend of E. H. Harriman*, 39–41. Klein notes that to get to Paul Smith's in those days "required a train trip to Saratoga and then Whitehall, a boat journey to Plattsburg, a short hop on a branch rail to the mines of Ausable Forks, and then a forty-two-mile trek by coach through the forest over a rough corduroy road."

15. For the story of the Tompkins Square Boys Club, see Kennan, *E. H. Harriman*, Vol. 1, 25–58

and Klein, *The Life and Legend of E. H. Harriman*, 41–43.

16. Campbell, *Mary Williamson Harriman*, 3.

17. Lovett, *Forty Years After: An Appreciation of the Genius of Edward Henry Harriman*, 13.

18. Moody and Turner, "Masters of Capital in America," *McClure's Magazine*, January 1911, 336.

19. *Ibid.*, 335, where it is also noted that the two had apparently attended the Saturday night dinners at the Travelers' Club together.

20. Klein, *The Life and Legend of E. H. Harriman*, 49.

21. Ackerman, *Historical Sketch of the Illinois Central Railroad*, 142–143.

22. Moody and Turner, "Masters of Capital in America," *McClure's Magazine*, January 1911, 337–338.

23. Harriman's role in the continued development of the Illinois Central is explored in depth in Klein, *The Life and Legend of E. H. Harriman*, especially pp. 62–94.

24. Lovett, *Forty Years After: An Appreciation of the Genius of Edward Henry Harriman*, 21.

25. Klein, *The Life and Legend of E.H. Harriman*, 64–66.

26. Klein, *The Life and Legend of E.H. Harriman*, 45.

27. *Ibid.*, 46.

28. Kennan, *E. H. Harriman*, Vol. 2, 31 traces the name back to Mrs. Parrott's family maiden name. Klein notes a more personal connection in that "Arden was the forest where Shakespeare had set *As You Like It*, the play from which Harriman's father had drawn his ill-fitting name. Harriman was not a well-read man, but it is hard to believe he did not know the play or draw his inspiration from it. He was in fact quoted late in life as saying, 'Arden to me is the Arden of *As You Like It* … a retreat from the world worries [*sic*].'" Klein, *The Life and Legend of E. H. Harriman*, 69.

29. Kennan, *E. H. Harriman*, Vol. 1, 75.

30. Loving, "W. Averell Harriman Remembers Life with Father," *Fortune*, May 8, 1978, 202.

31. Klein, *The Life and Legend of E.H. Harriman*, 67.

32. Latham, *The Panic of 1893: A Time of Strikes, Riots, Hobo Camps, Coxey's "Army," Starvation, Withering Droughts and Fears of "Revolution,"* 4. Kennan summarizes the ultimate carnage of the mid-1890s as "six mortgage companies, thirteen loan and trust companies, and five hundred and fifty-four banks failed, and one hundred and fifty-six railroads, with a capitalization of $2,500,000,000, went into the hands of receivers." Kennan, *E. H. Harriman*, Vol. 1, 117.

33. Klein, *The Life and Legend of E. H. Harriman*, 91–92.

34. Lefevere, "Harriman," *American Magazine*, June 1907, 121.

35. Quoted in Kobler, *Otto the Magnificent*, 23–24. Morgan overstated the case on the railroad's physical condition, perhaps as part of the justification for not undertaking the task. The

Union Pacific was in reasonably well-maintained shape, comparable to other roads in the Western U.S. See Klein, *Union Pacific: The Rebirth 1894–1969*, 49–50 and sources cited.

36. Klein, *Union Pacific: The Rebirth, 1894–1969*, 24.

37. The Schiff-Harriman conversation is quoted in Klein, *The Life and Legend of E.H. Harriman*, 112. A similar account of this conversation appears in Moody and Turner, "Masters of Capital in America," *McClure's Magazine*, January 1911, 340–341.

38. *Ibid.*

39. Kahn, "Edward Henry Harriman," as reprinted in the *Railway Library*, Slason Thompson, ed., Vol. 2, 1911, 317.

40. *Ibid.*, 313.

41. *Ibid.*

42. Kennan, *E. H. Harriman*, Vol. 1, 140.

43. *Ibid.*, 141.

44. Klein, *The Life and Legend of E. H. Harriman*, 120–122, based on sources including the trip diary kept by Mary and Cornelia.

45. Klein, *The Life and Legend of E. H. Harriman*, 123.

46. The easiest way to understand how staggering this expenditure was is to compute the difference between the buying power of a dollar in 1898 and today. The U.S. Bureau of Labor Statistics provides a means for doing that, using a Computer Price Index (CPI) inflation calculator for comparable years going back as far as 1913. The Bureau calculates that $1 in 1913 had the same buying power then as $24.95 in 2019. Other calculators adapt or extend the Bureau's methodology to estimate buying power with reference to years prior to 1913. The "Purchasing Power Calculator" at measuringworth.com tabs $1 in 1898 as having the same buying power as $32.01 in 2019 dollars: making the buying power of $25,000,000 in 1898 equal to $800,250,000 in 2019.

47. Kahn, "Edward Henry Harriman," as reprinted in the *Railway Library*, Slason Thompson, ed., Vol. 2, 1911, 316.

48. Klein, *The Life and Legend of E. H. Harriman*, 130–147 provides details of many of the major Union Pacific projects beginning in 1898, including Sherman Hill-Dale Creek, under the original $25 million appropriation and subsequent additional board-approved expenditures.

49. By 1909 Harriman had spent $160 million—including $18 million for line changes, $62 million for construction and acquisition of new lines, $40 million for rolling stock, $8 million for second track, and $32 million for other betterments. In the area of equipment alone, the Union Pacific acquired 522 new locomotives, 258 passenger cars, and 12,499 freight cars. Statistics from Klein, *Union Pacific: The Rebirth 1894–1969*, 65 and sources cited. Klein concludes that "For that money he got a modern railroad, perhaps the most efficient of its size in the nation, equipped in every way to handle the flood of traffic that

crashed down on it between 1898 and 1910." [These numbers represent the then current dollar value of the expenditures; for an approximation of what it would cost to duplicate that effort in today's dollars, see note 46, above].

50. Kahn, "Edward Henry Harriman," as reprinted in the *Railway Library*, Slason Thompson, ed., Vol. 2, 1911, 309.

CHAPTER 1

Materials on the lives of many of the members of the Harriman Expedition's scientific party are legion, reflecting the depth and breadth of their lives and accomplishments, and the place each holds in their respective disciplines. Those materials include many stand-alone biographies, such as Keir B. Sterling's *Last of the Great Naturalists: The Career of C. Hart Merriam*, John Taliaferro's *Grinnell: America's Environmental Pioneer and His Restless Drive to Save the West*, Stephen J. Pyne's *Grove Karl Gilbert: A Great Engine of Research*, William Frederic Badè's *The Life and Letters of John Muir*, and other works which are identified in the Bibliography. Also particularly important are the extensive biographical memoirs on many members of the party which were written for the National Academy of Sciences *Biographical Memoirs* series, and are available online at www.nasonline.org/publications/biographical-memoirs.

1. Harriman's explanation is contained in his "Preface" to Merriam, ed., *Harriman Alaska Series*, Vol. I, xxi–xxii.

2. *Ibid.*

3. Goetzmann and Sloan, *Looking Far North: The Harriman Expedition to Alaska, 1899*, 5.

4. Goetzmann and Sloan cite Sterling, *Last of the Naturalists: The Career of C. Hart Merriam*, 119. However, in his brief discussion of the origin of the Harriman Expedition, Sterling makes no mention of either "doctor's orders" or of Dr. Morris—in fact, Morris does not appear to be mentioned anywhere in Sterling's book. What Sterling does say at page 119 as to the motivation or reason for the trip is that "Edward H. Harriman, president of the Union Pacific Railroad, decided in that year 'to get a little rest and recreation' from his railroad building 'by making a summer cruise' to Alaska." For the quoted language of "to get a little rest and recreation" and "by making a summer cruise," Sterling accurately cites Kennan, *E. H. Harriman*, Vol. 1, 185–187, where, as with Sterling, Kennan makes no reference to "doctor's orders." In the endnote citing Kennan, Sterling also states (page 361) that he could find "no corroboration" for a version of the origins of the Expedition propounded in Palmer, "In Memoriam: Clinton Hart Merriam," *The Auk*, Vol. 71, No. 2, May 1954, 131–132, where the author claims that it was Mrs. Harriman who "arranged with Dr. Merriam to outline a vacation trip for Mr. Harriman, whose physician had ordered him to take an extended rest from financial activities," and that it was Merriam and Mrs. Harriman who decided "upon a sea trip to Alaska for several weeks." The Palmer version is also at odds with what Harriman and Merriam wrote about the origins of the Expedition, and with the lack of any evidence that Mrs. Harriman and Merriam had become acquainted at any time prior to the Expedition's departure.

5. Klein, *The Life and Legend of E. H. Harriman*, 131, quoting September 1898 correspondence from Harriman to Union Pacific president Horace G. Burt.

6. Goetzmann and Sloan, *Looking Far North: The Harriman Expedition to Alaska, 1899*, 8, where it is also stated that "A small rail line had recently been built in the Yukon gold rush country, with the incredible hope that it would eventually be extended beneath the Bering Sea to Siberia, and Harriman actually seems to have been eager to assess the potential for this daring operation to link the continents." The authors cite Stefansson, *Northwest to Fortune*; Kennan, *E.H. Harriman's Far Eastern Plans*; and Lovett, *Forty Years After: An Appreciation of the Genius of Edward Henry Harriman*. As to these sources, Stefansson's hypothesis that the Harriman Expedition might have been part of a grand design for a New York to Paris railway is based on circumstantial evidence: apparently piecing together things such as Congressional action in 1898 that made it possible for railroad builders to obtain a right-of-way in Alaska; the Expedition's stop to ride the White Pass Railroad out of Skagway; and the Expedition party's eventual visits to both the coast of Siberia and, then, directly across the ocean, to Port Clarence in Alaska. Kennan provides no link or connection between Harriman's early 20th Century demonstrable interest in a world-wide system and the 1899 Expedition. And Lovett, while noting that at the end of his life in 1909 Harriman was "dreaming of new world-wide plans of transportation expansion," does not speak to any tie to the 1899 Expedition and makes no reference whatever to an Alaska-Siberia railroad.

7. Kennan in *E. H. Harriman's Far Eastern Plans*, 6–7 notes that Harriman proposed to "reconstruct and reequip" the South Manchuria Railway with American capital, making it the eastern part of a proposed trans–Asiatic line, and that "Having secured this essential link, he intended to buy the Chinese Eastern, which he thought the Russians, having lost Port Arthur, would gladly sell, and then acquire transportation rights over the Trans-Siberian and the Russian Government roads from North Manchuria to the coast of the Baltic Sea. These acquisitions, in connection with the Pacific Mail Steamship Company and the American railroad systems that he already controlled, would give him a continuous line more than three quarters of the way around the globe, and it would be a comparatively easy matter, thereafter, to connect up the termini by

establishing a line of steamers across the Atlantic from the United States to Russia." Harriman traveled to Japan in the summer of 1905 and meetings there resulted in a "Memorandum of Preliminary Understanding" with the Japanese government for purchase of the South Manchuria Railway, but that fell through because of a provision in the Treaty of Portsmouth providing that transfer of that railway from Russia to Japan could be made only with the consent of the Chinese government—which was not forthcoming. See also Oliver, *The Bering Strait Crossing: A 21st Century Frontier Between East and West*, 124–128, where it is noted that Harriman's plans traced to completion of the Trans-Siberian Railroad to Vladivostok in 1903 and the end of the Russian-Japanese War.

8. Oliver, *The Bering Strait Crossing: A 21st Century Frontier Between East and West*, 118–124, where the author suggests that the "most likely source" for the post-Expedition rumors about "Harriman's (apocryphal) railroad ambitions in Alaska" was an August 16, 1899 *New York Times* report on Harriman's return from Alaska, which was headlined: "**E.H. HARRIMAN RETURNS— Pleased with the Alaska Tour and the Rail Outlook**." Oliver states that the "Rail Outlook" in the headline was misleading, and referred not to Alaska, but, as part of the same press interview, to Wyoming.

9. Klein, *The Life and Legend of E. H. Harriman*, 182. Klein is also the author of the authoritative, multi-volume work on the history of the Union Pacific.

10. Merriam, "Introduction" to the *Harriman Alaska Series*, Vol. I, xxviii.

11. Klein, *The Life and Legend of E. H. Harriman*, 183.

12. *Ibid.* Harriman may have been aware of, and perhaps took some small added inspiration from, the Wellman Polar Expedition of 1898–1899, involving a traveling party of less than a dozen men, and which had the dual purposes of exploring Franz Josef Land and making a "dash" to the North Pole. The Wellman party was well into its journey as the Harriman Expedition was taking shape. While Wellman characterized it as "incidental" activity, he did note that "scientific work of the usual character was to be carried on by a competent corps of observers." This expedition was underwritten by the National Geographic Society and a group of individuals, including J. Pierpont Morgan and W.K. Vanderbilt. See Wellman, "The Wellman Polar Expedition," *The National Geographic Magazine*, Vol. X, December 1899, 481 et seq.

13. With regard to the winter of 1899, including conditions in Washington, see Kuchin, Weiss and Wagner, "The Great Arctic Outbreak and East Coast Blizzard of 1899," *Weather and Forecasting*, Vol. 3, December 1988, 305–318.

14. Merriam and Roosevelt would share a lifelong, though at times intellectually rocky, friendship based upon their mutual interests in ornithology and the natural sciences, dating from 1878 when Merriam, all of twenty-three years old, wrote a favorable review of *The Summer Birds of the Adirondacks*, a booklet written by Roosevelt when TR was himself only twenty. See Brinkley, *The Wilderness Warrior: Theodore Roosevelt and the Crusade for America*, 107–108.

15. *Ibid.*

16. In 1905 the Division was officially renamed the Bureau of Biological Survey. In 1939–1940 its work and responsibilities were transferred from the Department of Agriculture to the Department of the Interior, where it was joined with the former Fish Commission to become the U.S. Fish and Wildlife Service.

17. Merriam, "Recollections and Impressions of E. H. Harriman," 1, unpublished manuscript, Merriam Papers, Bancroft Library, University of California, Berkeley.

18. *Ibid.*

19. *Ibid.*, 2.

20. *Ibid.*, 3.

21. Merriam Home Journals, March 31, 1899, Merriam Papers, Library of Congress. While having significant latitude and authority, Merriam would continue to regularly consult with Harriman on potential invitees.

22. Harriman, "Preface" to Merriam, ed., *Harriman Alaska Series*, Vol. I, xxii.

23. Merriam, "Recollections and Impressions of E. H. Harriman," 2, unpublished manuscript, Merriam Papers, Bancroft Library, University of California, Berkeley.

24. *Ibid.*, 3.

25. "History of the Cosmos Club," Cosmos Club Web site at www.cosmosclub.org.

26. Uhler, "In Memoriam: The Life of Albert K. Fisher," *The AUK*, April 1951, 210–213.

27. See Penry, "The Father of Government Mapmaking: Henry Gannett," *The American Surveyor*, November 2007.

28. Ridgway to William Brewster, April 27, 1899, Museum of Comparative Zoology Archives, Harvard University, Cambridge, MA, correspondence files of William Brewster, as quoted in Lewis, *The Feathery Tribe: Robert Ridgway and the Modern Study of Birds*, 61.

29. Grinnell diary, September 17, 1891, Grinnell papers, Braun Research Library, Autry Museum of the American West.

30. Ludlow, William, *Report of a Reconnaissance from Carroll, Montana Territory, on the Upper Missouri, to the Yellowstone National Park*, Washington, D.C.: Government Printing Office, 1876, 37, as noted in Reiger, ed., *The Passing of the Great West: Selected Papers of George Bird Grinnell*, 118–119.

31. The Boone and Crockett Club was probably the first organization formed with the specific purpose of promoting national legislation on the environment. See Reiger, *American Sportsmen and the Origins of Conservation*, 153.

32. By early 1889 membership (which was free)

was pushing 50,000 and publication of the magazine, which was handled by the *Forest and Stream* staff, had become such a drain on time and money that Grinnell was forced to discontinue publication. Loss of the magazine and the cohesiveness it brought greatly impacted the membership of individual societies, but the movement received a new impetus in 1896 with the formation of a strong Massachusetts Audubon Society, which served as a model for other states. Grinnell's original concept of a number of similar, local organizations under a national umbrella reached fruition in 1905 in the National Association of Audubon Societies, an organization that continues well more than a century later as the National Audubon Society: its flagship publication, *Audubon*, traces its roots to Grinnell's *Audubon Magazine*.

33. Merriam, "To the Memory of John Muir," *Sierra Club Bulletin*, Vol. 10, No. 2, January 1917.

34. Muir, *Edward Henry Harriman*, 10.

35. Brinkley, *The Quiet World: Saving Alaska's Wilderness Kingdom, 1879–1960*, 12.

36. See Roosevelt's bibliographic essay "Hunting Lore," the concluding chapter of his *The Wilderness Hunter*.

37. Barrus, *John Burroughs: Boy and Man*, 324.

38. Merriam to Emerson, April 14, 1899, Emerson Papers, Amherst College Archives and Special Collections.

39. See Palache to Emerson, May 2, 1899, Emerson Papers, Amherst College Archives and Special Collections.

40. Kincaid's work, collections, and Cockerell's involvement were described in the "School and College" section of the *Boston Evening Transcript*, December 31, 1897.

41. Kincaid, unpublished "Autobiography" (typescript) 44, Kincaid Papers, Special Collections, Allen Library, University of Washington.

42. Some question has been raised as to whether Grinnell was in fact a member of Merriam's climbing party that midsummer evening. He is identified as among that group, and thus meeting Curtis for the first time, in a number of sources—for example, Goetzmann and Sloan, *Looking Far North: The Harriman Expedition to Alaska, 1899*, 12: Egan, *Short Nights of the Shadow Catcher: The Epic Life and Immortal Photographs of Edward Curtis*, 23 et seq.; Andrews, *Curtis' Western Indians*, 21; Lawlor, *Shadow Catcher: The Life and Work of Edward S. Curtis*, 28–31; Boesen and Graybill, *Edward S. Curtis: Photographer of the North American Indian*, 17–22. Grinnell's highly-respected biographer John Taliaferro argues otherwise (Taliaferro, *Grinnell: America's Environmental Pioneer and His Restless Drive to Save the West*, 540—a footnote to his text at page 272) citing two facts. The first is that Grinnell's diary and correspondence show that he was "not anywhere near the Cascades or Seattle" during the time in question. That observation regarding the contents of Grinnell's writings is correct, though he clearly was in the West that summer visiting Wyoming, the Blackfeet reservation and the St. Mary's Lakes country in Montana, and the Trans-Mississippi and International Exposition in Omaha. Like Taliaferro, I find no specific reference in Grinnell's diary to Mount Rainier or the encounter with Curtis, though that could simply reflect the omission of a relatively short and unrecorded side trip of sorts. While Grinnell was a prolific diarist, his diaries are at times less than complete, if not totally devoid, in their reference to certain events or identification of the participants in other events. For example, in the summer of 1904 Grinnell and his wife Elizabeth travelled to Yellowstone—but no diary of that trip has been found. Another example that directly involves Curtis relates to the medicine lodge ceremony on the Blackfeet reservation in the summer of 1900. While on board the *George W. Elder* near the end of the Harriman Expedition in July 1899, Grinnell and Curtis discussed meeting at this event (as reported in Chapter 17 of this book), and Grinnell wrote to Curtis in the spring of 1900, again urging him to attend. The evidence that Curtis did so is clear in his papers, his photographs, and other evidence: but there is no mention whatever of Curtis in Grinnell's diary covering the week or ten days they spent together with the Blackfeet. Taliaferro also points to Curtis's late-in-life correspondence with Harriet Leitch, former librarian at the Seattle Public Library: specifically a letter from the then 82-year-old Curtis to Leitch dated April 10, 1951 in which he states "You are quite right in thinking that I met George Bird Grinnell on the Expedition." Taliaferro believes that Curtis "clearly meant the Harriman Alaska Expedition" and that this, not on Mount Rainier, was where they met for the first time. However, also not without some ambiguity, in that same correspondence Curtis explained how he happened to be on the Harriman Expedition, particularly how the men he had rescued on Mount Rainier—and who he identified not specifically by name but by referring Leitch to a picture of Merriam, Grinnell, and others taken on the *Elder*—were involved in the planning of the Expedition. An important source bearing on the question of those involved in the encounter on Mount Rainier is the narrative in the Boesen and Graybill work referenced earlier in this note. Graybill was Florence Curtis Graybill—Edward Curtis's daughter. With access to a variety of family and personal papers, Curtis's collected correspondence, and a number of other resources, Boesen and Graybill describe the encounter on the side of Mount Rainier in 1898, identifying both Merriam and Grinnell as among the group that Curtis helped. Thereafter, they record, "During the rest of the winter, having found much in common to discuss on the mountain, Edward and Grinnell kept in touch by mail. In the spring Edward received a letter from Grinnell saying that E.H. Harriman, the railroad magnate, planned a scientific expedition to Alaska, then in the world spotlight for the discovery of

gold." The Boesen and Graybill discussion concludes by quoting from Grinnell's letter: "Mr. Harriman commissioned Mr. Merriam and myself to round up qualified people to go along. We would like to have you with us as chief photographer." The Boesen and Graybill narrative would seem to be authoritative on the question of Grinnell being a part of the Mount Rainier climbing party, and that encounter being where and when Curtis and Grinnell met for the first time.

43. For an extended description of the Merriam-Grinnell encounter with Curtis on Mt. Rainier, see Egan, *Short Nights of the Shadow Catcher: The Epic Life and Immortal Photographs of Edward Curtis*, 23–34.

44. Gifford to Dellenbaugh, April 29, 1899, Dellenbaugh Collection, Beinecke Rare Book and Manuscript Library, Yale University.

45. Starks, Expedition Log, 1, Starks Papers, Green Library, Stanford University.

46. Merriam Home Journals, April 23, 1899, Merriam Papers, Library of Congress.

47. Grinnell in "The Harriman Alaska Expedition Itinerary," *Forest & Stream*, February 24, 1900 at page 142 notes that "There were of necessity some declinations of the invitations given...."

48. Merriam Home Journals, March 31, 1899, Merriam Papers, Library of Congress.

49. Chapman to Fisher, August 19, 1899, Albert K. Fisher Papers, Library of Congress.

50. Keenan, *The Life of Yellowstone Kelly*, xxi.

51. Merriam Home Journals, May 3, 1899, Merriam Papers, Library of Congress.

52. Kelly's recollections of the May 9 and 10 meetings with Harriman are in his "Memoirs Describing Expeditions and Military Service in Alaska and the Philippines," 105–106, unpublished manuscript, Beinecke Rare Book and Manuscript Library, Yale University

53. Copies of this letter are in multiple locations, including the Benjamin K. Emerson Papers, Amherst College Archives and Special Collections, and the Albert K. Fisher Papers, Library of Congress.

54. Harriman to Dellenbaugh, May 18, 1899, Dellenbaugh Collection, Beinecke Rare Book and Manuscript Library, Yale University. An identical letter was sent to each of the members of the Expedition's scientific party.

CHAPTER 2

Somewhere along the way in the twentieth century, the once prevalent habit of keeping a diary began to fade and wane; along, some would say, with the art of legible handwriting. But in 1899, many of the members of the Harriman Expedition were committed diarists: Merriam, Brewer, and others kept excellent personal diaries and journals. Among those, Frederick Dellenbaugh's, in its more than 300 pages, is perhaps the most comprehensive and is extraordinary in its thoroughness, clarity, and detail. In addition to relating the

events of each day and his personal experiences, Dellenbaugh enriched his writing and the record of the Expedition by such additions as pasting in copies of meal menus, inserting the printed programs for shipboard events, and collecting the autographs of the members of the party, including the Harriman's and their entourage, in the final pages of the diary.

While diaries provided a record of events and memories, relatively contemporary communication with those left behind at home could be accomplished only through another art destined for a near complete demise in the later years of the next century: handwritten letters. Despite being at times faced with no idea of when the letters they wrote might actually be put into the mail delivery system, much less received by their addressees, a number of Harriman's guests generated a significant stream of correspondence, often revealing—as letters home to loved ones are wont to do—emotions, interactions, activities, triumphs, embarrassments, and failures that might otherwise have escaped mention. Although there were others, the primary or most frequent (sometimes involving multiple letters to the same person on the same day) letter writers were Charles Palache, Charles Keeler, Louis Agassiz Fuertes, and John Muir.

1. Palache to Helen Markham, May 23, 1899, Palache Papers, Bancroft Library, University of California, Berkeley

2. Dellenbaugh journal, May 23, 1899, Dellenbaugh Collection, Beinecke Rare Book and Manuscript Library, Yale University.

3. Trudeau was the son of physician, pioneering tuberculosis researcher, and long-time Harriman friend Edward Livingston Trudeau, of Saranac Lake, NY. The presence of a "Trained Nurse" was noted in the official listing of members of the Expedition in Volume I of the *Harriman Alaska Series* (see the Appendix to this book), but without reference to the nurse's name. Ms. Adams was identified by name in *The Harriman Alaska Expedition: Chronicles and Souvenirs—May to August 1899*, at page 13. She was also identified by name in William Ritter's diary (undated loose sheet), Ritter Papers, Bancroft Library, University of California, Berkeley.

4. The maids were not specifically included or referenced in the official listing of members of the Expedition discussed in the preceding note and reprinted in this book's Appendix. They were, however, identified in *The Harriman Alaska Expedition: Chronicles and Souvenirs—May to August 1899*, at page 13, and in various diaries and journals as Augusta Larson, Mrs. H.D. Budd, and Adelaide Mangold. See Merriam's expedition diary/journal, entry for June 2, 1899, Merriam Papers, Library of Congress, and Ritter's diary (undated loose sheet), Ritter Papers, Bancroft Library, University of California, Berkeley. The listing in *The Harriman Alaska Expedition: Chronicles and Souvenirs* also includes reference to one "Stevens,"

who is identified as "Mr. Harriman's valet." No other reference to Stevens has been found in any of the diaries, journals, letters, or other written records of the Expedition.

5. The combined nature of Pullman's business is succinctly described in Welsh et al, *The Cars of Pullman*, 6: "The company built, owned, and leased a large fleet of sleeping and parlor cars, which it provided to railroads under contract. The railroads handled the reservations and carried travelers from place to place aboard Pullman cars. Pullman was essentially a giant hotel company." As such, Pullman could shift its fleet of cars and onboard Porters and other personnel around the country, depending on demand.

6. Merriam, expedition diary/journal, May 23, 1899, Merriam Papers, Library of Congress; Klein, *The Life and Legend of E. H. Harriman*, 185 and sources cited. Harriman was having a private car built, but it would not be available until August, when the Expedition returned from Alaska.

7. *The Harriman Alaska Expedition: Chronicles and Souvenirs May to August 1899*, 7.

8. Nelson expedition diary, May 23, 1899, Eberly Family Special Collections Library, Pennsylvania State University. Composition of the special train is also noted in Klein, *The Life and Legend of E. H. Harriman*, 185, citing the UP's June 2, 1899 "Itinerary and Consist of Special Train Carrying the Harriman Alaska Expedition." George Pullman chose to give names to his cars, rather than simply assigning them numbers, for subjective and objective reasons that included the overall image of the company, the idea that it gave each car a personality, and because it enhanced operating and accounting efficiency through the use of different categories of names to signify different categories of cars. A September 7, 1895 *New York Times* story on "How the Pullman Cars Are Named" reported that Pullman's daughter Florence was in charge of naming the cars, and that she evidenced "a decided preference for names which sound euphoniously, and which have a soft and musical quality." Groups of sleepers might carry the names of countries, rivers, historic towns, flowers, or any of a number of categories: the cars in the Harriman special have a Shakespearian ring—"Borachio" being a character in *Much Ado About Nothing*, while "Horatio" was Hamlet's true friend. The *Times* story noted that "There is a fine distinction displayed in the naming of cars for special services. For instance, dining cars are in all cases named after celebrated cooks... and the cooks of famous men and women." The Harriman dining car "Gilsey" may have been named in honor Peter Gilsey, founder of the Gilsey House hotel and restaurant in New York City. As to smoking cars, those, according to the *Times*, "...are given names which suggest luxury and leisurely enjoyment"—which would certainly encompass the "Utopia" on Harriman's special.

9. Welsh et al, *The Cars of Pullman*, 38.

10. Kearney, "Reminiscences of the Harriman Expedition," 1, Waldo L. Schmitt Papers, Smithsonian Institution Archives. Kearney gathered his memories and transmitted them to Schmitt in 1948.

11. Burroughs Journal, May 23, 1899, Burroughs Papers, Archives and Special Collections Library, Vassar College Libraries.

12. Dellenbaugh journal, May 23, 1899, Dellenbaugh Collection, Beinecke Rare Book and Manuscript Library, Yale University. Dellenbaugh pasted his copy of the Bill of Fare into his journal.

13. Palache to Helen Markham, May 23, 1899, Palache Papers, Bancroft Library, University of California, Berkeley

14. Merriam, "Recollections and Impressions of E. H. Harriman," 4, unpublished manuscript, Merriam Papers, Bancroft Library, University of California, Berkeley.

15. *Ibid.*

16. Palache to Helen Markham, May 24, 1899, Palache Papers, Bancroft Library, University of California, Berkeley.

17. Nelson expedition diary, undated entry but most likely May 24 or May 25, 1899, Eberly Family Special Collections Library, Pennsylvania State University.

18. Palache to Helen Markham, May 24, 1899, Palache Papers, Bancroft Library, University of California, Berkeley. Multiple letters of the same date.

19. Burroughs, "Narrative of the Expedition," in Merriam, ed., *Harriman Alaska Series*, Vol. I, 1.

20. *Ibid.*, 3.

21. Dellenbaugh journal, May 25, 1899, Dellenbaugh Collection, Beinecke Rare Book and Manuscript Library, Yale University.

22. Burroughs, "Narrative of the Expedition," in Merriam, ed., *Harriman Alaska Series*, Vol. I, 6–7.

23. Palache to Helen Markham, May 26, 1899, Palache Papers, Bancroft Library, University of California, Berkeley.

24. *Ibid.*, although a separate letter of the same date: Palache wrote to Helen twice on the 26th, both letters relating to the events of the previous day.

25. Palache to Helen Markham, May 28, 1899, Palache Papers, Bancroft Library, University of California, Berkeley.

26. Burroughs, "Narrative of the Expedition," in Merriam, ed., *Harriman Alaska Series*, Vol. I, 7.

27. Palache to Helen Markham, May 28, 1899, Palache Papers, Bancroft Library, University of California, Berkeley.

28. Dall diary, May 28, 1899, Dall Papers, Smithsonian Institution Archives.

29. Starks, Expedition Log for May 28, 1899, Starks Papers, Green Library, Stanford University.

30. Burroughs, "Narrative of the Expedition," in Merriam, ed., *Harriman Alaska Series*, Vol. I, 14; Palache to Helen Markham, May 30, 1899, Palache Papers, Bancroft Library, University of

California, Berkeley; Klein, *The Life and Legend of E. H. Harriman*, 186. Klein notes that A. L. Mohler, President of the Oregon Short Line, joined the party in Lewiston. The Short Line, which was owned by the Union Pacific, was laying branch lines in the area in competition with the Northern Pacific, and Harriman and Mohler had a chance to take a look at the work as they moved down the Snake. The description of the interruption caused by the train wreck is taken from Keeler to Louise Keeler, May 31, 1899, Keeler Papers, Bancroft Library, University of California, Berkeley—where it is part of a long letter describing what, when he and John Muir joined the party in Portland, Keeler had heard about the main group's cross-country trip.

31. Palache to Helen Markham, May 30, 1899, Palache Papers, Bancroft Library, University of California, Berkeley; Burroughs, "Narrative of the Expedition," in Merriam, ed., *Harriman Alaska Series*, Vol. I, 16.

32. Muir to Walter Hines Page, May 25, 1899, as noted in Bade, *The Life and Letters of John Muir*, Vol. II, 320–321.

33. Keeler to Louise Keeler, May 27, 1899, Keeler Papers, Bancroft Library, University of California, Berkeley.

34. Keeler to Louise Keeler, May 28, 1899, Keeler Papers, Bancroft Library, University of California, Berkeley.

35. Muir journal, May 26, 1899, Muir Papers, Special Collections, Holt-Atherton Center for Pacific Studies, University of the Pacific. Copyright 1984 Muir-Hanna Trust.

36. Keeler to Louise Keeler, May 27, 1899, Keeler Papers, Bancroft Library, University of California, Berkeley.

37. The conversations with Holabird are noted in Muir's journal of May 26, 1899, Muir Papers, Special Collections, Holt-Atherton Center for Pacific Studies, University of the Pacific, Copyright 1984 Muir-Hanna Trust, and in Keeler's May 27th letter to Louise Keeler, Keeler Papers, Bancroft Library, University of California, Berkeley.

38. *The Oregonian*, May 30, 1899.

39. Keeler to Louise Keeler, May 31, 1899, Keeler Papers, Bancroft Library, University of California, Berkeley.

40. Fredell, Diary of a Trip to Alaska, Beinecke Rare Book and Manuscript Library, Yale University.

41. Kelly, "Memoirs Describing Expeditions and Military Service in Alaska and the Philippines," unpublished manuscript, Beinecke Rare Book and Manuscript Library, Yale University.

42. Guberlet, *The Windows to His World: The Story of Trevor Kincaid*, 109, pinpoints the *Elder* as tying-up at the Seneca Street wharf.

43. Factual information concerning the *George W. Elder* is drawn from a number of sources, most notably from Elder, "SS *George W. Elder*: A Chronology," *PowerShips*, Fall 2014, 46–50. The author of this comprehensive article on the

history and service of the *Elder* was George William Elder, who was distantly related, but with no blood line connection, to the ship's namesake.

44. Keeler to Louise Keeler, May 31, 1899, Keeler Papers, Bancroft Library, University of California, Berkeley.

45. Muir journal, May 31, 1899, Muir Papers, Special Collections, Holt-Atherton Center for Pacific Studies, University of the Pacific. Copyright 1984 Muir-Hanna Trust.

46. Emerson Papers, Special Collections, Amherst College Library.

47. Palache to Helen Markham, May 31, 1899, Palache Papers, Bancroft Library, University of California, Berkeley

48. Merriam expedition diary/journal, May 31, 1899, Merriam Papers, Library of Congress; Kennan, *E. H. Harriman*, Vol. I, 190; Klein, *The Life and Legend of E. H. Harriman*, 187.

49. Burroughs, "Narrative of the Expedition," in Merriam, ed., *Harriman Alaska Series*, Vol. I, 17–18. As to the "menagerie," Nelson estimated that there were thirty sheep in the flock. Nelson expedition diary, May 31, 1899, Eberly Family Special Collections Library, Pennsylvania State University.

50. Roland Harriman, *I Reminisce*, 3–4.

51. Burroughs, "Narrative of the Expedition," in Merriam, ed., *Harriman Alaska Series*, Vol. I, 18.

52. The invaluable resource for this and later discussions relating to the deck and cabin plans are the blueprints of the *Elder's* passenger accommodations which reside in the Historic Documents Collection of the San Francisco Maritime National Historical Park, Fort Mason, San Francisco, California.

53. Keeler to Louise Keeler, May 31, 1899, Keeler Papers, Bancroft Library, University of California, Berkeley (Keeler's second May 31 letter to Louise).

54. Fuertes to his parents, May 31, 1899, Fuertes Papers, Division of Rare and Manuscript Collections, Cornell University Library.

55. Fuertes to his parents, June 1, 1899, Fuertes Papers, Division of Rare and Manuscript Collections, Cornell University Library.

56. Kincaid quoted in Guberlet, *The Windows to His World: The Story of Trevor Kincaid*, 47.

57. Dellenbaugh journal, May 31, 1899, Dellenbaugh Collection, Beinecke Rare Book and Manuscript Library, Yale University. Averell Harriman would recall that the band music played on departure was the Star Spangled Banner. Abramson, *Spanning the Century: The Life of W. Averell Harriman, 1891–1986*, 68.

CHAPTER 3

Of the various books and other writings drawn on for this chapter and its brief overview of the history of Alaska, as well as the nature and depth of the exploration of the territory, those of particular value to this work were the third edition of *Alaska: A History* by Claus-M Naske and Herman Slotnick, and Morgan Sherwood's *Exploration of Alaska, 1865–1900*. The former is encyclopedic and pulls together many other sources; the latter is a focused study of the nature of Alaskan exploration and the key players and agencies in that effort during the period of American ownership to the close of the nineteenth century, culminating with the Harriman Expedition. Douglas Brinkley's sweeping account in *The Quiet World: Saving Alaska's Wilderness Kingdom, 1879–1960*, is another outstanding reference and resource for anyone interested in wilderness preservation and "the Great Land."

1. Elliott, *The Condition of Affairs in the Territory of Alaska*, 3.
2. Gannett, "General Geography," in Merriam, ed., *Harriman Alaska Series*, Vol. II, 297.
3. Rogers and Cooley, *Alaska's Population and Economy: Regional Growth, Development and Future Outlook*, Vol. 2, *Statistical Handbook*, 7.
4. Dall, "The Discovery and Exploration of Alaska," in Merriam, ed., *Harriman Alaska Series*, Vol. II, 185.
5. As to Bering's expeditions, see Fisher, *Bering's Voyages: Whither and Why*; Steller, *Journal of a Voyage with Bering, 1741–1742*; Naske and Slotnick, *Alaska: A History*, 3rd Edition, 33–47.
6. Steller, *Journal of a Voyage with Bering, 1741–1742*, 144–145.
7. Dall, "The Discovery and Exploration of Alaska," in Merriam, ed., *Harriman Alaska Series*, Vol. II, 193.
8. Black, *Russians in Alaska, 1732–1867*, 129; Langdon, *The Native People of Alaska*, 24.
9. Dall, "The Discovery and Exploration of Alaska," in Merriam, ed., *Harriman Alaska Series*, Vol. II, 194.
10. Naske and Slotnick, *Alaska: A History*, 3rd Edition, 69.
11. Fedorova, *The Russian Population in Alaska and California: Late 18th Century–1867*, 154 is the source for the Russian population figure of 700. Brinkley, *The Quiet World: Saving Alaska's Wilderness Kingdom, 1879–1960*, 32 gives the slightly higher number of eight hundred Russian settlers.
12. Bolhovitinov, *Russian-American Relations and the Sale of Alaska, 1843–1867*, 64; Naske and Slotnick, *Alaska: A History*, 3rd Edition, 87–88.
13. Bolhovitinov, *Russian-American Relations and the Sale of Alaska, 1843–1867*, 101–102; Naske and Slotnick, *Alaska: A History*, 3rd Edition, 88.
14. Bolhovitinov, *Russian-American Relations and the Sale of Alaska, 1843–1867*, 212–217.
15. Ransom, "Derivation of the Word Alaska," *American Anthropologist*, July 1940, 550–551.
16. Black, *Russians in Alaska, 1732–1867*, 285–286.
17. Dall, "The Discovery and Exploration of Alaska," in Merriam, ed., *Harriman Alaska Series*, Vol. II, 203.

18. Naske and Slotnick, *Alaska: A History*, 3rd Edition, 102.
19. *Ibid.*, 99–100.
20. *Ibid.*, 112.
21. Organic Act of 1884, 23 U.S. Stat. 24.
22. Naske and Slotnick, *Alaska: A History*, 3rd Edition, 142 and Appendix E, citing Rogers and Cooley, *Alaska's Population and Economy: Regional Growth, Development and Future Outlook*, Vol. 1.
23. From "A Short History of the Klondike Gold Rush," Klondike Gold Rush National Historical Park—Seattle Unit section of the National Park Service web site, www.nps.gov/klse.
24. Curtis, "The Rush To The Klondike Over The Mountain Passes," *Century Magazine*, March 1898, 697.
25. Gannett, "General Geography," in Merriam, ed., *Harriman Alaska Series*, Vol. II, 276.
26. Naske and Slotnick, *Alaska: A History*, 3rd Edition, 131.
27. Grinnell, "The Salmon Industry," in Merriam, ed., *Harriman Alaska Series*, Vol. II, 337.
28. Naske and Slotnick, *Alaska: A History*, 3rd Edition, 107 and sources cited.
29. Sherwood, *Exploration of Alaska, 1865–1900*, 71.
30. *Ibid.*, 187.
31. Brinkley, *The Quiet World: Saving Alaska's Wilderness Kingdom, 1879–1960*, 26.

Chapter 4

John Burroughs and George Bird Grinnell, while naturalists, environmentalists, and early conservationists, were also writers by profession, and they were the two members of the Harriman Expedition who would write most broadly and comprehensively about the journey and the activities of those gathered aboard the *George W. Elder*. Burroughs was the Expedition's designated historian, and he was clearly conscious of his position as the literary spokesman of the party in writing the chronological "Narrative of the Expedition" for the official publication, the *Harriman Alaska Series*, and undoubtedly had in mind that this would be the piece that would be most widely read by the public and quoted in the popular press, and would create widespread impressions of the journey, its participants, and the "unknown country" the Expedition visited. Those pressures or considerations notwithstanding, he created a superbly written document that not only tells an accurate story but provides ample evidence of his inimitable way with words and the ability to repeatedly turn a creative, uniquely descriptive phrase. Grinnell succeeded in the same way in multiple essays he wrote for the *Harriman Alaska Series* and, to perhaps an even greater extent, in a fifteen-part series he wrote for *Forest & Stream* magazine and which began appearing in that publication in February 1900. Unlike Burroughs in the Narrative, Grinnell did not need to write sequentially or chronologically. Instead, he wrote by subject, and his magazine articles cover a wide range of topics from Indians to fur seal destruction to the adventures of the hunters and to life aboard the *Elder*. Although his approach differed from Burroughs's, he succeeded in equal measure and, via the magazine's significant circulation, likely reached an even wider audience. Taken as a whole, Grinnell's contributions complement Burroughs's Narrative, and stand with it for their literary as well as historical merit.

1. Merriam, "Introduction" to the *Harriman Alaska Series*, Vol. I, xxix. This was the same Pritchett who had been considered by Harriman and Merriam, and was identified in the April 23, 1899 *New York Herald* story as among those who would be members of the party, but who—if actually invited—had declined the invitation.

2. Keeler to Louise Keeler, June 1, 1899, Keeler Papers, Bancroft Library, University of California, Berkeley.

3. Burroughs, "Narrative of the Expedition," in Merriam, ed., *Harriman Alaska Series*, Vol. I, 19.

4. Palache to Helen Markham, June 1, 1899, Palache Papers, Bancroft Library, University of California, Berkeley.

5. Nelson expedition diary, June 1, 1899, Eberly Family Special Collections Library, Pennsylvania State University.

6. Dall diary, June 1, 1899, Dall Papers, Smithsonian Institution Archives.

7. Burroughs, "Narrative of the Expedition," in Merriam, ed., *Harriman Alaska Series*, Vol. I, 62–63.

8. Grinnell, "The Harriman Alaska Expedition: Life on Shipboard," *Forest & Stream*, June 16, 1900, 464–465.

9. Nelson expedition diary, June 2, 1899, Eberly Family Special Collections Library, Pennsylvania State University.

10. Elder, "SS *George W. Elder*: A Chronology," *PowerShips*, Fall 2014, 47.

11. Palache to Helen Markham, June 3, 1899, Palache Papers, Bancroft Library, University of California, Berkeley.

12. Burroughs, "Narrative of the Expedition," in Merriam, ed., *Harriman Alaska Series*, Vol. I, 21.

13. Fuertes's explorations on Princess Royal Island were reported in a letter to his parents, apparently dated June 3, 1899, quoted in Boynton, *Louis Agassiz Fuertes: His Life Briefly Told and His Correspondence Edited*, 44–45.

14. Fuertes to his parents, June 7, 1899, Fuertes Papers, Division of Rare and Manuscript Collections, Cornell University Library.

15. Fuertes autobiographical manuscript, Fuertes Papers, Division of Rare and Manuscript Collections, Cornell University. See also Peck, *A Celebration of Birds: The Life and Art of Louis Agassiz Fuertes*, pages 45 et seq. for analysis of Fuertes's approach as "A Painter of Life," and additional discussion at pages 99 et seq. of the application of that approach in Fuertes's work on the Harriman Expedition.

16. Keeler to Louise Keeler, June 3, 1899, Keeler Papers, Bancroft Library, University of California, Berkeley.

17. "Metlakatla" was spelled "Metlakahtla" by some, and the village was originally referred to as "New Metlakatla." In addition, the diaries and letters of Expedition party members contain other variations based on individual attempts at committing the name to a string of letters that in one writer or another's mind reflected how it sounded. "Metlakatla" is used consistently here, and it is the name and spelling that the village carries to this day.

18. Palache provided an extensive abstract of Nelson's talk in a letter to Helen Markham, June 3, 1899, Palache Papers, Bancroft Library, University of California, Berkeley. Other details in this brief history of the founding of "New" Metlakatla are drawn from the web site of the Metlakatla Indian Community at www.metlakatla.com/community origins.

19. Burroughs, "Narrative of the Expedition," in Merriam, ed., *Harriman Alaska Series*, Vol. I, 25.

20. *Ibid.*, 24.

21. Grinnell, "The Natives of the Alaska Coast Region," in Merriam, ed., *Harriman Alaska Series*, Vol. I, 155.

22. Burroughs, "Narrative of the Expedition," in Merriam, ed., *Harriman Alaska Series*, Vol. I, 26.

23. *Ibid.*, 25.

24. *Ibid.*, 24.

25. Grinnell, "The Natives of the Alaska Coast Region," in Merriam, ed., *Harriman Alaska Series*, Vol. I, 153–154.

26. "Mr. Harriman Talks of Alaska," *New York Daily Tribune*, August 14, 1899, 12.

27. Metlakatla Indian Community web site, www.metlakatla.com.

28. Keeler to Louise Keeler, June 4, 1899, Keeler Papers, Bancroft Library, University of California, Berkeley.

29. Dellenbaugh journal, June 4, 1899, Dellenbaugh Collection, Beinecke Rare Book and Manuscript Library, Yale University.

30. *Ibid.*

31. Burroughs journal, June 22, 1896, Burroughs's papers, Archives and Special Collections Library, Vassar College Libraries.

32. Burroughs, "Narrative of the Expedition," in Merriam, ed., *Harriman Alaska Series*, Vol. I, 18.

33. Warren, *John Burroughs and the Place of Nature*, 116.

34. Burroughs journal, December 25, 1914, Burroughs's papers, Archives and Special Collections Library, Vassar College Libraries.

35. Muir, *Travels in Alaska*, 18.

36. Burroughs, "Narrative of the Expedition," in Merriam, ed., *Harriman Alaska Series*, Vol. I, 27; Keeler to Louise Keeler, June 5, 1899, Keeler Papers, Bancroft Library, University of California,

Berkeley; Dellenbaugh journal, June 5, 1899, Dellenbaugh Collection, Beinecke Rare Book and Manuscript Library, Yale University; Dall, "Alaskan Notes," *The Nation*, August 17, 1899.

37. Muir journal, June 5, 1899, Muir Papers, Special Collections, Holt-Atherton Center for Pacific Studies, University of the Pacific. Copyright 1984 Muir-Hanna Trust.

38. Fuertes, Alaskan Journal, June 5, 1899, Fuertes Papers, Division of Rare and Manuscript Collections, Cornell University.

39. Palache to Helen Markham, June 5, 1899, Palache Papers, Bancroft Library, University of California, Berkeley.

40. Burroughs, "Narrative of the Expedition," in Merriam, ed., *Harriman Alaska Series*, Vol. I, 28.

41. Dellenbaugh journal, June 6, 1899, Dellenbaugh Collection, Beinecke Rare Book and Manuscript Library, Yale University.

42. Palache to Helen Markham, June 6, 1899, Palache Papers, Bancroft Library, University of California, Berkeley.

43. "Alaska's Renowned First Large-Scale, Low-Grade Gold Mine," *The Juneau Empire*, December 31, 2003.

44. Palache to Helen Markham, June 6, 1899, Palache Papers, Bancroft Library, University of California, Berkeley.

45. *Ibid.*

46. Dellenbaugh journal, June 6, 1899, Dellenbaugh Collection, Beinecke Rare Book and Manuscript Library, Yale University.

47. "Alaska's Renowned First Large-Scale, Low-Grade Gold Mine," *The Juneau Empire*, December 31, 2003.

48. Burroughs, "Narrative of the Expedition," in Merriam, ed., *Harriman Alaska Series*, Vol. I, 29.

49. Palache to Helen Markham, June 5, 1899, Palache Papers, Bancroft Library, University of California, Berkeley.

50. Kincaid, unpublished "Autobiography" (typescript) 49, Kincaid Papers, Special Collections, Allen Library, University of Washington. Kincaid was in the party that had stayed in Juneau and, thus, was not himself on board the *Elder* when the dog was discovered; assumedly he heard the story from someone who was on the ship at the time.

Chapter 5

There is a wealth of resources on the Klondike Gold Rush, "Soapy" Smith, the history of Skagway, and the sidelights and side stories pertaining to all three. Particularly useful to the historical sketch presented at the beginning of this chapter were William Hunt's *North of 53°: The Wild Days of the Alaska-Yukon Mining Frontier, 1870–1914*; Roy Minter's *The White Pass: Gateway to the Klondike*; Pierre Berton's *Klondike: The Last Great Gold Rush, 1896–1899*; and the resources and staff of

the Klondike Gold Rush National Historical Park, which has units in both Skagway and Seattle.

1. *The Harriman Alaska Expedition: Chronicles and Souvenirs May to August 1899*, 298A.

2. Burroughs, "Narrative of the Expedition," in Merriam, ed., *Harriman Alaska Series*, Vol. I, 30–31.

3. *Ibid.*

4. *Ibid.*, 31.

5. Muir journal, June 7, 1899, Muir Papers, Special Collections, Holt-Atherton Center for Pacific Studies, University of the Pacific. Copyright 1984 Muir-Hanna Trust.

6. London, "Which Make Men Remember," in *The God of His Fathers and Other Stories*, 68.

7. Grinnell, "The Harriman Alaska Expedition: Itinerary," *Forest & Stream*, February 24, 1900, 142–143.

8. Merriam expedition diary/journal, June 7, 1899, Merriam Papers, Library of Congress

9. Burroughs, "Narrative of the Expedition," in Merriam, ed., *Harriman Alaska Series*, Vol. I, 34. Many of the specimens collected by the three-man Osgood party were lost weeks later when their boat swamped on the Yukon River.

10. Dellenbaugh journal, June 7, 1899, Dellenbaugh Collection, Beinecke Rare Book and Manuscript Library, Yale University.

11. It would be January of 1903 before the dispute was settled with the signing of the Alaska Boundary Treaty. Then U.S. Secretary of State John Hay viewed the outcome with satisfaction: "We give up 30 square miles of our claim, which we don't want, and the Canadians have to give up 30,000 square miles of their claim, which is of enormous value." Hay to Clara Hay, October 18, 1903, John Hay Papers, Library of Congress.

12. Dellenbaugh journal, June 7, 1899, Dellenbaugh Collection, Beinecke Rare Book and Manuscript Library, Yale University.

13. Grinnell diary, June 7, 1899, Grinnell papers, University of Montana.

14. Dall, "Alaskan Notes," *The Nation*, August 17, 1899, 128.

15. Dellenbaugh journal, June 7, 1899, Dellenbaugh Collection, Beinecke Rare Book and Manuscript Library, Yale University.

16. Palache to Helen Markham, June 6, 1899, Palache Papers, Bancroft Library, University of California, Berkeley

17. Palache to Helen Markham, June 7, 1899, Palache Papers, Bancroft Library, University of California, Berkeley

18. Palache to Helen Markham, June 10, 1899, Palache Papers, Bancroft Library, University of California, Berkeley

19. Ritter diary, June 7, 1899, Ritter Papers, Bancroft Library, University of California, Berkeley.

20. Starks Expedition Log, June 7, 1899, Starks Papers, Green Library, Stanford University.

21. Palache to Helen Markham, June 10, 1899, Palache Papers, Bancroft Library, University of California, Berkeley

22. Gannett, "General Geography," in Merriam, ed., *Harriman Alaska Series*, Vol. II, 258.

23. Grinnell, "The Harriman Alaska Expedition: Life on Shipboard," *Forest & Stream*, June 16, 1900, 465.

24. Muir, *Edward Henry Harriman*, 10–11.

25. Dellenbaugh journal, June 8, 1899, Dellenbaugh Collection, Beinecke Rare Book and Manuscript Library, Yale University.

Chapter 6

This chapter begins and ends—in its first and last sentences—with John Muir, and his thoughts and observations logically permeate the record of a near week-long sojourn by the Harriman Expedition in what was truly "John Muir Country." Though he kept many journals and other forms of notes, Muir was, as John Burroughs would observe, "greater as a talker than as a writer," and much of his journal keeping was literally "on the fly" in notebooks he sometimes tied to his belt on his journeys, and in which he scribbled shorthand thoughts and observations, not always dated, and most of which he didn't revise or expand upon. Fortunately, these unpublished works were carefully edited, and organized by others, in particular William Frederick Badé and Linnie Marsh Wolfe. And Burroughs may have slyly been crediting Muir's speech and lamenting only the relative paucity, not the quality, of his written work. In truth, throughout his life Muir displayed considerable literary talent, though many of his books were published after the Expedition, including *Travels in Alaska* and his short and remarkable tribute, *Edward Henry Harriman*.

1. Muir, *Travels in Alaska*, 153. Henry Fielding Reid was a leading seismologist and a pioneer geophysicist.

2. Burroughs, "Narrative of the Expedition," in Merriam, ed., *Harriman Alaska Series*, Vol. I, 35.

3. Fuertes to his parents, undated letter but apparently June 8, 1899, Fuertes Papers, Division of Rare and Manuscript Collections, Cornell University Library.

4. Muir, *Travels in Alaska*, 77, 86.

5. Brinkley, *The Quiet World: Saving Alaska's Wilderness Kingdom, 1879–1960*, 6 and sources cited.

6. Muir, *Travels in Alaska*, 86–87. Muir's Tlingit guides, echoing Vancouver, referred to the area as "the big ice-mountain bay" or the "Ice Bay."

7. *Ibid.*, 142.

8. Muir, "Notes on the Pacific Coast Glaciers," in Merriam, ed., *Harriman Alaska Series*, Vol. I, 128; Gannett, "The Harriman Alaska Expedition," *Journal of the American Geographical Society of New York*, Vol. 31, No. 4, 352–353.

9. Brinkley, *The Quiet World: Saving Alaska's Wilderness Kingdom, 1879–1960*, 6 and sources cited.

10. Merriam expedition diary/journal, June 9, 1899, Merriam Papers, Library of Congress; Merriam, "Recollections and Impressions of E. H. Harriman," 8, unpublished manuscript, Merriam Papers, Bancroft Library, University of California, Berkeley.

11. Grinnell, "The Harriman Alaska Expedition: Big Game Hunters," *Forest & Stream*, March 16, 1900, 183.

12. Nelson expedition diary, June 8, 1899, Eberly Family Special Collections Library, Pennsylvania State University.

13. Merriam, "Recollections and Impressions of E. H. Harriman," 8, unpublished manuscript, Merriam Papers, Bancroft Library, University of California, Berkeley.

14. Dellenbaugh journal, June 9, 1899, Dellenbaugh Collection, Beinecke Rare Book and Manuscript Library, Yale University.

15. Palache to Helen Markham, June 10, 1899, Palache Papers, Bancroft Library, University of California, Berkeley

16. Typically, a Nunatak is the rocky peak of a mountain protruding out of the glacial field.

17. Muir journal, June 9, 1899, Muir Papers, Special Collections, Holt-Atherton Center for Pacific Studies, University of the Pacific, Copyright 1984 Muir-Hanna Trust.

18. Roland Harriman, *I Reminisce*, 6–7.

19. Muir, *Edward Henry Harriman*, 12.

20. Dellenbaugh journal, June 9, 1899, Dellenbaugh Collection, Beinecke Rare Book and Manuscript Library, Yale University.

21. Burroughs, "Narrative of the Expedition," in Merriam, ed., *Harriman Alaska Series*, Vol. I, 37.

22. Dellenbaugh journal, June 9, 1899, Dellenbaugh Collection, Beinecke Rare Book and Manuscript Library, Yale University.

23. Muir journal, June 9, 1899, Muir Papers, Special Collections, Holt-Atherton Center for Pacific Studies, University of the Pacific, Copyright 1984 Muir-Hanna Trust.

24. Egan, *Short Nights of the Shadow Catcher: The Epic Life and Immortal Photographs of Edward Curtis*, 36; Lawlor, *Shadow Catcher: The Life and Work of Edward S. Curtis*, 35.

25. Palache to Helen Markham, June 10, 1899, Palache Papers, Bancroft Library, University of California, Berkeley The account of the geologists' foray on Friday the 9th is based on, and the quotations in this text paragraph are from, this lengthy letter from Palache to Helen Markham.

26. Grinnell, "The Harriman Alaska Expedition: Big Game Hunters," *Forest & Stream*, March 16, 1900, 183.

27. Nelson expedition diary, June 9, 1899, Eberly Family Special Collections Library, Pennsylvania State University.

28. Kelly, "Memoirs Describing Expeditions and Military Service in Alaska and the Philippines," 114, unpublished manuscript, Beinecke Rare Book and Manuscript Library, Yale University.

29. Grinnell, "The Harriman Alaska Expedition: Big Game Hunters," *Forest & Stream*, March 16, 1900, 183.

30. Merriam expedition diary/journal, June 9, 1899, Merriam Papers, Library of Congress.

31. *Ibid.*

32. Dellenbaugh journal, June 9, 1899, Dellenbaugh Collection, Beinecke Rare Book and Manuscript Library, Yale University.

33. Burroughs, "Narrative of the Expedition," in Merriam, ed., *Harriman Alaska Series*, Vol. I, 39.

34. Boynton, *Louis Agassiz Fuertes: His Life Briefly Told and His Correspondence Edited*, 47, quoting a letter from Fuertes to his parents dated "June 7 10:00 p.m." The letter is either incorrectly dated, since it clearly refers to Muir's June 9 lecture, or it may have been started on the 7th and completed over the following days.

35. Muir to Louise Muir and daughters, June 14, 1899, Muir Papers, Special Collections, Holt-Atherton Center for Pacific Studies, University of the Pacific, Copyright 1984 Muir-Hanna Trust.

36. Fuertes to his parents, June 11, 1899, Fuertes Papers, Division of Rare and Manuscript Collections, Cornell University Library.

37. Fuertes to his parents, June 12, 1899, Fuertes Papers, Division of Rare and Manuscript Collections, Cornell University Library.

38. Palache to Helen Markham, June 14, 1899, Palache Papers, Bancroft Library, University of California, Berkeley.

39. *Ibid.*

40. Muir to Louise Muir and daughters, June 14, 1899, Muir Papers, Special Collections, Holt-Atherton Center for Pacific Studies, University of the Pacific, Copyright 1984 Muir-Hanna Trust.

41. Wolfe, *John of the Mountains: The Unpublished Journals of John Muir*, 386.

42. Palache to Helen Markham, June 14, 1899, Palache Papers, Bancroft Library, University of California, Berkeley.

43. *Ibid.*

44. Muir journal, June 12, 1899, Muir Papers, Special Collections, Holt-Atherton Center for Pacific Studies, University of the Pacific, Copyright 1984 Muir-Hanna Trust.

45. Merriam, "Recollections and Impressions of E. H. Harriman," 8, unpublished manuscript, Merriam Papers, Bancroft Library, University of California, Berkeley.

46. Burroughs, "Narrative of the Expedition," in Merriam, ed., *Harriman Alaska Series*, Vol. I, 40.

47. Dellenbaugh journal, June 11, 1899, Dellenbaugh Collection, Beinecke Rare Book and Manuscript Library, Yale University.

48. Keeler, "Notes on Muir Glacier," Keeler Papers, Bancroft Library, University of California, Berkeley.

49. Nelson expedition diary, June 10, 1899, Eberly Family Special Collections Library, Pennsylvania State University. It appears that Nelson noted the date incorrectly; Sunday was June 11, not the 10th.

50. Muir journal, June 14, 1899, Muir Papers, Special Collections, Holt-Atherton Center for Pacific Studies, University of the Pacific, Copyright 1984 Muir-Hanna Trust.

Chapter 7

The Reverend Dr. George Nelson had interests, approaches, and perspectives which differed from many of the others who traveled on the *Elder*. Often he remained on the ship to think, read, and write while others were off collecting or hunting or simply sightseeing. And when he did go ashore it was with a curiosity and purpose that was at times uniquely his own. The entries in his diary—whether concerning life on board ship or while ashore—often speak to details and incidents that find little or no mention in the writings of other members of the party, and which add much to the day-to-day story of the Harriman Alaska Expedition. For example, at the outset of the journey it was Nelson who walked the platform at Grand Central Station in New York City to inspect the train and record the names of the special's Pullman cars. And this chapter's tale of life in Sitka benefits from Nelson's notes on Governor Brady's reception, and of a missionary-like trip to the local jail.

1. Palache to Helen Markham, June 15, 1899, Palache Papers, Bancroft Library, University of California, Berkeley.

2. Muir journal, July 15, 1879, Muir Papers, Special Collections, Holt-Atherton Center for Pacific Studies, University of the Pacific, Copyright 1984 Muir-Hanna Trust.

3. Keeler to Louise Keeler, June 17, 1899, Keeler Papers, Bancroft Library, University of California, Berkeley.

4. Ritter diary, June 14, 1899, Ritter Papers, Bancroft Library, University of California, Berkeley.

5. Wyatt, "Introduction" to Grinnell, *The Harriman Expedition to Alaska: Encountering the Tlingit and Eskimo in 1899*, xl.

6. Nelson expedition diary, June 14, 1899, Eberly Family Special Collections Library, Pennsylvania State University.

7. Schiff, "Yalies in Alaska's History: John Green Brady," *Yale Alumni Magazine*, January/February 2007.

8. Muir journal, June 15, 1899, Muir Papers, Special Collections, Holt-Atherton Center for Pacific Studies, University of the Pacific, Copyright 1984 Muir-Hanna Trust.

9. Muir journal, June 15, 1899, Muir Papers, Special Collections, Holt-Atherton Center for Pacific Studies, University of the Pacific, Copyright 1984 Muir-Hanna Trust.

10. Palache to Helen Markham, June 15, 1899, Palache Papers, Bancroft Library, University of California, Berkeley.

11. Fuertes Alaskan Journal, June 16, 1899, Fuertes Papers, Division of Rare and Manuscript Collections, Cornell University.

Special Collections, Holt-Atherton Center for Pacific Studies, University of the Pacific, Copyright 1984 Muir-Hanna Trust.

12. Grinnell, "The Harriman Alaska Expedition: Big Game Hunters," *Forest & Stream*, March 10, 1900, 183–184.

13. Dellenbaugh journal, June 15, 1899, Dellenbaugh Collection, Beinecke Rare Book and Manuscript Library, Yale University.

14. Merriam expedition diary/journal, June 15, 1899, Merriam Papers, Library of Congress.

15. Ritter diary, June 15, 1899, Ritter Papers, Bancroft Library, University of California, Berkeley.

16. Muir journal, June 16, 1899, Muir Papers, Special Collections, Holt-Atherton Center for Pacific Studies, University of the Pacific, Copyright 1984 Muir-Hanna Trust.

17. Keeler, "Recollections of John Muir," *Sierra Club Bulletin*, John Muir Memorial Number, January 1916.

18. Palache to Helen Markham, June 17, 1899, Palache Papers, Bancroft Library, University of California, Berkeley.

19. Keeler to Louise Keeler, June 16, 1899, Keeler Papers, Bancroft Library, University of California, Berkeley. All of this was contained in two separate letters to Louise, both dated June 16. The one Keeler wrote while standing on the wharf was completed in time to leave Sitka on the *Topeka* when it left for Seattle early that afternoon. The other was apparently deposited at the Sitka post office later in the day, to await the next southbound ship.

20. Nelson expedition diary, June 16, 1899, Eberly Family Special Collections Library, Pennsylvania State University; Dellenbaugh journal, June 17, 1899, Dellenbaugh Collection, Beinecke Rare Book and Manuscript Library, Yale University.

21. Burroughs, "Narrative of the Expedition," in Merriam, ed., *Harriman Alaska Series*, Vol. I, 50.

22. Keeler to Louise Keeler, June 17, 1899, Keeler Papers, Bancroft Library, University of California, Berkeley.

23. Dellenbaugh journal, June 16, 1899, Dellenbaugh Collection, Beinecke Rare Book and Manuscript Library, Yale University.

24. Ritter diary, June 17, 1899, Ritter Papers, Bancroft Library, University of California, Berkeley.

25. Burroughs, "Narrative of the Expedition," in Merriam, ed., *Harriman Alaska Series*, Vol. I, 50.

26. Kincaid, unpublished "Autobiography" (typescript), 50, Kincaid Papers, Special Collections, Allen Library, University of Washington. While Kincaid referred to a "phonograph," the device involved was clearly Harriman's Graphophone, which was an adaptation of Edison's phonograph. According to Dauenhauer, *Haa Tuwunáagu Yís, for Healing Our Spirit*, the speeches and songs recorded by Harriman are the oldest known sound recordings of Tlingit. It was not, however, the first time one of those present had used a Graphophone to record tribal songs. In the late summer of 1897, Grinnell went west, packing a Graphophone with a forty-inch, leatherette horn, and dozens of wax cylinders. First on the Northern Cheyenne reservation and then on a visit to the Blackfeet, "he filled nearly eighty cylinders, recording more than one hundred songs." Taliaferro, *Grinnell: America's Environmental Pioneer and His Restless Drive to Save the West*, 244–245, referencing Grinnell diary of September 22, 1897, Grinnell papers, Braun Research Library, Autry Museum of the American West.

27. Nelson expedition diary, June 16, 1899, Eberly Family Special Collections Library, Pennsylvania State University.

28. Dellenbaugh journal, June 16, 1899, Dellenbaugh Collection, Beinecke Rare Book and Manuscript Library, Yale University.

29. Keeler to Louise and Merodine Keeler, June 17, 1899, Keeler Papers, Bancroft Library, University of California, Berkeley.

30. Muir journal, June 17, 1899, Muir Papers, Special Collections, Holt-Atherton Center for Pacific Studies, University of the Pacific, Copyright 1984 Muir-Hanna Trust.

31. Nelson expedition diary, June 17, 1899, Eberly Family Special Collections Library, Pennsylvania State University. Soon after the departure of the Harriman Expedition from Sitka, the sometimes crowded conditions and lengthy trial waits that Nelson saw and learned of, along with the general lack of law and order, especially in the remote communities, would lead C.S. Johnson, judge for the District Court of Alaska, headquartered in Sitka, to determine that he should hold court throughout the territory. That summer, Judge Johnson, accompanied by U.S. Attorney A.J. Daly and Governor Brady, traveled to Dawson, and from there down the Yukon River, holding court at various settlements. They went on to St. Michaels, Nome, Dutch Harbor, and points in between before returning to Sitka, covering in total over seven thousand miles. See Naske and Slotnick, *Alaska: A History*, 3rd Edition, 131.

32. Grinnell, "The Harriman Alaska Expedition: Indians," *Forest & Stream*, March 31, 1900, 244.

33. Palache to Helen Markham, June 17, 1899, Palache Papers, Bancroft Library, University of California, Berkeley.

34. *Ibid.*

35. Burroughs, "Narrative of the Expedition," in Merriam, ed., *Harriman Alaska Series*, Vol. I, 52.

CHAPTER 8

Conspicuously absent from the abundance of source material noted and quoted in these pages is much of anything written by members of the Harriman family. In terms of personal papers, none of them were regular diarists, and since they were all together on the *Elder* they shared their experiences in-person on a daily basis, with little reason to write letters "home." And writing for publication was not their forte—E. H. Harriman, for example, was known to have written, in his lifetime, only one magazine article. There are scattered interviews that touch upon the Expedition, an example being the one reported in this chapter involving Averell Harriman's memory of Muir and Burroughs walking the deck of the *Elder*, and some first-person recollections of the Expedition as noted by Roland Harriman in his autobiography, *I Reminisce*, and in biographies such as Rudy Abramson's *Spanning the Century: The Life of W. Averell Harriman 1891–1986*. E. H. Harriman's brief "Preface" to the *Harriman Alaska Series* publication provides important thoughts on the origins and purpose of the Expedition, as well as an overview of the voyage. For the most part, however, the activities, impressions, and thoughts of the Harrimans come to us through the writings of other members of the party. That record is fairly extensive and detailed; no doubt due to participation of the Harriman family members in almost every facet of the Expedition's daily activities, and by a natural motivation on the part of the writers to note what their leader and benefactor and his family were doing and saying.

1. Burroughs, "Narrative of the Expedition," in Merriam, ed., *Harriman Alaska Series*, Vol. I, 52.

2. Brewer, "The Alaska Atmosphere," in Merriam, ed., *Harriman Alaska Series*, Vol. II, 284.

3. Burroughs, "Narrative of the Expedition," in Merriam, ed., *Harriman Alaska Series*, Vol. I, 52.

4. Averell Harriman "Reminiscences" as quoted in Lindsey, "The Harriman Alaska Expedition of 1899, Including the Identities of Those in the Staff Picture" *Bioscience*, June 1978, 383.

5. Burroughs, "Narrative of the Expedition," in Merriam, ed., *Harriman Alaska Series*, Vol. I, 52.

6. Grinnell, "The Harriman Alaska Expedition: A Small Talk About Glaciers," *Forest & Stream*, March 3, 1900, 165.

7. Keeler to Louise Keeler, June 21, 1899, Keeler Papers, Bancroft Library, University of California, Berkeley.

8. Muir, "Notes on the Pacific Coast Glaciers," in Merriam, ed., *Harriman Alaska Series*, Vol. I, 121.

9. Palache to Helen Markham, June 21, 1899, Palache Papers, Bancroft Library, University of California, Berkeley

10. Dall diary, June 19, 1899, Dall Papers, Smithsonian Institution Archives; Gannett, "General Geography," in Merriam, ed., *Harriman Alaska Series*, Vol. II, 261; Klein, *The Life and Legend of E. H. Harriman*, 192.

11. Muir journal, June 19, 1899, Muir Papers, Special Collections, Holt-Atherton Center for Pacific Studies, University of the Pacific, Copyright 1984 Muir-Hanna Trust.

12. *Ibid.*, entry for June 20, 1899.

13. Burroughs, "Narrative of the Expedition," in Merriam, ed., *Harriman Alaska Series*, Vol. I, 58.

14. *Ibid.*, 59.

15. Muir journal, June 23, 1899, Muir Papers, Special Collections, Holt-Atherton Center for Pacific Studies, University of the Pacific, Copyright 1984 Muir-Hanna Trust.

16. Burroughs, "Narrative of the Expedition," in Merriam, ed., *Harriman Alaska Series*, Vol. I, 60–61.

17. Grinnell, "The Natives of the Alaska Coast Region," in Merriam, ed., *Harriman Alaska Series*, Vol. I, 165.

18. Burroughs, "Narrative of the Expedition," in Merriam, ed., *Harriman Alaska Series*, Vol. I, 58.

19. Grinnell, "The Harriman Alaska Expedition: Big Game Hunters," *Forest & Stream*, March 10, 1900, 184.

20. Keeler to Louise Keeler, June 21, 1899, Keeler Papers, Bancroft Library, University of California, Berkeley.

21. Merriam, "Recollections and Impressions of E. H. Harriman," 10–11, unpublished manuscript, Merriam Papers, Bancroft Library, University of California, Berkeley.

22. Palache to Helen Markham, June 21, 1899, Palache Papers, Bancroft Library, University of California, Berkeley.

23. Palache to Helen Markham, June 23, 1899, Palache Papers, Bancroft Library, University of California, Berkeley.

24. Palache to Helen Markham, June 24, 1899, Palache Papers, Bancroft Library, University of California, Berkeley.

25. Burroughs, "Narrative of the Expedition," in Merriam, ed., *Harriman Alaska Series*, Vol. I, 63.

26. *Ibid.*, 62.

Chapter 9

As part of its exploration of Prince William Sound, the Harriman Expedition attached names to geographic features which were either previously completely unknown or, as in the case of some particular glaciers, that were known to exist but had never been named. Recognition of those names fell under the authority of the U.S. Board of Geographic names, which was established in 1890, via an Executive Order signed by President Benjamin Harrison, to address the complex issues of geographic feature names during the surge of exploration and settlement of western territories after the Civil War. Inconsistencies and contradictions among many names, spellings, and applications became a serious problem for surveyors, map makers, and scientists who required uniform, non-conflicting geographic nomenclature. Henry Gannett was Chief Geographer of the United States, and he served as the first Chair of the newly-created Board—which dealt not only with the existing problems that had led to the Board's creation, but also with recognition of newly-discovered and/or named features, and definition of their location by geographic coordinates, topographical identifiers, historical and descriptive information, and other attributes. His role in the Expedition's discussions of names for College Fiord and Harriman Fiord, as well as for the glaciers in those fiords and elsewhere, combined with his careful surveys, assured that the names would "stick."

1. Burroughs, "Narrative of the Expedition," in Merriam, ed., *Harriman Alaska Series*, Vol. I, 64. Elliott thought the bird was a Fulmar Petrel, but the ornithologists Merriam, Fisher, and Fuertes identified it as an albatross—Fuertes Alaskan journal, June 24, 1899, Fuertes Papers, Division of Rare and Manuscript Collections, Cornell University Library.

2. Grinnell, "The Harriman Alaska Expedition: Prince William Sound," *Forest & Stream*, March 17, 1900, 205.

3. Muir to Louise and daughters, June 24, 1899, Muir Papers, Special Collections, Holt-Atherton Center for Pacific Studies, University of the Pacific. Copyright 1984 Muir-Hanna Trust.

4. Palache to Helen Markham, June 24, 1899, Palache Papers, Bancroft Library, University of California, Berkeley.

5. Merriam expedition diary/journal, June 24, 1899, Merriam Papers, Library of Congress.

6. Muir journal, June 24, 1899, Muir Papers, Special Collections, Holt-Atherton Center for Pacific Studies, University of the Pacific. Copyright 1984 Muir-Hanna Trust.

7. Grinnell, "The Salmon Industry," in Merriam ed., *Harriman Alaska Series*, Vol. II, 345–346.

8. Burroughs, "Narrative of the Expedition," in Merriam, ed., *Harriman Alaska Series*, Vol. I, 65–66.

9. Palache to Helen Markham, June 29, 1899 (writing of Sunday the 25th), Palache Papers, Bancroft Library, University of California, Berkeley.

10. Dellenbaugh journal, June 25, 1899, Dellenbaugh Collection, Beinecke Rare Book and Manuscript Library, Yale University.

11. Burroughs, "Narrative of the Expedition," in Merriam, ed., *Harriman Alaska Series*, Vol. I, 67.

12. Gannett, "The Harriman Alaska Expedition," *Journal of the American Geographical Society of New York*, Vol. 31, No. 4, 1899, 346, 354.

13. Grinnell, "The Harriman Alaska Expedition: Prince William Sound," *Forest & Stream*, March 17, 1900, 205.

14. Muir journal, June 25, 1899, Muir Papers, Special Collections, Holt-Atherton Center for Pacific Studies, University of the Pacific. Copyright 1984 Muir-Hanna Trust.

15. Palache to Helen Markham, June 29, 1899 (writing of Sunday the 25th), Palache Papers, Bancroft Library, University of California, Berkeley.

16. Muir journal, June 25, 1899, Muir Papers, Special Collections, Holt-Atherton Center for Pacific Studies, University of the Pacific. Copyright 1984 Muir-Hanna Trust.

17. Burroughs, "Narrative of the Expedition," in Merriam, ed., *Harriman Alaska Series*, Vol. I, 68.

18. *Ibid.*, 69.

19. Gannett, "General Geography," in Merriam, ed., *Harriman Alaska Series*, Vol. II, 262.

20. Burroughs, "Narrative of the Expedition," in Merriam, ed., *Harriman Alaska Series*, Vol. I, 69.

21. Dellenbaugh journal, June 26, 1899, Dellenbaugh Collection, Beinecke Rare Book and Manuscript Library, Yale University; Muir journal, June 26, 1899, Muir Papers, Special Collections, Holt-Atherton Center for Pacific Studies, University of the Pacific. Copyright 1984 Muir-Hanna Trust.

22. Grinnell, "The Harriman Alaska Expedition: Prince William Sound," *Forest & Stream*, March 17, 1900, 205.

23. Burroughs, "Narrative of the Expedition," in Merriam, ed., *Harriman Alaska Series*, Vol. I, 70.

24. Gannett, "The Harriman Alaska Expedition," *Journal of the American Geographical Society of New York*, Vol. 31, No. 4, 1899, 354. A decade later, geologist U.S. Grant (apparently no relation to the general and U.S. President) added the names of the remaining Seven Sisters—Bernard, and Holyoke—to two smaller glaciers also located on the western side of College Fiord.

25. Nelson expedition diary, June 26, 1899, Eberly Family Special Collections Library, Pennsylvania State University

26. A sketch of the pennant, signed by Dellenbaugh, appears in *The Harriman Alaska Expedition: Chronicles and Souvenirs May to August 1899*, 301.

27. Burroughs, "Narrative of the Expedition," in Merriam, ed., *Harriman Alaska Series*, Vol. I, 71.

28. Grinnell, "The Harriman Alaska Expedition: Prince William Sound," *Forest & Stream*, March 17, 1900, 205.

29. Gannett, "The Harriman Alaska Expedition," *National Geographic Magazine*, December 1899, 510.

30. Gannett, "The Harriman Alaska Expedition," *National Geographic*, December 1899, 510.

31. Muir, *Edward Henry Harriman*, 13.

32. *Ibid.*, 14–15. Merriam would record that Harriman himself "took the wheel" and pushed the ship on through the inlet. Merriam, "Recollections and Impressions of E. H. Harriman," 14–15, unpublished manuscript, Merriam Papers, Bancroft Library, University of California, Berkeley.

33. Keeler to Louise Keeler, June 27, 1899, Keeler Papers, Bancroft Library, University of California, Berkeley.

34. Muir, *Edward Henry Harriman*, 15.

35. Muir journal, June 26, 1899, Muir Papers, Special Collections, Holt-Atherton Center for Pacific Studies, University of the Pacific. Copyright 1984 Muir-Hanna Trust.

36. Burroughs, "Narrative of the Expedition," in Merriam, ed., *Harriman Alaska Series*, Vol. I, 72.

37. *Ibid.*

38. See Merriam expedition diary/journal, June 13, 1899, Merriam Papers, Library of Congress. The visit of Reid's party to Glacier Bay and Muir's cabin is discussed in Chapter 6 of this book.

39. Gannett, "The Harriman Alaska Expedition," *National Geographic*, December 1899, 510.

40. Burroughs, "Narrative of the Expedition," in Merriam, ed., *Harriman Alaska Series*, Vol. I, 73.

41. *Ibid.*, 71. Burroughs says the damage was sustained at a time before the *Elder* reached the vicinity of the Barry Glacier, and characterizes the propeller blade as "broken." Others place the incident at various points, including during the passage through the Barry Arm to Harriman Fiord, and there are some references to the propeller blade as not damaged but "lost." Whatever and wherever, the condition of the propeller, while of necessity requiring repair, was not an overriding emergency.

42. Merriam expedition diary/journal, June 26, 1899, Merriam Papers, Library of Congress; Muir journal, June 26, 1899, Muir Papers, Special Collections, Holt-Atherton Center for Pacific Studies, University of the Pacific, Copyright 1984 Muir-Hanna Trust.

43. Muir journal, June 26, 1899, Muir Papers, Special Collections, Holt-Atherton Center for Pacific Studies, University of the Pacific. Copyright 1984 Muir-Hanna Trust.

44. Merriam, "Recollections and Impressions of E. H. Harriman," 14–15, unpublished manuscript, Merriam Papers, Bancroft Library, University of California, Berkeley; Brewer diary, June 26, 1899, Brewer Papers, Manuscripts and Archives, Sterling Memorial Library, Yale University.

45. Nelson expedition diary, June 28, 1899, Eberly Family Special Collections Library, Pennsylvania State University.

46. Burroughs, "Narrative of the Expedition," in Merriam, ed., *Harriman Alaska Series*, Vol. I, 74–75.

47. Grinnell, "The Harriman Alaska Expedition: Prince William Sound," *Forest & Stream*, March 17, 1900, 206.

48. *Ibid.*

49. Nelson expedition diary, June 28, 1899, Eberly Family Special Collections Library, Pennsylvania State University. Apparently the injury was not serious, since it was not subsequently referred to in any of the letters, diary entries, articles, etc., kept and written by the party.

50. Palache to Helen Markham, June 29, 1899, Palache Papers, Bancroft Library, University of California, Berkeley. The narrative of the party's explorations and stay on Heather Island is drawn from this long letter, in which Palache provided Helen with a day-by-day recap of their activities.

51. Kelly, "Memoirs Describing Expeditions and Military Service in Alaska and the Philippines," 117–121, unpublished manuscript, Beinecke Rare Book and Manuscript Library, Yale University; Keenan, *The Life of Yellowstone Kelly*, 209–210.

52. Muir journal, June 29, 1899, Muir Papers, Special Collections, Holt-Atherton Center for Pacific Studies, University of the Pacific, Copyright 1984 Muir-Hanna Trust.

53. Muir, "Notes on the Pacific Coast Glaciers," in Merriam ed., *Harriman Alaska Series*, Vol. I, 132.

Chapter 10

The authoritative, most complete collection of the poems and poetic essays written and shared during the Expedition is found in *The Harriman Alaska Expedition: Chronicles and Souvenirs May to August 1899*. In addition, Frederick Dellenbaugh was painstaking in including copies of the poems in his diary. Like Dellenbaugh, Louis Fuertes also accounted for most of the poetry in his journal, which can be found online in the Fuertes papers in the Cornell University Library web site. In that web site many of the poems in the Fuertes journal are presented in both handwritten and transcribed versions, though at times the transcription may not accurately reflect or correctly interpret the handwriting.

1. Grinnell, "The Harriman Alaska Expedition: Life on Shipboard," *Forest & Stream*, June 16, 1900, 464. Grinnell's reference is to Muir's famous story of the dog Stickeen, which was originally published by Muir as "An Adventure with a Dog and a Glacier" in the August 1897 issue of *Century Magazine*, and later as the book *Stickeen: The Story of a Dog*.

2. *Ibid.*

3. *The Harriman Alaska Expedition: Chronicles and Souvenirs May to August 1899*, 26. Mrs. Harriman's use of the word "Receipt" as opposed to "Recipe" in the title of her poem reflected her literary background and the prevalence in the 18th and 19th centuries of what 21st century archivists refer to as a "medical receipt book"—a handwritten, often home-made collection of recipes, diet suggestions, home remedies, behavioral changes, and other cures for various ailments. In other words, a combination Martha Stewart cookbook and WebMD, sprinkled with a little behavioral science and personal conduct tips.

4. *Ibid.*, 46–47.

5. Grinnell, "The Harriman Alaska Expedition: Life on Shipboard," *Forest & Stream*, June 16, 1900, 465.

6. Nelson expedition diary, June 29, 1899, Eberly Family Special Collections Library, Pennsylvania State University.

7. *The Harriman Alaska Expedition: Chronicles and Souvenirs May to August 1899*, 57. Ship's carpenters were often nicknamed or referred to as "Chips."

8. Grinnell, "The Harriman Alaska Expedition: Life on Shipboard," *Forest & Stream*, June 16, 1900, 465.

9. Merriam expedition diary/journal, June 29, 1899, Merriam Papers, Library of Congress.

10. Keeler to Louise Keeler, June 29, 1899, Keeler Papers, Bancroft Library, University of California, Berkeley.

11. Burroughs, "Narrative of the Expedition," in Merriam, ed., *Harriman Alaska Series*, Vol. I, 76.

12. Grinnell, "The Harriman Alaska Expedition: Prince William Sound," *Forest & Stream*, March 17, 1900, 206, contains the account of the visit to the DeWees camp.

13. Burroughs, "Narrative of the Expedition," in Merriam, ed., *Harriman Alaska Series*, Vol. I, 78.

14. *Ibid.*, 79.

15. Muir journal, July 1, 1899, Muir Papers, Special Collections, Holt-Atherton Center for Pacific Studies, University of the Pacific. Copyright 1984 Muir-Hanna Trust.

16. Burroughs, "Narrative of the Expedition," in Merriam, ed., *Harriman Alaska Series*, Vol. I, 77, 79.

17. Fernow, "Forests of Alaska," in Merriam, ed., *Harriman Alaska Series*, Vol. II, 235 et seq. Fernow's assessment of the quality and economic value of Alaska's forests would and, at different times, would not come true, due to the influence of a variety of factors including on-again, off-again federal subsidies to the logging industry. For an excellent twenty-first century discussion of Fernow's conclusions see Alaback, "Fernow's Prediction and the Search for a Sustainable Timber Industry in Southeast Alaska," in Litwin, ed., *The Harriman Alaska Expedition Retraced*, 49 et seq.

18. Dellenbaugh journal, July 1, 1899, Dellenbaugh Collection, Beinecke Rare Book and Manuscript Library, Yale University.

19. Burroughs, "Narrative of the Expedition," in Merriam, ed., *Harriman Alaska Series*, Vol. I, 81.

20. *Ibid.*, 81–82.

21. Ritter diary, July 1, 1899, Ritter Papers, Bancroft Library, University of California, Berkeley.

22. Dellenbaugh journal, July 1, 1899, Dellenbaugh Collection, Beinecke Rare Book and Manuscript Library, Yale University.

23. Grinnell, "The Harriman Alaska Expedition: In Uyak Bay," *Forest & Stream*, April 7, 1900, 262.

24. Palache to Helen Markham, July 4, 1899 (writing of the events on July 2), Palache Papers, Bancroft Library, University of California, Berkeley.

25. Muir journal, July 2, 1899, Muir Papers, Special Collections, Holt-Atherton Center for Pacific Studies, University of the Pacific. Copyright 1984 Muir-Hanna Trust.

26. Palache to Helen Markham, July 4, 1899 (writing of the events on July 3), Palache Papers,

Bancroft Library, University of California, Berkeley.

27. Grinnell, "The Harriman Alaska Expedition: In Uyak Bay," *Forest & Stream*, April 7, 1900, 262.

28. Kelly, "Memoirs Describing Expeditions and Military Service in Alaska and the Philippines," 122–124, unpublished manuscript, Beinecke Rare Book and Manuscript Library, Yale University.

29. Muir journal, July 3, 1899, Muir Papers, Special Collections, Holt-Atherton Center for Pacific Studies, University of the Pacific. Copyright 1984 Muir-Hanna Trust.

30. Burroughs, "Narrative of the Expedition," in Merriam, ed., *Harriman Alaska Series*, Vol. I, 85.

31. Keeler to Louise Keeler, July 3, 1899, Keeler Papers, Bancroft Library, University of California, Berkeley.

32. Grinnell, "The Harriman Alaska Expedition: In Uyak Bay," *Forest & Stream*, April 7, 1900, 262.

33. Ritter diary, July 4, 1899, Ritter Papers, Bancroft Library, University of California, Berkeley.

34. Nelson expedition diary, July 4, 1899, Eberly Family Special Collections Library, Pennsylvania State University.

35. Dellenbaugh journal, July 4, 1899, Dellenbaugh Collection, Beinecke Rare Book and Manuscript Library, Yale University. Hay, one of Lincoln's secretaries, was serving as Ambassador to England in July 1898, before becoming Secretary of State in the McKinley administration in September of that year.

36. Nelson expedition diary, July 4, 1899, Eberly Family Special Collections Library, Pennsylvania State University.

37. Brewer, "4th of July Oration on the Hurricane Deck of the George W. Elder," Brewer Papers, Sterling Memorial Library, Yale University.

38. Dellenbaugh journal, July 4, 1899, Dellenbaugh Collection, Beinecke Rare Book and Manuscript Library, Yale University.

39. *The Harriman Alaska Expedition: Chronicles and Souvenirs May to August 1899*, 71.

40. Dellenbaugh journal, July 4, 1899, Dellenbaugh Collection, Beinecke Rare Book and Manuscript Library, Yale University.

41. Muir journal, July 4, 1899, Muir Papers, Special Collections, Holt-Atherton Center for Pacific Studies, University of the Pacific, Copyright 1984 Muir-Hanna Trust; Merriam expedition diary/journal, July 3, 1899, Merriam Papers, Library of Congress.

42. Muir, *Edward Henry Harriman*, 35–37.

43. Muir journal, July 4, 1899, Muir Papers, Special Collections, Holt-Atherton Center for Pacific Studies, University of the Pacific.

44. Keeler to Louise Keeler, July 4, 1899, Keeler Papers, Bancroft Library, University of California, Berkeley.

45. Palache to Helen Markham, July 4, 1899 (writing of the events on July 3), Palache Papers, Bancroft Library, University of California, Berkeley.

46. Burroughs, "Narrative of the Expedition," in Merriam, ed., *Harriman Alaska Series*, Vol. I, 17.

47. Dellenbaugh journal, July 5, 1899, Dellenbaugh Collection, Beinecke Rare Book and Manuscript Library, Yale University.

48. Burroughs, "Narrative of the Expedition," in Merriam, ed., *Harriman Alaska Series*, Vol. I, 86.

Chapter 11

One of the best recorded expositions of the fearsome nature of the Bering Sea, and possibly the earliest, can be found in the O.W. Frost and Margritt Engel translation (published in 1988) of Georg Wilhelm Steller's *Journal of a Voyage with Bering, 1741–1742.*

1. Muir journal, July 5, 1899, Muir Papers, Special Collections, Holt-Atherton Center for Pacific Studies, University of the Pacific. Copyright 1984 Muir-Hanna Trust.

2. Palache to Helen Markham, July 5, 1899, Palache Papers, Bancroft Library, University of California, Berkeley.

3. Keeler to Louise Keeler, July 8, 1899, Keeler Papers, Bancroft Library, University of California, Berkeley.

4. Nelson expedition diary, July 5, 1899, Eberly Family Special Collections Library, Pennsylvania State University.

5. Palache to Helen Markham, July 5, 1899, Palache Papers, Bancroft Library, University of California, Berkeley.

6. Fuertes Alaskan Journal, July 5, 1899, Fuertes Papers, Division of Rare and Manuscript Collections, Cornell University.

7. Palache journal, July 5, 1899, Palache Papers, Bancroft Library, University of California, Berkeley.

8. Grinnell, "The Harriman Alaska Expedition: In Uyak Bay," *Forest & Stream*, April 7, 1900, 262.

9. *Ibid.*

10. Dellenbaugh journal, July 5, 1899, Dellenbaugh Collection, Beinecke Rare Book and Manuscript Library, Yale University. Arrangements were apparently made to send the packers south on a ship that was lying at anchor near one of the Uyak Bay canneries.

11. Merriam, "To the Memory of John Muir," *Sierra Club Bulletin*, January 1917.

12. Palache journal, July 6, 1899, Palache Papers, Bancroft Library, University of California, Berkeley.

13. Muir journal, July 7, 1899, Muir Papers, Special Collections, Holt-Atherton Center for Pacific Studies, University of the Pacific. Copyright 1984 Muir-Hanna Trust.

14. Palache journal, July 7, 1899, Palache Papers, Bancroft Library, University of California, Berkeley.

15. Dellenbaugh journal, July 7, 1899, Dellenbaugh Collection, Beinecke Rare Book and Manuscript Library, Yale University.

16. Merriam expedition diary/journal, July 7, 1899, Merriam Papers, Library of Congress.

17. Kearney, "Reminiscences of the Harriman Expedition," Waldo L. Schmitt Papers, Smithsonian Institution Archives.

18. Muir to his family, July 8, 1899, Muir Papers, Special Collections, Holt-Atherton Center for Pacific Studies, University of the Pacific. Copyright 1984 Muir-Hanna Trust.

19. Fuertes to his parents, July 10, 1899, Fuertes Papers, Division of Rare and Manuscript Collections, Cornell University Library.

20. Merriam expedition diary/journal, July 8, 1899, Merriam Papers, Library of Congress.

21. Dellenbaugh journal, July 8, 1899, Dellenbaugh Collection, Beinecke Rare Book and Manuscript Library, Yale University.

22. Keeler to Louise Keeler, July 8, 1899, Keeler Papers, Bancroft Library, University of California, Berkeley.

23. Burroughs, "Narrative of the Expedition," in Merriam, ed., *Harriman Alaska Series*, Vol. I, 93.

24. Keeler's account is in an unpublished manuscript, *Friends Bearing Torches*, Keeler papers, Bancroft Library, University of California, Berkeley. Burroughs had a different version of the incident. He told his biographer Clara Barrus that he already had his bag ashore when Muir got wind of his plans, retrieved the bag, and brought it back just as Burroughs was about to disembark; since the ship was clearing away, Burroughs had no choice but to stay aboard. Barrus, *The Life and Letters of John Burroughs*, Vol. I, 381.

25. Muir journal, July 8, 1899, Muir Papers, Special Collections, Holt-Atherton Center for Pacific Studies, University of the Pacific. Copyright 1984 Muir-Hanna Trust.

26. Burroughs, "Narrative of the Expedition," in Merriam, ed., *Harriman Alaska Series*, Vol. I, 94.

27. Merriam, "Bogoslof, Our Newest Volcano," in Merriam, ed., *Harriman Alaska Series*, Vol. II, 291 et seq. The area has undergone continued weathering and change, and by the early 21st century had become one island.

28. *Ibid.*, 331.

29. *Ibid.*

30. *Ibid.*, 334.

31. Muir journal, July 8, 1899, Muir Papers, Special Collections, Holt-Atherton Center for Pacific Studies, University of the Pacific, Copyright 1984 Muir-Hanna Trust; Nelson expedition diary, July 8, 1899, Eberly Family Special Collections Library, Pennsylvania State University.

32. Dellenbaugh journal, July 9, 1899, Dellenbaugh Collection, Beinecke Rare Book and Manuscript Library, Yale University.

33. Keeler, *Friends Bearing Torches*, unpublished manuscript, Keeler papers, Bancroft Library, University of California, Berkeley.

34. Some accounts credit Harriman with obtaining the permit, while others indicate that

Merriam was responsible. Merriam seems the more likely given his position in the government, his service on the Bering Sea Commission that had dealt with sealing operations and jurisdictional rights in the Bering Sea, and his previous visits to the Pribilofs.

35. Grinnell, "The Harriman Alaska Expedition: To Bogoslof and the Pribilofs," *Forest & Stream*, May 5, 1900, 344.

36. Burroughs, "Narrative of the Expedition," in Merriam, ed., *Harriman Alaska Series*, Vol. I, 96.

37. Muir journal, July 9, 1899, Muir Papers, Special Collections, Holt-Atherton Center for Pacific Studies, University of the Pacific. Copyright 1984 Muir-Hanna Trust.

38. Merriam expedition diary/journal, July 9, 1899, Merriam Papers, Library of Congress.

39. Grinnell, "The Harriman Alaska Expedition: To Bogoslof and the Pribilofs," *Forest & Stream*, May 5, 1900, 344.

40. Dellenbaugh journal, July 9, 1899, Dellenbaugh Collection, Beinecke Rare Book and Manuscript Library, Yale University.

41. Burroughs, "Narrative of the Expedition," in Merriam, ed., *Harriman Alaska Series*, Vol. I, 97–98.

42. *Ibid.*, 98–99.

43. Dall diary, July 9, 1899, Dall Papers, Smithsonian Institution Archives; Merriam expedition diary/journal, July 9, 1899, Merriam Papers, Library of Congress.

44. Merriam, "Recollections and Impressions of E. H. Harriman," 16, unpublished manuscript, Merriam Papers, Bancroft Library, University of California, Berkeley.

45. Muir journal, July 9, 1899, Muir Papers, Special Collections, Holt-Atherton Center for Pacific Studies, University of the Pacific. Copyright 1984 Muir-Hanna Trust.

46. Burroughs, "Narrative of the Expedition," in Merriam, ed., *Harriman Alaska Series*, Vol. I, 99.

47. Gannett, "General Geography," in Merriam, ed., *Harriman Alaska Series*, Vol. II, 271.

48. Dellenbaugh journal, July 10, 1899, Dellenbaugh Collection, Beinecke Rare Book and Manuscript Library, Yale University.

49. Muir journal, July 9, 1899, Muir Papers, Special Collections, Holt-Atherton Center for Pacific Studies, University of the Pacific. Copyright 1984 Muir-Hanna Trust.

50. *The Harriman Alaska Expedition: Chronicles and Souvenirs May to August 1899*, 153 contains the full text of the poem. The poem is also reprinted, in its entirety, in Barrus, *The Life and Letters of John Burroughs,* Vol. I, 381–382. Muir would respond—at length—after the Expedition was over in "The True Story of J.B. and the Behring Sea" (Reprinted in Wolfe, ed., *John of the Mountains: The Unpublished Journals of John Muir,* 422–426).

51. Grinnell, "The Harriman Alaska Expedi-

tion: Plover Bay and Port Clarence," *Forest & Stream*, June 2, 1890, 422.

52. Grinnell, "The Harriman Alaska Expedition: Life on Shipboard," *Forest & Stream*, June 6, 1890, 465.

CHAPTER 12

As a resource or window on all things Alaskan, including remote and little-known areas such as St. Matthew and Hall Islands, one cannot overlook *Alaska Geographic* magazine. For thirty-some years this quarterly publication provided, often by devoting an entire issue to a single subject, original articles and color photographs on topics including Native peoples and cultures, phenomenon such as the aurora borealis, discrete and at times obscure historical events, wildlife from salmon to grizzly bears, and distinct geographic areas and features including the Bering Sea and the Seward Peninsula. A glossy publication, it differed from but had much in common with the *National Geographic Magazine* in its aims, purposes, and approach. It ceased publication in 2003, but many of its 118 issues remain outstanding resources and are variously available from the Alaska Geographic Society, bookstores, and specialty shops in Alaska, and online through antiquarian and rare book dealers and sellers.

1. Muir journal, July 11, 1899, Muir Papers, Special Collections, Holt-Atherton Center for Pacific Studies, University of the Pacific. Copyright 1984 Muir-Hanna Trust.

2. Muir, *The Cruise of the Corwin,* 63, referencing a coaling stop on June 27, 1881.

3. Dellenbaugh journal, July 11, 1899, Dellenbaugh Collection, Beinecke Rare Book and Manuscript Library, Yale University. Merriam echoed Dellenbaugh in calling it "the most barren and desolate place of its size" he had ever seen. Merriam expedition diary/journal, July 11, 1899, Merriam Papers, Library of Congress.

4. Burroughs, "Narrative of the Expedition," in Merriam, ed., *Harriman Alaska Series*, Vol. I, 100.

5. Grinnell, "The Harriman Alaska Expedition: Eskimo—Plover Bay and Port Clarence," *Forest & Stream*, June 2, 1900, 422; Grinnell, "The Natives of the Alaska Coast Region," in Merriam, ed., *Harriman Alaska Series*, Vol. I, 175–176.

6. Burroughs, "Narrative of the Expedition," in Merriam, ed., *Harriman Alaska Series*, Vol. I, 100.

7. *Ibid.*, 101.

8. Grinnell, "The Harriman Alaska Expedition: Eskimo—Plover Bay and Port Clarence," *Forest & Stream*, June 2, 1900, 422.

9. Burroughs, "Narrative of the Expedition," in Merriam, ed., *Harriman Alaska Series*, Vol. I, 101.

10. Grinnell, "The Natives of the Alaska Coast Region," in Merriam, ed., *Harriman Alaska Series*, Vol. I, 176–177.

11. Muir journal, July 11, 1899, Muir Papers, Special Collections, Holt-Atherton Center for Pacific Studies, University of the Pacific. Copy-

right 1984 Muir-Hanna Trust. It does not appear that Muir, in his earlier voyage aboard the *Corwin* in 1881, had visited this particular village.

12. Burroughs, "Narrative of the Expedition," in Merriam, ed., *Harriman Alaska Series*, Vol. I, 102.

13. Grinnell, "The Harriman Alaska Expedition: Eskimo—Plover Bay and Port Clarence," *Forest & Stream*, June 2, 1900, 422.

14. *Ibid.*, 423.

15. Grinnell, "The Natives of the Alaska Coast Region," in Merriam, ed., *Harriman Alaska Series*, Vol. I, 178.

16. Muir journal, July 12, 1899, Muir Papers, Special Collections, Holt-Atherton Center for Pacific Studies, University of the Pacific. Copyright 1984 Muir-Hanna Trust.

17. Burroughs, "Narrative of the Expedition," in Merriam, ed., *Harriman Alaska Series*, Vol. I, 103.

18. Grinnell, "The Natives of the Alaska Coast Region," in Merriam, ed., *Harriman Alaska Series*, Vol. I, 179.

19. Burroughs, "Narrative of the Expedition," in Merriam, ed., *Harriman Alaska Series*, Vol. I, 103.

20. Grinnell, "The Natives of the Alaska Coast Region," in Merriam, ed., *Harriman Alaska Series*, Vol. I, 182–183.

21. Burroughs, "Narrative of the Expedition," in Merriam, ed., *Harriman Alaska Series*, Vol. I, 105.

22. Fuertes Alaskan journal, July 12, 1899, Fuertes papers, Division of Rare and Manuscript Collections, Cornell University Library.

23. Merriam, "Recollections and Impressions of E. H. Harriman," 20, unpublished manuscript, Merriam Papers, Bancroft Library, University of California, Berkeley.

24. Muir journal, July 12, 1899, Muir Papers, Special Collections, Holt-Atherton Center for Pacific Studies, University of the Pacific. Copyright 1984 Muir-Hanna Trust.

25. Merriam, "Recollections and Impressions of E. H. Harriman," 20, unpublished manuscript, Merriam Papers, Bancroft Library, University of California, Berkeley.

26. *The Harriman Alaska Expedition: Chronicles and Souvenirs May to August 1899*, 172–174. The "Song of the Innuit" also appears in Merriam, ed. *Harriman Alaska Series*, Vol. II, 367–370, where it is accompanied by the explanatory note: "Innuit is the name by which the Eskimo calls himself and his people from Greenland to Mount St. Elias. The topek is the winter house of turf and walrus hide, as contrasted with the igloo or snow-house, used where there is no wood. All Innuit believe in evil spirits which dwell inland from the shores; in Greenland they are supposed to inhabit the Nunataks or peaks which rise like islands out of the bosom of the glaciers. In times of starvation Innuit ethics allow a mother to expose an infant, for whom she cannot supply food, in the snow to die. The child's mouth is usually stuffed with grass, as otherwise its spirit would return and be heard crying about the house at night."

27. Burroughs, "Narrative of the Expedition," in Merriam, ed., *Harriman Alaska Series*, Vol. I, 105.

28. Grinnell, "The Natives of the Alaska Coast Region," in Merriam, ed., *Harriman Alaska Series*, Vol. I, 183.

29. Muir journal, July 13, 1899, Muir Papers, Special Collections, Holt-Atherton Center for Pacific Studies, University of the Pacific. Copyright 1984 Muir-Hanna Trust.

30. Merriam expedition diary/journal, July 13, 1899, Merriam Papers, Library of Congress.

31. Grinnell, "The Harriman Alaska Expedition: In Uyak Bay," *Forest & Stream*, April 7, 1900, 263.

32. Dellenbaugh journal, July 13, 1899, Dellenbaugh Collection, Beinecke Rare Book and Manuscript Library, Yale University.

33. Elliott, *The Condition of Affairs in the Territory of Alaska*, 16.

34. Dellenbaugh journal, July 14, 1899, Dellenbaugh Collection, Beinecke Rare Book and Manuscript Library, Yale University.

35. Fuertes to his parents, July 18, 1899 (writing of Hall Island on the 14th), Fuertes Papers, Division of Rare and Manuscript Collections, Cornell University Library.

36. Keeler, "Days Among Alaska Birds," in Merriam, ed., *Harriman Alaska Series*, Vol. II, 233.

37. Hall, "The Harriman Alaska Expedition," *The Yale Scientific Monthly*, February 1900, 170.

38. Keeler, "Days Among Alaska Birds," in Merriam, ed., *Harriman Alaska Series*, Vol. II, 233.

39. Elliott's story is retold in Rhode, "St. Matthew and Hall Islands: Oasis of Wildness," *Alaska Geographic*, Vol. 14, No. 3, 72.

40. Dellenbaugh journal, July 15, 1899, Dellenbaugh Collection, Beinecke Rare Book and Manuscript Library, Yale University.

41. Fuertes Alaskan journal, July 15, 1899, Fuertes Papers, Division of Rare and Manuscript Collections, Cornell University Library. Description of the Sabine's coloring from Keeler, "Days Among Alaska Birds," in Merriam, ed., *Harriman Alaska Series*, Vol. II, 234.

42. Muir journal, July 15, 1899, Muir Papers, Special Collections, Holt-Atherton Center for Pacific Studies, University of the Pacific. Copyright 1984 Muir-Hanna Trust.

43. Burroughs, "Narrative of the Expedition," in Merriam, ed., *Harriman Alaska Series*, Vol. I, 113. There were probably, if not undoubtedly, polar bears on St. Matthew at the time of the Harriman Expedition's visit, but their numbers were in decline. As to the last of the polar bears of St. Matthew Island, biologist and writer Elaine Rhode reported that tracks of a bear were seen in the winter of 1942–1943 and one bear was spotted on the island in March 1976, but none thereafter. She notes that "Alaskan polar bear biologists have

proposed that the animals may have been of a separate stock, bonded to the islands. When the original clan was wiped out, that bond was erased. Bears that might have repopulated the islands were so heavily hunted in succeeding years that the opportunity was lost." Rhode, "St. Matthew and Hall Islands: Oasis of Wildness," *Alaska Geographic*, Vol. 14, No. 3, 73.

CHAPTER 13

Secondary characters sometimes make unexpected, cameo appearances in the progress of events, and such was the case with Joseph Stanley-Brown and his joining the Harriman party in Dutch Harbor. The Stanley-Brown Papers at the Library of Congress provide detail of his time with Garfield and the history of the Stanley-Brown family. And his early relations with his future wife are noted in Ruth Feis, *Mollie Garfield in the White House*. Chicago: Rand McNally & Company, 1963.

1. Muir journal, July 16, 1899, Muir Papers, Special Collections, Holt-Atherton Center for Pacific Studies, University of the Pacific. Copyright 1984 Muir-Hanna Trust.

2. Kearney field book, July 17, 1899, National Museum of Natural History branch, Smithsonian Libraries.

3. Starks Expedition Log, July 10–18, 1899, Starks Papers, Green Library, Stanford University.

4. Merriam expedition diary/journal, July 17, 1899, Merriam Papers, Library of Congress.

5. See Millard, *Destiny of the Republic: A Tale of Madness, Medicine and the Murder of a President*, 91, 256–257. Stanley-Brown attended Yale's Sheffield Scientific School (where he may have become acquainted with William Brewer), and after graduation married Mollie Garfield. Starks noted that Stanley-Brown was "in charge" of the North American Company's station and that he and his wife "live here a part of each year." Starks Expedition Log, July 10–18, 1899, Starks Papers, Green Library, Stanford University.

6. Fuertes Alaskan journal, July 17, 1899, Fuertes Papers, Division of Rare and Manuscript Collections, Cornell University Library.

7. Burroughs, "Narrative of the Expedition," in Merriam, ed., *Harriman Alaska Series*, Vol. I, 114.

8. Palache journal, July 7, 1899, Palache papers, Bancroft Library, University of California, Berkeley.

9. *Ibid.*, July 8, 1899.

10. *Ibid.*, July 9, 1899.

11. *Ibid.*, July 11, 1899.

12. *Ibid.*, July 12–16, 1899. Palache's journal exhibits some confusion in dates. While he did not reveal any details of his discovery, the "wished-for key" was the evidence of volcanic activity.

13. Noted in Muir journal, July 18, 1899, Muir Papers, Special Collections, Holt-Atherton Center for Pacific Studies, University of the Pacific. Copyright 1984 Muir-Hanna Trust.

14. Dellenbaugh journal, July 18, 1899, Dellenbaugh Collection, Beinecke Rare Book and Manuscript Library, Yale University. Dellenbaugh, who was not part of the Sand Point party, recorded what members of that party reported on their return to the *Elder*.

15. Palache journal, July 18, 1899, Palache papers, Bancroft Library, University of California, Berkeley.

16. For a summary of the reports by Ritter, Saunders and Kincaid see Muir journal, July 18, 1899, Muir Papers, Special Collections, Holt-Atherton Center for Pacific Studies, Copyright 1984 Muir-Hanna Trust.

17. Dellenbaugh journal, July 18, 1899, Dellenbaugh Collection, Beinecke Rare Book and Manuscript Library, Yale University.

18. Muir journal, July 18, 1899, Muir Papers, Special Collections, Holt-Atherton Center for Pacific Studies, University of the Pacific. Copyright 1984 Muir-Hanna Trust. Muir's journal contains a summary of the reports by Ritter, Saunders, and Kincaid.

19. Palache journal, July 18, 1899, Palache papers, Bancroft Library, University of California, Berkeley.

20. Fuertes to his parents, July 18, 1899, Fuertes Papers, Division of Rare and Manuscript Collections, Cornell University Library.

21. Palache journal, July 19, 1899, Palache papers, Bancroft Library, University of California, Berkeley.

22. Dellenbaugh journal, July 19, 1899, Dellenbaugh Collection, Beinecke Rare Book and Manuscript Library, Yale University, provides a succinct summary of the early publication plan.

23. Muir journal, July 19, 1899, Muir Papers, Special Collections, Holt-Atherton Center for Pacific Studies, University of the Pacific. Copyright 1984 Muir-Hanna Trust.

24. Klein, *The Life and Legend of E.H. Harriman*, 198.

25. Palache journal, July 20, 1899, Palache papers, Bancroft Library, University of California, Berkeley; Grinnell, "The Harriman Alaska Expedition: Homeward Bound," *Forest & Stream*, June 23, 1900, 482.

26. Dellenbaugh journal, July 20, 1899, Dellenbaugh Collection, Beinecke Rare Book and Manuscript Library, Yale University.

27. Washburn, "Fox Farming in Alaska," in Merriam ed., *Harriman Alaska Series*, Vol. II, 357–365.

28. Grinnell, "The Harriman Alaska Expedition: Some Fur Bearers," *Forest & Stream* March 24, 1900, 222.

29. Palache journal, July 20, 1899, Palache papers, Bancroft Library, University of California, Berkeley.

30. Muir journal, July 21, 1899, in Wolfe, ed., *John of the Mountains: The Unpublished Journals of John Muir*, 414.

31. Dellenbaugh journal, July 21, 1899, Dellen-

baugh Collection, Beinecke Rare Book and Manuscript Library, Yale University.

32. Muir journal, July 22, 1899, Muir Papers, Special Collections, Holt-Atherton Center for Pacific Studies, University of the Pacific. Copyright 1984 Muir-Hanna Trust.

33. Merriam expedition diary/journal, July 22, 1899, Merriam Papers, Library of Congress; Palache journal, July 22, 1899, Palache papers, Bancroft Library, University of California, Berkeley.

34. Grinnell, "The Harriman Alaska Expedition: Life on Shipboard," *Forest & Stream*, June 16, 1900, 465.

35. Burroughs, "Narrative of the Expedition," in Merriam, ed., *Harriman Alaska Series*, Vol. I, 115.

36. Brewer's daily temperature readings were faithfully included at pages 288–289 of *The Harriman Alaska Expedition: Chronicles and Souvenirs May to August 1899*. Brewer's meticulous nature and attention to detail included, at the end of the listing, the signature of W.H. Averell, apparently as a witness attesting to the accuracy of the entries. Brewer also made a margin note next to the temperature he recorded for one day, to clarify that that reading was taken somewhat later than the usual 7:30 a.m.

37. Kearney, "Reminiscences of the Harriman Expedition," 3, Waldo L. Schmitt Papers, Smithsonian Institution Archives.

38. Burroughs, "Narrative of the Expedition," in Merriam, ed., *Harriman Alaska Series*, Vol. I, 115.

39. Palache journal, July 23, 1899, Palache papers, Bancroft Library, University of California, Berkeley.

40. Muir journal, July 23,1899, Muir Papers, Special Collections, Holt-Atherton Center for Pacific Studies, University of the Pacific. Copyright 1984 Muir-Hanna Trust.

41. Dellenbaugh journal, July 21, 1899, Dellenbaugh Collection, Beinecke Rare Book and Manuscript Library, Yale University. In his journal entry for July 25, Dellenbaugh would note that the engineer "appears not to have been internally injured."

42. On September 10 a major quake with an epicenter near Yakutat and Disenchantment Bays, and registering 8.2 on the Richter Scale (an "earthquake of the century"), resulted in significant changes in the level of the land which were "the greatest recorded in historical times, the maximum uplift amounting to over 47 feet," though fortunately "in the small village nearest at hand there was no loss of life." Tarr and Martin, "The Earthquakes at Yakutat Bay, Alaska in September 1899," U.S. Geological Survey Professional Paper 69, U.S. Government Printing Office, 1912. Trevor Kincaid would note in his autobiography that "I was later shown photographs of the cliff opposite which our vessel had been anchored [in Yakutat Bay] and it showed beds of barnacles and mussels forty feet above sea level. Islands heaved up and down like sinking ships. Evidently we had a narrow escape." Kincaid, unpublished "Autobiography" (typescript) 47, Kincaid Papers, Special Collections, Allen Library, University of Washington.

43. Muir journal, July 24, 1899, Muir Papers, Special Collections, Holt-Atherton Center for Pacific Studies, University of the Pacific. Copyright 1984 Muir-Hanna Trust.

44. Palache journal, July 24, 1899, Palache papers, Bancroft Library, University of California, Berkeley.

45. *Ibid.*

46. Coville quoted in Chowder, "North to Alaska," *Smithsonian Magazine*, June 2003.

47. Muir journal, July 24, 1899, Muir Papers, Special Collections, Holt-Atherton Center for Pacific Studies, University of the Pacific. Copyright 1984 Muir-Hanna Trust.

48. *Ibid.* July 25, 1899.

49. Palache journal, July 25, 1899, Palache papers, Bancroft Library, University of California, Berkeley.

50. Muir journal, July 25, 1899, Muir Papers, Special Collections, Holt-Atherton Center for Pacific Studies, University of the Pacific. Copyright 1984 Muir-Hanna Trust.

Chapter 14

Douglas Cole's *Captured Heritage: The Scramble for Northwest Coast Artifacts* (1985) remains much the most thorough and useful resource on the subject.

Accomplishing NAGPRA: Perspectives on the Intent, Impact, and Future of the Native American Graves Protection and Repatriation Act (2013), by Sangita Chari and James Lavallee, provides a broad study of the Act's practical application, with contributions reflecting the approach and viewpoints of Native American tribes, museums, federal agencies, and others.

1. Dellenbaugh journal, July 2, 1899, Dellenbaugh Collection, Beinecke Rare Book and Manuscript Library, Yale University.

2. *Ibid.*, July 26, 1899.

3. *Ibid.*

4. Grinnell, "The Harriman Alaska Expedition: Indians," *Forest & Stream*, March 31, 1900, 245.

5. Dellenbaugh journal, July 26, 1899, Dellenbaugh Collection, Beinecke Rare Book and Manuscript Library, Yale University; Nelson expedition diary, July 26, 1899, Eberly Family Special Collections Library, Pennsylvania State University.

6. Dellenbaugh journal, July 26, 1899, Dellenbaugh Collection, Beinecke Rare Book and Manuscript Library, Yale University.

7. Grainger, "Forward," [sic] in *A Time Remembered: Cape Fox Village 1899*.

8. Worl, "Standing With Spirits, Waiting," in Litwin, ed., *The Harriman Alaska Expedition Retraced: A Century of Change, 1899–2001*, 37.

9. Grainger, "Forward," [sic] in *A Time Remembered: Cape Fox Village 1899*.

10. See, for example, Palache journal, July 26, 1899, Palache papers, Bancroft Library, University of California, Berkeley, and Ritter diary, July 26, 1899, Ritter papers, Bancroft Library, University of California, Berkeley.

11. Grinnell, "The Natives of the Alaska Coast Region," in Merriam ed., *Harriman Alaska Series*, Vol. I, 152.

12. Ritter diary, July 26, 1899, Ritter papers, Bancroft Library, University of California, Berkeley.

13. Muir, *Travels in Alaska*, 43.

14. Muir journal, July 26, 1899, Muir Papers, Special Collections, Holt-Atherton Center for Pacific Studies, University of the Pacific. Copyright 1984 Muir-Hanna Trust.

15. Dellenbaugh journal, July 26, 1899, Dellenbaugh Collection, Beinecke Rare Book and Manuscript Library, Yale University.

16. *Ibid.*

17. Nelson expedition diary, July 26, 1899, Eberly Family Special Collections Library, Pennsylvania State University.

18. Kelly, "Memoirs Describing Expeditions and Military Service in Alaska and the Philippines," 125, unpublished manuscript, Beinecke Rare Book and Manuscript Library, Yale University.

19. Abramson, *Spanning the Century: The Life of W. Averell Harriman, 1891–198*, 68.

20. Cole, *Captured Heritage: The Scramble for Northwest Coast Artifacts*, 309, n.54; "A Tale of Two Totem Poles," *Washington Post*, September 17, 2004, WE 32; Chowder, "North to Alaska," *Smithsonian Magazine*, June 2003.

21. Merriam expedition diary/journal, July 27, 1899, Merriam Papers, Library of Congress.

22. Kincaid's poem appears in *The Harriman Alaska Expedition: Chronicles and Souvenirs May to August 1899*, 238–239.

23. Wyatt, "The Harriman Expedition in Historical Perspective," Introduction to *George Bird Grinnell—The Harriman Alaska Expedition to Alaska: Encountering the Tlingit and Eskimo in 1899*, xliv.

24. Worl, "Standing With Spirits, Waiting," in Litwin, ed., *The Harriman Alaska Expedition Retraced: A Century of Change, 1899–2001*, 37.

25. "A Tale of Two Totem Poles," *Washington Post*, September 17, 2004, WE32.

26. Litwin, "Expedition Log Two: Sunrise at Cape Fox Village," in Litwin, ed., *The Harriman Alaska Expedition Retraced: A Century of Change, 1899–2001*, 27.

27. Litwin, "View From A Seattle Hotel Window," in Litwin, ed., *The Harriman Alaska Expedition Retraced: A Century of Change, 1899–2001*, 3.

28. As to the return of the totems and the repatriation ceremonies, see Litwin, ed., *The Harriman Alaska Expedition Retraced: A Century of Change, 1899–2001*, 27–44.

Chapter 15

1. The Dixon Entrance is an approximately 50-mile-wide strait between Prince of Wales Island to the north and Graham Island (now part of the Haida Gwaii island group) to the south. The Entrance provides access from the open Pacific Ocean to the Inside Passage.

2. *The Harriman Alaska Expedition: Chronicles and Souvenirs May to August 1899*, 247.

3. Dellenbaugh journal, July 27, 1899, Dellenbaugh Collection, Beinecke Rare Book and Manuscript Library, Yale University; Merriam expedition diary/journal, July 27, 1899, Merriam Papers, Library of Congress.

4. Merriam expedition diary/journal, July 28, 1899, Merriam Papers, Library of Congress.

5. The A.K. Fisher papers in the Library of Congress contain a copy of this July 29 letter.

6. Palache journal, July 28, 1899, Palache papers, Bancroft Library, University of California, Berkeley.

7. Muir journal, July 27, 1899, Muir Papers, Special Collections, Holt-Atherton Center for Pacific Studies, University of the Pacific. Copyright 1984 Muir-Hanna Trust. Muir's journal entry is dated the 27th but clearly applies to the events of the 28th—he had run entries for a couple of days together and at this point the dates in his journal were consistently a day behind the events he was writing about.

8. *The Harriman Alaska Expedition: Chronicles and Souvenirs May to August 1899*, contains, at page 236, the "Official Programme" for the Captain's Celebration. That album also reprints various of the evening's poems and songs, including (at pages 268–269) the "A Farewell" lyrics.

9. Palache journal, July 28, 1899, Palache papers, Bancroft Library, University of California, Berkeley.

10. *Ibid.*, July 29, 1899.

11. Burroughs, "Narrative of the Expedition," in Merriam, ed., *Harriman Alaska Series*, Vol. I, 118.

12. Palache journal, July 29, 1899, Palache papers, Bancroft Library, University of California, Berkeley.

13. Burroughs, "Narrative of the Expedition," in Merriam, ed., *Harriman Alaska Series*, Vol. I, 118.

14. Dellenbaugh journal, July 27, 1899, Dellenbaugh Collection, Beinecke Rare Book and Manuscript Library, Yale University.

15. Muir journal, July 30–31,1899, Muir Papers, Special Collections, Holt-Atherton Center for Pacific Studies, University of the Pacific. Copyright 1984 Muir-Hanna Trust.

16. *Seattle Post Intelligencer*, July 31, 1899.

17. Merriam expedition diary/journal, July 31, 1899, Merriam Papers, Library of Congress; Nelson expedition diary, July 31, 1899, Eberly Family Special Collections Library, Pennsylvania State University.

18. Kelly, "Memoirs Describing Expeditions and Military Service in Alaska and the Philippines," 126, unpublished manuscript, Beinecke Rare Book and Manuscript Library, Yale University.

19. Merriam expedition diary/journal, August 2, 1899, Merriam Papers, Library of Congress; Dall diary, August 2, 1899, Dall papers, Smithsonian Institution.

20. Nelson expedition diary, August 2, 1899, Eberly Family Special Collections Library, Pennsylvania State University.

21. Merriam expedition diary/journal, August 2, 1899, Merriam Papers, Library of Congress. Harriman stayed to meet with officers of both the Union Pacific and the Oregon Railway & Navigation Company, including a trip along the Navigation line. Within a few months Navigation became a part of the Union Pacific system, with Harriman as chairman of its board. Klein, *The Life and Legend of E.H. Harriman*, 157.

22. Dellenbaugh journal, August 3, 1899, Dellenbaugh Collection, Beinecke Rare Book and Manuscript Library, Yale University.

23. Nelson expedition diary, August 5, 1899, Eberly Family Special Collections Library, Pennsylvania State University.

24. *Ibid.*, August 8, 1899.

25. Muir to the Big Four, August 30, 1899, Muir Papers, Special Collections, Holt-Atherton Center for Pacific Studies, University of the Pacific. Copyright 1984 Muir-Hanna Trust. The collection contains the Big Four's "compound" letter to Muir and the full text of his response.

26. Burroughs Journal, August 9, 1899, Burroughs Papers, Archives and Special Collections Library, Vassar College Libraries.

27. Burroughs to Fisher, September 24, 1899, A.K. Fisher Papers, Library of Congress.

28. Fuertes to his parents, July 31, 1899, Fuertes Papers, Division of Rare and Manuscript Collections, Cornell University Library.

29. Muir to the Big Four, August 30, 1899, Muir Papers, Special Collections, Holt-Atherton Center for Pacific Studies, University of the Pacific. Copyright 1984 Muir-Hanna Trust.

30. Merriam Home Journals, November 29, 1899, Merriam Papers, Library of Congress.

31. *Ibid.*, entry for May 23, 1900. Merriam listed the attendees as Mr. and Mrs. Harriman, Mary and Cornelia Harriman, W.H. and Elizabeth Averell, Dorothea Draper, William Devereaux, George Bird Grinnell, Louis Agassiz Fuertes, Swain Gifford, Frederick Dellenbaugh, William Brewer, John Burroughs, Wesley Coe, Dr. Morris, the Rev. Nelson, J. Stanley-Brown, and Merriam.

CHAPTER 16

1. See, for example, *Kansas City Journal*, July 31, 1899; *Deseret Evening News*, July 31, 1899; *Denver Republican*, July 31, 1899; *Omaha Bee*, August 8, 1899.

2. "E. H. Harriman Returns," *New York Times*, August 16, 1899.

3. Harriman, "Preface," in Merriam, ed., *Harriman Alaska Series*, Vol. I, xxi–xxii.

4. "The Harriman Expedition," *New York Daily Tribune*, August 15, 1899.

5. "In Alaska's Wilds: What the Harriman Expedition Discovered," *Boston Evening Transcript*, August 12, 1899.

6. Kincaid, unpublished "Autobiography" (typescript) 48, Kincaid Papers, Special Collections, Allen Library, University of Washington.

7. The "count" of 100 bird skins is provided by Peck, *A Celebration of Birds: The Life and Art of Louis Agassiz Fuertes,* 14.

8. Litwin, "Expedition Log Nine," in Litwin, ed., *The Harriman Alaska Expedition Retraced*, 127.

9. In 1911 the *Proceedings* became the *Journal of the Washington Academy of Sciences.*

10. In many cases these papers formed the basis for articles in the *Harriman Alaska Series.*

11. *National Geographic Magazine*, Vol. 10, No. 12, December 1899; *Journal of the American Geographical Society of New York*, Vol. 31, No. 4, 1899.

12. Merriam, "Introduction," in Merriam ed., *Harriman Alaska Series*, Vol. I, xxxi.

13. Gannett, "General Geography," in Merriam, ed., Harriman *Alaska Series*, Vol. II, 276–277.

14. Colt, *The Economic Importance of Healthy Alaska Ecosystems*, 19.

15. Grinnell, "The Salmon Industry," in Merriam ed., *Harriman Alaska Series*, Vol. II, 339.

16. *Ibid.*, 343, 354.

17. Gilbert, "Lake Ramparts," *Sierra Club Bulletin*, January 1908, 225–226.

18. Gilbert, "Glaciers and Glaciation," in Merriam, ed., *Harriman Alaska Series*, Vol. III, 113.

19. *Ibid.*, 111.

20. *Ibid.*, 109.

21. *Ibid.*, 160–161, 220–223.

22. *Ibid.*, 210–218.

23. Sterling, *Last of the Naturalists: The Career of C. Hart Merriam*, 123. The *Harriman Alaska Series* has a complicated production and publication history. Originally, from 1901 to 1905, it was privately printed by Doubleday, Page & Company of New York, and carried the common single-word title *Alaska*, with individual volumes subtitled by their contents: for example, Volume I was fully-titled *Alaska: Narrative, Glaciers, Natives*. In 1910, following Harriman's death, Mrs. Harriman transferred publication of the remaining volumes to the Smithsonian Institution. The Smithsonian reissued all of the Doubleday-published volumes with new title pages to better identify the work, and the *Harriman Alaska Series* became the distinctive common and commonly-referenced title for the entire work. The last of the *Series*, Volume XIV, appeared in two separately bound parts, the second of which contained photographic plates. This should have led to a fourteen-volume set, with fifteen books. However, as noted, Volumes VI and VII were never published. Thus, the *Series* is actually comprised of thirteen books. Quotations and page references in the instant work are from the original Doubleday Page publication.

24. Pyne, *Grove Karl Gilbert: A Great Engine of Research*, 174.

25. Merriam Home Journals, entry for December 29, 1899, Merriam Papers, Library of Congress.

26. *Ibid.*, entry for December 19, 1899.

27. *New York Herald*, April 23, 1899, 6.

28. Merriam expedition diary/journal, July 9, 1899, Merriam Papers, Library of Congress.

29. Muir to Johnson, February 24, 1905, quoted in Badè, *The Life and Letters of John Muir*, Vol. II, Chapter XVII.

30. Peck, "Conservation Comes to Alaska," in Litwin, ed., *The Harriman Alaska Expedition Retraced: A Century of Change, 1899–2001*, 194.

CHAPTER 17

1. The "Harriman Fund" paid Merriam an annual salary of $5,000 and provided an additional $7,000 a year for assistants and research expenses. Sterling, *Last of the Naturalists: The Career of C. Hart Merriam*, Rev. Ed., 281.

2. Muir, *Edward Henry Harriman*, 22–24.

3. Johnson, "John Muir As I Knew Him," *Sierra Club Bulletin*, January 1916.

4. As to Gilbert's residency with the Merriams, see Merriam's Home Journals, November 7, 1899 et seq., Merriam Papers, Library of Congress; Pyne, *Grove Karl Gilbert: A Great Engine of Research*, 204.

5. Gilbert, "The Investigation of the California Earthquake of 1906," in David Starr Jordan, ed., *The California Earthquake of 1906* [San Francisco, 1907], 256. Also discussed in Pyne, *Grove Karl Gilbert: A Great Engine of Research*, 231.

6. Coolidge speech quoted in *New York Times*, May 16, 1925, p. 23.

7. *New York Times*, April 12, 1938.

8. Quoted in Boesen and Graybill, *Edward S. Curtis: Photographer of the North American Indian*, 23.

9. Grinnell, "Portraits of Indian Types," *Scribner's Magazine*, March 1905, 270.

10. Quoted in Boesen and Graybill, *Edward S. Curtis: Photographer of the North American Indian*, 32.

11. Original copies of *The North American Indian* are scarce, and many of those are in the hands of private collectors. However, Northwestern University has digitized the entire work and it is available online at http://curtis.library.northwestern.edu. In 2016, Curtis collector and expert Christopher Cardozo announced an ambitious effort at republication of a limited number of finely bound complete sets of the original work, and those sets became available in 2018.

12. Christie's was the auctioneer, with the sale reported in its web site at www.christies.com.

13. Burroughs, "Real and Sham Natural History," *Atlantic Monthly*, Vol. 91, March 1903, 298–309.

14. Roosevelt, dedication letter in *Outdoor Pastimes of an American Hunter*. Roosevelt would jump directly and feet-first into the fray in an interview, "Roosevelt on the Nature Fakers," *Everybody's Magazine*, Vol. 16, June 1907, 770–774, and with a later essay of his own, "Nature-Fakers," *Everybody's Magazine*, Vol. 17, September 1907, 423–430.

15. Barrus, *The Heart of Burroughs's Journals*, 278.

16. Guberlet, *The Windows to His World: The Story of Trevor Kincaid*, 116

17. With regard to Starks's career, see "Memorial Resolution: Edwin Chapin Starks," online at www-marine.stanford.edu/memorials/StarksE.pdf

18. As to Cole's career, see McCabe, "Wisconsin's Forgotten Ornithologist: Leon J. Cole," *The Passenger Pigeon*, Fall 1979, 129–131, where the author relates how, on the Expedition, Cole struck up a friendship with Louis Agassiz Fuertes and that years later Cole "often displayed with pride a hand-painted deck of playing cards created by Fuertes and used by the members of the party in the absence of a commercial deck."

19. Wetmore, "Biographical Memoir of Robert Ridgway," National Academy of Sciences Biographical Memoirs, Vol. XV—Second Memoir, 63.

20. *Birds of North and Middle America* would eventually be expanded, after Ridgway's death, and using his plan and notes, to eleven volumes.

21. Ridgway, *Color Standards and Color Nomenclature*, 1. The publication has been carefully digitized and is available at the Columbia University Digital Library Collections web site at https://dlc.library.columbia.edu

22. Fuertes produced thousands of paintings, drawings, and watercolors over the course of the 30 years prior to his death in 1927, and these can be found in collections throughout the United States. One of the most significant concentrations of those works is at the Academy of Natural Sciences of Philadelphia, including hundreds of original works commissioned by the Biological Survey and on long-term loan to the Academy from the U.S. Fish and Wildlife Service. Another major depository is Cornell University, where Fuertes's correspondence, papers, and over one thousand watercolors and studies are housed at the Olin Library; with other significant collections on campus at the Laboratory of Ornithology and the Herbert F. Johnson Museum of Art. Among other substantial collections are those at the Field Museum in Chicago and at the National Geographic Society, which owns over 200 original watercolors produced by Fuertes under commissions for the Society's magazine.

23. Boynton, *Louis Agassiz Fuertes: His Life Briefly Told and His Correspondence Edited*, 306; Chapman, "In Memoriam: Louis Agassiz Fuertes," *The Auk*, January 1928.

24. Keenan, *The Life of Yellowstone Kelly*, 269–270.

25. *Ibid.*, xvii, where Keenan also judges that two other novels by Peter Bowen which appeared some thirty years after the movie came out, were "cleverly written," but in Keenan's opinion "notable only for their outrageous twists on Kelly's life."

26. *New York Times*, May 29, 1900.

27. Trudeau, *An Autobiography*, 275. This autobiography was that of the younger Trudeau's father.

28. Elder, "SS *George W. Elder*: A Chronology," *PowerShips*, Number 291, Fall 2014, 49–50, provides the most thorough post–Harriman Expedition historical information about the *Elder*.

Chapter 18

In terms of the intertwined stories of E. H. Harriman and the Union Pacific in the early years of the 20th Century, the field belongs to biographer/historian Maury Klein in his *The Life and Legend of E. H. Harriman* and in *Union Pacific: The Rebirth 1894–1969*, the second volume of his exhaustive three-part history of that iconic railroad.

1. As to the Central Pacific and the acquisition of the Southern Pacific, see Kennan, *E. H. Harriman*, Vol. I, 232–260; Klein, *The Life and Legend of E. H. Harriman*, 210–218; Snyder, "Harriman: 'Colossus of Roads,'" *The American Monthly Review of Reviews*, Vol. 35, January 1907, 42–43.

2. Kennan, *E. H. Harriman*, Vol. I, 302.

3. Chernow, *The House of Morgan: An American Banking Dynasty and the Rise of Modern Finance*, 91.

4. Kennan, *E. H. Harriman*, Vol. I, 312–313.

5. Klein, *Union Pacific: The Rebirth 1894–1969*, 101–107, provides an excellent summary of the machinations surrounding the Burlington acquisition and the Northern Pacific corner.

6. *New York Herald*, May 9, 1901.

7. Chernow, *The House of Morgan: An American Banking Dynasty and the Rise of Modern Finance*, 88.

8. Kennan, *E. H. Harriman*, Vol. I, 395. Kennan pegged the profit at $58,000,000. In Snyder, "Harriman: 'Colossus of Roads,'" *The American Monthly Review of Reviews*, January 1907, 48, the author estimated the profit at $80,000,000.

9. Kahn, "Edward Henry Harriman," an address delivered before the Finance Forum in New York on January 25, 1911, as reprinted in the *Railway Library*, Slason Thompson, ed., Vol. 2, 39.

10. *Wall Street Journal*, May 4, 1905. Harriman's situation was not unusual for the times; the article listed other captains of industry and their board positions, including William K. Vanderbilt with fifty-six seats and National City Bank's James Stillman with fifty-five.

11. *New York Sun*, April 8, 1905. A detailed discussion and analysis of the Equitable Life struggle is contained in Klein, *The Life and Legend of E. H. Harriman*, 329–343.

12. Kahn, "Edward Henry Harriman," an address delivered before the Finance Forum in New York on January 25, 1911, as reprinted in the *Railway Library*, Slason Thompson, ed., Vol. 2, 19.

13. In a transaction that passed with little notice, Ryan later sold half his shares to Harriman. The secrecy of this sale was such that some years later when J.P. Morgan approached Ryan about buying his stock he had no idea that half of the total was owned by Harriman. Morgan eventually acquired those shares from Harriman's widow. See Klein, *The Life and Legend of E. H. Harriman*, 341.

14. Kahn, "Edward Henry Harriman," an address delivered before the Finance Forum in New York on January 25, 1911, as reprinted in the *Railway Library*, Slason Thompson, ed., Vol. 2, 19–20.

15. Kennan, *E. H. Harriman*, Vol. I, 416.

16. Kahn, "Edward Henry Harriman," an address delivered before the Finance Forum in New York on January 25, 1911, as reprinted in the *Railway Library*, Slason Thompson, ed., Vol. 2, 19–20.

17. Keys, "Harriman: Part III—The Building of His Empire," *The World's Work*, March 1907, 8659–8663.

18. For the details of the Fish financial transactions and the conflict that unfolded over the next three years see Klein, *The Life and Legend of E. H. Harriman*, 344–355 and Kennan, *E. H. Harriman*, Vol. II, 42–63.

19. *New York World*, November 8, 1906.

20. Klein, *The Life and Legend of E. H. Harriman*, 353.

21. The break with Roosevelt is treated in depth and length in Kennan, *E. H. Harriman*, Vol. II, 174–274, and in Klein, *The Life and Legend of E. H. Harriman*, 360–371 and Klein, *Union Pacific: The Rebirth 1894–1969*, 172–176.

22. Klein, *The Life and Legend of E. H. Harriman*, 359.

23. *Ibid.*, 294–297 provides an account of the stops and starts of the week-long appendicitis battle.

24. Lovett, *Forty Years After: An Appreciation of the Genius of Edward Henry Harriman*, 17–18; Klein, *The Life and Legend of E. H. Harriman*, 373–374; Kennan, *E. H. Harriman*, Vol. II, 66–76; Abramson, *Spanning the Century: The Life of W. Averell Harriman*, 81–82.

25. Snyder, "Harriman: 'Colossus of Roads,'" *The American Monthly Review of Reviews*, January 1907, 37.

26. *Ibid.*, 38, 44, 47.

27. Keys, "Harriman: Salvage of the Two Pacifics," *The World's Work*, April 1907, 8802.

28. *The Economist*, June 1, 1907; Kennan, *E. H. Harriman*, Vol. II, 306.

29. *Financial World*, September 3, 1909. Klein, *The Life and Legend of E. H. Harriman*, 410–414 provides an extended discussion of the saving of the Erie.

30. Klein, *The Life and Legend of E. H. Harriman*, 410; Kennan, *E. H. Harriman*, Vol. II, 323.

31. Klein, *The Life and Legend of E. H. Harriman*, 440, noting Satterlee, *J. Pierpont Morgan: An Intimate Portrait*, 513–514 as to the details of this meeting.

32. Abramson, *Spanning the Century: The Life of W. Averell Harriman 1891–1986*, 92 reprints the full text of Harriman's will as reported, on the occasion of Mary's death, in the *New York Evening Post*, November 8, 1932.

33. Additional acreage at Arden, together with gifts from neighboring property owners, was subsequently added to the Park. In 1977, Averell and Roland facilitated the creation of another Harriman State Park, this one in northeastern Idaho, with the donation of 10,000 acres that had served as a cattle ranch and private retreat for the Harrimans and the families of other Union Pacific investors.

34. Campbell, *Mary Williamson Harriman*, 12.

35. The American Orchestral Society was dissolved in 1930. At that time "its general objectives" were taken over and carried on by a new organization, the National Orchestral Association. Campbell, *Mary Williamson Harriman*, 66.

36. As quoted in Campbell, *Mary Williamson Harriman*, 83–84.

37. *New York Times*, December 20, 1934.

38. "Who was Mary Harriman?" *Connected: The Junior League Magazine*, Association of Junior Leagues International, July 2014. See also "Founder Mary Harriman: A Spirited Reformer Ahead of Her Time," https://www.ajli.org/?nd=p-who-legacy-mary-harriman

39. *Ibid.*; additional biographical information is taken from the "Mary Harriman" online biography at the National Women's History Museum. The Museum's web site is located at https://www.womenshistory.org/students-and-educators/biographies

40. Campbell, *Mary Williamson Harriman*, 14.

Bibliography

Manuscript and Archival Collections

Amherst College, Archives and Special Collections, Frost Library, Amherst, MA—Benjamin Kendall Emerson Papers

Autry Museum of the American West, Braun Research Library, Los Angeles, CA—George Bird Grinnell Diaries

Cornell University, Division of Rare and Manuscript Collections, Kroch Library, Ithaca, NY—Bernhard Eduard Fernow Papers; Louis Agassiz Fuertes Papers

Harvard University, Schlesinger Library, Radcliffe Institute for Advanced Study, Cambridge, MA—Palache Family Papers

Huntington Library, San Marino, CA—George Bird Grinnell Papers; Charles A. Keeler Papers

Library of Congress, Manuscript Division, Washington, D.C.—Clara Barrus and John Burroughs Papers; Albert K. Fisher Papers; W. Averell Harriman Papers; John Hay Papers; C. Hart Merriam Papers; Joseph Stanley-Brown Papers

Massachusetts Historical Society, Boston, MA—Benjamin Kendall Emerson Family Papers

Pennsylvania State University, Eberly Family Special Collections, Paterno Library, State College, PA—George F. Nelson Harriman Expedition Diary and Artifacts

San Francisco Maritime National Historic Park, San Francisco, CA—*George W. Elder* Blueprints

Seattle Public Library, Ferguson Seattle Room Collection, Seattle, WA—Edward S. Curtis Letters to Harriet Leitch, 1948–1951

Smithsonian Institution Archives, Washington, D.C.—Frederick V. Coville Papers; William H. Dall Papers; Harriman Alaska Expedition Collection; Waldo LaSalle Schmitt Papers

Smithsonian Institution, Archives of American Art, Washington, D.C.—R. Swain Gifford Papers

Smithsonian Institution, National Museum of the American Indian, Washington, D.C.—Mary Harriman Rumsey Collection

Smithsonian Institution Libraries, National Museum of Natural History Branch, Washington, D.C.—A.K. Fisher Field Book, Harriman Alaska Expedition (Division of Mammals Archives); Thomas H. Kearney Field Books, Harriman Alaska Expedition (Department of Botany)

Stanford University, Green Library, Palo Alto, CA—William Healey Dall Papers; Edwin Chapin Starks Papers

University of California-Berkeley, Bancroft Library, Berkeley, CA—Charles Augustus Keeler Papers; C. Hart Merriam Papers; Charles Palache Papers; William E. Ritter Papers

University of Montana, Archives and Special Collections, Mansfield Library, Missoula, MT—George Bird Grinnell Collection

University of the Pacific, Special Collections, Holt-Atherton Center for Pacific Studies, Stockton, CA—John Muir Papers

University of Washington, Special Collections, Allen Library, Seattle, WA—Edward S. Curtis Papers; Harriman Expedition Collection; Trevor Kincaid Papers

Vassar College, Archives and Special Collections Library, Poughkeepsie, NY—John Burroughs Papers

Yale University, Beinecke Rare Book and Manuscript Library, New Haven, CT—Frederick Samuel Dellenbaugh Collection; C. H. Fredell Diary of a Trip to Alaska; Luther S. Kelly Papers

Yale University, Manuscripts and Archives, Special Collections, Sterling Memorial Library, New Haven, CT—William Henry Brewer Papers; George Bird Grinnell Papers

Harrimanalia

The Harriman Alaska Expedition: Chronicles and Souvenirs— May to August 1899

This private family album or scrapbook of over 300 pages, produced under Mrs. Harriman's supervision, contains photographs, drawings and watercolors, maps, the programs for shipboard events such as the Fourth of July celebration, poems and the lyrics to songs composed by the Expedition party, listings of the crew of the *George W. Elder*, logs of distances traveled, records of daily temperatures, and other information. *Chronicles and Souvenirs* can most easily be found in the W. Averell Harriman Papers (Box 1034) at the Library of Congress, and has been digitalized for online access through the Library web site at rs6.loc.gov/mss/amrvm/vmh/vmh.html.

A Souvenir of the Harriman Alaska Expedition May to August 1899

This is a two-volume, limited edition photo album that was privately produced by Harriman following the Expedition for distribution to members of the family and the scientific party. It contains 253 selected photographs, for the most part taken by Edward S. Curtis, though also containing photos contributed by other Expedition members, including Harriman himself and C. Hart Merriam. The Souvenir Album may be found—often among the papers of Expedition members—at a number of locations including the Library of Congress, the Bancroft Library at the University of California–Berkeley, the Beinecke Rare Book and Manuscript Library at Yale University, and in Special Collections at the University of Washington.

BOOKS

Abramson, Rudy. *Spanning the Century: The Life of W. Averell Harriman, 1891–1986.* New York: William Morrow & Co., 1992.

Ackerman, William K. *Historical Sketch of the Illinois Central Railroad.* Chicago: Fergus Printing Co., 1890; Forgotten Books Reprint, 2015.

Adams, Mark. *Tip of the Iceberg: My 3,000 Mile Journey Around Wild Alaska, the Last Great American Frontier.* New York: Dutton, 2018.

Ambrose, Stephen E. *Nothing Like It in the World: The Men Who Built the Transcontinental Railroad 1863–1869.* New York: Simon & Schuster, 2001 (First Touchstone Edition).

Andrews, Ralph W. *Curtis' Western Indians.* Superior Publishing Co., 1962.

Badè, William Frederic. *The Life and Letters of John Muir.* Boston and New York: Houghton Mifflin Company, 1924.

Ballou, Maturin Murray. *The New El Dorado: A Summer Journey to Alaska.* Boston and New York: Houghton, Mifflin and Co., 1890.

Barrus, Clara. *John Burroughs: Boy and Man.* Garden City, New York: Doubleday, Page & Co., 1920.

_____, ed. *The Heart of Burroughs's Journals.* New York: Houghton Mifflin Co., 1928.

_____. *The Life and Letters of John Burroughs.* 2 vols. Boston: Houghton Mifflin Co., 1925; Reprint—New York: Russell and Russell, 1968.

Bartsch, Paul, Harald Render and Beulah Shields. *A Bibliography and Short Biographical Sketch of William Healey Dall.* Washington: Smithsonian Institution, 1946.

Berton, Pierre. *Klondike: The Last Great Gold Rush, 1896–1899.* Toronto: McClelland and Stewart Ltd., 1972.

Black, Lydia T. *Russians in Alaska, 1732–1867.* Fairbanks: University of Alaska Press, 2004.

Boesen, Victor, and Florence Curtis Graybill. *Edward S. Curtis: Photographer of the North American Indian.* New York: Dodd, Mead & Co., 1977.

Bolhovitinov, N.N. *Russian-American Relations and the Sale of Alaska, 1843–1867.* Translated and edited by Richard A. Pierce. Kingston, Ontario: Limestone Press, 1996.

Borneman, Walter R. *Alaska: Saga of a Bold Land.* New York: Perennial, 2004.

Boynton, Mary Fuertes. *Louis Agassiz Fuertes: His Life Briefly Told and His Correspondence Edited.* New York: Oxford University Press, 1956.

Brinkley, Douglas. *The Quiet World: Saving Alaska's Wilderness Kingdom, 1879–1960.* New York: HarperCollins, 2011.

_____. *The Wilderness Warrior: Theodore Roosevelt and the Crusade for America.* New York: HarperCollins, 2009.

Brooks, Alfred H. *Blazing Alaska's Trails,* 2d ed. Fairbanks: University of Alaska Press, 1973.

Bruchey, Stuart, ed. *Memoirs of Three Railroad Pioneers.* Reprint—New York: Arno Press, 1981.

Burroughs, John. *Camping & Tramping With Roosevelt.* Boston and New York: Houghton Mifflin, 1905.

Campbell, Persia Crawford. *Mary Williamson Harriman.* New York: Columbia University Press, 1960.

Chari, Sangita, and James M.N. Lavallee. *Accomplishing NAGPRA: Perspectives on the Intent, Impact, and Future of the Native American Graves Protection and Repatriation Act.* Corvallis, OR: Oregon State University Press, 2013.

Chernow, Ron. *The House of Morgan: An American Banking Dynasty and the Rise of Modern Finance.* New York: Grove Press, 1990.

Cohen, Stan. *Gold Rush Gateway: Skagway and Dyea, Alaska.* Missoula, MT: Pictorial Histories Publishing Company, 1986.

Cole, Douglas. *Captured Heritage: The Scramble for Northwest Coast Artifacts.* Seattle: University of Washington Press, 1985.

Crain, Esther. *The Gilded Age in New York: 1870–1910.* New York: Black Dog & Leventhal Publishing, 2006.

Dall, William Healey. *The Yukon Territory: The Narrative of W.H. Dall, Leader of the Expedition to Alaska in 1866–1868.* London: Downey & Co., 1898.

Dauenhauer, Nora Marks, and Dauenhauer, Richard. *Haa Tuwunáagu Yís, for Healing Our Spirit.* Seattle: University of Washington Press, 1990.

Eckenrode, H.J., and Pocahontas Wright Edmunds. *E. H. Harriman: The Little Giant of Wall Street.* New York: Greenberg, 1933.

Egan, Timothy. *Short Nights of the Shadow Catcher: The Epic Life and Immortal Photographs of Edward Curtis.* New York: Houghton Mifflin Harcourt, 2012.

Fedorova, Svetlana G. *The Russian Population in*

Alaska and California: Late 18th Century—1867. Kingston, Ontario: Limestone Press, 1973.

Fisher, Raymond H. *Bering's Voyages: Whither and Why.* Seattle: University of Washington Press, 1977.

Gidley, Mick. *Edward S. Curtis and the North American Indian, Incorporated.* New York: Cambridge University Press, 2000.

Goetzmann, William H., and Kay Sloan. *Looking Far North: The Harriman Expedition to Alaska, 1899.* New York: Viking Press, 1982.

Grainger, John, ed. *A Time Remembered: Cape Fox Village 1899.* Saxman, AK: Cape Fox Corporation, 1981.

Graybill, Florence Curtis, and Victor Boesen. *Edward Sheriff Curtis: Visions of a Vanishing Race.* New York: Thomas Y. Crowell Company, 1976.

Grinnell, George Bird. *The Harriman Expedition to Alaska: Encountering the Tlingit and Eskimo in 1899,* with introductions by Polly Burroughs and Virginia Wyatt. Fairbanks: University of Alaska Press, 2007.

Guberlet, Muriel L. *The Windows to His World: The Story of Trevor Kincaid.* Palo Alto CA: Pacific Books, 1975.

Hall, Elton W. *R. Swain Gifford: 1840–1905.* New Bedford, MA: Old Dartmouth Historical Society, 1974.

Harriman, E. Roland. *I Reminisce.* Garden City, NY: Doubleday & Co., 1975.

Hinckley, Ted C. *The Americanization of Alaska: 1867–1897.* Palo Alto, CA: Pacific Books, 1972.

Hunt, William R. *North of 53°: The Wild Days of the Alaska-Yukon Mining Frontier, 1870–1914.* New York: Macmillan, 1974.

Isto, Sarah Crawford. *The Fur Farms of Alaska: Two Centuries of History and a Forgotten Stampede.* Anchorage: University of Alaska Press, 2012.

Jenks, Cameron. *The Bureau of Biological Survey: Its History, Activities, and Organization.* (1927). Arno Press Reprint edition, 1974.

Jensen, Richard J. *The Alaska Purchase and Russian-American Relations.* Seattle: University of Washington Press, 1975.

Keenan, Jerry. *The Life of Yellowstone Kelly.* Albuquerque: University of New Mexico Press, 2006.

Kelly, Luther S. *Yellowstone Kelly: The Memoirs of Luther S. Kelly.* Edited by M.M. Quaife. New Haven: Yale University Press, 1926.

Kennan, George. *E. H. Harriman: A Biography.* 2 vols. Boston and New York: Houghton Mifflin Co., 1922.

_____. *E. H. Harriman's Far Eastern Plans.* Garden City NY: The Country Life Press, 1917. [This title is an original small book version of what became Chapter XVII in Vol. 2 of Keenan's *E. H. Harriman: A Biography*].

Klein, Maury. *The Life and Legend of E. H. Harriman.* Chapel Hill: University of North Carolina Press, 2000.

_____. *Union Pacific: The Rebirth, 1894–1969.*

Minneapolis: University of Minnesota Press edition, 2006. [Originally published by Doubleday & Company, 1989].

Kobler, John. *Otto the Magnificent.* New York: Charles Scribner's Sons, 1988.

Kushner, Howard J. *Conflict on the Northwest Coast: American-Russian Rivalry in the Pacific Northwest, 1790–1867.* Westport, CT: Greenwood Press, 1975.

Latham, Frank B. *The Panic of 1893: A Time of Strikes, Riots, Hobo Camps, Coxey's "Army," Starvation, Withering Droughts and Fears of "Revolution."* New York: F. Watts, 1971.

Lawlor, Laurie. *Shadow Catcher: The Life and Work of Edward S. Curtis.* New York: Walker and Company, 1994.

Lewis, Daniel. *The Feathery Tribe: Robert Ridgway and the Modern Study of Birds.* New Haven: Yale University Press, 2012.

Litwin, Thomas S., ed. *The Harriman Alaska Expedition Retraced: A Century of Change, 1899–2001.* New Brunswick, NJ: Rutgers University Press, 2005.

London, Jack. *The God of His Fathers and Other Stories.* New York: McClure Phillips & Co., 1901.

Lord, Nancy. *Green Alaska: Dreams From the Far Coast.* New York: Counterpoint, 1999.

Mercer, Lloyd. *E. H. Harriman: Master Railroader.* Boston: Twayne Publishers, 1985.

Merriam, C. Hart, ed. *Harriman Alaska Series.* 13 Volumes. New York: Doubleday, Page and Company, and Washington, D.C.: Smithsonian Institution, 1901–1914.

Millard, Candace. *Destiny of the Republic: A Tale of Madness, Medicine and the Murder of a President.* New York: Doubleday, 2011.

Minter, Roy. *The White Pass: Gateway to the Klondike.* Fairbanks: University of Alaska Press, 1987.

Morris, Edmund. *Theodore Rex.* New York: Random House, 2001.

Muir, John. *The Cruise of the Corwin: Journal of the Arctic Expedition of 1881 in Search of De Long and the Jeannette.* Boston and New York: Houghton Mifflin, 1917.

_____. *Edward Henry Harriman.* Garden City, NY: Doubleday, Page & Co., 1912.

_____. *Stickeen: The Story of a Dog.* Boston and New York: Houghton Mifflin, 1909.

_____. *Travels in Alaska.* Boston and New York: Houghton Mifflin, 1915. Republication, San Francisco: Sierra Club Books, 1988.

Naske, Claus-M., and Herman E. Slotnick. *Alaska: A History.* 3rd ed. Norman: University of Oklahoma Press, 2011.

Oliver, James A. *The Bering Strait Crossing: A 21st Century Frontier Between East and West.* London: Information Architects, 2007 revised edition (paperback).

Parsons, Cynthia. *George Bird Grinnell: A Biographical Sketch.* Millbrook, N.Y.: Grinnell and Lawton, 1993.

Peck, Robert McCracken. *A Celebration of Birds:*

The Life and Art of Louis Agassiz Fuertes. New York: Walker & Co, 1982.

Punke, Michael. *Last Stand: George Bird Grinnell, the Battle to Save the Buffalo, and the Birth of the New West.* New York: Smithsonian Books, 2007.

Pyne, Stephen J. *Grove Karl Gilbert: A Great Engine of Research.* Iowa City: University of Iowa Press, 2007.

Reiger, John F. *American Sportsmen and the Origins of Conservation,* third edition. Corvallis: Oregon State University Press, 2001.

Reiger, John F., ed. *The Passing of the Great West: Selected Papers of George Bird Grinnell.* New York: Westchester Press, 1972.

Renehan, Edward J., Jr. *John Burroughs: An American Naturalist.* White River Junction, VT: Chelsea Green Publishing Co., 1992.

Ritter, Harry. *Alaska's History: The People, Land, and Events of the North Country.* Anchorage: Alaska Northwest Books, 1993.

Rodgers, Andrew Denny III. *Bernhard Eduard Fernow: A Story of American Forestry.* Princeton, N.J.: Princeton University Press, 1951.

Roosevelt, Theodore. *Outdoor Pastimes of an American Hunter.* New York: Charles Scribner's Sons, 1905.

_____. *The Wilderness Hunter.* New York: G.P. Putnam's Sons, 1893.

Sachs, Aaron. *The Humboldt Current: Nineteenth-Century Exploration and the Roots of American Environmentalism.* New York: Penguin Books, 2007.

Sale, Roger. *Seattle, Past to Present.* Seattle: University of Washington Press, paperback edition (with corrections), 1978.

Satterlee, Herbert J. *J. Pierpont Morgan: An Intimate Portrait.* New York: Macmillan, 1939.

Scidmore, E. Ruhamah. *Alaska: Its Southern Coast and the Sitkan Archipelago.* Boston: D. Lathrop and Company, 1885.

Sherwood, Morgan B. *Exploration of Alaska, 1865–1900.* Fairbanks: University of Alaska Press, 1992.

Speidel, William C. *Sons of the Profits: The Seattle Story 1851–1901.* Seattle: Nettle Creek Publishing, 1967.

Stefansson, Vilhjalmur. *Northwest to Fortune: The Search of Western Man for a Commercially Practical Route to the Far East.* New York: Duell, Sloan and Pearce, 1958.

Steller, Georg Wilhelm. *Journal of a Voyage with Bering. 1741–1742.* ed. O. W. Frost, trans. Margritt A. Engel and O.W. Frost. Stanford, CA: Stanford University Press, 1988.

Sterling, Keir B. *Last of the Naturalists: The Career of C. Hart Merriam.* Rev. Ed. New York: Arno Press, 1977.

Taliaferro, John. *Grinnell: America's Environmental Pioneer and his Restless Drive to Save the West.* New York: Liveright Publishing Corp, 2019.

Trudeau, Edward Livingston. *An Autobiography.*

Garden City: Doubleday, Doran & Company, 1915 [Reprint by Leopold Classic Library].

Turner, Frederick. *Rediscovering America: John Muir in His Time and Ours.* New York: Viking Press, 1985.

Warren, James Perrin. *John Burroughs and the Place of Nature.* Athens, GA: University of Georgia Press, 2006.

Wayner, Robert J., ed. *Car Names, Numbers and Consists.* New York: Wayner Publications, 1972.

Webb, Melody. *The Last Frontier: A History of the Yukon Basin of Canada and Alaska.* Albuquerque: University of New Mexico Press, 1985.

Welsh, Joe, Bill Howes, and Kevin J. Holland. *The Cars of Pullman.* New York: Crestline Press edition, 2015.

White, Christopher. *The Melting World: A Journey Across America's Vanishing Glaciers.* New York: St. Martin's Press, 2013.

Whymper, Frederick. *Travel and adventure in the Territory of Alaska.* Wentworth Press edition, 2016 [Original publication by J. Murray, 1868].

Wolfe, Linnie Marsh, ed. *John of the Mountains: The Unpublished Journals of John Muir.* Madison: University of Wisconsin Press, 1979. [Reprint of the original, Boston, MA: Houghton Mifflin, 1938].

_____. *Son of the Wilderness: The Life of John Muir.* 2d. ed. Madison: University of Wisconsin Press, 2003.

Worster, Donald. *A Passion for Nature: The Life of John Muir.* New York: Oxford University Press, 2008.

Young, Samuel Hall. *Alaska Days with John Muir.* New York: Fleming H. Revell, 1915 [Republication—Salt Lake City: Peregrine Smith Books, 1990].

Articles, Reports, and Speeches

Burroughs, John. "Real and Sham Natural History," *Atlantic Monthly,* Vol. 91 (March 1903).

Chapman, Frank M. "In Memoriam: Louis Agassiz Fuertes." *The Auk,* Vol. XLV, No. 1 (January 1928).

Chowder, Ken. "North to Alaska." *Smithsonian,* June 2003.

Curtis, Edward S. "The Rush To The Klondike Over The Mountain Passes." *Century Magazine,* Vol. 55, No. 5 (March 1898).

Dall, William Healey. "Alaskan Notes." *The Nation,* Vol. 69 (August 17, 1899).

Dickerson, Gordon E. and Arthur B. Chapman. "Leon Jacob Cole, 1877–1948: A Brief Biography." *Journal of Animal Science,* Vol. 67, No. 7 (1989).

"Discoveries in Our Arctic Regions: The Harriman Alaska Expedition." *The World's Work,* Volume 1 (November 1900).

Elder, George W. "*SS George W. Elder:* A Chronology." *PowerShips,* Number 291 (Fall 2014).

Frome, Michael. "George Bird Grinnell: Grandfather of Conservation." *Field and Stream,* June 1970.

Gannett, Henry. "The Harriman Alaska Expedition." *National Geographic Magazine,* Vol. X, No. 12 (December 1899).

_____. "The Harriman Alaska Expedition." *Journal of the American Geographical Society of New York,* Vol. 31, No. 4 (1899).

Gilbert, Grove Karl. "Lake Ramparts." *Sierra Club Bulletin,* Vol. VI, No. 4 (January 1908).

Grinnell, George Bird. "The Harriman Alaska Expedition," a fifteen-part series. *Forest and Stream,* Vol. LIV, Numbers 8–25 (February 24-June 23, 1900).

_____. "Portraits of Indian Types." *Scribner's Magazine,* Vol. XXXVII, No. 3 (March 1905).

Grosvenor, Gilbert H. "The Harriman Expedition in Cooperation with the Washington Academy of Sciences." *National Geographic Magazine,* Vol. X, No. 4 (June 1899).

Hall, William Edwin. "The Harriman Alaska Expedition." *Yale Scientific Monthly,* Vol. 6, No. 5 (February 1900).

"Harriman's Last Fight." *Current Literature,* Vol. 47, No. 4 (October 1909).

James, George Wharton. "Charles Keeler: Scientist and Poet." *The National Magazine,* Vol. 35 (November 1911).

Johnson, Robert Underwood. "John Muir As I Knew Him." *Sierra Club Bulletin,* John Muir Memorial Number, Vol. 10, No. 1 (January 1916).

Josephy Jr., Alvin M. "The Splendid Indians of Edward S. Curtis." *American Heritage Magazine,* Vol. 25, Issue 2 (February 1974).

Kahn, Otto H. "Edward Henry Harriman." An address delivered before the Finance Forum in New York on January 25, 1911. Reprinted in the *Railway Library,* Slason Thompson ed., Vol. 2. Chicago: Gunthorp-Warren, 1911. Also reprinted as "The Last Figure of an Epoch: Edward Henry Harriman," in Otto H. Kahn, *Our Economic and Other Problems: A Financier's Point of View.* New York: George H. Doran Company, 1920.

Keeler, Charles. "Recollections of John Muir," *Sierra Club Bulletin,* John Muir Memorial Number, Vol. 10, No. 1 (January 1916).

Keys, C.M. "Harriman," a four-part series. *The World's Work,* Vol. 13 (January-April 1907).

Kincaid, Trevor. "The Harriman Alaska Expedition." *Mazama,* Vol. 2, No. 2 (April 1901).

Kuchin, Paul J., Alan D. Weiss and Joseph J. Wagner. "The Great Arctic Outbreak and East Coast Blizzard of 1899." American Meteorological Society, *Weather and Forecasting,* Vol. 3 (December 1988).

Lefevere, Edwin. "Harriman." *American Magazine,* Vol. 64, No. 2 (June 1907).

Lindsey, Alton A. "The Harriman Alaska Expedition of 1899, Including the Identities of Those in the Staff Picture." *Bioscience,* Vol. 28, No. 6 (June 1978).

Lovett, Robert A. "Forty Years After: An Appreciation of the Genius of Edward Henry Harriman." Address delivered at the National Newcomen Society dinner in New York City, November 17, 1949. New York: Newcomen Society in North America, 1949. Printed for the Newcomen Society by Princeton University Press.

Loving, Rush, Jr. "W. Averell Harriman Remembers Life With Father." *Fortune,* May 8, 1978.

McCabe, Robert A. "Wisconsin's Forgotten Ornithologist: Leon J. Cole." *The Passenger Pigeon* (Wisconsin Society for Ornithology), Vol. 41, No. 3 (Fall 1979).

Merriam, C. Hart. "To the Memory of John Muir." *Sierra Club Bulletin,* Vol. 10, No. 2 (January 1917).

Moody, John, and George Kibbe Turner. "Masters of Capital in America." *McClure's Magazine,* Vol. 36, No. 3 (January 1911).

Muir, John. "An Adventure with a Dog and a Glacier." *Century Magazine,* Vol. 54 (August 1897).

Osgood, Wilfred H. "Clinton Hart Merriam—1855–1942." *Journal of Mammalogy,* November 17, 1943.

Palmer, Theodore Sherman. "In Memoriam: Clinton Hart Merriam." *The Auk,* Vol. 71, No. 2 (May 1954).

"Papers from the Harriman Alaska Expedition," thirty papers by various authors. *Proceedings of the Washington Academy of Sciences,* Vols II—IV (1900–1902).

Peck, Robert McCracken. "A Cruise for Rest and Recreation: The Harriman Expedition of 1899." *Audubon Magazine,* Vol. 84, No. 2 (1982).

Penry, Jerry. "The Father of Government Mapmaking: Henry Gannett." *The American Surveyor,* November 2007.

Rennick, Penny, ed. "The Bering Sea." *Alaska Geographic,* Vol. 26, No. 3 (1999).

Rhode, Elaine. "St. Matthew and Hall Islands: Oasis of Wildness," in "Alaska's Seward Peninsula." *Alaska Geographic,* Vol. 14, No. 3 (1987).

Schiff, Judith Ann. "Yalies in Alaska's History: John Green Brady." *Yale Alumni Magazine,* January/February 2007.

Sloan, Kay. "Mr. Harriman Requests the Pleasure of Your Company." *American Heritage,* Vol. 33 No. 4 (June/July 1982).

Snyder, Carl. "Harriman: 'Colossus of Roads.'" *The American Monthly Review of Reviews,* Vol. 35 (January 1907).

Uhler, Francis M. "In Memoriam: The Life of Albert K. Fisher." *The AUK,* Vol. 68 (April 1951).

Wellman, Walter. "The Wellman Polar Expedition." *The National Geographic Magazine,* Vol. X (December 1899).

"Who was Mary Harriman?" *Connected: The Junior League Magazine,* July 2014.

Wilson, Robert. "Birdman of America." *American Scholar,* Vol.75, No.2 (Spring 2006).

Wynne, Michael J. "De Alton Saunders: Phycological Trailblazer." *Phycological Society of America Newsletter,* Vol. 46, No. 2 (Summer/Fall 2010).

GOVERNMENT DOCUMENTS

Allen, Henry T. *Report of an Expedition to the Copper, Tanana, and Koyukuk Rivers. Washington*, D.C.: U. S. Government Printing Office, 1887. This report was subsequently published, in another form, in "A Military Reconnaissance of the Copper River Valley, 1885." *Compilation of Narratives of Exploration in Alaska.* Senate Reports., 56th Cong., 1st Session, 1900, no. 1023, Serial 3896.

Elliott, Henry Wood. *The Condition of Affairs in the Territory of Alaska.* Washington, D.C.: U.S. Treasury Department/Government Printing Office, 1875.

Tarr, Ralph S., and Lawrence Martin. "The Earthquakes at Yakutat Bay, Alaska in September 1899." United States Geological Survey Professional Paper 69, U. S. Government Printing Office, 1912.

GENERAL REFERENCES

Boyer, Paul S. ed. *The Oxford Companion to United States History.* Oxford: Oxford University Press, 2001.

Colt, Steve. "The Economic Importance of Healthy Alaska Ecosystems." Institute of Social and Economic Research, University of Alaska, Anchorage, 2001.

Dictionary of American Biography. Allen Johnson, Dumas Malone, and others eds. New York: Charles Scribner's Sons.

Healey, David. *Great Storms of the Chesapeake.* Charleston, SC: The History Press, 2012.

The Houghton Mifflin Dictionary of Biography. Boston: Houghton Mifflin Co., 2003.

Langdon, Steve J. *The Native People of Alaska.* 3rd ed. Anchorage: Greatland Graphics, 1993.

National Academy of Sciences, *Biographical Memoirs.* National Academy of Sciences: Washington, D.C.

Ransom, J.E. "Derivation of the Word Alaska." *American Anthropologist*, July 1940.

Rogers, George W. and Richard A. Cooley. *Alaska's Population and Economy: Regional Growth, Development and Future Outlook*, Vol. 2, *Statistical Handbook.* Fairbanks, AK: Institute of Social, Economic, and Government Research, 1963.

NEWSPAPERS

Boise Statesman
Boston Evening Transcript
Denver Republican
Deseret Evening News
Juneau Empire
Kansas City Journal
New York Daily Tribune
New York Herald
New York Times
New York World
Omaha Bee
Omaha World-Herald
Portland Oregonian
San Francisco Daily Evening Bulletin
Seattle Argus
Seattle Post-Intelligencer
Seattle Star
Seattle Times
Wall Street Journal
Washington Post

Index

Numbers in **bold italics** indicate pages with illustrations